ONE HUNDRED MILES FROM

MANHATTAN

ONE HUNDRED MILES FROM
MANHATTAN

Guillermo Fesser

LITTLE BRIDGE PRODUCTIONS

Previously published in Spanish by Santillana Ediciones Generales, S.L., 2008, Madrid, Spain

Library of Congress Control Number: 2014933926

ISBN Hardcover: 978-1-936940-70-7
ISBN Softcover: 978-1-936940-72-1

Cover art: Victor Monigote
Book design: Danielle Ferrara
English translation: Kristin Keenan

Little Bridge Productions
35 N. Parsonage St.
Rhinebeck, NY 12572

www.100milesmanhattan.com
fesser@100milesmanhattan.com

Printed in the United States of America
Distributed by Epigraph Publishing Service

To the Hill-Howe clan,
my American family

With special love to my children,
Max, Nico and Julia, and my
wonderful wife, Sarah, with
whom I have the fortune of
sharing two worlds.

Contents

Foreword

In the early 1980s, the great Spanish radio journalist Guillermo Fesser startled listeners in post-Franco Spain by reporting the news in a new way: He made it entertaining. He wasn't condescending. He was funny, intellectually curious, and fearless. And he conveyed compassion and respect for his subjects, even those with whom he disagreed. Guillermo became a national treasure, beloved by his countrymen, from the inhabitants of Gypsy settlements to the bureaucrats scurrying through halls of the Spanish Congress. They devoured his radio shows, books, TV specials, films, works of theater, and newspaper articles as quickly as the irrepressible 53-year-old could produce them.

When Guillermo and his partner, Juan Luis, announced plans in 2002 to end their radio show after more than two decades of broadcasting daily, King Juan Carlos I paid homage: "I'm really sorry they'll be stopping their show, but they've done a fantastic job and I'll always remember them with fondness and friendship."

Luckily for the King and Guillermo's other fans, Guillermo's plan to take a break from storytelling didn't last long. Within the first hour of relocating from Madrid to a small town 100 miles north of New York City with his wife and their three kids, Guillermo's intended time-out became time he used to capture stories as a journalist. As he struggled to reconcile what he learned from the people he met with his preconceptions about the U.S., their tales became fodder for a bestseller in Spain: *A Cien Millas de Manhattan.* In essence, it his personal meditation on the unexpected Americas he discovers.

Now the book has just been translated into English, giving Guillermo a crack at surprising you about a place you know. You should let him. Who better than a kind-hearted foreigner to help you marvel at our own land and learn something about your fellow Americans?

Guillermo will introduce you to a compelling cast, including Sunny Fitzsimmons, a professor-turned-Texas rancher who is reintroducing buffalo to the West. Sunny, whom Guillermo visits at his 17,000-acre Shape Ranch, has managed to convince the state's governor to grant wild animal status to the magnificent creatures, improving his odds. You'll learn why Sunny's way of raising bison differs from fellow rancher and CNN founder Ted Turner's method, as well as this gem about the social needs of bison: "They die of a broken heart if they are left alone."

Guillermo also takes you beneath the streets of Manhattan with Steve Mosto, an expert on the massive steam pipe systems that power thousands of the city's buildings. And you'll install, on the ninth floor of the Wall Street Journal's offices, the elegant memorial that sculptor John Corcoran created to honor reporter Daniel Pearl, who was murdered after being kidnapped in Pakistan while reporting for the paper. You'll make maple syrup with John, too.

Here's where I should mention that I'm a big fan of Guillermo's, too: I worked for his radio show for a few years in Madrid and became friends with him and his wife, Sarah. They took me under their wing and treated me like family as I got my bearings in their wonderful city. Like Sarah, I also grew up in Rhinebeck, N.Y., the quaint former dairy farming community that became both a subject and a base camp for Guillermo's adventures across the country that appear in this book's pages. Apart from a handful of people I've known for years, such as my parents, who run Upstate Films, Rhinebeck's movie theater, Guillermo taught me plenty about people and places I never knew existed. *—Nick Leiber*

Prologue

It was a sunny morning back in May of 2002 in downtown Madrid and tourists were piling back into Gran Via's outdoor cafes, unaware of all the frenzied activity taking place in the offices of the fancy buildings lining the avenue. People who had arrived in Spain from all over the world were dunking their orders of churros into coffee with curiosity. I was observing them from a window on the ninth floor and, from their unhurried movements, I detected that sweet happiness sparked by not having a tight schedule, that inner smile that motivates you to consider spending the entire day doing nothing more than enjoying time with a loved one. "Guillermo?" "Yes?" "Mr. Delkader is waiting for you in his office." "Ah, thanks." The secretary's voice brought me back to reality and to 32 Gran Via, headquarters of the biggest media conglomerate in the Spanish-speaking world: the PRISA group. Television channels, radio broadcasting stations, magazines, newspapers, book publishers... The radio station occupied two floors. The studios were on the eighth. On the ninth, the executives of Union Radio granted or denied talk show hosts the sacred privilege of sitting in front of a couple microphones that, through multiple broadcasters, reached millions of listeners in Spain, Portugal, Latin America, and the United States.

Back then, Augusto Delkader, a friendly, shrewd journalist, steered the radio company's course. I had been to the ninth floor many times. To negotiate contracts. To pitch projects. To fight for stories. His office was decorated in shades of gray, which supposedly had been chosen to invoke a sense of calm in his visitors, but whose coldness triggered an uneasy feeling in me that May morning. Unlike previous visits to the office, this time my nervousness couldn't be attributed to anxiety about whether or not the boss would accept my conditions. Instead, I was experiencing quite the opposite—the uncertainty of whether that man would let me leave without a fuss. Or better said, let *us* leave, because there were two of us.

I was accompanied by Juan Luis, my colleague and business partner since our journalism school days. After graduating we landed a contract for $100 a month at a new radio station, Antena 3, and began to broadcast a show we called *Gomaespuma* on Saturdays at two o'clock in the morning. The Antena 3 executives gave us space at that inconvenient hour because they couldn't find anyone else who wanted to do a live show for so little money, but we accepted with the hope of capturing the attention of some night owl. Gomaespuma means "foam rubber" in Spanish. I came up with that name because I wanted our show to be very elastic and flexible, including discussion of serious news as well as comedy and all sorts of emotions. Foam rubber's air bubbles reminded me of sparkly champagne bubbles, which I associated with the late-night show and the fresh new radio style that we were creating.

Within a few years, *Gomaespuma* had built an audience of 500,000 followers who never missed our Saturday night radio date. We'd regularly get complaints from the managers of the gigantic discos on the Mediterranean coast: "Just who in the hell are you all? At two o'clock in the morning the dance floors empty out and everyone goes to their car to listen to you. Couldn't you broadcast at a different time? You're going to bankrupt us!" "Fine," we responded, "maybe you could give the DJ a break and play the show through your speakers?" And that's what they did.

In the mid-1980s we jumped to the afternoon shift and, at long last, in the '90s, we moved to the morning. With each change, we acquired more faithful addicts. Once a month we broadcast a live show outside the studio and the amount of people who attended never ceased to amaze us. We filled theaters, basketball courts, stadiums... We couldn't believe it. We seemed more like a rock group than two radio show hosts. Our fans deserved extra credit because, apart from the putting up with shoving and other inconveniences unique to open air events, they had to get up at an ungodly hour to see us. We started at seven o'clock in the morning and when we arrived at the broadcasting site, at around six-thirty, we always found people who asked us to please sneak them in with us because it was already full. "Come in with me and I'll tell them you're a sound engineer. ... Get up on the stage and stay quiet over one side. ... Take my notebook and say that you're my assistant. ... Come, I'll tell them you're my sister." We snuck in everyone we could until security caught on, yelled at us and ripped up the tickets of the supposed members of our team.

In Barcelona we did an early morning show on the beach. It was winter, a cold wind was blowing and it was still dark out when we played the opening theme music. In front of us, where we knew the audience was, we could hear clapping, whistles and cheers, but we had no clue as to how many people had come to listen to us. When the reddish sun dawned on the horizon and the attendees' profiles were silhouetted against it, we realized that sitting on the sand with their eyes fixed on us were 5,000 souls. In the Plaza Mayor in Madrid 10,000 people showed up. In the sports center in Valencia we had 15,000 attendees. The same thing happened in Sevilla in the Expo tent. And in Vigo...25,000! How could there be 25,000 people coming to a park to listen to a radio show at six o'clock in the morning?

The trick, I suppose, was an explosive mix of humor and journalism. We used to get people to smile as a way to tackle the toughest subjects each day. We acted like comedians on the airwaves, but we didn't settle for regurgitating news headlines written by others. We traveled around the world looking for our own sources of information. We broadcast shows from the trenches of the war in Yugoslavia, from the abject poverty of the streets of Calcutta, or from the boats filled with

Africans in search of the promised land in Europe, but we always did it with a smile on our lips. We pushed ourselves so that the demands of the news didn't get in the way of us always seeing the bottle half full. And when it turned into an almost impossible mission, we temporarily shifted toward entertainment and went to cover the Olympics in Sydney or the Oscars in Los Angeles.

We infected the audience with our optimism but, above all, we noticed that people liked us for something very simple but unusual among other leaders in the media: when we interviewed King Abdullah of Jordan in his palace, we treated him with the same respect as we did Rosa, the cleaning lady, when she came by to dust in the main studio on Gran Via in Madrid and we complimented her work on the air. And we also involved our listeners in our effort to make a better world for all of us. We couldn't report a tragic piece of news and then go on to the next one as if it were nothing. We collected thousands of pairs of sunglasses and we went to Mauritania with a team of ophthalmologists who were going to operate on desert dwellers' cataracts. We showed up in Havana with a boat loaded with toys to distribute within Cuba's schools. We convinced the Spanish army to lend us a cargo plane and we distributed tons of formula for hungry babies in Serbia's hospitals…

"Good morning, boys, everything going well?" "All is well, Augusto, thanks." "Sit down, please." The chairman of Union Radio had been told that *Gomaespuma*'s team wasn't happy working for the company and his goal was to placate. He wanted to resolve the problem, smooth the way to negotiate the next season. But he had been misinformed. There wasn't any problem. We had simply made a decision after 20 years of professional commitment. "We're going," we told him. He didn't want to believe it. "What's happening? Is something going on? Is about money?" "We're leaving, that's all." He continued without acknowledgement. He had reasons to cast doubt on the truth of our affirmation: *Gomaespuma* was at its peak and it had just broken advertising revenue records. He took out a checkbook. "That's not it," we said. "We need to stop." We had both just turned 42. We had just played the ninth hole of our lives and we wanted to take a break to think about the second part of the game. We needed time—free time to think, to enjoy churros dipped in coffee like the tourists exploring Madrid's streets nine stories below. Some things money just can't buy. "Do you have other offers? Are you thinking about signing with another broadcaster?" No. "We're going home," we told him. "And if we come back, you'll be the first to know."

Two months later, in July of 2002, I said goodbye to 20 years of radio and moved with my family to my wife's hometown in search of the quiet life of a small place. During broadcasting hours I had been learning that in radio shows, which are supposedly built upon words, the silences play an equally important role. A headline has more of an impact if you hold your breath for three seconds before launching it at the world. In interviews, the small moments of dead air substituted for the breaths, the smiles and the yawns that give our lives vitality. In a bipolar world where good and bad, yin and yang, nothingness and infinity coexist, I had been shaping the theory that human thinking advances when a balance is reached between its two complementary halves: speaking and listening. I'd spent 20 years telling my own stories and something inside of me warned me that it was time to start paying attention to the stories of others.

With this goal, to listen, I settled into a small New York town on the edge of the Hudson River one summer afternoon. I was there with the idea that my children and myself would get a better understanding of their mother's roots. My wife. During that time, I also planned to write a movie script, but I almost couldn't find time for it. Before I knew it, I found myself swept up into a sea of fascinating stories. Unexpected stories. In an America that I didn't even suspect could exist.

1

August

John Raucci, the driver who picks us up from JFK Airport, was born in 1950 in Brooklyn, into an Italian and thoroughly Catholic family. That's why he throws me for a loop when he mentions that he was a member of Reverend Moon's Unification Church. He shatters my preconceptions and gives me a cultural shock that is not unusual for Europeans who travel to the United States with a pre-conceived notion of Americans. You expect to run into Woody Allen or Beyoncé or a tie-wearing pair of Mormons who distribute little flyers in people's mailboxes. You expect the stereotypes that the mass media feeds us. No way. The cultural combinations are so unpredictable that the blonde, blue-eyed driver taking us to our destination in the Hudson River Valley followed precepts dictated from far-away North Korea.

Raucci arrives at the wheel of a Lincoln Continental, with a trunk as big as my parents' cellar. Maybe this American tendency to enlarge objects stems from the need to keep things proportional to a natural environment into which it seems the Creator injected steroids. Here, the rivers are almost as wide as they are long and domestic cats appear to be blown up like balloons by gas station air pumps. Everything is big. Thicker is better, like the ad for Long John Silver claims. Despite the spacious trunk, we play three rounds of Tetris with the bags to fit them all in. Take one out. Put another in. Not that one. Take it back out and try putting the first one in the other way around. Even so, some of the bags don't fit and we have no choice but to intersperse them between us in the car. We're all squashed together, like sardines in a can, full of expectation before the new adventure that awaits us. Raucci exchanges a few pleasantries with us, and then starts talking. We are suffering from jet lag and travel exhaustion, so we can barely open our mouths. I simply listen. On a two-hour drive, if you can ignore three children kicking the back of your seat, you can learn a lot from your interlocutor.

Actually, my conversation with Raucci begins when one of my children, despite loud protests from the other two, decides to remove his shoes. Oh, what a stench! However, our driver smiles and launches into a story about the benefits of walking barefoot, which leads him to rewind to his memories of being a long-distance runner at school. Raucci was good at sports, and quickly understood that he would find no better springboard to college than excelling at one of them.

That was during baseball's glory days, when stadiums were packed to the brim. This sport, which rarely has an exciting play, created infinite betting possibilities and gave working class the chance to return home with a wad of cash. Raucci was well-suited for pitching, but opted instead for the subtler glory of shaving a few seconds off the clock on the 1,500-meter track. "Baseball forces you to be closed up in a stadium," he confesses as we finally break free of the monumental traffic jam around the airport. "Running lets you go out into the world. The landscape is not pre-determined for the runner; he picks his course in each training session and can change it at will." Maybe because of this, during his long outdoor training sessions, Raucci was often overcome by a sensation of having found his rightful place in the universe and being in harmony with the cosmos. He ran against the elements and against himself. He got good grades and never suffered any injury that forced him to give up running, the rhythm of which perfectly suited his easy-going personality and developed the spirituality that had accompanied him since early childhood. Running and the serenity displayed by his Catholic teachers at school led him to follow the call to religion at age 15 in Leonardtown, Maryland. There, he completed the juniorate and then the novitiate course at the seminary of Theodore James Ryken, founder of the Xaverian order.

When Raucci came of age, he donned the robes of a Franciscan brother and became Little John—in the midst of a social revolution that questioned the established order. The intellectual Little John found that he demanded more freedom of worship than the Xaverian Brothers Minor could offer him. In the priesthood, Raucci had to strike a difficult balance between what psychology told him and what the spiritual path had opened for him, and found himself profoundly confused. Finally, the need to follow his own instincts overpowered his devotion to the emotion-stifling practice that religion had become for him. Heartbroken, he felt compelled to hang up his beloved black robe in less than a year after joining the brothers.

Raucci enrolled in the psychology department at Saint Francis College, "the small college of big dreams five minutes from Manhattan" in Brooklyn Heights. Once he had a degree under his belt, he left Brooklyn to travel through Europe. His aim was to practice French, the language that had so fascinated him in the classroom. He could do so to his heart's content in Paris. He also traveled through Switzerland. When he finally reached the state of grace that speaking a foreign language with ease affords, his money ran out and he had no choice but to say *a tout a l'heure* to the Old Continent and return home.

Back in New York, where Raucci muddled through the time fog that envelops those who ponder their future, a follower of the Unification Church approached him to talk about peace. At the time, Raucci did not know how to believe in God, and said as much. His new friend treated him with sympathy and also spoke enviably fluent French, so Raucci accepted his company as a means to improve his own use of the subjunctive, *que je lise, que nous lisions*, and memorize a few tongue twisters: *un soupir souvient souvent d'un souvenir.* ("A sigh often originates from a memory.") Raucci also learned that the new faith was based on the belief that Jesus Christ had appeared on Mount Mydou in North Korea before a young boy named Sun Myung Moon. Jesus had enjoined Moon to complete the evangelizing mission that had been interrupted by his crucifixion. According to Raucci's new friend, it was not God's predestined will that Jesus be crucified. All that stuff about Pontius Pilate washing his hands had caught the Creator off guard. That's why God's plan for the kingdom of peace went awry and complete salvation was delayed until the Second Coming. The day the apparition took place, early on Easter Sunday, April 17, 1935, the chosen one was 15 years old (or 16, according to the Korean way of counting) and the divine command threw him into a long period of doubt. According to Sun Myung Moon's own testimony, he clung to the hem of Jesus' clothing and wept inconsolably. "Oh, God, why would you give me a mission of such paramount importance?" He stayed like that for days, buried beneath a mountain of fears. He was able to overcome his anguish through prayer. After making a pilgrimage throughout North Korea 18 years later, Sun Myung Moon proclaimed to the world that he had accepted the divine challenge to save his people and bring God's peace to the Earth! He then set off for Japan and the United States so he could tell the world about the greatness of the Korean people. Sun Myung Moon had resumed the testimony of the King of Kings and proclaimed himself the new envoy of heaven.

Moon's followers told Raucci that the aim of the Unification Church was to reunite under a single leadership the various Christian trends. Their secret formula consisted of injecting into Christianity the spirituality inherent in Far Eastern religions—an explosive mix of two opposites—to create a new order with the best each house had to offer. That is apparently why the Son of God had opted to go to Mount Mydou in search of an heir. For Raucci, the idea of attempting to unify religions was a seductive proposal and, whether due to the incentive of being able to express himself with someone in the language of Alex de Tocqueville, or because the story of Moon revived the admiration he had felt for Jesus during his year as a Franciscan, he embraced the Unification Church.

From the beginning, what attracted Raucci most to Moon's doctrine was the fact that the Messiah was not presented as a savior. To

Christians, Jesus had come to pay for the sins of the people. The Jews still awaited the arrival of a messenger from God who would rescue them from earthly hardships. But Sun Myung Moon's mission was simply to act like a good father. This followed a simple syllogism that Moon expressed in two premises and a conclusion: A: If Adam and Eve had not succumbed to the temptation of the Devil, they would have been good parents. B: If Adam and Eve had been good parents, all of their descendants would have inherited goodness naturally and evil would not exist in our world. C: If Moon, the True Father, acted like a good father, he could transmit goodness in a natural way to his followers and therefore interrupt the chain of evil inherited from the days of the Garden of Paradise. Thus, good parents would transform society and it would not be necessary for a savior to come save the world from any curse. We would all be good people. Moon shelved Plato's theory, *homo hominis lupus est*, man is a wolf to men. He abandoned Thomas Hobbes' idea of the inherent selfishness of human beings. From now on, the apple would not fall far from the tree. From a good father would come a wonderful son. Thus began the pursuit of World Peace through Ideal Families. Amen.

After the agreeable initial contact, the Unification Church ordered Raucci to teach new followers and he happily complied. Spreading the word was like returning to the pulpit, and he doggedly devoted himself to lecturing on street corners, with a chalkboard. But Raucci's sigh of relief was short-lived. Fortune, like the boulder that chased Indiana Jones, pushed Raucci up against a wall. In December 1975, a *New York Daily News* reporter, John Cotter, became an undercover recruit in the Unification Church and attended one of Raucci's classes. A sarcastic cartoon of Raucci appeared in the press. There was no doubt about it—it was him, half smiling, with his hair neatly parted on the side, sporting the devil's horns. The cartoon illustrated a devastating article on Reverend Moon's cult. In Brooklyn, all alarms went off. To Raucci's parents, their son had been abducted. His friends saved up money to hire a deprogrammer, a specialist in cults who would immediately remove him from what they considered to be a dangerous group. It wasn't easy to be a Moonie.

"A Moonie?" inquires Max with a yawn behind my seat. "I thought we were going to get sunnies…" Raucci looks at me, confused. "No offense," I tell him. "We have been discussing on the plane the possibility of getting some worms and going fishing in a lake. Go to sleep, Max."

The Unification Church was accused of being a youth-abducting sect, isolating young people from their families. After reciting mantras from seven in the morning until midnight, members would purportedly become zombies who were forced to sell flowers on the street. Parents across the country banded together and hired deprogrammers to recapture their children. Information on the mysterious church included dark descriptions of its founder. Some people drew Hitler mustaches on ads carrying Moon's picture. It was even rumored that Moon was in collusion with the North Korean secret police and that his true objective was to control the American political system. These serious accusations forced Congress to hold hearings to find out who this Reverend Moon really was.

Some journalists asked legitimate questions about how Moon managed to live in a luxurious $850,000 estate in Tarrytown (tax free since it was owned by a religious institution). They could not understand where he had obtained the money to buy that and another Hudson River estate valued at $650,000, as well as the Columbia University Club for $1.2 million. Information emerged linking Moon to 20 business ventures and purporting that he served the advisory boards of several Korean companies that produced tea, paint and military weapons. At the same time, baseless urban legends circulated about the church. One of the most notorious claims was that Procter & Gamble had made a pact with Moon. Apparently, the True Father had assured the company that if it used the Unification Church symbol on all of its products, business would prosper. Otherwise, the Devil would steal its profits. There was indeed a moon and stars logo on P&G product packages, but it had in fact been designed in the United States in 1850, and had been used since that date as a trademark for candles.

Raucci had to defend himself before both his family and strangers. He invited his parents to visit the seminary on the banks of the Hudson, the headquarters that Reverend Moon founded in Barrytown in 1975. He was able to convince his parents that the teachings imparted there varied little from the ideas they shared every Sunday during the celebration of the Eucharist, but he was exhausted from fighting against the accusations that rained in from every side. The struggle led Raucci to become deeply enamored with Sun Myung Moon and to believe that the unification of the world was within reach. He decided to move into the church's seminary.

Immersed in mystic lucubration, Raucci spent three pleasant years in Barrytown. At first he had doubts and was ready to give up. But then something inexplicable happened. Raucci heard within himself the deep voice of his late grandfather, Dominick Granato: "Johnny, stay here, this is where you belong." Raucci answered, "But Grandpa, I'm confused…" The deep voice of the patriarch on his mother's side left little room for interpretation: "Stay here, son, your place is here." It was a shocking event that forced him to accept Moon as God's prophet, the only person who could pull our crumbling world together. Raucci devoted more hours to study and spent his free time tending to the upkeep of the seminary. He was surrounded by young men and women, some of whom had raging tempers, but with whom he nevertheless had to learn to live with as if they were brothers and sisters. Finally, he could breathe a sigh of relief. However, in July 1982, just as he was about to come up for a second breath of air, a major scandal broke: the mass wedding in Madison Square Garden.

The blessing of marriage was crucial to Moon's strategy. If your religion is based on the creation of parents and you decide to promote faith by counting by twos, you have to pair up the members of your church. When the occasion presented itself, Raucci knew that a Japanese woman was right for him. He wanted a companion who was cultured, soft-spoken and obliging. He was convinced that the level of leadership he had earned by defending Moon's philosophy was enough for the True Father to grant him his wish: "Okay, Raucci, you've earned it: here's your Japanese woman. You deserve it." But this did not happen.

Madison Square Garden, the world's most famous arena, was the scene of the Unification Church's mass wedding—three floors above Penn Station, where, incidentally, Don Pepi's Deli serves a prosciutto and mozzarella sandwich that's so good it can cure the hiccups. For New Yorkers, it's known simply as "The Garden." On July 1, 1982, 4,150 people from 70 countries thronged together, eager for the blessing of Sun Myung Moon and his wife, Hak-ja Han, who, with complacent smiles, were waiting inside the arena, wearing white satin robes and ornamental crowns. It was the largest wedding in history. It was not Moon's first Blessing Ceremony, but it was the one that called attention to the movement. It graced the front pages of the *New York Times*, *New York Post* and *Daily News*. Skeptical journalists had fun with Moon's last name, referring to his followers as "moonies." The 2,075 couples ranged in age from 21 to 62, averaging 30 years old. Two-thirds of the couples were of different races or cultures. The women were dressed like conventional brides, in modest, empire-waist white satin gowns with high necklines and lace veils. They held bunches of flowers in their right hand and hooked their left arm through their partner's. The men's navy blue suits were in sharp contrast to their pristine white shirts, gloves and shoes. They wore burgundy ties whose inscription on the back read: World Peace through the Ideal Family. Moon had proclaimed himself the successor of Jesus of Nazareth and symbolized the dream of unifying the Earth through mass interracial marriages.

The grooms had in their pockets the nuptial rings engraved with the Unification symbol: a radiating square within a circle that symbolizes God reaching out to the cosmos in 12 directions (for the 12 Apostles). The grooms would exchange them with the women they had met just a week earlier at the New Yorker Hotel, the emblematic building that the Unification Church had purchased in 1975. There, the True Father had paired up hundreds of young people at his whim, including John Raucci, who went to the New Yorker's Art Deco salons thinking his great moment had arrived. "Reverend Moon," he prayed, "please remember that I want a Japanese woman." He watched as the prophet advanced between the two lines that had formed in the ballroom for the inspection. The men stood at the right, the women at the left, as Moon strode between them, attracting hundreds of anxious stares from his followers as they waited for a gesture from the divine messenger to step out of the line. To Raucci, they were like iron particles dependent on a magnet to know which way to go. Moon would turn one way, then the other. Sometimes he would stop in front of someone, but then sigh and resume walking. He seemed to be trying to concentrate, to find inspiration to make the right decisions. When he motioned to a young man to approach, he would scan him slowly, from top to bottom, before selecting a young woman and drawing her to the young man's side. Then he analyzed their reactions. If he were not convinced there was good chemistry between the two, he would ask the young man to go back to his spot, and then call another candidate. This time he would get it right. Perfect. Moon expressed his satisfaction to each lucky couple and sent them to the room designated for the couples' rapid acceptance procedure. The couples had just a few minutes alone to decide if they were in agreement with Moon's choice. Although the pairing was considered an act of faith and Moon was not pleased when his will was questioned, if anyone was bold enough to disagree, he would consent to selecting a new partner for that person.

Moon's followers claimed that he could read people's minds just by studying their faces for a few seconds. A rounded shape beneath the eye would mean sincerity. Completely round: infantilism. Flat beneath the eye: alert to some danger, on the defensive. A U-shaped nose like Bob Hope's: a need to be the center of attention. A thin upper lip and thicker lower lip: a gift for persuasion. White below and above the pupil: a sign of discomfort, probably because the person is lying. And so on. Based on these principles, Moon was supposedly able to match compatible characteristics, aiming for the couple's long-term relationship rather than on their achieving momentary passion.

When the so-called True Father stopped before him, Raucci smiled broadly, awaiting a reciprocal response. Moon only grimaced, however, and had a faraway look. Raucci felt lost: "I ... I, Reverend Father, want a Japanese woman." Finally, the True Father smiled at his disciple. Relieved, Raucci relaxed. He was at peace. The danger was past. Moon turned to the young women and calmly went down the line. He stopped before an elegant woman with Asian features who lowered her head timidly, observed Raucci out of the corner of his eye, and then kept walking. Suddenly he stopped again and pointed to a short woman with straight dark hair. She looked like a country bumpkin. Moon beckoned her to the center of the room and gestured for Raucci to approach. "Me?" Raucci thought. "You're asking me to go up there? But I, True Father, want a Japanese woman." "Come," Moon insisted, stretching out his hand to invite him to meet his designated partner.

At that moment, Raucci asked God to open up the ground of Manhattan to swallow him up forever. Since his prayers had not been answered, he concentrated his energies on Plan B: Get out of there somehow. But there were no exits, only a long narrow corridor that led the couple to the decision-making room. Raucci and the woman went in and he closed the door after them, ready to spit out the truth. He wanted to tell her, "Look, I'm sorry, but you aren't the person I had in mind. You are not Japanese." But he couldn't do it. The words would not come. But he had to do it. The smiling face before him was not new. He had seen that face in the halls of the church headquarters and knew that she was a slow, methodical woman who did not have his level of education. He had to be honest with her. "I'm sorry; it's nothing personal. It's just that I want to marry a Japanese woman." But before he could open his mouth, she shook her head in amazement and happily exclaimed: "I can't believe it!" Raucci recoiled. Getting out of this predicament was going to be much more difficult than he had anticipated.

The woman's name was Madeline, and she stood in front of him, talking. "Four months ago, I dreamed about you in New York City." Raucci was aghast. "Who is this person? What is she talking about?" "In my dream you told me you were my husband," Madeline continued, "and I happily responded that I was your wife." Whaaat? The end of her dream was the beginning of his nightmare. Lord Almighty! "Then, the morning after the dream," Madeline smiled, "we ran into each other at the Columbia University building that the church bought and I said hi to you. Don't you remember?" Yes, in an overly friendly way, he suddenly recalled. Raucci had been entering the headquarters when they ran into each other. Out of the blue, this woman ran up to him, offering an excessively effusive greeting—Hhiii!—like someone running into an old friend. Hhiii!! He was confused. Is this woman crazy, he wondered. "How's it going?" he had responded, and walked quickly away. "Since your reaction was so cold," Madeline lowered her voice, "I thought that beautiful dream would never come true. That is, until today when, as you see, we are here together. Everything makes sense now. Oh, John, you've made me the happiest woman on Earth!" Raucci felt faint. The wallpaper on the hotel wall faded from view.

"Are you all right?" "Yes, sorry, Madeline, it's nothing." "Are you sure?" "Yes, let's go." How could he possibly break that woman's heart into a million pieces? They returned to the master. "We gladly accept your decision, Aboji." On the outside, two smiling faces. On the inside, only Madeline was happy. Raucci's soul felt so crushed that when he knelt before Moon to receive the blessing, it seemed like his heart would roll right out of his mouth. Nevertheless, the tragic future Raucci had predicted for himself was not imminent. At least that is what he thought, pragmatically. The marriage commitment would in no way change the course of his life in the coming months. Like the other 2,000-odd couples, Raucci and his bride would be required to live separately and avoid sexual relations for a period of three and a half years. This was considered the time necessary to forge mutual understanding and make love bloom. It was also a time during which Raucci and Madeline would have to recruit at least three new members for the Unification Church.

At 11:27 a.m. on the day of the mass wedding, with the summer heat beginning to take its toll, the Garden opened. The couples that had formed lines at several entrances merged once they were inside the grounds to form an impressive column eight deep. Upon entering the field, they passed under a flower arch and the music started. A band of 30 musicians solemnly played the "Wedding March" that the romantic Mendelssohn composed for the *Suite for a Midsummer's Night Dream*. On the stage, like glittering giants stuffed into their imperial robes, Moon and Mrs. Hak-Ja Han, his wife and the church's True Mother, waited as the procession approached, holding bowls of perfumed water along with several wands with strings tied to them. As the couples paraded before the royal couple, the Moons dipped the wands in the water and shook them over the heads of the participants to give them their blessing. Hundreds of tiny drops imbued with divine grace flew, like magical confetti, over the happy procession. From the stands, which sported flags and colorful banners, thousands of family members, most of them resigned, observed the ceremony. The couples walked down to the Garden's boxing ring, where many nights of glory had taken place until Don King moved the ring to Las Vegas. For this occasion, a huge cream-colored rug covered the platform. It took 43 minutes for all of the couples to be seated. Missing were 50 couples who had forgotten to request their marriage license, and one bride, Cara Mahlahan, who had been abducted in the street, allegedly at her parents' behest, by three men who knocked her fiancé to the ground, threw her in the back of a light blue van and sped away.

The show started. Moon jumped up and down and strode back and forth on the stage as he addressed his audience in Korean. Then, as his words were calmly interpreted by an aide, his speech began to make sense. "Do you pledge to inherit heavenly tradition?" The speech focused on the cosmic commitment that the couples were about to make and the detailed description of the terrible eternal punishment that breaking it would entail. Each exhortation ended with a studied pause, with a measured silence that preceded a question posed to the auditorium. The response, "Yes! Yes, Father!" rose like an eerie roar, voiced by the 4,000 throats that packed Madison Square Garden for each of the four vows the couples made. The final vow bid them to be the center of love before society, the nation, the world and the universe. The couples then faced each other and exchanged rings.

The ceremony lasted an hour and a half. At the end, the tenor Enzo Stuarti sang "Be My Love" and the participants bowed in four directions to their families to express their respect. "Wait a minute!" I ask my driver. "'Be My Love'—the song that Mario Lanza used to sing?" "U-huh." He nods. "You must be kidding me!" I say. "Why? Do you know it?" "Do I know it? There was a guy on my radio station who had a film music show and he used to play that song all the time. It is stuck in my head." And to prove it, I go ahead and reproduce the lyrics with better intention than talent: *"Be my looooooove, and with your kisses set me burning. One kiss is all that I need to seal my fate. And, hand-in-hand, we'll find love's promised land. There'll be no one but youuuuuuuuuuuu for me, eteeeeeeeeeernally ... If youuuuu will be myyyyyyyyyy love."* "Papá, you're so annoying!" whispers Julia from the back seat, abruptly ending my concert.

After the tenor's performance, thousands of multicolor balloons were released in the Garden. The True Father closed the ceremony wishing everyone peace. In just two or three generations, these marriages would miraculously cause more people to marry people from countries considered to be their enemies, and all hatred would melt away. Peace was the signal the newlywed couples were waiting for—in unison, they bowed, putting the palms of their hands on their knees, and, as if pushed by an ocean swell, jumped up, creating a tsunami of arms that swayed to shouts of *Mansei!*—"Victory will be eternal It was a spontaneous expression of enthusiasm with no physical or psychological force capable of stopping it. Since Moon did not want impassioned kisses, given that sexual purity is at the core of his doctrine, he favored rhythmic movement and shouts to allow the newlyweds to release their adrenaline. *Mansei!* Everyone raised their arms to form a wave, like people at a World Cup soccer match. *Mansei!* And the party, which cost $1.2 million—or $600 per couple—was over. "You may go in peace."

That same afternoon, Raucci decided to devote body and soul to his church. And then, nine years later, in 1991, the Unification Church ex-communicated him. "Thanks, John, but don't bother coming back to the seminary." What had happened? Well, Moon taught his disciples that the energy springing forth from God is only useful when it is used to return it to our fellow man in the form of love. By doing so, people would feel a burning desire to give a bit more each time; capable of improving their character and, therefore, of being eligible to enter an idyllic universe of peace on Earth. The Kingdom of Heaven, but here and now.

In this ideal world, each dawn would be more beautiful than the previous one because love would be expanding with every passing minute. Money would not exist and people would survive thanks to the disinterested support of their group. Those who could drive a car would offer their services as drivers; those who knew how to cook would cook. They would work for love rather than a salary. Before such positive expectations, Raucci and other enthusiastic colleagues passionately devoted themselves to the principles of love. However, despite their efforts, they did not achieve the promised results.

It is easy for whoever receives a divine revelation, Raucci told me, to get very into himself. To become arrogant. To believe that the whole world is less than him. Most of the Unification Churches had begun with extreme spiritual zeal. Good intentions, which, after time and the tremendous social growth of the movement, had become overshadowed. The ideal future that the founding fathers had proposed contrasted with some leaders' lifestyles. Because of their bad example, people could not understand anymore what Moon, who always kept his humility, was trying to teach them. Some leaders did business and acquired some decidedly unspiritual commitments in the name of the Unification Church. One group of followers opposed the movement's secularization because of the Reverend's most beloved son, who had died in a traffic accident while trying to help some people who had been injured. Raucci and others signed a petition addressed to the church's heads. Their manifesto stated that the executive board of the congregation did not live in keeping with the conduct that they preached. These comments did not go over well with the coterie of advisors surrounding Moon. They viewed them as a threat, and the signees were expelled, accused of having created a sect outside the church, of having been brainwashed—ironically the same charges the official movement had been accused of by journalists and many sectors of civil society.

Raucci suddenly found himself on the street, with nothing. He could not reconnect with his family and friends, nor could he enter the Unification Church's seminary. His beloved faith denied him bread and water. He was a prodigal son. A traitor. A persona non grata. He was without a present, and faced with the impossibility of reencountering his past, he would have to seek refuge in the future, and in his children: Joseph Christopher (also known as Joe), David and Gideon. Raucci never lost faith in the teachings and ideals of the Unification Church, and he educated his children following its principles. But not until he had seen them grow up, leave home and form relationships, and had heard the excellent things people said about them, did he begin to recover his lost pride. He then understood that the goodness that others admired in his offspring was not his work alone. He took another look at Madeline, his wife, and committed to change his pre-conceived vision of her. Surprisingly, he quickly began to learn what it meant to fall in love. He then came to the firm conviction that in the spiritual world, someone had planted the seed of the dream that the young Madeline had told him about in a room at the New Yorker Hotel. He now believed her dream had been a sign for him to accept the marriage, which, over time, would make him a lucky man.

* * *

Two hours after we leave JFK, the Lincoln Continental approaches a bridge over the Hudson River. Wow. Nature here is overwhelming. Once we passed the last house in the city, New York quickly became a forest so thick and so full of life that I could get my Ph.D. in biology just by observing the run-over animal species lying on the shoulders of the road. Which in a way makes me realize the lack of wildlife that we have in over-hunted Europe. Here, skunks, squirrels and chipmunks are still part of the landscape. It doesn't surprise me that Walt Disney had chosen them as main characters for his movies, even though I read somewhere that he actually did it to avoid lawsuits. You see, the run-over raccoons lining the shoulders of the road cannot file suit against the producers when they are depicted as the thieves in a film. "How do you like the view?" Raucci asks me with a smirk. "I love it," I respond, admiring the continuous under-deck truss that links the old capital of Kingston with the hamlet of Rhinecliff. "Look," says Raucci. "On the opposite bank, there to the north, is the seminary. Behind those trees, do you see it? If you look closely, you can see the seminary and its wharf." "What seminary? I can't see anything." Sarah and the children have long been asleep in the backseat and I can hardly pay attention to my interlocutor because I'm so absorbed in admiring the view. This is a river? So wide? *Madre mía*! The immense mass of water seems more like a succession of lakes, one flowing into another into infinity. It's a colossal current nearly a mile wide, dividing the lushness of extraordinary greens. A wild, almost pornographic undergrowth sprawls over its banks. Crossing this bridge is better than riding a roller coaster. For the moderate price of $1, round-trip, you can experience a sensation similar to flying in a small plane without having to leave the ground. And it is never gets old; quite the contrary. I highly recommend it. Many people have to cross it every day. In the fog. In the sun. In the apocalyptic light of a storm. Snow. In the burning colors of autumn. Over icy waters. I am like a kid in a bumper car; I could spend the whole day crossing this metallic giant from one side to the other. I happily pay the toll again, and again. Each time I cross, I feel lucky and I'm very grateful that engineer David B. Steinman cleverly designed the side handrails to ensure that they do not block the panoramic view from the car. Towandaaaa!

High on the bridge, it is easy to envision the privileged natural environment in which Raucci's three sons grew up and became interested in sports—the youngest, Gideon, in basketball and the oldest and middle sons, Joe and Dave, in long-distance running like their father. Raucci, trying to be coherent with the type of trades that would fit in the Ideal World that he was helping the Unification Church to create, decided to get involved only with works that would directly touch people's souls. Little important tasks like driving people to the airport, repairing wind instruments or coaching the kids' sports teams. This last mission is the one that reconnected him with the Brooklyn boy who ran the two and a half miles that separated him for the target, feeling with each stride that his heart was beating in time with nature.

Dave and Joe enthusiastically followed their father's advice until they began to experience health problems. First they were diagnosed with asthma. Then, after running long distances, sharp pains in the shins kept them from continuously training—far from ideal with a sport in which progress is only achieved through constancy. His sons' health problems were a complete surprise to Raucci, who had not experienced them when he competed for his school. How was it possible for Raucci, running without the aid of anything other than a pair of flat-soled Keds, to face so easily the challenges to which his sons succumbed, even though they had help from ergonomic shoes? Had his poor boys been born with physical limitations? Driven by curiosity, Raucci began research and was amazed to discover that his offspring were not the only people affected by injury. Both statistics and the testimonies of runners and trainers demonstrated that 21st-century American athletes were suffering many more injuries than their predecessors. Until the 1970s, the United States had produced Olympic medalists in cross-country running, but by the 1980s, American athletes began to lag behind and the fruits of the podium began to be reserved almost exclusively for Africans.

Raucci thought about this phenomenon for a long time. It seemed strange to him, to put it mildly. Maybe he did not have a higher calling, but he did have a profound understanding of sports. He lost sleep over his sons' issues. He looked for help in books. And then, one morning in the spring of 2000 he thought of what he had learned from Moon: Wisdom does not say one thing and nature another. Both should work in perfect balance. Yes! Raucci was convinced he had just solved the puzzle. "I've got it," he said to Madeline, who was at a loss as to how to respond to her husband's excitement. "I'm going to train the boys again." "But if they can't?" "But they can." He called Joe and Dave and proposed a plan with two non-negotiable rules: they must run barefoot and they could only inhale through their noses. Confused, the boys agreed to give it a try because, after all, Raucci is their father.

After seven consecutive seasons without injury, 21-year-old David Raucci won the gold medal in the 1,500-meter race at the International World Sports competition in Seoul, with a time of 03:57. On the podium, he received hugs and tributes from Abebe Gessesse, the trainer who led the Ethiopian Haile Gebrselassie to glory. Raucci had a chance to talk to Abebe about the race and the latter blurted out, "Send me the young Raucci and I'll turn him into a world champion." It was something the old fox of the track would not venture lightly. He knew he could shave about five seconds off David's time per year. If he could avoid injury, by the time he was 27, the age of wonder of many long-distance runners, David could reach the level of the world record-holder Guerrouj, the Moroccan who left the clock in Rome frozen at 03:26 in 1998.

* * *

Back in the Lincoln, we take a right at the light for Route 199 and head down River Road. Nico wakes up. He overhears our conversation and asks me what it is all about. "Oh, I'm telling your father, volunteers Raucci, that we should spend as much time barefoot as we can." "Really? I don't think so," replies Nico, pinching his nose with one hand and using his other hand to point to the bare foot of his seatmate. We pass Ferncliff Forest before finally reaching Rhinebeck. Home sweet home. We park in front of a light-gray, two-story house. Of course a basketball hoop hangs on the garage wall. The only sign of the former residents is the door-knocker bearing the last name Kane, and the television cable that sticks out from under the carpet. The house smells of wood, fresh paint and summer's end. We begin to unpack the suitcases.

We say goodbye to Raucci but arrange to meet again soon. Very soon. So soon that just a few days later, I find myself sitting with Nico and watching Raucci's sons jog across the grass at 6:00 a.m. They are running barefoot together with a bunch of kids in the park surrounding Red Hook High School. It's cool out and the dew-moistened grass turns the soles of their feet green. Sitting next to me, Raucci retells the story he told me on the way home from the airport. In his last year of high school, his older son Joe decided to run professionally, but when he increased his training from 45 miles to 70 miles a week, he began feeling pain—a pain that the experts believed was the normal price to pay for the constant pounding of the foot against the ground. But this was not Raucci's experience.

The statistics confirmed that African runners rarely suffered injuries, while North Americans experienced them excessively. Raucci wondered what factor made the athletes of the two continents so different and discovered two intersecting lines in his chart: Africans trained barefoot, while the decline of U.S. distance runners suspiciously coincided with the appearance of so-called ergonomic sports shoes on the market. Until the 1980s, everyone had used Keds; after that, the sole became inflated, the inside of the shoe cushioned, the heels snugger, but yet … injuries increased! Progress acted against nature. Intrigued by the finding, Raucci decided to do some research. Africa was far beyond his reach; so he figured out that, if the fact of running barefoot was related

25

to ancient traditions, it could be worth taking a look into the Native American cultures whose history was closer at hand. And, sure enough, he learned that, before the arrival of the Europeans, the members of many tribes inhabiting the continent would run great distances every day. In 14th-century America, the legs were the only means of transport, so running was the ideal solution if you wanted to do errands quickly. For the pre-Columbian Indian, it was normal to run an average of 300 miles a week; more than four times the 70 miles that had injured his son. Surprisingly, in none of the remaining transcriptions of healing protocol treatment of the different Native Americans tribes that he examined, could he find neither a single mention of leg injuries nor a description of their possible treatment. Did that mean that the first Americans didn't get injured for running? Raucci also discovered that, like the African athletes, the Native Americans always ran barefoot, or at most, with only the simple protection of some thin moccasins that did not interfere with the adequate flexing of their muscles. Thus, the first inhabitants of the Americas considered that the feet had not been conceived by the Creator to bear any weight—not even that of shoes. For Native Americans, the feet, like the hands, could be covered to protect them from rough terrain or extreme weather, but this was never done on a regular basis.

The human foot is designed to detect, through a multitude of sensors incorporated into the sole, the morphology of the surface it steps on: sand, rock, grass, mud—information that it immediately transmits to the brain to determine the strength with which the foot should hit the ground. Under optimal running conditions, the brain will request the foot to land softly and always from front to back; first the ball and finally the heel. When the terrain is rough, the brain orders other muscles to help the poor feet to keep us upright on the uneven surface. Then, we either balance ourselves with our arms; or shift the trunk forward, or flex the legs to lower the center of gravity. Any posture is okay as long as it prevents us from stomping too hard. Although, if that happens, the sole pain would advise us to step more softly next time. Ouch!

The shoes interrupt this process. They blunt all our sole's sensors … causing the brain to panic. What the hell! As a result, in a desperate attempt to collect information from the surface, a cerebral instinct command is triggered to our feet: hit the ground with extra force, and hit it now! And they do. And they don't stop stomping since, protected by the cushioned shoes, they don't feel any pain. But something else gets damaged through the shocked skeleton while the feet try unsuccessfully to gather ground data.

In Red Hook, the group of barefoot runners climb the campus hill, jog around some trees and then head back down the hillside. They all seem happy … except for one who just got stung by a wasp. Dang! Raucci manages to remove the stinger, squeezes the runner's foot to eliminate the venom and then applies ice followed by a baking soda poultice. Not a big deal. What did I tell you? The runner who got stung is running again. Uphill. Downhill. He runs up and down innumerable times until he reaches the 15 miles his trainer ordered him to run. By then enough time has passed for my slacks to soak up the morning dew from the wooden bench and I feel the cold dampness on my backside. It is a strange moment that I take advantage of to ponder my vocation as a journalist with a simple question: What the heck am I doing here at 6:30 in the morning? Haven't I given up the radio to leave early risings behind, among other reasons? And then I hear a voice inside me, similar to that of Raucci's grandfather, but with a Castilian accent, which says sarcastically: "Well, in the U.S., you're going to have to get up at the crack of dawn plenty, buddy." Although I haven't been here long, I've already realized that Americans love the rooster hour. Many go to sleep as soon as the sun sets and jump out of bed before it rises. Here the afternoon, as the name suggests, begins literally after 12:00. By contrast, for Spaniards, the halfway point of the day occurs after lunch, at about 3:00 p.m., and you begin to say good afternoon after 4 p.m. It's a cultural gap of three hours, which foolishly led me to accept Raucci's invitation to meet him and the runners "first thing in the morning." How could I have known that this

27

referred to 6:00 a.m., not 9:00 a.m.? As far as I'm concerned, I'm still on vacation, and during the summer, at least in Spain, 6:00 in the morning is not first thing in the morning—it's very late at night! It's the time you go to bed after a wild night out.

At last the young athletes break formation and approach the bench where we are sitting. We greet each other. The first thing I notice is that their feet have lives of their own. The toes move independently, like the serpents in Medusa's hair. The difference between their feet and those of the rest of humanity is obvious. If you look down in a swimming pool on a hot day, the toes of most everyone are pressed together due to the narrow-pointed toe mold of the shoes most people normally wear. Frequently, the sides of the feet flatten and, rather than retaining their natural cylindrical volume, adopt the geometric shape of McDonald's french fries. But not the feet of the Red Hook runners. After two seasons of freedom, their feet have expanded like dehydrated sponges when you toss them in water. The soles of their feet paint the silhouette of an inverted pyramid. A prism starts at the heel and thickens through the arch to end splayed, like the leaves of a palm tree, in a little branch of toes—five clearly rounded, separated toes, with individual movement. These kids' feet are appendices that move separately at the will of their owners, toes that wave happily at the camera when you point it in their direction. Click, click.

Barefoot training makes the young runners' feet land flat on the ground, and allows a light, smooth movement from the tip of the toes to the heel. This muscular action strengthens their calf muscles, thereby giving them extra force to increase the length of their stride. Energy is put at the service of speed, rather than being wasted by repeatedly pounding the ground. Because the runners have recovered forward traction, they have become much faster. They take off easier and have recovered agility in the sprint. Plus, there is a significant caloric savings that can be used to hasten the final sprint.

Barefoot running has many wonders, but they are still far from being accepted by the sport's experts. New Zealander Arthur Lydiard, the inventor of jogging, who trained many Olympic champions, predicted that when a flexible running shoe was designed to permit the normal function of the foot muscles, runners would reduce their time by a full minute in the 10K race. Shoe manufacturers have invested too many millions in this industry for new evidence to come to light that would threaten their business. Neither do institutions want to run risks. Even the poorest schools in the U.S. have a grass field or cinder track. What with liability, a barefoot student runner stepping on a piece of glass could mean the end of a coach's career or a school's sports program, or even the shutting down of a school. Athletes have no choice but to adapt to these circumstances. Sudanese-American runner Lopez Lomong is a good example. The athlete who was chosen to lead the U.S. team at the 2008 Beijing Olympics learned to run barefoot in his native country and trained barefoot until he left Africa at 16. During the races sponsored by Foot Locker in New York State, Raucci asked Lomong what made him start wearing running shoes and the champion responded: "I was forced to by law." He did not want to, but he had no choice.

In late 1999 in California, it was rumored that Stanford University was about to impose barefoot training for field competitions. This measure would have revolutionized the heart of American athleticism because Stanford's sports department is deservedly known as the Home of Champions. If Stanford had competed as an independent nation in the London 2012 Olympics, it would have earned fifth place in the world ranking for gold medals. Some claim that the decision to abandon running shoes was almost a reality, but in the end, the university opted for a less risky alternative as a result of the collaboration between its athletes and Nike, whose founder was a Stanford alumnus. The result was the design of a revolutionary running shoe whose sole attempts to provide the same freedom of movement as the naked foot. Nike Free was born and its promotional launching praised the benefits of running barefoot.

"Call me crazy," says Raucci. "But to me, Nike Free reminds me of the story of the Emperor's New Clothes. The ad announces that running barefoot is the most natural, healthiest way to run, but that it is not recommended. However, it suggests that you should run *as if* barefoot, but with shoes on. Wearing a running shoe that seems like you're not wearing it and whose price, in many cases, is at least $100—hello?!?"

At the Red Hook park I entertain myself by watching the runners' toes moving independently and taking a lot of photographs. Click. Click. "A runner wearing shoes," says Raucci, "is the same as a baseball batter wearing a coat." Innumerable nerve endings are distributed on the soles of the feet, which are massaged when we touch the ground, and which produce beneficial effects on the internal organs. "No one would consider putting a one-inch display protector on an iPhone screen," says Raucci. "Likewise, putting a shoe between our feet and the ground makes us give up our built-in acupuncture. It is just the opposite of what Asian cultures do. In Asia, people take every opportunity to revive the body through its acupuncture points." In fact, Raucci adds, one of the many reasons the Chinese use chopsticks is that they massage some of the nerve endings in the hand, sending pleasant sensations to the brain, which, when mixed with the senses of taste, touch and smell, make eating a much more sensorial and pleasurable experience.

Each muscle is complemented by another. When one stretches, the other contracts, and vice versa. If we force the mechanisms in just one direction, we will create an imbalance in the musculature. And that, Raucci informs me, is precisely what shoes do by forcing us to change the frontal support of the toes for the back of the heel. The use of shoes relaxes the ligaments in the front of the foot, whose main mission is support. By not carrying out this function, we are losing the ability to spread the toes. Moreover, tensing the front muscles of the shin excessively results in the progressive atrophy of the calf muscle. When the heel hits the ground, the vibration impacts the ankle, which causes inadequate pressure on the metatarsus. This creates problems, which, when diagnosed, are referred to as the familiar conditions of tendinitis or sprains. "We should spend as much time barefoot as we can," Raucci insists. "Otherwise, sooner or later, the chain of collateral damage will extend dangerously upwards until it finally destroys the musculature of the back," he says. "It will atrophy the muscles to the extent that, in the case of women who frequently wear high heels, it can even change the position of the trunk and, consequently, the placement of the internal organs. Wow!"

Okay, I'm thinking, enough about running. The jet lag has left me a bit dazed. I arrived just two days ago, I tell Raucci. I have lots of things to do and I cannot devote my whole life to thinking about feet. Besides, the idea was for me to come here to write a movie script based on the life of my cleaning lady, an older woman from Madrid. If this keeps up, I might just have to begin the movie with Cándida running across a sandy beach to hear Reverend Moon speak. The truth is that there is not much more room on my hard drive. When you meet someone who takes you from the airport to your home, he is supposed to talk to you about the traffic or perhaps ask you how long it took your plane to travel along the 40th parallel and the 5,779 kilometers that separate New York from Madrid. This is commonly known as "small talk." But instead, destiny wanted my meeting Raucci to take another course and now, in the east field of Red Hook High School, he tells me that even if we are finished talking about running barefoot, he has yet another subject to discuss with me. Another subject?! But what else could he tell me that he hasn't already? "It has to do with the Native Americans," he says. "You already told me they ran a lot," I protest. "Three hundred miles a week, I think you said." He nods. "But apart from running, they also rested," he says. "So?" "Well, it's just that we don't rest," he says. "Well, we do, but not enough." "Oh, dear God!"

"In addition to the evolutionary error of coming down out of trees and putting on shoes, the white man also screwed things up by inventing the chair," Raucci tells me. According to traditional Chinese medicine, backaches arrived in the West when we stopped squatting to rest. In Asia, as well as Africa and South America, it is common to see people squatting, whether it is a group of adults waiting for a bus or a gang of kids playing with a spinning top. But in the West, the so-called civilized world, people sit on chairs and benches in seats that disrupt the natural tensions and relaxations of the musculature of the legs and trunk. Squatting, with the knees together and the backside resting on the heels, realigns the bones and strengthens the muscles we have pounded on during daily activity. It performs the same function as the stretching that cats and dogs do when they get up: it realigns the body. "The chair has caused considerable damage," Raucci tells me. "You don't say," I respond, standing up and feeling reluctant to erase from my list of heroes the two Bauhaus architects who designed the Barcelona chair, an icon of modernism. "Please don't go yet," Raucci says. "Sit down for a minute." "No," I reply. "I really have to go and besides, if I stayed, I'd have to squat." He laughs as we say goodbye.

"Goodbye, guys!" I thank all the runners for their kind attention and wish the one who got stung by the yellow jacket the best of luck. I turn to go. But Raucci does not want me to leave without offering his definitive conclusion on all the subjects discussed. "We uselessly try to alleviate many of our pains," he explains, "by applying treatments to the specific place where it hurts. A crass mistake. Back pains could be overcome if we would just pay attention to where they originate. Down there. The more sophisticated the shoe, the more cushioned the sole and the more it hugs our ankle, the worse it is for our health." "Okay," I say. "Let's keep in touch." As I walk toward the car, I silently thank the Camper shoemaker that the soles of my Majorcan moccasins are as flat as the Castile plains. Still, nothing makes me think that this conversation is just the appetizer for other, more surprising revelations to come. Or that, thanks to our encounter, I will spend some weeks of my American stay immersed in a book about nasal breathing written in Rio Grande, Brazil, in 1860 and published in London 10 years later. What's to become of my cleaning lady film script, *Cándida*?

2

September

Julia says she wants to be a teacher when she grows up. Her stuffed animals are her students on the kitchen floor. "It's okay," she says to the yellow giraffe. "Just calm down. Take a deep breath and everything is going to be back to normal." The giraffe looks bewildered. "Where did you hear that phrase?" I ask my daughter. "That's what my teacher at school says to a hyperactive boy in my class," she says, casually. "When he gets anxiety attacks, the teacher tells him, 'Take a deep breath and everything is going to be back to normal.'" "Oh, I see," I respond, trying to play down the issue. I step out into the street. Another blue and green day of clear skies and leafy trees. This landscape has the same tones as Church's paintings. Spain is red and yellow like Sorolla's massive paintings on display at the Hispanic Society of America in New York City. Artists capture the lighting of life with their oils—the sun on the Mediterranean beaches, where couples embrace on the sand versus the woods on the banks of the Hudson, where couples go cruising in little boats.

Emulating Julie Andrews in the opening scene of *The Sound of Music*, but moving in a more manly fashion, I search for the ray of sunshine that slips through the walnut trees in the backyard. I take a deep breath. Everything is going to be fine. I'm in New York—not the city, but the state. I have ended up in the town where my wife was born. It's called Rhinebeck, which in German means "brook of the Rhine" because the first Palatine settlers got a case of European homesick blues. It's 100 miles from Manhattan, halfway between New York City and Albany, the state capital. It puzzles me that in the United States, with only four exceptions, the most populous city of a state is not the one with a star on the map. Weird? According to James Howard Kunstler, author of the amazing history book *The Geography of Nowhere*, the founding Americans didn't want politicians near the business centers, so when their cities flourished, many states exiled their capitals to the provinces. So, for instance, Chicago is not the capital of Illinois. And in Pennsylvania, although the most interesting streets continue to be the ones of Philadelphia, the administration is found in Harrisburg.

Rhinebeck is an enclave in a valley of rolling hills that remind me of a model train set. There are small wooden houses painted in pastel tones and churches with tall bell towers. Farms like the one where Babe the pig lived, with red barns, silos like giant lipsticks and white fences to keep in the horses. Serpentine roads cutting through forests of ancient locust, chestnut, maple and oak trees. The foliage here extends beyond infinity. What I learned in the cement jungle will be rather useless for defending myself against ticks and poison ivy in a rural community of 7,000 people. Like Billy Crystal in *City Slickers*, I'm going to have to face challenges, the first of which is to understand that the cardinal points serve for something more than simply decorating weathervanes.

A month after our arrival in the Hudson Valley, I can proudly affirm that I finally know where North is. It wasn't easy, I admit, because I'm a bit *despistado* (absentminded) when it comes to directions. Well, *despistado* in Spanish. In English, I would probably be considered a 3.5 dyslexic, with the right to use a handicapped sticker so that I can park my car right in front of the door of the Stop & Shop—a sticker that a surprising number of people here seem to have. It's so common that it's as if you can cut your fingernail too short, go to the doctor and be prescribed a handicap sticker. At my driving test, my poor sense of direction drove the Kingston policeman who accompanied me in the car crazy. When he asked me to turn left, I went right. "Careful, that's a one-way street!" "But, officer," I said, "didn't you tell me to turn there?" The poor man, who didn't want to flunk me but merely to ensure that I would not become a threat on wheels, ordered me to pull over to the curb. "Okay," he said, "hands up." Imagining myself being carted off to Guantanamo Bay, I said to the officer, "You're going to arrest me for a little traffic violation?" "No way, dude," he said. "Just put your hands up and I'm going to teach you once and for all how to tell which one is left." "Oh, okay," I exclaimed, relieved. Then he asked me to extend my thumbs and index fingers to form the bottom corner of a square. "What letter does the word 'left' begin with?" he asked. Like Bert and Ernie on *Sesame Street*, I told him it begins with an L. "Good," he said. "Now, in which of your hands have you drawn an L with your fingers?" I looked at both hands. The policeman shook his head methodically, from side to side, as if he were playing the part of a metronome. Tick, tock, tick, tock... This is the country of show business and even the police are natural showmen. Tick, tock, tick, tock... Feeling under pressure, I confirmed that the fingers on my right hand formed an arrow. By contrast, those on my left formed a clear letter L. "In this one," I said. "Correct," he responded, obviously relieved. "So, let's go, start the car and when I say 'to the left,' do me a favor and turn towards the direction of the hand that makes a letter L, got it?" "Okay, understood." We took off. Left. Right. Left. Right. *Suuuunny Day, sweepin' the clouds awayyyyyy, on my way to where the air is sweeeeeet. Can you tell me how to get, how to get to Sesame Street?*

My driver's license arrived a few days later in the mail. Ever since then, I've been able to live like a normal citizen and buy beer at the gas station. Your face might have more wrinkles than a California raisin, but they'll still ask you for your driver's license to verify that you are at least 21. "Hey, Warren," I say to the attendant at the Mobil station on the edge of the town. "License, please." I know it's the law—no ID, no beer—but it's still ridiculous. At the gas station, there are two unbreakable rules. First, you need a State of New York ID to buy alcohol. Second, you can never enter with a propane tank. So the worst thing I have surmised that you can do is to try to buy beer without an ID and with a propane tank hidden beneath your raincoat. It could be considered a double felony. It would be an important case for our friend Karen Valle to resolve. Karen, whose son Adam is in Julia's class, has a formidable sense of humor. She jokes with Sarah that when our children grow up, they'll devote themselves to investigating fraud. They'll park the car in front of the gym and spend the morning dunking donuts in their coffee until they spot someone leaving the facility who has skipped work that day. Then they'll jump out of the car and confront the guy: "Aha! So your back was hurting and you called in sick, did you? Come with us." I laugh, but her fantasy doesn't surprise me because there are so many detective shows on television that people naturally become fans. The shows that begin with a terrible crime seem to be the ones most repeated on cable TV, combined with infinite reruns of *The Fugitive*. The one with Richard Kimble seems to be on every other day. We've seen Harrison Ford jump into the water from the top of that dam to avoid getting caught by Tommy Lee Jones countless times. Mr. Ford must be a wreck from taking the plunge all those times.

Every time I go to buy beer at the gas station, even though it's always the same one in town, and no matter whether I was just there yesterday, they have to verify that I look like the photo on my driver's license. I look dreadful in that picture, but I will undoubtedly see that image of me as young and smiling when it's time to renew my license in a few years. ID photos, like fine wines, get much better with age. "ID, please." "Here it is." "Thanks." It's a good idea to take the whole affair of having to prove that you're over 21 as a confidence-building exercise. If you feel depressed about the passage of time, go to your neighborhood Mobil for a six-pack. You'll feel optimistic again, at least for a few hours. And if you don't like beer, go to Village Pizza, where the owner, with his unmistakable, deep radio announcer's voice, greets you, no matter what your age, with a friendly "Hello, young lady/young man." But back to the gas station and my six-pack: "What's up, Warren?" "Wait, I have to put the beer in a paper bag. You can't take it like that." Finally, I leave, rejuvenated by the ID exercise, but with the sensation of having committed some misdeed what with having to conceal the liquor. I look inside the brown bag at the label on the bottles and tell Samuel Adams, "It's okay, Sam, take a deep breath and everything is going to be back to normal." Mr. Adams appears to relax a little.

The driver's license is so important in the United States that you can obtain one even if you don't drive. Yes...There is actually a driver's license for non-drivers! All you have to do is go to the Department of Motor Vehicles to get it.

But let's get back to the subject of sense of direction. In Upstate New York, if you don't have a compass incorporated into your hard drive, you're out of luck. Here, when people give you directions, they assume you navigate on land like Sinbad does the sea. They tell you to pass Country Comfort Furniture going south, then turn west on Chestnut Street and head north at the intersection with Crosmour Road and turn in to the fifth driveway on the east side of the street. Okay, I'm on my way; let's see if I make it. Of course, once you're used to it, the method is quite precise and prevents mix-ups. Once I was supposed to meet a friend from Seville in Madrid at the Puerta del Sol, which is the icon of the Spanish capital, yet we couldn't find each other for five hours. The reason was that in Andalusia and Extramadura, from which most of the conquerors of the New World hailed, there's no distinction between the pronunciation of the letters Z and S. So *Gonzalez* sounds the same as *Gonsales*. The Z (theta) sound, it seems, is a Castilian contribution from King Charles V. He governed Spain like Schwarzenegger did in California for many years: with an Austrian accent. The courtesans of Castile, sucking up to the King, started to mimic his defective speech rather than to correct it. Thus, the Spanish lisp was born, which we inhabitants of the center of the Iberian Peninsula love to flaunt. With the southern pronunciation, the Puerta del Sol can refer either to the famous square in Madrid where I waited for a friend (*Puerta der Só*) or the entrance to the Madrid zoo on the outskirts of the city (*Puerta der Zó*), where my friend was in fact waiting for me.

The compass doesn't allow for confusion. I've found a landmark, my own personal North Star, to help me find my North: Williams Lumber, the mecca of do-it-yourselfdom. The place where all men must go at least a couple of times a week to feel they are playing the role that nature has assigned them: to make repairs in their homes. There you will always find a new tool that is surprisingly indispensable for filling that hole in the garage wall or that strange piece you were looking for to fix that kitchen cabinet door that didn't want to close. It doesn't matter if you don't know what the hell you're looking for. At Williams, they call each screw by its name. Not a nut gets past them. Just share your concern with any of the employees wearing burgundy-colored shirts that inhabit the store's aisles and they will take you to the exact location where you'll find that little thingy you were looking for. "Was it a pivoting hoist ring?" "I guess it was, thank you." Williams Lumber is my North Pole, and besides, since I go there so often, I sometimes receive coupons with Ace points. What more can you ask for? When leaving the town, before turning on the ignition, I always think, so where is Williams? Once I locate it, I can configure a map in my head. To return home, my reference point is Ruge's Auto Shop. Sometimes I look at the sign in the front, other times I look at the owner, who frequently crosses the main street to go to the garage of the Subaru dealership and from the Subaru dealership to the garage. He's easy to spot: Lewis Ruge is the only human being who wears shorts in hot weather and ice storms alike. I'm going to freak out the day I see him wearing long pants. I will interpret it as a sign that a new Ice Age is upon us. Or the end of the world. Or both.

During the second week of September, coinciding with a sudden drop in temperature, the streets of Rhinebeck fill with old cars—hundreds of perfectly-preserved clunkers which, when they circulate together around the Victorian-style houses, transport you to the past. Some drivers dress in early-20th-century clothing too, including vests, fingerless gloves, aviator glasses and checkered caps. At the intersection in the center of town, those coming and going in different directions meet but do not form traffic jams.

The four-way stop, which is like the European roundabout but without the decorative fountain in the middle, works beautifully. Only occasionally does some wise guy just pretend to stop, and when that happens, the policeman on duty writes him a ticket to fill the municipal coffers. There are small red and black cars from the 1940s with exposed engines, long vanilla and turquoise-colored Cadillacs, lemon yellow Pontiacs and emerald green Oldsmobiles. A 1920s Coca Cola truck passes in front of me, carrying yellow wooden crates on which is painted in red: *Every Bottle Sterilized*. It's as if the collection of toy cars on the top shelf of Williams Lumber comes to life and takes to the streets. A local *Toy Story*. A miracle.

Each fall, everyone celebrates the Nationals, motorized jewels born before 1972. Gradually, the 68 hectares of grass at the Dutchess County Fairgrounds become speckled with the colorful presence of more than 1,500 vehicles, which share space with auto parts dealers. The cars, some of which are for show, others for sale, attract people from every corner of the East Coast. For a modest fee, many people even sleep at the fairgrounds in their campers.

Taking advantage of the flood of cars, which parade slowly past our house, Julia abandons her stuffed friends to sell lemonade with Makenzie, our neighbors' granddaughter, and a couple of friends from her nursery school, Isabel and Grace. Sarah has placed a low table with a plastic cooler on the sidewalk and the girls offer thirsty drivers a glass of lemonade for 50 cents. They spend hours chanting the same line: "Lemonade, ice cold lemonade, only fifty cents!" Each time a customer approaches and the girls make a sale, their faces light up with an ear-to-ear grin. They no doubt plan to squander their profits at Stickle's, an original five-and-dime store where time stands still. A place where kids can find everything they dream about.

At four, Julia seems to have a clear understanding of things. During breakfast, she told her older brothers, Nico and Max, that she was sorry to inform them that she was the only intelligent person in the family. My sons, who landed in the United States at the ages of eight and ten, respectively, didn't pay much attention to the comment. They went out to the garage and got busy painting the walls white. It was their idea: "*Papá*, we can't leave it like that, you know?" What? When we moved in, we found the garage walls sheet-rocked. Nothing special: it looked just like every other garage in this valley. After all, it's just a room we will use to hang tools, store garbage cans and put the second-hand car to sleep, which, like nearly everyone else's vehicle, is a Subaru that we bought at Ruge's. But my kids suspect that the room will form part of our life more than we realize and that, in some way, it needs to be integrated into the house. It seems that in New York State, architects place the main entrance on the front of the house because that's what they learned in school, not because it's necessary. No one uses it. Here, the car functions as our legs, and everyone enters the house through the garage. This is especially clear when you leave the village and drive around the streets of the outskirts of town. Because some house designs were selected from a catalogue, they are not especially designed to adapt to the specific topography of the land on which they sit. And since most owners prefer entering through the garage—also because the shorter the driveway, the fewer hours spent shoveling snow in winter—the useless front door may be located just about anywhere. Sometimes on top of a rock. Other times next to a cliff. Or in other such unexpected places that it seems the homes landed randomly from the sky, like Dorothy's house in the Land of Oz.

We like to take daily walks around Wynkoop Lane, and so do some of our neighbors. It's a beautiful street that begins in the village but hits the town border halfway down. It is a challenge for the authorities of the different local governments to agree on whether the village or the town municipal departments should remove the trash and clear away the snow on this street. It's a mile away from Route 308, which cuts through the forest and extends until the last farm, and passes a little stone house that looks like it belongs to Hansel and Gretel. Taking walks in Rhinebeck is a common practice. The only thing is that it occurs at high speed, making you feel like a 33-rpm record being played at 45 rpm.

Ready, set, go! Tighten your shoelaces, grab a bottle of water, and we're off! Many people walk in pairs, particularly women, some of whom take their running shoes to work with them to put them on at lunchtime so they can dash out for a power walk. They rush along the streets, up Livingston, down Chestnut, with faces red as apples, advancing at a military pace to reach their mysterious targets.

There are three shifts of walking couples. First are the early birds, who set out at the crack of dawn. The second shift of walkers goes out at lunchtime, while the third takes a spin before dinner after work. During the rest of the day you'll rarely see anyone voluntarily walking down the street, unless they're taking the dog out. We usually run into the same people on our walks: the inseparable cousins Colleen Kane and Erin Decker—who some newcomers refer to as if they were a lovely unisex couple—or Elwood and Maggie. Elwood Smith is an illustrator who has created a wonderful universe of characters. Since he is a great artist and deals with publishers in the city, everyone assumes he is also a native New Yorker, but he actually grew up in Michigan, in a town even smaller than Rhinebeck, and he is more country than corn. He told me so himself one day during a break in our walk because, thank God, just like Spaniards, Americans don't need to be properly introduced to engage in conversation. Otherwise, the same thing that happened to Joe Hambrook with his neighbor would have happened to me. Joe created the Muzzy monster for the BBC. He lived in Greenwich, England, where Eastern and Western time meet. I visited him once to ask him to collaborate on a Spanish TV project, and he told me the following story. Every morning of his life, he would leave his little house on the banks of the Thames at 6:30 a.m. At exactly the same hour, his neighbor from across the street would emerge from his house. They would say hello. "Good day." "Good day." Then they would go their separate ways—the neighbor to his car, Joe to the nearest train station on his way to the BBC studios in London. A few years later, the Hambrooks spent a sabbatical year in Tuscany. One day, as he was taking his dog for a walk along a small path between the vineyards, Joe spotted someone reading the newspaper. He thought he recognized him; indeed, when he got close enough, he realized it was his neighbor from Greenwich. What on earth was this guy doing in Italy? Joe walked past him. "Good day." The neighbor lifted his eyes from the newspaper. "Good day." Both of them kept going as if they'd never seen each other, and they never saw each another again. "We couldn't stop to talk," Joe explained to me, "because we had never been properly introduced."

In Rhinebeck, except for some Mexican workers who travel by bicycle, everyone drives, even if they live two blocks from their destination. To walk—in other words, to power walk—is practiced only near the traffic light at the intersection of Route 9 and Market Street, especially toward the north or east. For unknown reasons, locals don't tend to walk south or west, although the shops in that direction are just as interesting as the others. To the west, the town appears to end at the Bagel Shop. There's nothing beyond it. It's Comanche territory. The Wild West. To the south, as Montgomery Street turns into Mill Street, walkers seem to lose interest. Once they pass Olde Mill Wine & Spirits—where Charles Derbyshire always offers the best advice for your taste and your budget— it's hard to keep going. It's as if people were afraid to move beyond that point. As if losing sight of the reference of America's oldest continuously operated hotel, the Beekman Arms, filled them with anxiety. As if they became oxygen-starved as they approached South Street, forcing them to turn around in search of fresh air.

People do walk, but only short distances. From the car to Hammertown—"Love where you live!"—the modern country furniture store where you wish you could afford to buy every item on display. From Fosters to the Smoke Shop. From Upstate Films to Terrapin Restaurant to try a tapa of Macadamia-nut-tempura calamari dipped in pineapple sauce. From the Department Store, where you can find that lumberjack shirt that every foreigner has dreamed about wearing someday, to Samuels's for coffee or hot chocolate. From Oblong Books, to Gigi's for a thin-crusted, crunchy "Skizza pizza" bianca of pear, arugula, fig, goat cheese and truffle-scented oil. Yum… From Calico to pick up a chocolate cake to Paper Trail to admire the books brilliantly deconstructed into sculptures by Ramón Lascano. And back to the car again. On weekends, most of the pedestrians are visitors from New York City who can be spotted from a mile away in their country gentleman outfits or their stilettos. Like the pilgrims from Rome embarking on Via Cruces, they stop religiously at each of the numerous real estate agencies' displays to look at photos of houses for sale. So many tourists come to Rhinebeck these days that it is hard to find a parking space, and the folks at Rhinebeck Bank have put a security gate manned by a guard to ensure that only bank customers occupy the bank-owned parking lot. But the locals have figured out the trick. They park, greet the guard, since he is like family, use the ATM machine and then go about whatever errand really brought them there. To Northern Dutchess Pharmacy so George or Walter can refill their prescriptions. To the Curthoys' wine and liquor store, where an abundance of Chilean and Spanish wines are sold. Quality for price, these beverages outstrip the French, Italian and Californian. Or to admire the windows of Hummingbird, Peggy and Bruce Lubman's jewelry store, whose exquisite elegance compels you to check out the display cabinet, even if you weren't planning to buy anything.

So that's how it works: people mill around on Rhinebeck's sidewalks, strolling from one side of the street to the other, but keep within the four blocks surrounding the traffic light.

Like I said, in Rhinebeck, the car serves as your legs. Welcome to the U.S.A. In the 1940s, Detroit lobbyists took over the American transport system by buying the lines of the electric railway systems of the big cities to impede their expansion to smaller towns, leaving undesirable buses, with infrequent stops, as the only alternative to cars. Yet in the United States, most people live scattered all over the countryside, isolated from one another and have to travel several miles to go to the supermarket, send a package or go to church. In the Hudson Valley, people live in the middle of the woods, on the edge of a lake or at the top of a hill overlooking the immense Hudson—formidable spots where you are lost without a car. People here are not afraid of distances. One-fifth of all Hudson Valley residents take an average of 45 minutes to reach their workplace, the same amount of time it took me in the city what with traffic jams and all. And that's just the people who travel within the area. Those who work in Manhattan have one hour and 40 minutes on the train each way—every day! It is a life of sacrifice for these people, who want a rural, friendly lifestyle for their children, but don't want to give up the professional career and income that the great metropolis provides. In one way, though, the commuters are the lucky ones because they can calmly read a book or chat with adults on the train each day. When you are the parent of small children, having three hours a day to read something, anything, or to be able to have a conversation with someone, anyone, can be a privilege rather than a sacrifice.

Given the pressing need to move about in a motorized fashion, driving begins early in this country, at 16. It is quite a shock to see such young kids behind the wheel on the highway. "Wasn't that so-and-so's son?" "Yes, it was." That's why all 10th graders have an astonished expression—because even they themselves cannot believe that adults would let them drive so young. When they get their license they jump for joy around the neighborhood. They pass you in their car one, two, three times. Any excuse is good enough to hit the road. The car is the only way to earn a few bucks doing errands, take granny shopping in Kingston or take a girlfriend to a movie. You leave the house and return to it on four wheels, always entering through the garage. We could ask Warren Smith, our architect neighbor, to eliminate the front door of our house so we can take advantage of the extra stretch of wall space in the house. Maybe we could use it to hang a photograph by Rob Hite, the Esopus-based artist who makes images of the fantasy houses he builds with sticks and roots. No one would know the difference from the outside. We could just screw in a fake front door out of respect for street aesthetics—just like everyone does with shutters. Yes. In Rhinebeck there are many window shutters that don't actually shut. Shhhh...

44

By the time they have finished their first can of primer, Nico and Max are already tired of their paintbrushes. They decide to continue their labor *mañana*, but as the days pass, the original idea loses steam. But I'm getting ahead of the events here. Just as we were about to become the owners of the only garage with a painted interior in the whole Valley, the boys realized that in this part of the world, no one, not even us, minds in the very least entering the house by crossing a mishmash of firewood, bicycles and snow shovels. Here, the content is more important than the container; having a comfortable home is more important than the way you access it. This gives Americans the advantage over us Spaniards, who are more worried about the way things look. My mother and sister once spent weeks making a costume for my niece who acted in a school play, playing a character of the French playwright Molière, with a bell-shaped skirt and a white wig. The costume was so showy that everyone talked about it. A photo of it even appeared in the newspaper. But no one said a word about my niece's acting ability, and wasn't that what we were supposed to talk about? Live and learn. So in Rhinebeck, the garage remained half-finished. The southern wall boasts a coat of primer and the northern wall is natural sheetrock. That wise renunciation enabled us to avoid the terrible dilemma of choosing the tone of white. Because in the United States, the country of multiple choices, not even white can just be … white. No. You have to choose between Decorator's White, Dove White … and so on.

The American pragmatism that led us to leave the garage as it was and devote ourselves to more important things is an intrinsic part of my wife's personality and truly fascinates me. I learned about it immediately after she graduated from college and we moved into an apartment together in Madrid. Every time we liked someone, I would belt out that handy Spanish catchphrase, "Maybe we'll furnish the house soon and when we're done, we'll have you around one of these days." But Sarah would surprise me by suggesting to them: "Better yet, why not come over for dinner tonight?" At first, this just blew me away. In Spain, the house has to be in perfect order to receive guests. And since it is never quite perfect, everyone socializes on the streets. If you go to Spain and see the restaurants full, it is not a clear sign of an economic boom. No. It is simply that everything is celebrated outside the house—not only weddings, but First Communions, birthdays, dinners with friends, get-togethers to watch a soccer game. You can spend years in my country and never receive an invitation to dinner at someone's house. But you will not leave the restaurant and the bar for the whole weekend. Consider yourself warned.

This practical view also reflects the philosophical movement begun in the late 19th century by Charles Sanders Pierce and William James, who measured the effectiveness of a thought in terms of its capacity to contribute to daily happiness. If it makes us happier, it is good. Thus, ever since we arrived, our Rhinebeck neighbors have been trying to make us happy. We have had a packed schedule of friendly dinners ever since. Friends of Sarah's. Friends of her brother Harry, whom the family calls Huck. Friends of friends of somebody else's friend. Parents of our kids' school friends. Friends of a friend we met at the house of a friend of a friend, who, it turns out, lives nearby. Everyone helped cushion our moon landing. Americans don't need to take out a loan to organize a big party. They open their house, provide their good will and don't blush when they ask their guests to bring wine or salad or contribute to the barbecue with chicken or hotdogs. The important thing is to have a good time.

Nico rushes in to ask me for permission to buy a foosball table. "What's that?" The people in the yellow house on the corner are having a yard sale, like several of our neighbors who have taken advantage of the influx of people who came to see the old cars. If a cargo ship were hired to go to Haiti carrying everything that people here offer in garage sales, Haiti would become one of the world's leading economies overnight and a member of the G8. Around here, people enter into a fit of cleaning in the fall and decide to rid themselves of some of their belongings. They put a price on everything, although, thanks to the ancient custom of bargaining, they end up giving practically everything away for free, as long as you take it with you. Sometimes they even put up a "Free" sign, confident that the object will disappear quickly. The neighbors in the yellow house will let us have the foosball table for $20, Nico says. So cheap? "Well, the sign says $50, but I've got $20 saved and Sandy agreed." "Sandy?" He points to the woman who waves at us from the corner with a wide smile. Oh, well. "Thanks, Sandy Blair, it's a deal." We now have a foosball table.

We enter the house with our new acquisition. Sarah has prepared a Spanish tortilla, a frittata with potatoes and onions, like the law mandates. A cold beer is the perfect accompaniment to the appetizer. We sit outside. The yard smells of recently cut grass and brings me back to the days when I played rugby on the fields of the Universidad Complutense. Next to the patio of blue stone, a local natural rock that resembles chalkboard but is much thicker, there is a butterfly bush in bloom. It got its name because its intensely mauve-colored posies easily attract *Lepidoptera*. Here they consider it a decorative plant and sell it at The Phantom Gardener. In Europe it's a weed. Perhaps that's why it migrated to this continent, to recover its dignity. They are tough plants that grow in the dumps on the outskirts of our cities. In post-war London, for example, the butterfly bushes were the first to refill the bombs craters courtesy of the German Air force. In our Rhinebeck bush, two orange-winged butterflies flutter about. There is also an oversized bumblebee that looks more like a penguin larva. In the Americas, even the insects are huge. Oh, wait a second. That's not a bumblebee, says Sarah. What do you mean? Look closely. I do: it is a textbook example of a bumble bee. Bumble … beeee. No, it's not; it's a hummingbird. A bird? Yep? *Mamma mia*, so it is!

Our yard, hummingbird included, is in the back. Normally, homes are built near the sidewalk, with a little bit of land in front and a paved driveway to the side, for parking cars or putting up basketball hoops. We Mediterranean folk usually build our houses as far as possible from the street to keep people from snooping in the windows. In Rhinebeck, the front of the house usually has a covered porch for sitting and waving at passersby. Here, you say hi to the people who walk by. In Spain, when we run into acquaintances, we say *adios* to keep them from stopping to tell us their life story. Here, that would be impolite. But the risk of living in small-town America is that if you ask people how they're doing, they may actually tell you. Another difference in customs: in Spain, you enter an elevator silently and say goodbye as you step out. In America, you say hi when you enter and you leave silently. These are curious but unimportant subtleties, with a few exceptions, like the time I kissed my father-in-law on the lips. It happened the first time we met. A long time ago, thank goodness. To place that incident in context, I will take a minute to explain what I call "the space theory." I don't mean astronomical space or black holes, but rather the personal space that people need to maneuver comfortably.

Until 2050, when U.S. demographics will have changed radically, most Americans will still be of European origin, particularly from northern Europe where it rains all the time. That means they have inherited a way of exteriorizing feelings in public that is more subdued than those of us who come from the countries that border Africa. Perhaps because the English always need to carry an umbrella, they find it difficult to hug people. When you have a conversation with someone here, your interlocutor won't like it if you touch him or give him little punches on the shoulder as you talk. And the distance between you and him should be wide. Let's say that during a conversation between two Italians or two Greeks, the natural distance between them would be about the size of a third person. But in a conversation between two Americans, two people could fit into the space between them. Americans need more distance. More separation. And watch out with what you do with your hands. It's as if you were packing a pistol. You feel uncomfortable if you invade someone else's personal space. It is not a question of disliking the other person. To the contrary, Americans tend to make a big deal about having a good sense of humor. After all, many of their ancestors hailed from the British Isles, whose inhabitants are the only people in the world who apologize to a table when they run into it. *"Oh, I am dreadfully sorry."* Americans love jokes and they adore teasing one another. It's just that they aren't used to physical contact and greeting each other with two kisses on the cheek. That strikes me as quite odd because, on the other hand, on New Year's Eve, when the clock strikes midnight, you have to kiss the women next to you on the lips. Whoever she is. I'm starting to suspect that, five minutes before midnight, everyone begins to position themselves strategically to avoid locking lips with an undesired person.

When I first met my father-in-law, Bud Howe, a big guy who played football in his youth, he smiled and held out his hand. Back then, in the early 1980s, the only English I knew was the line from a James Taylor song: *And it don't look like I'll ever stop my wandering* and the refrain from the Gloria Gaynor disco hit, *I Will Survive*. So, emboldened by Gaynor's recommendation, I gave my father-in-law two cheek-kisses to break the ice Spanish style. How was I to know that Americans, when they do kiss, do so from right to left? Why hasn't anyone written travel books explaining that in this corner of the universe, kisses are given the other way around? So when I went to kiss him—doing as I've always done, first on the west cheek and then on the east—he positioned himself to receive the kisses the other way around, and we met in the middle. How embarrassing. Once the mishap in customs passed, he asked me if I liked football. Since I still didn't know that what Real Madrid plays is called soccer here, I nodded. He turned on the TV and I sat through the first three-quarters of a Cowboys-Giants game. I had no idea when to get excited and when to get nervous. He explained the rules of the game and I responded affirmatively to everything. During the last quarter, I gave up and, with the excuse that I was exhausted from the long trip, discreetly retired to my room. Since then, we've had the opportunity to get to know each other better and to express our affection without the need for kisses.

Our backyard, protected from the stares of those walking by on the sidewalk, is also a strategic location for the grill. Barbecuing is done often, in good weather and bad, even in mid-winter, when a curious combination of body heat is produced: your face burns above the grill while your backside freezes facing the snow. It's truly bipolar: *bi* for bizarre, for the ridiculousness of the situation, and *polar*, like the white bears, for the cold you endure.

Our yard has no fences. Between the branches of the walnut trees planted along the edges of the yard you can glimpse other yards and other houses. Since the Pilgrims and early settlers lived under the permanent threat of attack from Indians, coyotes and bears, with no police or army, neighbors had to help each other defend themselves—without walls, so that everyone could see other people from their property. In Southern Europe, the Arabic custom of building walls against thieves persists to this day. Everywhere there are high walls so that the bad guys can't jump over them. In America, the opposite is true: properties are out in the open so no one can approach them without being seen. So that anyone approaching with bad intentions, man or beast, can be met with the whistle of a bullet. The story of the three pigs is obviously European. Here, the wolf, no matter how savage, could not have gotten so close to the first pig's house without being reported by a neighbor.

On the patio, I finish off the beer. Fall is upon us. Above us, flocks of Canada geese fly toward Poughkeepsie. I just can't understand how the Pilgrims, arriving on the Mayflower, didn't realize that they were settling in a horribly cold place. Against the light blue sky, the geese draw a gigantic arrow pointing toward the exit—to the south and warmer climates, as if trying to warn us to get out of there before it's too late. Meanwhile, in the treetops, squirrels hoard acorns and nuts. On the ground, snakes return to their hideouts and moths and grasshoppers begin to lay eggs. The leaves of the dogwood, the first tree to change color, begin turning an intense red. Soon wild duck hunting season will begin. Before we realize, it will be time to replace the window screens with glass storm windows. The air is cool. The sun does not warm with the same intensity. The gangs of kids who play in the street stow the baseball bat in the garage until next season and take out the elongated football. The imposing size of the trees and the fact that no brick limits my view moves me, and for a moment, I feel like I live on a *Tarzan* movie set.

3

October

During the first week of October, daybreak reveals a red "X" painted on the bark of the 100-year-old tree on our street. George Wyant, the village foreman of the highway department, put it there. A horse lover who patrols the streets in his green pickup and cowboy hat, George has his own horse farm and personally attends to his mare when she gives birth. Thanks to George, I've learned that animals' placentas are odorless so that when they give birth, defenseless in the middle of the forest, there is no smell to attract enemies. Otherwise, they would face certain death, like the maple tree on which George has drawn the X. It is a sign that, very soon, people will climb its branches with power saws and ropes and take it down in pieces. The immense sadness that I feel witnessing the disappearance of such an organic giant is balanced by observing the woodcutters' expert skills. Not even a splinter of bark hits the roof of the nearest house. The tree disappears within a few hours, as if it had never been planted. As if the Earth had swallowed it up.

Several of the houses in the area were built around 1850 and the average lifespan of the trees planted along the streets is 150 years. Do the math. Thus, at the dawn of the new century, they are falling down, one after another. These giants have gone from being jewels in the landscape to terrible threats. They could fall at any moment, splitting a house in two like a knife through butter. Good thing there is a local reforestation program. The village of Rhinebeck will give you a 6-foot tree if you dig a hole next to the sidewalk and promise to water it. Of course, depending upon how it grows, village officials reserve the right to trim it as they see fit. Here, telephone, electricity and television cables still circulate above ground. The aerial tangle is so surprising I've even seen tourists taking photos. Debates about burying the cables are heard on the radio every time a storm causes a blackout and leaves thousands of families without light or electricity. It seems like infrastructure was neglected during prosperous times (profit, profit, profit, without reinvesting in improvements) and now companies don't have the money to undertake this project. However, some people don't think the cables should be buried because it would make it harder to reach damaged sections and consequently will drive up repair costs. For this reason, the utility workers are forced to emulate Edward Scissorhands, reshaping the treetops so that wires and cables can cross over them without touching the branches. Rhinebeck has donut-trees, with round holes in the center of the treetops; one-armed trees, with branches growing only on one side; slingshot trees, which extend in a Y-shaped form and wig-trees, whose tops look like heads whose faces someone has cut away, leaving only the hair. Tim Burton would be very proud of this crew.

Thank goodness that some lovely arboreal specimens still remain. My favorites are the splendid sequoia in the Hills' yard, which you can see from Route 9 at the curve before the hospital, and the ginkgo in the yard of Dr. Sussin, the chiropractor. No one would dare to mark an X on any of those giants, at least not for a long time. If that gingko manages to thrive like its relatives do in Asia, the incredible insect resistance of its bark and its capacity to form aerial roots could ensure a lifespan of nearly 2,500 years. Can you imagine?

The sequoia was planted as a seedling in the 1920s by Anna Hill, my wife's grandmother, who got this rare genus of redwood coniferous species, by then believed to be extinct already in China, as a gift from the New York Botanical Garden due to her generous contributions. The Sussins' ginkgo is a true wonder. Its branches sport leaves resembling oriental fans that the autumn has dyed bright yellow. It is at the corner of Mulberry and Livingston streets, where I pass on my way to town. A few yards further down, I take advantage of a heavy stone block next to the sidewalk to retie my shoelaces. It's one of the pedestals that residents used in Victorian times to climb onto their horses. It is carved of bluestone, as are the enormous slabs that form the sidewalk. The thick flagstones are placed in a row like piano keys, which, despite their weight, have been shifted in some places by the troublemaking roots of the silver maples, swampy trees that crush everything in their path. On some stretches of sidewalk, the stone has been replaced by cement. I suppose that liability has something to do with this decision. However, on the sidewalks, as in politics, you can observe two opposing trends among the new house buyers: those who remove the uneven old bluestone and replace it with flat cement and those who remove the even cement and bring back the classy bluestone. The pedestal on which I'm leaning is a fancy one. Its north face is rounded, so as to avoid scraping the horse, I assume, and includes a middle step to enable people to climb its 21 inches comfortably. It belongs to the Mansard house, which would capture the attention of any passerby. It's the house where Helen Reed Delaporte lived, the first woman elected to a board of education in Dutchess County. She was the home's second owner. The millionaire O'Brien family built it in 1875 as a wedding gift for their son who did not stay there long because his wife, Sarah Lane, died. Apparently, the ghost of the dead woman has wandered through its rooms ever since. The house is higher than it is wide because it was designed to fit on a narrow lot while maintaining the hallmark roofline and the iron-crested tower of traditional Second Empire features, including the French style that the Louvre Museum made popular. It's an architectural jewel that claimed for itself the glory of having been the first house in the Village of Rhinebeck to use gas lighting. I don't know whether or not it's really haunted, but it reminds me a lot of the house Hitchcock used to film *Psycho*. Every time I walk by it, I can't help to look out of the corner of my eye to check whether Anthony Perkins is leaning out the window, wearing a wig and holding a knife on his hand. I thought I saw him once, but I was told it was only a Vassar professor who owned the house.

Kitty-corner to Helen Reed Delaporte's house is a much more colorful one—a masterpiece of marquetry in light green with red and orange details. Helen's sister, Sarah Reed Herrick, lived there. Their brother, Thomas Reed, one of the first members of the New York Stock Exchange, would frequently come to visit them. This corner was a powerful enclave in the late 19th century, and Rhinebeck owes the preservation of a large part of its architectural heritage to its distinguished inhabitants. It seems that John Jacob Astor IV, founder of the Astoria Hotel, who was swallowed up by the sea on his return trip from Europe on the *Titanic*, was born in Rhinebeck and was the owner of what is now Ferncliff Forest. Married for the second time, scandalously, to an 18-year-old woman, he decided to enlarge his estate. Astor's idea was to buy all the land between his property and the village, knock down the buildings on those lands and incorporate the new land into his estate. Delaporte, Herrick, Reed and other notable citizens prevented him from doing so. They bought the land before Astor could to prevent the demolitions and to give the community some public green areas. This is how the fairgrounds originated and the land was granted on which the hospital was built.

Uuuuuh... a ghostly voice startles me from behind, as if from beyond the grave. I turn towards the Second Empire house. "Is that you, Sarah Lane?" I ask, fearing I will run into the ghost of the late Mrs. O'Brien. No, it's not her, thank God. I breathe a sigh of relief. It's just my friend Jay Dorin, whose actual name would have remained Yacob Docsitsky if his grandparents had stayed in Russia. Both sides of his family came through Ellis Island—though at slightly different times. Jay's mother was born some years later in 1912 in an apartment on 112th Street and Saint Nicholas Avenue in an area of Harlem that was settled by a lot of the Jewish emigrants. The superintendent's wife, who was also a midwife, assisted her birth at home. His father, Nathaniel Dorin, was born on the Lower East Side. The neighborhood was made up mostly of Italians and Jews that often didn't mix well. There were also Germans and Irish as well as the original New Yorkers, mostly stemming from the Dutch, and they all lived in separate enclaves. When Jay was a kid, the Dorins decided to move to Brooklyn to look for a place of upward mobility. But the neighborhood was still full of poor and struggling emigrants. His mother remembers only having one change of clothes that her mother and grandmother washed each night, so she could start the next day fresh and clean.

Jay grew up hearing stories of those times in Brooklyn and was intrigued. He was told that Natie was tough, protected his family like a street fighter and became a semi-professional boxer. The family lived near President Street, where a group of gangsters called "Murder Incorporated" took roots. The gang was formed by Jewish immigrants and became deeply affiliated with the Italian Mafia as contract killers and enforcers. Jay asked questions about the past, but his father never said too much. Jay couldn't figure out why. Eventually, it was his father's father, Barnet, a troubled man who sometimes would go to the saloons at night, from whom Jay gleaned some information. Barnet alluded to the fact that his son knew one or two gangsters. Yes. And, even though they were not friends, he said, they would nod hello to each other in passing. So, at the end of the day, all Jay knew was that his daddy was an angry, tough guy with a lot of integrity. A man who dressed impeccably, carried himself confidently and worked hard. Jay was told that his father made it to middle school and then began earning money for his family. At the age of nine he would sell gum and newspapers on the elevated trains that run through Manhattan. Then he became a runner on Wall Street when messengers carried trade information between the brokerage houses. Natie also loved to dance, and was a competitive dancer at the Audubon Ballroom.

There were seven kids in Jay's father's family. Survival was paramount. Most of the kids slept in the same room and during the winter months, they all moved into the kitchen of the downtown tenement, as the stove was the only source of heat. The family tells a funny story of those times. Grandma Rose sent her daughter Helen to the butcher to pick up a chicken for dinner. It was a first for Aunt Helen, who was young but anxious for the responsibility of shopping. The butcher took the chicken out and Helen looked at it. "Just wait a minute! What are you trying to pull? Where are the other two legs?" Like her brothers and sisters, Helen had never seen any land besides the asphalt of New York City, so she figured out that a chicken probably had four legs. But that swindler of a butcher, that good for nothing guy without scruples, had the audacity to try to sell her a mutilated specimen. She wouldn't get the chicken. Aunt Helen went back home, told her mom … and that was it. She was not allowed to go shopping anymore for the family.

It seemed that everybody in the family had to work to overcome poverty, but Jewish law promotes education, and there was Grandma Rose. She was a devoted student of the Old Testament, one of the few women in her village back in Russia who had actually learned how to read, and the first woman in New York asked to sit with the Rabbis to help interpret Talmudic law. Grandma Rose decided it was her job to continue on the journey and point her descendants toward more ambitious targets than she had achieved herself. At that time, the City University of New York was open to teaching emigrant children at a very low rate. Grandma Rose saved every penny so she could pay at least for one child to go to college. Uncle Henry, who was probably the brightest one in the clan, was chosen to go. He worked very hard and became a high school chemistry teacher, then a professor of chemistry at New York University, and eventually wrote one of the most popular high school chemistry text books in the United States. Go Henry!

As Henry moved into the world of education, Jay's father, Natie, learned the shoe business as a teenager working for a variety of shoe stores in the city, and became set on opening his own store. In 1938, Natie was already married to Jay's mother, also called Rose. Rose's parents had saved a little money, so together with his brother-in-law, Natie was able to borrow $500 from them and open D&B Inc. at 128 West 57th Street. It was a major step for a kid who lived through the Depression eating only an apple and a roll over the course of a day. Wow! But that's all history. Now Jay is taking his little dog out for a walk. *Hola mi hermano*, he says to me, dusting off the Spanish phrase some Puerto Rican friends of his youth had taught him. "Hi Jay, you scared me to death. I thought you were a ghost." Jay can't help but smile. "Are you heading to town?" "Yes. I'll go with you." We walk together and Jay takes the opportunity to tell me about his Puerto Rican friend Rafael's encounter with a real ghost. Jay is a guidance counselor at Kingston Senior High School and the most prolific source of anecdotes I've ever met. Every time I'm with him, I'm disappointed that I haven't brought a tape recorder along. He lives two blocks from us and invited us to take a dip in his pool the summer we arrived. That's where we met his wife, Lisa Henderling, a successful illustrator who specializes in fashion illustrations. Google her.

Jay is Jewish and Lisa is not. Until only recently, Rhinebeck had few Jews. In the 1960s, there were only two Jewish families in town and although a few more families moved here later, it was not until after 9/11 that the process accelerated. After the attacks, many New Yorkers were looking for a small town to raise their children—a place of trust and comfort; a place where you know the people you have to deal with on a daily basis. A lot of Jewish families in New York City packed up and moved north, some of them to permanently reside in their summer or weekend homes. At the same time, Mexicans began to arrive in Rhinebeck. The exponential growth of local restaurants created a need for more kitchen staff. People started spreading the word and a lot of families arrived from Oaxaca and Morelos. The two migrations are still so recent that their cultural reality has not had time to filter into the popular knowledge of the community. Thus, in Max's fifth grade class, a girl recently mentioned that her brother was going to celebrate his Bar Mitzvah. "Really? Wow!" said one of her friends. "A Bar Mitzvah? I didn't know your brother was Mexican!"

Jay Dorin grew up in Washington Heights in a building a few doors up from the home of the great escape artist Harry Houdini. Natie's shoe store was doing well and the Dorins were part of the upwardly mobile middle class. At the end of the 1940s, new immigrants from Europe began flooding the neighborhood—people with strange tattoos on their arms and deep sadness in their faces. A lot of moms with kids, but not a lot of dads. There was a woman upstairs from Jay who was crazy, but her daughter told him that the Nazis had forced her to stand and watch her brothers and sisters executed for no reason. Another Italian neighbor's aunt had crooked hands. She had crossed the Alps to get into Yugoslavia, but got caught by the Nazis and all her fingers were broken during the interrogation. The concentrations camps were never spoken about. Everyone wanted to forget. Remembering was too painful and traumatic. So there was never an utterance about the Nazi horrors that had consumed Jay's neighbors' lives. The pain along with the physical and spiritual devastation could not be mentioned. It was another kind of exodus, a time to plant the seeds of desire to survive and move their lives forward.

Jay and his friends spent most of their time on the streets. An innocent "good morning" from a passerby was taken as an affront. "Good morning?????? What the hell do you mean by that?" An attitude of mistrust prevailed in the neighborhood where many cultures converged. The Jewish universe intermingled with the Puerto Rican, Greek, Irish and the Italian. And all of them ended up in front of the display case of a French bakery, where the inaccessible dreams of the majority of local inhabitants took the form of brioche.

In the 1950s New York still had a sense of segregation. African Americans had occupied mostly Harlem and some areas East of Broadway, but black people began to move into the houses on both sides of Jay's block as well as the beautiful brownstone houses around the corner. They were the great-grandchildren of slaves who were moving up north from the Carolinas, Virginia and Georgia to build their own middle-class families. It was common for many of the Jewish families who were making extra money to hire help from that black community. Jay's brother Barry was pretty wild and the Dorins hired a full-time nanny named Eveling. She was the only person who could keep Barry under control with a lot of discipline and a lot of love. They also hired a woman named Leola who helped his mother with the household chores once a week. She always listened to what Jay was saying and made him feel good about himself. When he told her a story, Leola would put her arms on her hips, shake her head, and say with great incredulity "Hmm, can you beat that."

There was a courtyard in the back of the building where, every once in a while, some of the black ladies would come and sing songs in perfect Yiddish. They memorized the lyrics at work and passed them through the sieve of blues, creating a moving spectacle of musical fusion. The sad Yiddish songs probably paralleled their own pain. People would lean out the windows that faced the courtyard to listen and toss down nickels wrapped in tissues to soften the blow of metal against concrete. A shower of rolled-up paper rained down appreciation for the heartfelt memories.

Jay went to a rough school. His parents felt he'd better learn all the skills necessary to survive and public school was the best place for that. He always saw New York as a living theatre where one could decide during the course of the day the role that he wanted to play and there would be a cast of thousands willing to lend support. It was a fun place full of excitement and games, and sometimes mischief, with a lot of freedom to be and freedom to become. There were days when Jay went out from morning to early evening and never crossed a street, yet had a full day. As Jay grew up, he had a large variety of mixed friends, like his father. Some would become very successful and some would go to the dark side of life. A contrast that was not so surprising in a neighborhood where characters as disparate as Alan Greenspan, the boy who ended up heading the Federal Reserve Bank, shared the sidewalk with Joe Rodríguez, the Puerto Rican gangster who only managed to become an apprentice of the bully on the corner. He carried a gun always and was obsessed with imminent death. Jay tells the story of one day when he was in his twenties and took a walk with Joe. "Are you ready to die, Jay?" Jay got scared. What is this guy talking about? "No, I'm not ready to die. What do you mean, Joe?" His heart was pounding and his mind racing to figure out what he had done wrong, what code he had broken. But then Rodriguez looked him in the eye and went into a philosophical rant. "Is your life complete, Jay? Do you feel that you did everything that you have to do? Are you living fully and properly, always being true to yourself and having no regrets? When you have the guys upstairs saying, 'Pencils down,' you have to be ready to go, Jay. We have to be brave, because we're going to die soon." "What are you saying, Joe? Stop it; nobody's going to die here. Don't be such a downer, man." But Joe insisted that death was on his heels and that he needed to prepare himself to face it with honor. "You never know when it's coming. And when it comes you have to accept it with elegance. With bravery. Like a man. We have to be strong, Jay." "Okay, Joe, okay." "We have to be on guard, Jay. We have to be on the alert to confront with dignity the instant in which the Grim Reaper comes for us." "Knock it off, Joe, please." But he wouldn't drop the subject. "We're going to die, Jay." "Listen, Joe, you can die if you want to, but just let me be!" Then one winter morning, just when Joe's anxiety had finally seemed to ease and he had made plans for staying on this Earth, he was killed. The bullets from his own bodyguard's gun threw him into the air. The man received a nice payout to do this heinous deed and finish Joe like a puppet. None of his friends knew whether the shots caught Joe prepared to begin his journey into the void. But they chose to believe that he was ready. Rest in peace.

By the time Joe died, the gang that used to meet under the George Washington Bridge had already dissolved. However, its members recall with resonating laughter the day when Buffalo, a kid with an unusually large rear end, was hit by a car. The accident was a source of hilarity for many weeks on the northern edge of Harlem. TV was around by then, but kids were allowed to watch only a certain amount. Everybody just wanted to be outside. There was so much to do on Riverside Drive at the park and the playground, on rooftops and in basements. Their favorite game was called Carlo Demalo. "You ran from one side of the street to the other side," Jay tells me, "and if you got caught in the middle by the other team they beat you up." That was the deal. They were also engaged in a war. They would pick up sticks and look for dog crap, which was plentiful and easy to find, dip the sticks into the crap and begin chasing one another. The object of the game was to avoid getting touched and hopefully land a hit on someone else.

One day they noticed that Buffalo had no stick … so he became the prime target. The gang chased him and Buffalo ran for his life. Contact with the deadly stick was not only disgusting, it also brought shame. So Buffalo ran here and there and then between two parked cars into the narrow street. His timing was really bad. A car was speeding down the block. The driver of the car hit his brakes. Buffalo, alerted by the sound of the horn, increased his speed towards the other side of the road to avoid the fatal impact. It looked as if his body would clear the vehicle, except that he had underestimated his anatomical proportions. His rear end failed to make it. The enormous backside Mother Nature had given him remained exposed. The Mercury whacked him right in the middle of his keister. Bam!!! Time froze as everyone watched him being thrown into the air in slow motion, contorting and grimacing along the way. He was tossed straight up and a bit forward with a perplexed look on his face. Whaaat? He landed on the ground in a seated position—on his very own airbag. It was a rump landing, two bounces, and in the end all was well. The driver, sweating with worry, apologized to everyone. The gang was so amazed that Buffalo was unscathed by the accident that he was left untouched by the deadly stick. He had earned a free pass. Life on the block continued, and the laughter over Buffalo lasted for months. It would calm down for a few days only to resume weeks later, when the memory would be refreshed. This lasted until the first thaws of spring, when Buffalo's story gave way to the gang's silent admiration for another potential victim: Rafael Vélez.

Rafael and his brother Jorge moved to the neighborhood when they all were teenagers. Rafael was a bony, scrawny humanoid and a *jebero*, a hick from the countryside of Puerto Rico. He saw his first flush toilet in his new apartment at 835 Riverside Drive and told the other kids stories of the *gaga-torey*, a man who came around with a big wagon to collect the town's waste. Rafael was the new kid and new kids had to be initiated into their new world. It happened one day when the gang was walking through the connected hallway between 845 and 839. A quick glance was enough for the group to decide to beat Rafael up. "Man, we're going to kick your ass, and that is the way it is." Rafael looked at the whole group, carefully assessing the situation as he was pushed up against the wall. And then he said in his thick Puerto Rican accent, "Ju can kick my ass if ju want to, but first I want to show ju something." They were confused, as that had never happened before. However, intrigued by the victim's excessive flattery and unexpected confession, the boys agreed with the requested stay of execution. And then it happened. Rafael quietly put his hand down to his fly and slowly unzipped it to reveal a member of unusual proportions. The force of gravity acted on the lower jaws of those present, distorting their mouths in amazement. In a semicircle, surrounding the boy who had instantly become a hero, they observed with astonishment an organ that must have been half of Rafael's body weight. Time stood still and space evaporated. Not longitude, latitude or height. Adios to the metric system, to the imperial system and Newton's laws. The universe yielded before the theory of unique thought. Incredible!

After a few moments during which coordinates ceased to exist, Rafael put it back into his pants, zipped up his fly and quietly walked out of the hallway. No one dared to lift a hand to him. No one wanted to act on the threats made. Fully excited, young Oscar pointed out that if Rafael ever got fully excited so much blood would have to flow to his "bad-boy" that he would faint from lack of blood on his brain. But that was it. No more comments emerged from their throats. That night, the gang members' thoughts ruminated on their pillows. The following day, the group unanimously adopted a resolution without discussion: Rafael Vélez was proclaimed the king of the neighborhood. Long live King Rafael!

I first got to hear these kinds of stories at Jay's house the night we took a dip in his pool and had dinner together. We had shrimp, but without the heads. Americans can't stand it when their food looks at them. The butcher and the fisherman don't work in public. Here in America, they go about eliminating all relationship between the animal and the cut of meat. At the supermarket, a mysterious door opens, and a guy in a white coat places trays of plastic-wrapped filets on the shelf. "Eyes that don't see, heart that doesn't feel," as the old Spanish saying goes. This custom is incomprehensible to me because happiness is most easily achieved when a person feels connected to nature, when he understands what is going on and knows that it forms part of a process. But here a missing link is created in the chain of life. The whole fish disappears and, as if by magic, orange fillets of salmon appear in the display case. What's more, those of us who like to cook are denied the best part to make a fish broth: the head. The system forces you to buy a prepared broth with preservatives, which does not taste the same. Not surprisingly, given this disconnection between food and the animal world, some city kids believe that the most common breed of cow is the "2 percent." It gives way to incidents like the one I heard when I accompanied my father-in-law to Blondie's, where he goes every morning to have breakfast and chat with friends. Buss, a retired plumber with a passion for hunting and fishing, told this story. It seems a couple who had come from New York City to hunt deer in Milan (a small town pronounced My-lan that these outsiders called Meelan with an affected Italian intonation) were stopped by police on the Taconic Parkway with a sheep, dead from a bullet wound secured to the car roof with bungee cords.

Hunting is an increasingly serious problem. Until only recently, many people born in this part of the world grew up with a fishing rod in one hand and a shotgun in the other. Hunters are necessary for lots of reasons, perhaps most importantly that by going out to the field frequently, they become familiar with nature and learn to respect it. The decline in hunting and fishing licenses is troubling. It's not good for the animals, because overpopulation causes starvation and the spread of diseases that make their existence miserable. Nor is it good for people, because car accidents increase and backyards are destroyed by deer, which even go into the village at night to munch on tulips.

The request for hunting licenses has declined drastically for three reasons. The first, which is indeed a serious matter, is the transmission of Lyme disease by deer ticks. Many hunters have stopped going into the woods to avoid the problem. The second reality is simply economic. In New York State, hunting for pure pleasure is not permitted. If you kill an animal, you are obligated to butcher it and use its meat. It is illegal to kill a deer and leave the carcass abandoned in field. But few people need to hunt to feed their family and survive over the long winter. The third reason is the increasing influence of the conservationist movement, which proposes to preserve nature as it is, without human intervention. This mentality does not take into account that human beings are part of nature and that, as a predatory animal, we also play a role in the chain of life. If human beings were meant to eat grass, we'd have eyes on the sides of our heads like ruminants rather than in the center of our face to spot our prey, like carnivores. It's another thing altogether if we make the cultural decision to give up meat. To each his own. But to attempt to deny the evidence that we are a predatory species is like asking a tiger to eat carrots or a robin to stop taking worms to her nest to feed her young. I am not defending those who go on an African safari to kill a lion, or someone who enjoys shooting an eagle in full flight. I refer to those who hunt a deer to help cull the invasive population and/or to enjoy its meat. These people also contribute to maintaining the network of U.S. national parks by paying a license fee. In hunting, the shot is the least important thing. Hunting means spending seven hours in a tree and understanding which chirp corresponds to each bird species, knowing the direction that the wind is blowing so you can place yourself where animals can't smell you, holding the trigger when you spot a female in heat, because you know a male will be right behind her. It means feeling you are part of the landscape and loving it.

Controlling hunting is necessary; prohibiting it would be a disaster. In 1996, a curious incident occurred, which proves how crucial it is to have the knowledge of the people in the area where you want to take action. The organization People for the Ethical Treatment of Animals (PETA) encouraged the citizens of Fishkill, New York, to consider changing the name of their town to "Fishsave" because the current one suggested cruelty to animals. But the reality was that the town's name didn't encourage the killing of fish at all. Fishkill was founded by the Dutch in the early 1600s. Many waterways throughout New York, Pennsylvania and New Jersey were named by the Dutch settlers and have "kill" in their names because that is the Dutch word for stream. Rhinebeck's local creek, the Landsman Kill, is one example. It would have been enough for PETA to consult with anyone who grew up in the Hudson Valley to avoid this entirely useless campaign which was led, no doubt, with good intentions.

Jay and I are approaching the bank parking lot. He has just finished telling me about his Puerto Rican friend Rafael's encounter with a ghost. It seems that on one occasion, Rafael came running out of his house nervous and white, and told the gang that his grandfather had died a couple of days ago. "Oh, no…" "It was okay," he said, "because he was old and sick. But last night I got up to go to the bathroom and found the ghost of *mi abuelo* sitting peacefully on the toilet." Rafael, terrified, couldn't piss. He ran to his room screaming and dove into bed. The gang waited a prudent amount of time until the story could be corroborated by Georgie, Jorge el Gordo, Rafael's older brother and antithesis. And, sure enough, the heavyset, tall and muscular guy claimed he had also had an encounter of that type with his grandfather. The same night, about an hour later, he walked to the bathroom and, to his amazement the ghost of the old man was still sitting at the toilet. So Georgy confirmed that the ghost story was true! The gang was fascinated. "So what happened?" And Georgy said, "Nothing. I don't care he was sitting there, man, I had to take a *chit*." So Gordo had not run. He had no fear for anything. Unperturbed, Georgy gestured to the spirit to get up off the commode so he could use it. "Take a hike, buddy," he'd said. But the *abuelito* didn't move. So he just sat on top of him and let loose. "And then what?" "Nothing," Georgy said. "He was gone!" And life continued as usual.

Jay waits outside while I do some business at Rhinebeck Bank. I watch him through the window. He's older than I am. He's broken the sound barrier of 60, but doesn't make a big deal about it. According to his own definition, he was simply invited to the party of life before I was and he's been enjoying it for longer. "I've had that luck," he tells me. That's it. Well, almost. He also believes that major changes arrive in 40-year installments. His parents experienced the roaring 1920s. Forty years later the 1960s took hold. And, doing the math, he believes we are in the midst of a 2K revolution that corresponds to his son's generation.

He ended up here after a journey of initiation that first led him to Woodstock in the 60s. During a time when many let themselves be led by the blues, Buddhism, Kerouac's *On the Road* and many other spiritual and experimental creations and events. The hippie movement brought to young people the idea of a world in which there was no place for urgency. Jay gladly embraced it at the time of the Woodstock rock festival—the real one, that of 1969, the one that included Richie Havens; Joan Baez; Santana; Janis Joplin; the Grateful Dead; Creedence Clearwater Revival; The Who; Jefferson Airplane; Joe Cocker; The Band; Blood, Sweat and Tears; Johnny Winter; Crosby, Stills, Nash & Young and Jimi Hendrix. Jay acted as if he was wearing a wristwatch whose 12 numbers represented the months of the year, not the hours in the day. If someone asked him, "Hey man, what time you got?" he would look at the hands on his imaginary watch and respond: "Mid-February." Or "Close to summer." And he was happy.

Jay finished a Master's degree in guidance counseling at NYU and hung it up on the wall not knowing if he would ever use it. A couple of years went on without him doing much and then he figured out that he'd better move on with his life. That's when he decided he wanted to go into film. Without having any foundation he thought he would love to do that kind of work. His friend Billy was an assistant cameraman at that time, so he approached him about it. Billy asked him, "Are you sure?" "Yes." So he got him an interview with Mike Jackson, one of the people in Bob Drew's Cinema Verité crowd. Mike asked Jay what he knew about filmmaking. Jay looked up at the sky, reached deep inside and told Mike the truth: "Nothing ... except I really want to do it." Mike looked at him and said: "Oh, that will do. Pack your bags; you're going to California with us January 1." For Jay, that was the start of the best years ever. His career as a still photographer lasted for over 20 years.

Back in New York he got into therapy. He tried counseling, personal growth workshops, bio-energetics and Loving Relationships Training with an introduction to Rebirthing. The city was too stressful, though. So Jay headed to Florida in search of a more positive lifestyle. In Miami he met Lisa. He attended a litany of personal growth programs, and went back to school at the University of Miami, earning a degree in Chemical Dependency Training. He took advantage of the course to assess the pathways in his life and learned that, no matter how long the tunnel, there would always be light at the end if you worked for it.

Yes. In a confusing world in which many young people lost their way in an ocean of drugs, he proposed to show them the exit—which is the Latin word for success (*exitus*), for finding your way out of a problem. In other words, Jay wanted to help adolescents achieve their full potential. He began to work both as a guidance counselor and photographer—the former for money and compassion, the latter for passion without money.

Lisa and Jay got married in 1989 and had a grand wedding. Life in Miami was active and productive and they created a large group of friends. Jay began working as a Project Trust specialist with kids at risk in Miami Beach High School. Using his new training, along with what he had gained in his years of therapy, he conducted a very successful and recognized program in drug and alcohol prevention, education and intervention. He felt that he saved many kids—people with whom, to this day, he is still in touch. Then his son Max was born and Lisa and Jay knew that the time had come to move on and seek their fortune in another state. But they made some moves that were not really thought through.

They first went to Mill Valley, outside of San Francisco. It was too expensive to live there. It seemed like an impossible place. Jay went to classes, got certified to sell insurance and mutual funds, and started working for Prudential, where the real money could be made. But he didn't have it in him to do this kind of a work and left the field. Soon he and Lisa realized that spending a year in California without making money is a feat only the very wealthy can afford. So they packed their bags again. At the time, everyone was saying wonderful things about Oregon. It was the hot spot of the moment and its population was growing at the dizzying rate of 3 percent annually. So giddy-up! They packed up their belongings and arrived in Ashland, a charming town in Southern Oregon. But they didn't fit in. It was PBB: Perfect But Boring. They found themselves roaming endlessly with no other goal than the next great meal. Everyone was politically correct. Jay called the place "the wounded hippie town." There was not a single family who had not adopted a rescue dog that had undergone some sort of physical abuse from the local animal shelter. There was Lithia Park that had Lithium in water so nobody was bi-polar. Its basic population was extremely liberal. In the areas around Ashland were those to the very far right. The town was made up of Native Americans and an assortment of local bikers, most of whom had been there for generations. There wasn't much to do in this area. The high point of his day was taking a walk with his two-year-old son in the afternoon to the sheep farm that was down the road from where they lived and looking at the sheep testicles. For some reason, sheep testicles are huge and Max at his two-year-old height could get a great angle of vision.

Consumed by boredom, Jay showed Lisa a poster with a white dove sitting on the neck of a guitar that had hung in his room in Woodstock, and they decided to try their luck on the western banks of the Hudson. But they were disappointed. The place appeared stuck in time. Twenty-five years after the big concert (which actually took place at Bethel, about an hour's drive away), the same guys were there, doing the same things and with the same attitude towards life. The women with their gray hair untouched by hair dye; the men had white beards and ponytails tied with rubber bands. And tourists were taking pictures of them. People Jay had known from the 1960s were there. They turned around, crossed the Kingston Bridge and looked for a spot on the east side of the river. And they began to do what you have to do to try to settle in. Max started school and, after a rocky start, Jay landed a decent job as a guidance counselor at Kingston High School.

I exit the Rhinebeck Bank and we head back home. Jay accompanies me because he lives a few blocks east of my house. A wooded area borders his backyard and a litter of foxes was born a few feet from his pool. In my garage, the rake awaits me; it's trembling just thinking about all the leaves it will have to help me rake from the yard to the curb. Leaves fall through September and all throughout October and later, when you think it is not possible for more to fall, they fall again in November. You rake them to the curb and men from the village take them away, passing by in a truck that looks like an elephant. A giant vacuum cleaner sucks up the leaves, which are converted to mulch that sits in giant mounds behind the village garage; you can buy it very cheap in spring. So the trees return to the earth they came from. Dust we are and to dust we shall return. Mulch holds humidity and help plants germinate better. It also prevents excess weeds. For this process to be possible in spring, you have to rake in autumn. Those who go to the IXL gym at this time of year do so to justify the monthly payment because you do the same amount of exercise raking leaves, with the added benefit that it's outside.

Jay looks at the diabolical scarecrow in a bale of hay we put out for Halloween, which is nearly here. We filled some old jeans and a shirt with hay and then glued a rubber mask on top. Since mid-October, the houses have been assaulted by jack-o-lanterns and gory decorations. With respect to Halloween, Jay and I talk about parallel universes and places where we all struggle against our dark side. He steers the conversation to the intriguing subject of space travel. He encourages me to spend a day at his house sometime soon to get involved in the process of rebirthing, which is a powerful breathing technique. "Okay … I don't know what to tell you, Jay," I say. He warns me that the first time I'm reborn, my joints may seize up and my knuckles may twist. "Oh." I want to tell him that I'll think about it, that I need more time to decide, but simultaneous translation betrays me and I give him a categorical confirmation in two words: "Okay, great." "Okay, great?" He sets up an appointment, just like at a doctor's office, for several weeks later.

There's no turning back. Dear God, why have you abandoned me? Will my knuckles twist? Will my joints seize up? My pulse quickens. I grab the shopping cart where I have loaded a lot of leaves this morning and empty the contents in the curb at my friend's feet. "Are you okay, brother?" "Yes, Jay, it's nothing." It's just that it would have been better to be reborn now because the twisted fingers would have been great for Halloween night.

All Hallow's Eve, the night before All Saints' Day. Halloween originates from the ancient Celtic custom of honoring the dead on the night of transition between summer and winter. At the time, it was believed that souls came down from heaven, united in the procession of spirits, which, covered by white shrouds, wandered along paths. People placed oil lamps at crossings to light the way, basically encouraging the spirits to leave as soon as possible. The poor sucker who ran into the macabre procession knew he was condemned to join it. Once this unfortunate encounter occurred, the dead would continue to appear night after night to irreversibly undermine his health. Of course, there was always the possibility of being saved, thanks to the old trick of conquering the ghost by way of his stomach. To this end, people roasted chestnuts in cemeteries and offered sweets to the dead. There were celebrations in which the wine flowed and participants blackened their faces with coal to scare one another. For centuries, the oil lamps, sweets and costumes formed part of the popular imagination of the Celtic world: Ireland and a large part of the Iberian Peninsula (Spain and Portugal)—until Pope Gregory IV Christianized the ceremony in the 840s and insisted that it made no sense.

After the Catholic Church eliminated all possibilities of associating the holiday with pagan beliefs, people had to invent a legend that would reconnect it with a celebration they were not willing to give up. The tale of Jack of the Lantern appeared in Ireland. Jack mocked the devil, which punished him by making him wander in the dark with a burning stick placed in a carved tuber. Jack took over the job of the souls in purgatory and Halloween continued. Later, after the discovery of the Americas, pumpkins arrived and this greatly facilitated the expansion of the celebration. Oil lamps illuminated animal skulls and it was fashionable to put wax candles in the hard rind of this newly-discovered vegetable. The lamps moved to the front doors of houses. The terrifying faces cut in *Cucurbitaceae* were designed to frighten the errant spirit of the crafty Jack. An illustrious neighbor of this valley, the writer Washington Irving, was responsible for transferring the tradition.

Here, as October 31 approaches, you have to go to a garden in search of pumpkins. We went to the Lobotsky Farm, which is in an ideal spot. You take White Schoolhouse Road and then go down a dirt road with tiremarks sunken in the mud until you reach the esplanade that offers a magnificent view of the mountains. It is an enormous field where innumerable climbing stalks form a framework like a giant spider web. Huge leaves lie dead with their wrinkled brown veins, the hairy cuttings dehydrated and without hope. All the energy that the sun has granted to these fields was used to produce the fruits whose loud color contrasts with the pale soil. Like orange sequins on a Flamenco dancer's dress. Huge round pumpkins as far as the eye can see. Whole families run around the field in search of the best specimen, one that perfectly fulfills their spherical ideal. You choose the one you like and put it in one of those little red carts, an exact reproduction of those used by the Romans, which children often play with. The cash register is next to the parking lot. At the end of the day, farm employees fill in the gaps in the landscape produced by the sales of the day. They truck in more pumpkins collected in other fields and arrange them strategically so that the natural display does not lose its charm. We choose three large pumpkins for $20. It occurs to me that somehow including a panoramic shot of this pumpkin field in my Cándida movie could be spectacular. After all I am thinking of ending the script with her coming to New York for a visit.

Now it's time for the mandatory stop at A.L. Stickle's to celebrate Halloween the right way. The display window of this five-and-dime looks like it's straight out of a Norman Rockwell cover for the *Saturday Evening Post*. It serves as a calendar for passersby since it marks all the main U.S. holidays. A few weeks ago, the display was dedicated to Columbus Day, which in New York, to my surprise, is the same as saying "Long live Italy!" Columbus Italian? October 12, the day Christopher Columbus landed in the Americas, is the National Day of Spain. Our July 4. Although Columbus was supposedly born in the city-state of Genoa, he is the most important figure in Spain's history. And he did the trip with our queen's money. Under our flag. So…

Anyway, today it is the witches' turn, but in a few weeks Stickle's decorations will announce Thanksgiving. Next will come toys for Christmas, hearts for Valentine's Day, leprechauns and four-leaf-clover hats for Saint Patrick's Day, colored eggs for Easter and so on and so forth, holiday after holiday, until the patriotic flags of July 4 appear again. Matt Stickle and Tim Flanagan decorate the window with all manner of items to celebrate the eve of All Saint's Day: masks, jars of acrylic blood and hairy spiders ready for hanging in windows. Strings of orange lights to wrap around trees and porch columns. Foam board tombstones with funny inscriptions to set up your own cemetery in the yard. "I told you I was sick." "Here lies the body of Jonathan Lake. Stepped on the gas, instead of the brake." At Stickle's, you can buy skeletons, mummies and ghosts. There are tablecloths and napkins illustrated with headless horsemen, and orange plastic pumpkin-shaped buckets for children to go trick or treating.

Every time we go to Stickle's, our kids enthusiastically greet Tim and Matt as if they are Sponge Bob and the Easter Bunny. They love to go there. Both men treat them wonderfully. Tim is always ready with a joke. He's got a way with kids, who seek him out as soon as they enter the store. Sometimes Tim hides and jumps out to scare them. Or he chases them down one of the aisles to the back, where the star attraction of the store hangs: the 53-inch wide rolls of oilcloth cut to order for your picnic table. But the real reason my kids love to come here is because they can touch everything. Fishing lines, cowbells, erasers, notebooks, Slinkies ... For Halloween, Matt helped Nico reach a candle in the form of a zombie head from the shelf. The face was green and the inside red. As the wax melts, it looks like the zombie is drooling blood from its mouth. Interesting. Max is enticed by a human arm. It is a white shirtsleeve filled with foam rubber, from which a plastic hand emerges. The idea is to stick it out of the trunk of the car so that people will think there's a dead body there. Doubly interesting. Oh, and we also pick up a makeup kit to transform the kids' faces into monsters. For children our kids' age, it is hard to think of a better way to have fun in Rhinebeck than to stop by Stickle's to pick up something and then celebrate at Fosters. To the delight of our offspring, the day we went to buy the Halloween items, we fulfilled the plan to the letter. I'll rewind to mid-October to tell you about it.

Fosters Coach House Tavern, open from 11:00 a.m. to 11:00 p.m. Tuesday through Sunday, and on Fridays and Saturdays until midnight. An old coach house for horse-drawn carriages, the building was reconstructed after World War II and returned to its original appearance in the late 1980s. As soon as you enter, you're greeted by owner Bob Kirwood, who wears an impeccable white apron. He's been wearing it since 1965. After exchanging pleasantries, you can turn right, toward the bar with its giant plasma TV—where customers on stools and a Beck's beer in hand follow sporting events—or left, where the old stables are lined with food tables. Sitting on a box between two wooden panels painted in red and topped by a black iron strip, you can enjoy the friendly atmosphere of this tavern. On the walls hang photographs of glorious afternoons at mythical horse tracks. Among these is Saratoga, which is a bit over an hour away on the thruway. Oh, and if you need to visit the restroom before looking at the menu, you'll run into the coach of Vicepresident Levi P. Morton transformed into a telephone booth at the foot of the stairs.

London Broil is the specialty at Fosters. You can make it at home, but it's not the same. You remove the fat from the meat, poke some holes in it with a fork and marinate it in wine. You leave it in the fridge overnight in a glass bowl covered with a kitchen towel. You then throw out the liquid and season it with black pepper, wrap it in tinfoil and broil it at 425 degrees for 15 to 20 minutes. But let me warn you, it won't come out like that at Fosters. It is my father-in-law's favorite dish. This time Bud asks the waiter for ice water for everyone. "Ready to order?" Ready. Everyone asks for the beef, except for my daughter, who prefers a plate of steamed clams with a bowl of melted butter for dipping. My turn. A shiver runs up my spine, from coccyx to skull. I just want a hamburger. But no. If you take too long, the waitress gets impatient and the rest of the diners get antsy. Ready? Let's go.

"A hamburger, please." Her turn: "How would you like it? Rare, medium, done or well done?" I like mine a bit rare, but not as bloody as the *Texas Chainsaw Massacre*, so I say, "Medium, but a bit rare." "You mean medium-rare?" "Yeah, that's it, great." Now for the bread. "White, rye, whole wheat or French?" I say white, just to say something. "In a roll or a bun?" "Oh, oh…" I ask for the bun because that's what hamburgers always come in. Great. "Any extra ingredients? Cheese, onion, lettuce, tomato, pickles?" "Onion, lettuce and tomato, thanks." "French fries?" "Yes, thank you." "Soup or salad?" I think she says "super salad" so I say, "That's fine." "What's fine?" "That would be good, bring me a super salad, please." "Both?" "What do you mean both?" "They are two different things," she explains. "Either soup or salad." "Oh, darn, the salad, then." "Green or pasta?" For the love of God! "Green," I say. "A small green salad, please." "Which dressing? Italian, vinaigrette, Thousand Island or ranch?" "Whatever has oil and vinegar." "The Italian." "That would be great, thanks." "You are very welcome."

The lunch is a pleasant affair. The bill arrives. The tip has to be added to the total. Twenty percent????? Where's the defibrillator because I'm about to pass out! It's not that I'm cheap, it's just that I'm not used to this. But I've been told that in the United States, waiters earn only a modest wage so their income depends on customers' generosity. No wonder they smile when they serve you and make a point of bringing you more butter, refilling your water glass and repeatedly asking you if everything is okay. No wonder there is so much staff turnover in the business. As soon as they find a better job, they're gone. In Madrid, you go to a restaurant and if you return 20 years later, the same waiter will serve you, although with less hair and a graying moustache. Here it's different. But when in Rome, do as the Romans do. So, 20 percent it is.

Back at home, it's time to carve the pumpkins. Thank God these pumpkins' rinds are not like those in Madrid, where you would have to take a hammer and chisel to them. The ones in this town have the texture of a watermelon rind. A kitchen knife goes through them beautifully. Sarah prepares them with the kids. First they cut a star-shaped lid from the top, which is easy to put back in place afterwards. They then use a spoon to empty the pumpkin cavity. The contents can be used for soup, but given the amount of pulp the kids drop on the floor, I don't think soup is in our future. We toast the seeds. Now they cut out the eyes, eyebrows, nose and mouth with big teeth. A little candle inside and it's good to go. You can also make much more sophisticated figures. For $5, Stickle's sells a kit to draw even more sophisticated patterns on the pumpkins than those in the stained glass windows of the Episcopal Church on Chestnut Street. Some people create true masterpieces. The house on the corner of

South and Beech has a porch full of characters so real they look like they belong in Madame Tussaud's Wax Museum.

For the tombstones, I went to Williams Lumber and got some sheets of white foam board that can be cut easily. I used gray watercolor to paint them so it wouldn't eat through the foam board and added a few drops of black ink to imitate the dappling of stone. Once dry, I wrote the text with pencil and then retraced the letters with a solder gun so they would be in low relief. I then painted the letters in black for contrast and they were ready for the yard. More sophisticated people put mounds of sand in front of the tombstones to simulate recent burials. Others glue a plastic raven to the tomb or hide a smoke machine behind them so fog won't be lacking. Oh … our neighbors have also made a tombstone but much smaller. We go up to look at it and are surprised to discover that it's real and permanent. Their cat, a huge animal that occasionally wandered across our yard, has died. It is a slate headstone with the animal's name, date and the inscription "In Loving Memory." Petsmart, the huge pet store in Kingston, has hundreds of them for all tastes, with all types of messages. "We'll see you in the next life." "Friend and companion." "We won't forget you." "My sweet angel, we'll miss you." Julia and Nico offer condolences to their friends Matt and Makenzie Roush for the parting of their cat.

Tonight we're having dinner at the Econopoulys' house. Tim and Nola grew up with Sarah in Rhinebeck. Nola Curthoys was in Sarah's class and was the first friendly face my wife introduced me to the first summer I visited. She was serving drinks behind the bar at the Starr Bar. She has long blond hair and a permanent smile. On the other side of the bar were several potential suitors hoping that she was smiling at them. Nola used a small shot glass to measure the alcohol for the gin and tonics. Here, there's no mercy when it comes to alcoholic drinks. The tonic comes out of a hose. They can serve you three gallons' worth if you want, but the alcohol is distributed as if it were perfume. Two drops and that's it. It's not like in the bars in Spain, where the waiter keeps pouring the gin until you tell him to stop. Here, if you want to be able to taste the alcohol in a drink, you have to ask for a double. Econopouly is a Greek name and for me it represents the ethnic and cultural fusion you find in Upstate New York. I don't know anyone more American than Tim. He's the closest to Jeremiah Johnson living in this valley, with his lumberjack shirt, passion for nature and annual lake expeditions by canoe in the Adirondacks. But Tim has a brother who is an orthodox monk on Mount Olympus. He has a part of him that is more Greek than yogurt. I would never have imagined it, but there you have it. When the Jews celebrate their Passover and the Christians their Easter, the Econopoulys prepare, at the house of another brother, Will, a gastronomic feast that seems to me to be the best possible way to break-the-fast. As the iPod in the kitchen plays the Stamatis Kokotas version of "Otrellos," a local lamb is slowly roasting over coal. From early morning until late afternoon, it turns on the spit until it is perfectly golden brown. Depending on the temperature every year, the diners accompany the banquet with a glass of Tsantali Roditis rosé or a red Myrto. The food never stops coming: meatballs, moussaka, roast garlic tzatziki, meat-and-rice stuffed dolmas... Yum! When the time comes, the lamb is taken down from the spit and Will removes the wires. Tim and his brother-in-law Richard expertly carve the animal. This is easy for Richard, whose father was the butchery instructor at the Culinary Institute. The steaks, filet mignon ... and everyone fighting for the pieces encrusted with cloves of garlic.

Tim's paternal grandparents were Greek. They grew up in small Peloponnesian villages a few miles apart, but met in New York. His grandmother never learned English. However, his grandfather would proudly sit to read the *Daily News* every day after work. When Tim and his siblings were little, their parents took them to visit their cousins in Greece, very poor people whose only valuable possessions were two goats with which the children played. Before leaving, the animals were served on the table to celebrate the happy reunion. In Greece, that boundless generosity comes from people of the Middle East, which stretches to the east. Iran is the highest expression of this generous spirit. Mr. Econopouly recalls that when he saw the goats, he called his children to the gathering, aware of the effort his relatives were making, and asked them to eat everything without complaint. To eat every last scrap of meat on the plate. And they did. Even today, the "clean bones" request is a family joke. Tim says his father is incapable of eating meat without stripping the bones bare. His plate doesn't have to go through the dishwasher.

Nola and Tim got married in the middle of the woods. It was like when Snow White became engaged to the woodcutter. A few weeks before the ceremony, I became familiar with a nasty weed that had attacked Nola and which, ever since, I've learned to avoid at all costs. It's called poison ivy. It impregnates you with oil, so the best remedy is a good shower with dishwashing liquid after having worked in the yard. Palmolive has become my best friend in the summer. Tim and Nola's house overlooks Crystal Lake, a magnificent place right in the middle of town, from whose windows you can practically dive into the water and start swimming. Or take a spin in a kayak. Before dinner, I have to pick up Nico from his friend Andrew's house, which is on the same street. Andrew Chestney is the son of Chris, the owner of the funeral home, a nice, tall guy who sponsors Max's basketball team. He must do it as a service to the community because I'm pretty sure he doesn't want to attract more customers. When I reach the house, I hear the echo of voices resounding from the far side of the yard. I walk around the side of the house and find a table full of people sitting around some bottles of wine. Chris and his wife Carol stand to greet me and with extraordinary hospitality (we may have met only a couple of times when picking up our kids from school), and ask me to sit with their friends to share a glass. Some faces are familiar to me and we exchange greetings. I'd love to stay, but I don't have time. I'm just about to tell them I'm rushing off because Nola and Tim are expecting us for dinner, but I keep quiet. In a small town like this, you quickly learn to be discreet. Everyone knows everyone else and you never know if someone might be offended for not being included in some plan. It's not a question of concealing information, it's just trying not to offer unsolicited information. Here, you may be having a cup of coffee with someone in the afternoon and say goodbye as if you weren't going to see him in a week, but that same evening, you see him again at a friend's dinner table. Neither of you had mentioned the dinner invitation. "What are you doing tonight?" "I've got a dinner, how about you?" "Yeah, me too." But you don't say where or with whom. The weekend in Rhinebeck is full of surprises ... and tension. You never know if you'll make the cut.

At Crystal Lake, it is a cool but pleasant evening and the bats flutter about. "Won't you stay for a glass of wine?" asks Chris Chestney again. Then, loosened up by the relaxed atmosphere on the porch, I say: "With Halloween around the corner, and what with your being a funeral director and those bats circling above, I wouldn't stay here even if you tied me to the chair." Chris gives me a serious look and then laughs. Phew. Being funny in a different language is one of the hardest things to pull off and there are many ways to mess up. Nico comes out of the house with Andrew. Carol asks me if my son can sleep over. Have I heard right? "Okay," I say. "How many nights?" I know that the politically correct thing is to say that your kids are the best thing that ever happened to you and that you would just like to be able to spend more time with them. That's what the politicians say when they are forced to drop out of the electoral race: that they will have more time to spend with their families. Knowing some of those politicians, you can't help but feel sorry for their families. But in the case of normal people, those of us who really do have relationships with our kids, there's nothing better than to get a break from them every now and then. Let someone else keep them overnight to give you a chance to miss them and want to see them even more the next day. "Thanks, Carol, Nico is all yours. Is breakfast included?" I head down South Street on my way to dinner, happy to be living among such kind people.

The Dapson-Chestney Funeral Home, like other American funeral businesses, was founded in the shadow of a small cabinet-making shop.

Previously, building coffins was a voluntary effort carried out by those who could do so, namely cabinetmakers and carpenters. In Rhinebeck, the old Carroll Furnishing factory became Carroll Furnishing and Undertaking. The verb "to undertake" means to commit oneself to and assume a responsibility. The term "undertaker" stuck as the appropriate euphemism to refer to the mortuary executive because he was the one who took care of the dead. The prefix "under" is just a coincidence with no relation to the fact that bodies are buried underground. Way back when burials shifted from being a social labor to a lucrative business, the undertakers definitively broke off from those who crafted wooden shelves, chairs and beds.

Rhinebeck has two funeral homes, one to the east and the other to the west of Market Street. Two businesses offering exequial services for a total population of 7,000? That might seem excessive, but not many years ago, mourning took place mainly in homes. Today, Dapson-Chestney Funeral Home organizes just one wake a year in a private home, as opposed to the 80 it holds annually at its facilities. Cremation has also been on the rise, accounting for 30 percent of funeral rites. Not all towns in the county have their own funeral home. In small towns such as Milan, Tivoli or Staatsburg, neighbors have to choose between the cemetery in Rhinebeck, Red Hook or Hyde Park. Curiously, decisions seem to coincide with the town where their children went to school. It makes sense as they most likely made friends through their children and consequently, wherever that was is where they developed their social life.

In a big city like New York, there are Italian, Jewish and Irish funeral homes, all of which originated in their own neighborhoods and which follow different traditions. Here, Chris has to adapt to different beliefs. Customs vary between Protestants and Catholics. The Church of Rome believes that the prayers of the living can help the souls of the dead to travel to heaven whereas the church of Martin Luther and Calvin considers it a waste of time to pray for the dead because it is too late to help them. Ministers have no trouble going to the funeral home to console the families whereas priests prefer families to go to the church. During the ceremony, the audience is reminded of who the deceased person was and of his or her personal or professional achievements. People recount funny or moving anecdotes about the deceased and recall the good times spent in their company. This sometimes conflicts with the stricter ideology of the Catholic Church, which insists that the rite should be a celebration of death rather than of life. It is assumed that the deceased has resuscitated and is now having a much better time in heaven. The earth is a valley of tears which, thanks to God, has ended and now there is glory in death.

There are innumerable subtle differences in the religious sphere, so Chris has to be open to the requests of the deceased's family. After all, his mission is to try to ease their suffering as much as possible. The director of a funeral home is something of a psychologist. Attempts to relay a final farewell of a family member with a celebration of life make for some exciting funerals on this side of the Atlantic. Sometimes the family provides the background music. This can be as simple as a recording of the favorite song of the guest of honor to play at the funeral home. Or it may be a more complex operation. A friend who plays the violin. A niece who sings. Or, in the funeral mass celebrated at the Cathedral Church of Saint John the Divine in New York for Jim Henson, on the high altar, the shaggy red Muppet who loves tickling, Elmo, sang together "Lydia the Tattooed Lady," the song that Groucho Marx immortalized in *At the Circus*.

Of course, says Chris, let us not forget, that we are in America the beautiful, the kingdom of show business. Lately, marketing gurus have identified niches in the realm of funereal extravagance. So Chris offers serigraph caskets in the colors of the deceased's favorite sports team or decorated with photos of his or her favorite actors or singers. The Batesville Company embroiders commemorative panels inside the lid, with the family coat of arms, the emblem of any organization, spiritual symbols, objects or landscapes associated with hobbies, or faces of loved ones. They can also make small niches in the corners of the caskets to place decorative figures referring to the spirit, personality or interests of the deceased and which the closest relatives will later take home as keepsakes. These may range from a sculpture of a bald eagle wrapped in the flag, to sporty, floral or spiritual motifs. For each casket, urn or cremation contracted, the staff at Batesville will plant a tree as part of the global reforestation program.

They also produce videos and photomontages that reconstruct the biography of the deceased, for families to show at the funeral home, give to those present or post on the Internet. Posters are printed with a photo of the deceased to decorate the room in which the celebration will take place, and keepsakes photographs are distributed among mourners. There are stamped t-shirts and personalized Bibles, candles and cushions. For those who cremate their loved ones, gold and silver pendants are sold that serve as reliquaries for carrying some ashes. In terms of caskets, the catalogue in Chestney's office offers more than 500 models, ranging in price from $200 for a pine box to $25,000 for the presidential-style coffin. The latest is made of hand-carved mahogany and has no religious motifs. There is an even more expensive version, which costs up to $100,000 given the gold-plated interior. Chestney tries not to influence choices. Some funeral homes are well known for taking advantage of the emotional fragility of the moment to sell the family the most expensive casket, something which a funeral home in a small town cannot get away with. Reputation is everything in a place like this. "If I take advantage of the situation," says Chris, "the next death in Rhinebeck will not be the concern of my business." Funeral homes can get away with that in a big city where people don't know them personally because the owners know the clientele will continue to come anyway. Not here. At any rate, he tells me, paying a lot for a casket is not always the fault of the funeral home. There are people who feel bad about what they did not do for the deceased in life and believe they can fix things by spending a fortune on the coffin. Of course, this is nothing compared with the eccentricities of the guy who, in a town closer to Manhattan, was buried at the wheel of his Formula 1 car. Here, people place objects that make them feel good in the caskets: bottles of beer, a pack of cigarettes, a lottery ticket … The Irish include a travel bag with objects the deceased will need on his journey to paradise, like they used to do in the pharaohs' tombs. A conventional funeral runs an average of $8,000.

At the moment, Rhinebeck doesn't have a problem with casket sizes. So far, all the deceased have fit in the normal-sized coffin, which measures 2 feet wide, or in the large size, which measures 2.5 feet. To date, no one has had to order the XXXL Goliath, measuring 3.5 feet across, with reinforced hinges and handles, which was developed in Indiana to hold the largest deceased, up to 650 lbs. The U.S. funeral industry began to readjust its technical specifications due to the considerable increase in weight, and therefore volume, of a large sector of the population. Twenty percent of the U.S. adult population is obese, for which reason the Woodlawn Cemetery in the Bronx was recently forced to increase the size of its plots from 3 feet to 4 feet wide.

Chris's profession is viewed well socially, and, except for a few inevitable jokes, his funeral home is associated with a business that contributes to everyone's well-being. This doesn't make up for the fact that for years, some of his friends could not understand why he had opted for such a disagreeable job. Now, he tells me, many have arrived to the dreadful age when they begin to lose their parents and finally appreciate his valuable labor.

Eighty percent of bodies are embalmed. Canada and the United States are the only countries in the world that routinely carry out this procedure. It is only mandatory in Minnesota, but funeral homes refuse to show the bodies if they haven't been embalmed. There's not much to it. Basically, the procedure uses a pump that extracts fluids from the body and exchanges them for chemical products. Previously, they would place two coins on the eyelids and tie the jaw shut with a cord until rigor mortis set in. Today superglue has simplified things.

Jewish funeral rites require funeral directors to work in a hurry. The body must be buried before sunset within 24 hours after death. Since families tend to be dispersed and attending a funeral often entails significant travel, there is an unwritten extension of the period to 48 hours. The synagogue in Kingston or Poughkeepsie sends someone to Chestney's to supervise the preparation of the body. According to the Jewish law of Halacha, the deceased is covered in white canvas and the undertaker, the chevra kadisha, initiates the *tahara* or purification rite. The cleansing is carried out without ever looking at the face of the deceased or uncovering him. Each time a body part is washed, a prayer is said: for the eyes, to cleanse the bad things he may have observed; for the mouth, for the bad words he may have spoken; for the nose, for the vile odors he may have inhaled; for the chest, for the bad impulses he may have had ... and so forth until the undertaker reaches the feet, which are washed to erase the bad steps taken. Once the body is purified, it is dressed in a type of pajamas, the *tachrichim*, consisting of white pants and a top made from 10 pieces of cotton in the case of men, and 12 pieces in the case of women. In Israel, the deceased are buried without caskets. In the U.S. and Europe, a hole is sometimes drilled in the bottom of the coffin to facilitate contact with the soil. American culture tends to protect the family from the more morbid parts of the ceremony. People do not attend cremations and at burials, people leave before the casket is lowered into the ground. Jews are the exception since mourners are expected to throw shovels of sand over the coffin.

Sometimes the burial takes place in special areas. It is not very common, of course, but it occurs with wealthy people who live on large estates and want to be buried there. Chris always urges against this: what happens if the children sell the house? Then they wouldn't have access to their parents' graves.

There are several cemeteries in the Rhinebeck area. All of them are in sloped meadows interrupted by discreet rows of vertical tombstones. Some are public whereas others belong to churches, such as that of St. Joseph's Chapel in Rhinecliff. This is the largest cemetery; it is private and admits all creeds. If the family has no money, the county covers the cost of a modest burial. War veterans get free burials. High-ranking military officers and heroes go directly to Arlington National Cemetery in Virginia. Many of the tombstones on Route 9 have eroded with the passage of time and the inscriptions are practically illegible. Sometimes you find a large tomb where the parents are buried and which has complete names and dates, and surrounding it, smaller graves with the initials of their children: N. H., J.M., T.C.

At last, Halloween night arrives and we have no choice but to take turns trick or treating. I go out with the kids in search of candy while Sarah stays home to serve those who come requesting it. Hundreds arrive at our house. We are right in the middle of town, in an area easily covered on foot, and the customers come in droves. Trick or treat. Let them come. We are prepared with mounds of chocolate bars, toffees and hard candies. Gangs of kids ring the doorbell. Among the groups, I recognize Ian Katomski, Susanne Callahan's son, dressed as a skunk. Susanne is another of Sarah's inseparable friends from childhood. I say hello and Ian sprays me with a water bottle. "Hey, this is a real skunk!" There are masks for every taste, but most are not scary. We learned that lesson too late. A few days ago, there was a children's costume contest in the American Legion parking lot, the home for war veterans, and our kids wanted to participate. Max and Nico are dressed as monsters and Julia as a witch. Nico is quite scary, with green makeup covering his face, and covered with wounds and pustules created with wax and fake blood. He is convinced he is going to win first place. When he stands in front of the jury, we know he doesn't have a chance. There are no deformed butlers or ghosts of any sort. One boy is dressed as a red fire hydrant, another as a medieval knight with horse included ... The winner is the boy whose ingenious father, Christian Fekete, a French architect, has hung red construction paper in the form of an apple from his neck. In the paper, he has made a hole for the left elbow, from which the boy's arm extends, covered in a sock that resembles a worm. "Wow!" I say. "Why didn't anyone tell us that Halloween costumes in the U.S. were more like those of Brazil's carnival than those of the *Rocky Horror Picture Show*?"

"Stupid *Papá*," Max and Nico say. "Why—are we dressed as monsters?" "It's your fault we are making fools of ourselves. You're so dumb, *Papá*."

The practice of asking for sweets, observed from a respectable distance by parents, is reserved for elementary school kids. By middle school, ages 11 and up, the kids have other plans. The gangs hang out near the old South Street cemetery and come armed with shaving cream, eggs and firecrackers. Occasionally, they get involved in some dispute and the police do everything they can to patrol the streets to prevent them. I have yet to face this reality. We go to the firehouse station instead. I've ridden the train of terror for the youngest kids. Upstairs, they pass out hot chocolate to anyone who wants it. The evening is freezing cold and the light from the lampposts shines on tiny snowflakes, the first of the season.

November 1 begins on a sad note. We hear suspicious noises and go out to see what's going on. Some hooligans have squashed Julia's jack-o-lantern against the front steps. We suspect two thugs who are nervously running up the street. Julia can't hold back her tears. "They did it," she says as she points in the kids' direction. "We don't know that," I tell her, lowering her hand. "Don't worry, we'll carve another pumpkin." The disagreeable episode unlocks the key for deciphering the meaning of the name of an alternative Chicago rock group whose name never made any sense in Spanish: The Smashing Pumpkins. What's that? Who would ever smash a pumpkin? Well, it turns out that in America some people will. I always thought that the name of the band was a surreal invention, like Blind Melon and the like. Apparently not. There really are pumpkin smashers out there. Julia and I go out to look around the area in search of clues.

Curiously, I had met the members of Blind Melon during the celebration of the second Woodstock Festival, also known as Mudstock, in the summer of 1994. The 25th anniversary of the mythical musical event of 1969 was not celebrated in Bethel, the site of the original concert, or in the Village of Woodstock, but rather 16.5 kilometers away, at the Saugerties Farm. Promoter Michael Lang had gone to H.H. Hill Real Estate in Rhinebeck to ask my brother-in-law for help finding a location, and Huck put him in touch with Winston Farm. So of course Huck had tickets. At the time, we were on vacation, visiting Sarah's family. One afternoon, Huck suggested we cross the Hudson with him to go to the concert and hang out in the VIP section used by the artists. Sarah declined because she was pregnant with our second child and the photos in the newspaper suggested a real risk of slipping in the mud amid the crowds. Some good friends of ours, Laura Lee Berlingieri and David Ferris, were spending the weekend with us. We met them in Madrid where they were teaching English at the Instituto Norteamericano. We were introduced to them by Metta Callahan, another Rhinebeck native who also lived in Spain's capital at the time. That summer, David and Laura Lee had decided to make a change in their lives and were studying for their MBAs at Thunderbird School of Global Management in Arizona, and had come to visit us. Later, they would work on Wall Street, then in London, Bombay and Hong Kong. Today they live in Melbourne, Australia. But back in August 1994, they gladly accepted the invitation to cross the Hudson and go to the Woodstock anniversary concert on the wharf that Lang had rented from the Unification Church for the event.

When we reached Rose Hill Lane, a handful of people were waiting for the boat. The four of us were engaged in conversation as we awaited the ferry when a man rushed up screaming something unintelligible. "What's wrong?" "Nothing," said the babbling stranger. "The helicopter with Jimmy Cliff is going to take off and there's a free space. Who wants to go?" Before we had a chance to react, Huck had disappeared. The chorus of "You Can Get It If You Really Want" must have been going through his head and made him forget that he had the festival tickets in his pocket. We began to laugh nervously. A bit confused, we got on the ferry with the group that had been waiting with us. They served us a glass of champagne. Very civilized. "What should we do?" "Enjoy this crazy life while it lasts." We greeted our travel companions. It turns out they were the members of Blind Melon, who were playing that night. They came to success with their song "No Rain" and opened for Neil Young, Lenny

Kravitz and the Rolling Stones. Very nice guys. The vocalist had the name of an immoral person: Hoon. Nevertheless, that afternoon while we crossed the Hudson, Hoon seemed like a calm, reserved guy. This was based more on observation than anything else because we exchanged no more than two and a half sentences with him before we arrived on the west bank. "See you later." "Good luck." "Thanks." That evening we would watch him perform while wearing his girlfriend's dress on stage. A year and a half later, Shannon Hoon would leave this world, the victim of an overdose.

We got off the ferry. The area was cordoned off. A bodyguard the size of a Louis XV armoire cut off the retinue. "Who are you?" he asked the Indiana vocalist in a dry voice. "We are Blind Melon," Hoon responded. The bodyguard tweaked his earpiece and activated the microphone of his walkie-talkie to give an order: "Limousine for Blind Melon, please." Seemingly out of nowhere, a black train-car sized vehicle on wheels pulled up. He lifted his arm and let them through. A driver opened the car door and they were gone seconds later. "Who are you? Excuse me?" The Incredible Hulk stood before me, connected to his radio in real time with the heads of the New York State Police. One word from him and the response would have been immediate from the hundreds of agents patrolling the area that had been overtaken by 50,000 rock music addicts. One gesture from that man and they would have the three of us face down on the grass, a boot to the head, handcuffs on the hands and shackles on the legs. "Who are you?" he repeated impatiently, staring at me. A helicopter rose up from behind the locust trees and passed over us. It had just left Jimmy and Huck enjoying a cold Coronita at the organization's headquarters and was going back to pick up the Red Hot Chili Peppers. The repetition of the question brought me back to reality: "Who are you?" My voice sounded weak and desperate: "We are friends of Huck." "Friends of whom?" My brother-in-law's name meant nothing to this representative of law and order. "I can't understand you," he said. "We are friends of Huck!" I said, raising my voice. He activated the walkie-talkie. "Security?" ... ggggg... "Copy?" ... Gggggggg.... "Security, copy?" … Gggggg… A metallic voice emerged from the other side. Yes, security. I copy you… Ggggg… Our legs were shaking. "Please…" ggggg … "Send over a limousine for the group Friends of Huck." A huge black car appeared. The officer raised his arm. He wished us good luck. "Roger, over and out." A friendly driver told us to get in. Yippee….

We went for it. Doubling over with laughter, the three members of the rock group Friends of Huck—Laura Lee Berlingieri, David Ferris and Guillermo Fesser—traveled in a car so long that it appeared to have been assembled by placing six Cadillac cabins together. It was as big as an Amtrak car. The guards were opening the roadblocks for us. We left Route 32, which was packed with thousands of cars trying to reach the site, and entered the festival headquarters. The limo stopped before what appeared to be a group of bungalows from a hotel on the Mayan coast. The driver kindly opened the door. A man greeted us and led us to one of the wooden huts. "I hope you find everything to your liking. Just let me know if you need anything." The only thing he didn't say was that we had clean towels in the closet. "Of course, thanks so much." We stood at the door not knowing what to do. On the little porch of the hut next to us, a guy with a mustache and bandana plucked an old Santana tune on his guitar. *Tantan tan tantan tatataaaaaan, tantan tan tantan tatatan… Samba Pa Ti.* The guy got it exactly right and he even looked a bit like the Mexican composer. It was him! Carlos Santana. "Hi, how's it going?" "Peace and love. Just warming up the fingers." "It sounds good. I think you should do that professionally," I said. "Yeah," he joked. "Let's see if the light shines down on us." "Yeah, sure." "What about you?" "Everything's fine. A bit… well, you know… everything's fine. Even better than we thought." "I'm glad." We turned away surreptitiously, as if we had something urgent to do, and quickly took off. Who was that character in the cabin next to us? The answer is blowing in the wind.

Mustache, goatee and endive-curly hair: There was Bob Dylan. He was doing his own thing, but it didn't matter to us. It was Bob Dylan, you know? We could have rolled on down like a rolling stone and we would have given him the same smile. How many times had I listened to *Desire?* That little song lasted eight minutes and 33 seconds. But I never got tired of it. As soon as it finished, I would place the needle at the beginning again. Until a scratch led to the record's retirement. "Hi." Nothing. It seemed like he was in a bad mood. A volunteer in the vicinity told us that he was angry because the organization had let his ex-wife into the VIP area. "Sara, Sara, sweet virgin angel, sweet love of my life. Sara, Sara, radiant jewel, mystical wife." The poet had complained to the handler that they had been separated for 30 years. "Doesn't that seem like enough time?" That day, the filters at several entrances were failing. Woodstock security was full of holes.

We decided to get away from headquarters before someone asked us to get on stage as the opening act for the Neville Brothers. We walked along the edge of the enormous mud pit. Like two boats stranded on the beach, right in the center of the pit, a pair of fat, bearded, tattooed guys in sleeveless shirts slept in two mud-incrusted canvas chairs. Two gigantic stages were operating at the same time. On the north stage, 100,000 scantily-clad, sweaty souls congregated. To avoid suffocating, we headed toward the south stage, where we breathed a sigh of relief when we discovered we'd only have to share the space with 40,000 other people. There we enjoyed "Mr. Senegal," Youssou N'Dour. "Seven seconds away. Just as long as I stay. I'll be waiting ..."

"What are you singing, *Papá?*" asks Julia, who prefers the theme song from *Dora the Explorer.* "Nothing," I say. We continue to inspect our backyard and the neighborhood in search of some clue as to the identity of the pumpkin smashers. No luck.

4

November

Steve Mosto, supreme consultant in issues related to steam in New York City, is a chemical engineer. But if you ask him what he does, he will tell you he is a musician—a composer who, due to circumstances beyond his control, was forced to head a company in Manhattan. Although Steve moves with the agility of a lynx among boilers and turbines, his natural habitat is the piano. He grew up listening to Beethoven, Mozart and Chopin, the music played at his home in Ringwood, New Jersey. When he turned four and started nursery school, he began to take piano lessons. Every Sunday morning, his father would take out his violin and accompany the great compositions of the masters recorded on vinyl records. Then it was little Steve's turn. He would bang on the keys, trying to emulate Bach, until one day he tired of classical music. He was 10 when he decided to send Vienna to hell and signed up for trumpet at school. He joined the school band and made his debut at the annual jazz concert. When he was 12, he formed his first rock group and took advantage of the circumstance to switch to the electric keyboard, without doubting his decision even for a second. They played sugar-coated versions of songs by Deep Purple, The Who, Kiss, Led Zeppelin, Rush, Styx and Pink Floyd. He also began to experiment with his voice. He had become hooked on the drug of music. He would immediately spend the money he earned, delivering newspapers on his bike before class or cutting the neighbor's grass after school, on amplifiers, microphones and loudspeakers.

Steve's first gig was a summer pool party. The band knew five songs and he played the bass on the keyboard with the aid of two fingers. That was the best idea he'd ever had. He became the King of Mambo. Girls swarmed around him and he didn't even need to converse with them coherently for them to stay at his side. Then it was time for his real debut, with hundreds of people listening in silence while he hammered the piano keys. The following autumn found him at the pulpit of St. Catherine Catholic Church. Every Sunday, an enthusiastic audience of 400 parishioners waited for the band to start during the Ringwood masses. He would mix religious hymns with melodies by Billy Joel and Elton John, to which listeners reacted with both surprise and gratitude. It took just a year for him to overcome his stage fright, and like the mythical figures of the Gospel, he leapt from the altar to the stage. He began to do shows in bars, telethons, clubs ... anyplace they would let him plug in his instruments. By the time Steve was 17, he had played at over 200 weddings. It was 1978 and he would sit with his buddy Mike in front of the record player listening over and over again to Eddie Van Halen, a genius who ripped the guitar like no one he'd ever heard before.

After graduating from high school with good grades, Steve was off to Rutgers University to pursue a degree in chemical engineering, the same subject his father had studied years before in Santiago, Chile, and his paternal grandfather before him in Italy, Steve III. At home, his family made it clear that they would not help finance his studies unless he chose a respectable career. And respectable meant engineering. So Steve opted to continue in the tradition. However, he also got a degree in music at the same time, just in case: jazz composition and piano. When he finished, he worked as an engineer for two years. But just as the goat takes to the mountain, musicians tend to be drawn to record contracts and when the young engineer was asked to make a record, his life took on a new direction. The contract arrived in an envelope from Nashville. He signed on with the recording company owned by actress Mary Tyler Moore. For four seasons, his jacket and tie collected dust as he toured the South accompanying the Oakridge Boys, the Judds, Pam Tillis, Poco and several other groups having a wonderful time that ended when the recording company decided to close its doors without warning. That's all folks. Without the support of the company, contracting offices turned their backs on him. Besides, in the South with an Italian name, he had zero possibilities of attracting the interest of the young people who went to music concerts. He could have changed his name from Steve Mosto to, let's say, Elvis Mockingbird; but no one thought to suggest this to him. So he returned to the East Coast. Round Two—back to engineering. Steve quickly found a job in Manhattan. The big companies had moved their headquarters elsewhere and engineers were scarce. He was sought out by and accepted an offer from a company that sold parts for underground steam conduction systems.

"Steam pipes?" I ask, surprised, interrupting a conversation into which no one invited me. "Yes, steam pipes," responds the guy who is taking pinnies from a cloth bag and passing them out among the children. He is one of the volunteer fathers who coach children's soccer on the fields of the Baptist Home. Like Bruce Washburn and John Graziano. I am here talking to John, who has the last name of a variety of grape, Graziano, and is the head winemaker at Millbrook Vineyards & Winery. We met at a delicious wine-tasting there. A couple of glasses later, between the merlot with its aromas of black cherry and cabernet franc with its notes of vanilla, John Graziano wanted to know what I did. I told him I was trying to write a movie script. It was to be a tribute to the maid who worked for my family her whole life. "Is it a documentary?" "No, it's fiction, but it's based on real events." I explained that Cándida was a very special person in my life—my very own Mary Poppins, except that instead of flying in on an umbrella, she came on the subway from the outskirts of Madrid. One of those women who emigrated from the rural poverty of post-war Spain to the great capital, willing to do anything to help her family get ahead, and always with a smile. Always with a kind word. Never for the money. She is one of those women who give up their own lives, working from sunup to sundown, so that their children will know what hope is—those women who live in a black-and-white world so that the next generation could exist in full-color HD. They are the world's engines. And John confessed to me that my description of Cándida also perfectly fit his grandmother, an Italian immigrant and tireless worker. He told me that growing up, the family joke at his house was that if you got up at midnight to go to the bathroom, Grandma Graziano would have made your bed before you got back.

Max picks up the last balloon from the bag and runs with his friend Eamon Graziano behind the rest of the troop. "Excuse me," I insist again, "but doesn't the steam in New York escape through the subway's ventilation grilles?" "No," Steve says. I don't want to be a pain but the subject is too intriguing to drop. I take a breath. It's okay, everything is going to be back to normal. On the grass, our children line up and try to mimic John Marvin as he dribbles the ball around the orange cones. "So," I ask timidly, "how does the steam escape?" In response, Steve holds out his hand: "My name is Steve Mosto." "Fesser," I respond. "My first name is unpronounceable." "Try it," he challenges me. "Ghe-yer-mo," I say. "Okay, Guillermo," he says without hesitating—one of the advantages of having a Chilean father. "What you see in the city is the steam that escapes from the pipes." "From steam pipes?" "Nope." "What do you mean? Which pipes?" "It's a long story," he says. "Could we grab a bite to eat one day so you could explain it to me?" "Okay, Thursday would be good." "Perfect." We arrange to meet for lunch on Thursday at Bread Alone Bakery for soup and sandwiches.

Let's talk about sandwiches. In America, the proportions are the inverse of Spain's. In other words, instead of eating bread with some meat inside, Americans wolf down a mountain of meat held together with a bit of bread outside. It's true that the delis cut the salami or prosciutto in super thin slices, perfect for savoring the flavor of the cured meat in all its glory, but when they put them on the bread, one slice on top of the other, they practically reassemble the whole ham. The mystery is why they

94

bother to cut it up in the first place. That Mediterranean ciabbata, rubbed with garlic and tomato, drizzled with extra virgin olive oil, a pinch of salt and an almost transparent slice of Iberico ham would be misunderstood here. They like big sandwiches ... so they can take half home for an extra free meal. The burritos at Gaby's Cafe are a perfect example. No one talks about it, but everyone always leaves the Mexican restaurant carrying a white styrofoam box. "Buenas noches, Lazaro." "Goodnight, sir."

Bread Alone, on E. Market Street, began when Dan Leader moved his family to the Catskill Mountains in 1983 with the dream of building a wood-fired brick oven bread shop. He achieved his dream and ever since has been baking all manner of fresh bread, following traditional recipes and using organic grains. Most people buy the bread already sliced for toasting at home. For every 12 loaves you purchase, Bread Alone gives you one free. There are also fresh-baked baguettes, ciabattas, focaccias with black olives and onions, nut breads. People come in the morning for a cup of coffee and a roll, croissants (the authentic ones that come apart if you pull on the horns), brioche with raisins, blueberry-filled muffins or eggs with bacon and toast. At midday, the bakery offers salads, moderately-sized panini and soups of the day. Mohammed serves Steve and me. He is an Egyptian, born just a few yards from the great pyramid of Giza. He has the whitest smile Mother Nature could offer without the aid of a teeth-cleaning treatment by Colleen at Dr. Ross's office. Mohammed earned a degree in philosophy at the University of Cairo, but chance led him to work as a movie stunt man for Ahmed Zaky, a celebrated actor in the Arab world, known for his interpretations of Nasser and Anwar El Sadat. Mohammed's first movie was filmed in 1994. It was called *Mr. Karate*, and Mohammed had to sport an enormous moustache and bulk up his eyebrows to resemble the lead actor. He learned to throw himself from moving cars, to jump off moving trains. "Everything has its trick," he says. "You just have to find a position that helps you cushion the fall ... except when you have to throw yourself down the stairs. If they hire you to do that, you do it anyway you can, but knowing there's no other way than to hurt yourself. It always hurts." "What can I get you?" Steve orders a pesto chicken salad whereas I opt for the cream of carrot soup with ginger and Parmesan slivers. "So, Mohammed," I ask, "if you knew you were going to hurt yourself falling down the stairs, why did you agree to do it?" "Easy," he says. "God ordered me to. Throughout my life, I've always asked God for guidance and so far I've been lucky." This reminds me of the response a bullfighter once made to a similar question: "Hunger hurts more than being gored by a bull."

On the movie sets in Cairo, Mohammed dreamed about emigrating to America, about having a career in Hollywood and waking up every morning in a little house with palm trees on Sunset Boulevard. After several years of saving Zaky from high-risk scenes, the Egyptian celebrity decided to help him out. He helped Mohammed get a visa, bought him an airline ticket and gave him the name of a Jordanian friend who lived in the Bronx. The same day Mohammed set foot in New York, he got a job offer. The Jordanian contact was a member of a large family. "How large, Mohammed?" "Some 2,000 members, more or less." "Wow!" "He lived in the New York area and owned many gas stations. He gave me a job at the one in Rhinebeck—the Getty Station." Amid the gas pumps, he found a girlfriend and the two of them considered going to Los Angeles so that Mohammed could study acting. Jean thought it was a good idea. "Jean?" I ask, surprised. "Pat Beecher's sister?" "Yeah, do you know her?" That's the thing about small towns. You move about like a chip in the game of Chutes and Ladders, never knowing which square you'll land on or where it will take you. Pat lives in the house at the corner where the school bus, with Annie at the helm, stops daily. Maybe this is a smile connection because Annie Holden has a smile as big as Mohammed's every morning as she opens the hydraulic door—pshhhh—as if transporting a group of screaming kids to school were a holistic experience. "Goooood moooorning!" "Good morning, Annie." The kids happily board the yellow monster with wheels that swallows them one by one and makes them disappear for a few hours. "Bye, Annie." It's a hard knock life for us. ...

Mohammed's girlfriend Jean lives in Red Hook with her mother and a chimpanzee that they use in therapy sessions for patients with psychiatric conditions. The only thing you can't do with a monkey is disagree with him, Jean said the day I met her. "Of course," I said, "I wouldn't want to ever take issue with a monkey." "No, really," she insisted, "they really can't stand that. They become violent. If the monkey decides to eat spaghetti on the floor, well, we have to let her. You see what I mean?" Mohammed brings us our order: the soup, the salad and the drinks. I tell him I had a Fulbright to do a master's degree in film at the University of Southern California and that information quickly strengthens the bond between us. "So you must know Eric," he says. "Eric? No, or at least I don't think so." "Julia's brother," he clarifies. But I still don't get it. "Julia Kane, the judge's mother?" "No, Julia Roberts, the movie actor." The fact that I'd pursued graduate studies in Los Angeles didn't mean that I rubbed elbows with Dustin Hoffman or enjoyed the privilege of calling Magic Johnson Earvin. The closest I ever came to Hollywood glamor was when I lived on the South Central campus and heard the stories of an electronic shop employee where Michael Jackson used to shop. It seems he appeared wrapped in a sheet, like a Sahara Bedouin, without apparently realizing that nothing attracts more attention in an electronics shop in Los Angeles than showing up dressed like a nomad. He asked where the latest video games were and ordered two or three of each game. He never paid. A personal secretary would come in afterwards to handle the financial transaction. That is my whole relation with the red carpet. So, I'm sorry to have to tell Mohammed that I have not had the pleasure of meeting Eric. Mohammed probably thinks I'm being modest. He tells me that Eric lives in the area, which I obviously must know from my contacts. Mohammed used to talk to him a lot when he made deliveries for another store. Eric would call him at odd hours to place an order, seizing the opportunity to talk about movies and with the hope of establishing a professional contact, Mohammed would happily open the shop. I thank him for the information while trying to imagine what role an Egyptian actor could play in a Spanish movie shot in the states. Maybe the yellow cab driver when Cándida arrives at JFK? Mmmmm ... We agree to get together soon, with Sarah and Jean, too. I'm also curious to meet the chimpanzee.

Steve and I take a seat at one of the tables. "Let's get to the point," I tell him. I take out the blue notebook I bought at Stickle's, like the one Tintin took with him on his complex missions, and I look at my interlocutor, inviting him to begin the story. I warn him that it will take me a while to take notes, for which reason the steaming carrot soup in front of me will surely get cold. This is in fact what happens.

It seems that steam lived among us well before the boiler existed. In 1784, James Watt, the Scotsman whose surname would be associated with the unit of power we all refer to when we ask for a light bulb at the hardware store, greatly improved the piston engine. With this feat, he paved the way for the Industrial Revolution that would change the face of the Earth forever. I'd seen illustrations of one of those engines, a famous Boulton & Watt, in a Hudson Valley mansion. In the Livingston Family estate, the second-largest privately-owned property in New York State during the Colonial period. By the end of the 18th century, the property included a forest covering 148,000 acres in Columbia County and another 494,000 acres in Green County on the other side of the Hudson. The hacienda still provides impressive views of the Catskill Mountains, which earned it the Frenchified name of Clermont. From Rhinebeck, you can get there in just a quarter of an hour by car. You have to drive parallel to the river via Route 9G and then follow the winding road lined with huge trees; cousins of the trees that nourished the boiler of the first steam ship successfully built in the United States.

Before I visited Clermont, I thought that Chancellor Livingston was simply the name of the elementary school my kids attended. Frankly, the only individual I've heard of with that last name was the explorer "Dr. [David] Livingstone, I presume," whom H.M. Stanley encountered on the banks of Lake Tanganyika. Later, I learned that Chancellor Robert R. Livingston had been quite a guy. Although I acknowledge my lack of culture, in my defense I could argue that when in I studied the 18th century at school in Spain, America was only mentioned in passing. In 1700, let's not forget, Spain was the empire. Don Carlos, the history professor we nicknamed Pinhead, claimed that George Washington had won the war against the English thanks to the Spanish dollars we secretly sent him from Madrid. Well, we forked out tons of money and the dollar was the Spanish currency at the time, but who knows. Throughout history, the dominant country has always tended to claim as their own the achievements that other countries managed with their own effort.

Robert Livingston was one of the five drafters of the 1776 Declaration of Independence. In his role as chancellor, the highest justice official in New York State, he had the honor of swearing in George Washington as the first United States president. He served as secretary of state in the first cabinet and later, in 1802, Jefferson sent him to Paris on the impossible mission of purchasing New Orleans. The third U.S. president was attempting to guarantee control of entry into the U.S. via the Mississippi River through the purchase of the port. Against all odds, his ambassador returned with all of Louisiana. Luck played a big role in this last exploit of Livingston, although this in no way takes away from his merit.

The territory known as La Louisiane was conquered by the French explorer La Salle in 1682 on behalf of King Louis XIV of France. It was a huge region that included the current states of Missouri, the Dakotas, Nebraska, Kansas, Iowa, Oklahoma, Arkansas, and parts of present-day Louisiana, Minnesota, Montana, New Mexico, Texas, Wyoming and Colorado. In other words, the whole central part of the U.S. map was French. Bonjour! To the east, Louisiana bordered the English colonies whereas to the West it lay along a stretch of immense pine forests that would later be known as Oregon. The Kingdom of Spain held the southern part, which stretched from Florida to California to the very tip of the Southern cone. We are talking about a time in which the colonies served as currency in the disputed territories of the great European powers. Thus, 80 years later, in 1763, when Europe signed a peace treaty after the seven-year military campaign in Prussia, victorious England imposed its rules. The loser, the

French king, ceded control of Louisiana to the Spanish monarch. Thirteen years later, the Declaration of Independence of the 13 American colonies was drafted. The new nation, aware of the strategic importance of the Mississippi River for reaching the sea, quickly negotiated an agreement with the Spanish governor to allow it to use the Port of New Orleans. The agreement, called the Right of Deposit, guaranteed Americans a crucial trade route with the Western territories. Thanks to this agreement, its ships freely navigated along the Mississippi carrying staples such as wheat, tobacco, bacon, feathers, cider, cheese and butter.

But history is capricious, and was even more so when Napoleon Bonaparte was given the privilege of defining it. In 1800, the astute French emperor signed a secret treaty with Charles IV of Spain, which returned Louisiana to him in exchange for creating a kingdom for the son-in-law of the Spanish monarch someplace in Italy. In the early 19th-century, there was an overbooking of monarchs and poor Luis Francisco Borbón-Parma had no place to govern. Napoleon expelled the Great Duke from Florence and ceded Tuscany to the Spaniard, who gratefully re-baptized it with the ancient Roman name of the Kingdom of Etruria. France once again owned Louisiana and Napoleon could invade the U.S. and impose French teaching in schools. The United States was immediately on guard.

New Orleans was again in French hands. From there, Napoleon tried to supply his colonies in the Antilles, recover Santo Domingo and move his fleet north along the Mississippi. Imagine, the presidential debate among Romney, Santorum, Gingrich and Paul would have started with the French national anthem, the *Marseillaise*, and Herman Cain's tax plan would have been *neuf, neuf, neuf*. But the French governor of Haiti faced a violent slave rebellion, which was secretly financed by the Jefferson government and, on the high seas, yellow fever had claimed the lives of thousands of Napoleon's soldiers. When Livingston arrived in Paris a year later, Bonaparte was forced to abandon his expansionist plans in the Americas to concentrate instead on an imminent war against the Perfidious Albion. The chancellor offered a check for $10 million for the

Port of New Orleans. He was met with a counteroffer to take the whole territory for a mere $5 million more. To make the sale official, they needed to put on a show. In 1803, France made public the secret agreement with Spain and officially took possession of Louisiana for three weeks and on November 30 of that year transferred ownership to the United States. Jefferson, paying three cents per acre, literally doubled the size of his country. With this government operation, Jefferson's defense objectives were fulfilled. And Haiti? It became independent, but since it was no longer a threat, Jefferson refused to officially recognize the new republic he himself had helped to establish. He didn't want the abolition of slavery on that island to spread problematic ideas to his territories.

After his shopping spree, the New York magistrate took advantage of his stay in the city of the Seine to do some personal business. Besides buying a copy of the *Diderot Encyclopedia*, which you can see today in the Clermont Library, he was interested in the Boulton & Watt engines and their possible application to river navigation. Upon his return, and with the aid of his friend Robert Fulton, Livingston was the first person to successfully demonstrate the commercial viability of a steam ship. In the winter of 1807, the *North River* of Clermont was built. It was 150 feet long and 16 feet wide and covered in bronze. It cost $120,000. The first river trip took place on August 17, 1807 at a speed of five miles per hour, taking 32 hours to go upriver from the Port of New York to Albany, with a 20-hour pit stop at Clermont Manor. Downriver took somewhat less time: 30 hours to travel the 153 miles. The crossing was a novelty because previously, cargo could only be shipped downriver, but now vessels could travel in both directions. And they could travel at night.

Between 1814 and 1834, the number of steamships arriving at the Port of New Orleans increased from 20 to 1,200. Their development greatly facilitated connections with Europe and migrations to the New World grew exponentially. They also changed life in the U.S. When the Erie Canal was opened, New York surpassed the trade volume of Boston and became the new financial capital of the world. A story of champagne and roses shadowed by a small detail: the engine boilers tended to explode. Boom! In the mid-19th century, travelers in New Orleans who boarded one of the boats Mark Twain popularized in his novels had only a 50 percent chance of reaching the Port of St. Louis, Missouri, alive.

"Hello!" says someone waiting in line near our table to pay for a container of hummus. I return the greeting. But who is greeting me? Oh, no. It's one of those people incapable of deciphering a foreign accent. No matter what I say or how I say it, I know she won't understand me. "What's that?" I've met this person many times and she always makes me nervous, to the point that, in her presence, I surprise myself by committing grammatical errors I've long since overcome. Basic mistakes familiar to native Spanish speakers, such as switching "she" and "he" or putting the vowel *e* before the initial *s* so that I say "Espain" instead of "Spain," "espade" in place of "spade" and "esparkling" instead of "sparkling." It's horrible. Besides, since this person doesn't understand me, she always assumes I can't understand her either so she talks to me reeaal slow, as if I were a special-needs child. "I haave commme to buyyy some clementines," she says. "Do you un-ders-tand cle-men-ti-nes?" "Oh, yes," I say, forcing a smile while I think, "The Ma-ri-sol clementines that you have in that mesh-covered wooden box come from my country, lady. I was brought up on them and they are more Spanish that the Inés de Rosales sweet olive oil crackers that Lynn Forman sells at Rhinebeck Health Foods." In New York City, I recently met the son of the man who first exported clementines to America. The great freeze that left Florida without oranges in 1962 opened a new market niche for small citrus fruits, which has thrived ever since. Since Mediterranean clementines mature before those of California, the Spanish ones hit the shelves first, followed by the American ones, and everybody's happy. The Spanish ones come to Rhinebeck in a roundabout way via Canada because the Italian lobby doesn't like Spanish goods to pass through New York customs—the same reason why many Rioja wines arrive via Atlanta, and the very same reason why, until recently, we could not export cured pork. The Italian lobby has always feared that Spain's Iberico ham would take a big bite out of the prosciutto market ($380 million annually) and for years managed to persuade members of Congress that the Iberian Peninsula was still in quarantine for the swine fever that was eliminated a century ago. How was the ban lifted? By diplomacy: It was the gift George W. Bush gave to Spanish President Aznar for taking a photo with him in the Azores. The Spanish master chef José Andrés introduced Iberico ham to his Jaleo restaurant in Washington and—thanks to his personal effort to promote the Mediterranean style of life—now anybody can buy it pre-sliced at many supermarkets, including … Go Italy Gourmet! The woman with the clementines pays for the hummus and, before leaving, asks me about Iran. Oh, she's confused me with my Iranian brother-in-law. I tell her that Iran is doing wonderfully well, thanks. She says goodbye and leaves. I say *A-dios* (literally: go with God), and cannot avoid humming, "Oh my darling, oh my darling, oh my darling Clementine…" Steve Mosto joins in: "Thou art lost and gone forever, dreadful sorry, Clementiiiiine…"

"Long before the boiler there was steam," Steve reminds me as he spears a piece of chicken. "Got that?" "Yeah, of course." I nod, taking a spoonful of cold carrot soup. Yum. "Can you tell me how much heat water needs to become steam?" Steve asks suddenly. All this about the interviewees asking the journalists questions doesn't sit well with me, but, whatever. "One hundred degrees," I say. "Oh, I mean, 100°C, which is the scale I'm familiar with. To translate those degrees to Fahrenheit, I need a notebook." "There's no hurry," he says. Okay. Take a deep breath and… The old way of doing it is to multiply by 2, that's 200; swallow a zero, 20, subtract the second result from the first one, 200 minus 20 equals 180; and then add 32. In other words, water boils at 212°F. "Right," he says. "Oh good," I respond, relieved. "Water does indeed boil at 212 degrees, but that's not what I asked you." Oh dear. Steve asks trick questions, like those on the SAT. "I don't understand." "I asked you at what temperature water changes from a liquid to a gas." "And I responded 212." "Yes, but no. Let me explain. If you heat a pot of water at home and stick a thermometer in it, you'll see that it begins to boil when the mercury hits 212. But evaporation takes a bit longer because to change states, the water needs to absorb much more energy. When it finally obtains enough energy (water is the substance that needs the most heat to evaporate because it is difficult to break the strings of hydrogen that link its molecules), it leaves the pot as a gas without the slightest shift in the mercury reading. What happened?" "I haven't got any idea, Steve, you're the expert here." I take advantage of the lull to take another mouthful of soup. Yum… it's got just the right amount of ginger. "What happens is that latent heat makes an entrance." "What kind of heat?" "Hidden heat, as real as the sensory one, but that isn't seen on the thermometer." "Like Dracula but in a gaseous state," I say. "Water is capricious like that," my lunch companion tells me. "It can be liquid or steam at 212°F, whatever suits it."

To travel the path from the boiling point to its transformation into steam, water needs five times more heat than it does to change from ice to boiling in the pot. In other words, it needs less heat to move from 32 degrees to 212 than to move from 212 to … 212! Can you believe it? That's what Steve says. The heat the water needs to evaporate is measured in a thermal unit known as BTUs. "Man," I say, gratefully, "now I finally understand what those BTUs are." The weekender who thinks the Hudson Valley is very Mediterranean had mentioned them. She and her partner kindly invited us to a barbecue at her house, where Sarah and I were the only ones not sporting official riding gear. They had a beautiful house and had just redone the kitchen and installed an industrial oven. Everything was top quality from Ackerman's Appliance in Hudson. "Look at this stove we bought," she said proudly as she gave us a mini-tour of the new section. "It reaches 1,200 BTUs." I would give my left arm to have a gas oven at home so I told her I thought that was great. But I was thinking to myself, do you need such a big contraption to heat the pre-made lasagna that we just ate?

Steve continues: "The latent heat is what heats Manhattan buildings. It travels upward, embedded in the steam, emanates from the radiators and heats the rooms." "Oh," I respond. "So New York City houses are heated with steam heat?" "Not all of them, but a lot are," he confirms.

I figured that one out fast. "So steam comes from the boilers in the basements, right?" "Nope." I put my foot in it once again.

Home heating systems face the same safety problems that affected steamboats. After James Watt invented the radiator in 1784, no one could figure out how to regulate the pressure to prevent accidents. According to Dan Holohan, in his manual *The Lost Art of Steam Heating*, in the 1880s, a boiler exploded in the United States every 48 hours. Buildings blew up thanks to that obsession water has with increasing its volume some 1,700 times when it becomes a gas. Let's see: basement boilers reached 340 degrees. The steam rose from there through pipes to the radiators. It fulfilled its role of passing latent heat to the apartments, cooled down, re-condensed in water and returned to the boiler through a back circuit. When it returned to the tank, the top cooled. More and more water entered and when the burner recovered strength, it boiled quickly, increasing its volume nearly 2,000 times and producing a bang like you wouldn't believe. The pistons abandoned the boiler at a cruising speed of 300 miles per hour and if they hadn't had any obstacle in their path, would have reached a height of 3,200 feet. Houses could have entered into orbit, which would have made the satellite era come much sooner. But someone finally established a measure to calculate pressure, thereby enabling it to be reduced from 60 pounds per second to 2 pounds per second, and calm prevailed. End of story? Not quite; it's just the beginning actually. The idea of creating steam power stations and easing tenants' fears of having infernal contraptions in their basements greatly contributed to the cause.

In 1881, to take advantage of an accountant's patent to measure steam consumption, a certain Mr. Andrews suggested producing steam on a large scale and piping it throughout the city. The first steam power station included 48 boilers connected to a 223-foot chimney that competed in height with the impressive steeple of Trinity Church. The plant was established at an opportune time, just when skyscrapers began to appear on the city's skyline due to rising land prices. Faced with a land shortage on the island, builders placed their hopes on constructing their buildings upward. In 1870, two circumstances took place that made their dream possible: the invention of the elevator and the use of iron structures. The seven-story Equitable office building was built. Astounded New Yorkers congregated there to ride on the freight elevator as if it were a carnival attraction. Five years later, the Tribune headquarters went up, at twice the height of the Equitable building. After that, one by one, the 4,500 giants that today reach up toward the heavens appeared. The secret: solid ground.

The State of New York contains an enormous variety of rock formations and enjoys excellent locations from which to contemplate them, for example, the volcanic basalt cliffs of the Hudson River. Manhattan Island is no exception and the concrete points at which the skyscrapers are located are not the result of coincidence. The subsoil of the city is composed of a lustrous-looking rock, with a high concentration of mica. It is ideal for anchoring buildings. This bedrock, which has inherited the Greek name of schist due to the ease into which it can be broken up into slabs, is found at ground level around Wall Street, after which it sinks some 260 feet and resurfaces at 34th Street. In the famous Manhattan skyline, it is easy to see from the East River the troubling gap in skyscrapers between the business district and the Empire State Building. More towering buildings were not erected in the place where money talks because in the early 1900s, there was no way to get concrete pillars through the dozens of yards of sand and gravel to reach the solid rock below.

I finish the soup but am still hungry. "You can have some of my chips if you want," Steve offers. I don't hesitate. Cape Cod, my favorites—the ones that have an illustration of Nauset Lighthouse on the bag and just the right amount of crunch. Yum. "Thanks." "You're welcome." The heating system distributed through steam pipes from the power station simplified the safety and maintenance issues of the enormous real estate complexes erected on the island. The boiler being located away from the building finally allowed tenants to rest easy at night. Besides, the skyscrapers were little cities in themselves. I could easily imagine the size of the boiler rooms they would need to supply heat to thousands of customers. The basement in the city is a space that is too expensive to waste on safety valves and pipes. Thanks to the steam stations, their owners could turn a profit by renting out basements as storage space. Moreover, the municipal government was enthusiastic about forever eliminating coal-loaded trucks from its streets. "Coffee?" "No, thanks."

In 1823, the New York Gas Light Company was established in an effort to modernize the obsolete system of lampposts, the whale oil for which was provided by the city of Hudson. In 1844, the company joined forces with the competition and Consolidated Gas was born. It was the age when Thomas Alba Edison was attempting to build electric power plants. He was persuaded to sign on to the project to jointly control the energy market. It then became Consolidated Edison, or ConEd, the company that has distributed steam in Manhattan since 1954. Steam is a commodity just like gas or electricity. It is measured in thousands of pounds per hour and flows from seven large power plants: five in Manhattan, one in Queens and another in Brooklyn. One hundred and five miles of pipes comprise the largest steam ring in the world. These distribute steam to nearly 2,000 buildings located from Battery Park to 96th Street. This conduction system has operated for over 100 years and it springs leaks occasionally.

I get it. The steam that turned Manhattan into a set for *Blade Runner* comes from the leaks of the underground heating system. Aha. "And what do you do?" "Just that." "Search for leaks?" "Exactly." "You go beneath the city?" "Sometimes." My eyes light up. "Do you think I could go with you on one of your leak-hunting expeditions sometime?" "Everyone is very worried about security," he says, "But I'll talk to the maintenance coordinator of Rockefeller Center and, just maybe, if I tell him you're with me, he'll agree to issue you a permit." "Really?" I'm like Dan Aykroyd. "Who ya gonna call? Steambusters!" I look at my watch. "Shoot! It's gotten late. I have to run to pick up Julia. ... Thanks Steve, we'll keep in touch. Mohammed, Salam Alaikum. Alaikum Salam!"

Rhinebeck community nursery school is in the basement of a white church where the bells intone melodies every hour at an interesting volume. I hope the neighbors like the repertoire; otherwise, they must be a nervous wreck. *Tin ton tin ...* Maybe the experience is similar to that of living next to a train track: after a few weeks you get used to the noise and don't even notice it. It seems the brain doesn't pay attention to anything it considers usual. Neuroscientists claim that the brain doesn't have the capacity to detect everything happening around it so it just focuses on whatever appears to be new.

The white church, located at the beginning of South Street, is a privileged witness to how frequently drivers use the street as a shortcut between Routes 9 and 308 to avoid the light downtown. The speed limit is 25 miles per hour, but cars can get revved up, so it's a good idea to walk carefully. The current building of the Reformed Church was constructed in 1808 with donations from parishioners. Since some members of the congregation could not provide money to buy bricks, they were asked to gather rocks from their fields. The result is that the eastern and southern facades are made of brick while the other two are of stone. Church members are very proud of this since it demonstrates their spirit of including people of all social conditions. In the yard that faces Route 9, there is a wooden shed that they use in early December to depict the Living Nativity. According to the pastor, it is a good opportunity to remember the reason for the season. In the back is an old cemetery with tombstones whose names have faded with the passage of time. The nursery school put a swing set there and when I arrive, I see Julia playing with the other children among the graves. Life and death are embraced in a natural way in the circle of life. Little Christopher Marvin is crying because Mrs. Greco, the teacher, told him that tomorrow they are going to take all the kids to drink hot chocolate and he doesn't want to get buuurnnned. His mother, Annie, consoles him. We also try to cheer him up as we walk away from the white clock tower of this church, which, as the sign located at the entrance states, has been serving Christ and the community since 1731.

5

December

In December, the bare branches of the trees lining the town's main street are strung with little white lights. At night, with all the shops' display windows decorated for Christmas, Rhinebeck becomes the most elegant place on Earth. Party invitations start arriving in early December. Once you've overcome the anxiety produced by the mathematical impossibility of attending every party you're invited to, you must deal with an agenda of extraordinarily precise activities. That is because the invitations specify what time you should arrive and, believe it or not, what time you should leave! They say: "Party from 6 to 9." And they are completely serious. Beginning at about 8:50, you'll notice that the pile of coats on the host's bed is getting smaller. "Goodbye." "Thanks for coming." By about 9:05, the closest thing to festive music you'll hear is the clinking of silverware being rinsed before it's loaded into the dishwasher.

Sometimes the invitations will say "Till the last man falls," but they don't really mean it. It's just a saying for, say, someone who's going on vacation in France and can enthusiastically proclaim, "Tonight we'll paint the town red!" No. We know that they aren't going to the Bastille with a can of paint. Here the last man tends to fall … into his bed as soon as he gets home. Hudson Valley residents get up so early that they experience the Cinderella Syndrome—and when the clock strikes 12:00, they turn into pumpkins and want to go to bed. And of course it's not a good idea to drink and drive. Since there's no public transportation, people stop drinking wine and beer halfway through the party; they say *adios* to gin and tonics and start to sip water, *glug, glug,* like fish, to recover their reflexes and be able to confidently sit behind the wheel. So just when you think the party is really getting interesting, they shut it down.

But let's get back to Christmas. The child born in Bethlehem has increasingly ceded the leading role to a fat, bearded guy from the North Pole. America has gone from singing Christmas hymns in church ("Silent Night, Holy Night!") to intoning "Jingle Bells, Batman smells" at home. Mailboxes overflow with season's greetings. Family and friends who used to wish my wife a traditional Merry Christmas now wish her a generic Happy Holidays ... a greeting that will do for Christmas, Hanukah, Kwanza or any other holiday. Sarah gets all sorts of letters from people she may not have seen for years since Americans tend to get restless and move around a lot. They effortlessly leave one state for another. Don't think it's easy to guess their origin. Curiously, Americans tend to tell me they are from the place where they currently live rather than sharing the name of their city of birth. If I ask someone from Kansas who has been living in Rhinebeck for 13 years where he's from, he'll tell me that he's from Rhinebeck without batting an eye. If I pose the question to a Chinese woman from Beijing who lives in Manhattan, she'll say she's from New Yolk.

Most of the Christmas cards are family portraits taken at one of the year's high points, for example, their holiday in Italy, where everyone looks fairly happy, except for the middle-school child who hates having his picture taken. In one card we received, the kid is smiling roguishly at the camera as he discreetly gives the finger to his mother. His parents must not have noticed it, and we prefer to keep mum on the subject.

The details of the narrative may vary, but all of them open with a joke, contain a tear-wrenching moment towards the middle and end on a hopeful note. There are moving stories, like that of Sally Goodrich, who lost her son Peter aboard the second plane that crashed into the World Trade Center. Sally is Sarah's cousin and her passion for education and her great capacity for love have led her to establish a foundation in her son's name. The Peter M. Goodrich Memorial Foundation offers scholarships to Afghan youth to study in U.S. high schools and colleges and is building a school for girls in Pashtun Province in Afghanistan. This woman's motivation gives you goosebumps and makes you believe that goodness is indeed possible. To build amid the ruins. To rise like the phoenix from the ashes of pain and to extend a hand to the enemy. A lesson in integrity that is impossible to digest without getting a lump in the throat and tears in the eyes. There are surprising stories, like that of Chuck, a multimillionaire who is disappointed because the ship he commissioned from a Greek shipbuilder is too big to navigate on the lake where he lives and so he had to return it. To drown his sorrows, he spends his free time designing an 18-hole golf course in his backyard. And there are also fun stories like that of Robin Kosseff, another Rhinebeck native who, after being arrested in California for demanding the closure of a nuclear power plant dressed as a Martian, left for Jordan to work on an archeological dig and learn about Middle Eastern culture. Indiana Jones really does exist. Americans' fighting spirit and capacity for adventure never ceases to amaze me.

The holidays find me lying down in Jay Dorin's guestroom practicing my rebirthing breath work. "You have to relax, brother," he tells me. "I'll set the breathing rhythm and you follow my example." Apparently, this will allow me to go back to the past and bring up images and sensations from childhood. Jay says that the cells of my body have a great capacity for storing the memory of every event that ever happened to me—a process that supposedly started three months after my conception in my mother's womb. So when I take a lot of air, the breathing will oxygenate the cells and awake the dormant information. Oh boy, let's go. Breathing is short and fast, a succession of breaths so quick that I think I'm going to hyperventilate and pass out. "As far as I know," I tell Jay, "the basis for this belief is that birth is a traumatic event and that, by revisiting it, you can cure the hurt of the past. Don't get me wrong, I agree that the moment of birth must be complicated for the star of the show; especially because, if you think about it, the process consists of transforming yourself from a fish to a mammal over the course of a few seconds. From floating in the maternal womb breathing water to receiving a smack on your bottom and being forced to gulp air. However, believing that this process has such an impact that it justifies subsequent failure of your driving test ... well, let's just say I have my doubts." "It's not exactly that," Jay answers. "But it is a healing process." Whatever. Too late for details. Here I am, pumping oxygen into my blood by inhaling and exhaling without pause, ready for mental clarity and emotional well-being.

I wake two hours later. I must have been cold because Jay has covered me with a blanket. Scientists generally agree that the brain is incapable of remembering anything that occurred before two years of age. Jay asks me about my trip and I have to admit that I'm not too sure I returned to the maternal womb. "Although I might have," I tell him, "because everything was very dark. ... What I can tell you with all certainty, Jay, is that the nap did me a world of good. And your Sleepy's mattress was a solid investment for your guests' backs." I thank my friend for his time and for the revitalizing cup of tea he offers to clear my head. I go back to my domestic duties. At any rate, rewinding life every now and then is not necessarily a bad thing. It's good to look back, like the Native Americans did, in order to be able to move forward without hesitation. In the case of Christmas, rewinding is essential because the starter gun for the Most Wonderful Time of the Year went off on the fourth Thursday in November.

* * *

The Plymouth Rock celebration between the Pilgrims and Native Americans in 1621 may not have been the only—or even the first—Thanksgiving meal. In Florida, one is claimed to have taken place in San Augustine on September 8, 1565. Another supposedly took place on a Virginia plantation in 1619. President Lincoln called for Thanksgiving to become a national holiday but it wasn't until 1941 that President Franklin D. Roosevelt officially named the fourth Thursday of November as the single date for all Thanksgiving celebrations on the calendar. It is an ideal opportunity for people to return home since it's based on a principle we all share: it encourages us to be giving, appreciative and grateful. What's more, you don't even have to buy presents and there's always a good football game on TV.

We don't have to travel far to meet up with family. In fact, we only have to walk five minutes to have dinner at Sarah's parents' house. As we head toward Platt Avenue on foot, we are surprised by the first snowstorm of the year. Suddenly, the world turns white and my children disappear in the blizzard, like Bambi when he lost his mother. "Helllooooooo…" At last we arrive safe and sound to the banquet. The king of the dinner is the turkey, which is accompanied by sweet potatoes, cornbread, cranberry sauce and vegetables. We finish off with a pumpkin pie, which was invented when the pilgrims began to use pumpkin rinds as bowls for heating milk and wanted to make good use of the pulp inside.

Traditionally, wild turkeys were hunted, but now most people head to the supermarket. A lot of turkeys have been genetically modified to increase the size of their breast—so much so that the males can't reach the females anymore to reproduce and the birds have to be artificially inseminated. A very sad sex life. Thank God our turkey is from the local Sepascot Home Farm. From Route 308, you can see the red barn and the Scottish Highland cattle grazing, with their long, shaggy hair. The good thing about Sepascot is that it's self-service. You arrive and locate the shed with a counter in front of an industrial-sized freezer. Inside is meat, eggs, chickens, whatever was produced that day. Everything has a price tag on it. You get what you need, weigh it, calculate what you owe, and leave the money in a basket, get change and go out. In customers they trust. There are no security cameras, so you can even go shopping in your pajamas.

Turkey is generally a rather bland meat, but a great cook can produce miracles. Huck roasts it, following the instructions in a manual by a French chef, which stresses the importance of the resting period. For me, the stuffing is the important part. John Katomski makes the best with mushrooms, bamboo shoots, chestnuts, shallots and almonds. He is a program developer and massage therapy instructor at the Swedish Institute in New York. Another early-morning commuter. But he encounters happiness in the kitchen and with him I've begun the gratifying task of growing a garden together. There's no greater satisfaction than eating what you've planted yourself. The closest definition to heaven may be a sliced heirloom tomato with a pinch of sea salt and a few drops of olive oil on top. Oh, man! Actually, John accompanies the turkey with some caramelized leeks. In my humble opinion, the leek is man's best friend. I still wake up salivating some nights just thinking about it.

* * *

Now we can fast-forward to December again. After the first snow, you have to follow weather forecasts closely. The snow bipolarity that I'm used to in Madrid (either it snows or it doesn't) becomes a huge variety of possibilities in New York. Here the snow can adopt numerous forms, depending on the level of moisture, the temperature and the wind. I have had no choice but to learn a string of new expressions (chance of flurries, snow squalls, snow showers, sleet, freezing rain…) to understand what to expect each morning. I also start to become familiar with the dreadful wind chill factor, which drives me nuts. Even though the thermometer may read the same in two places, you can actually feel colder in one than the other. Wind increases the level of discomfort we experience at low temperatures. Our skin is insulated by a surrounding layer of warm air, which, under normal conditions, remains the same temperature as the body: 91°F. If a cold wind blows that thin layer of air away, we lose heat. The wind chill factor depends on the speed at which the skin loses its heat energy. The harder the wind blows, the faster we lose heat. This is so because actually "cold" is simply a lack of heat. Or, as the Russian proverb goes: There is no cold weather, just wrong gear.

Thanks to the wind chill factor, I feel like it's about 20 below as I ride a sled down Burger Hill. But no. It's actually just 32 degrees. So the thing is: My gloves are toast. My fingers are starting to get as stiff as icicles and when I try to take my gloves off, the leather snaps like a Nabisco cracker. Sarah has a hard time taking off with Julia on a green plastic sled. Finally, the sled starts flying down the hill toward the parking lot. After a while, we go to try the Mills Mansion front lawn, in Staatsburg. When you get tired of climbing the hill, dragging the sled behind you, you can visit the mansion to enjoy the lavish Christmas decorations, typical of the wealthy families during the Gilded Age—a bit over the top. At Mills, we use inner tubes that inflate like giant donuts to fly downhill. After a few short minutes, we're at the bottom, near the banks of the Hudson. A tugboat passes nearby with a huge load. A full moon emerges from the gray sky.

Even though it's freezing cold, blue skies predominate. New York is one of the sunnier states Jeff Irish, the Canadian engineer who was director general of the X-ray department for General Electric, realized this fact. When he quit his job in Paris in 2000 and moved with his wife Mary Wright to the town where she grew up, he started thinking about designing and installing solar energy systems. Today, his company, Hudson Solar, with over 800 systems installed, is a leading solar company in New York. He claims to lead by example. Located in Rhinebeck, Hudson Solar's headquarters became in 2008 the first and only zero-net energy, carbon-free commercial building in New York State and the entire Northeast. It is a building that consumes less energy than it generates, using a solar electric system to generate power from the sun, geothermal heating and cooling and solar thermal collectors to heat water.

Jeff tells me all of this as we stand next to the bonfire in front of the frozen lake at Trish Curthoys and Richard Von Husen's Christmas party. The investment in renewable energy, if you count what you save on electric bills, he tells me, guarantees a seven percent annual return.

Much higher than what the banks offer for your money. Upfront rebates and tax incentives can total up to 70 percent off residential system costs, and approximately 60 percent of the total cost of a commercial system is covered by grants. According to Jeff, solar panels produce 90 percent of the total energy consumed in his household and got paid for themselves in seven years.

Obviously, New York doesn't enjoy as many sunny days as California—in fact, we only get about 75 percent as many. Nevertheless, the sunshine is more effective here because the low temperatures keep the photoelectric cells in better condition. And the snow helps, too. The white blanket backlighting with its reflection the trees and houses, putting the town in dreamlike cinematographer depth, boosts sunray efficiency by 25 percent. This means that the production of solar panels in Rhinebeck is only 10 percent below that obtained on the West Coast. California solar panels produce 12,500 kilowatts annually while New York panels make 10,000 kilowatts a year. Not too bad.

Trish heads a Rhinebeck accounting firm and her husband Richard owns Warren Kitchen & Cutlery. He gets around on a bike. Neither temperature nor distance bothers him. He rides as fast as a bullet. He views life as if it were the Tour de France. If you run into a guy biking on Route 9, wearing a yellow jersey and seemingly racing against the clock, you'll know you've met up with Richard Von Husen: the biking leader of the Rhinebeck road general classification. Not to mention his passion for climbing frozen waterfalls with an ice pick in each hand. He loves adventure sports, a passion he shares with his brother-in-law and neighbor, Hans Boehm. They especially enjoy going a long way to reach the spots with virgin snow for some downhill skiing. From the bonfire spot, you can see Cathy and Hans Boehms' house on the other side of the lake, and can just make out a Christmas tree through the window. Did Santa Claus put it up, following the family tradition? Hans was the last boy of his generation to grow up believing in the old bearded guy, years after all of his schoolmates had discovered the true origin of Christmas gifts. But despite the tip off and his own calculations, which led to the discovery of suspicious packages in the closet, he held on tight to his conviction that Father Christmas visited his home in the wee hours of December 25. The irrefutable proof was the 9-foot fir that seemed to have popped up by magic in his living room, strung with lights and decorations and surrounded by packages, every Christmas morning. He went to bed without a tree and woke up with one. How was that possible? Besides the colorfully wrapped gifts, Santa Claus brought the Boehm Family a dense fir that looked like it came from a fairy tale. Hans did the math and decided it was impossible for his father to have enough time to go into the woods at night, chop down the immense pine, drag it to the house, decorate it with the help of Hans' good mom and be in bed before the kids went to wake them up early to open presents. No way! Or was it possible? Years later, his long experience as a psychiatric nurse at Benedictine Hospital in Kingston taught Hans that human beings are capable of amazing, seemingly impossible feats if they are determined enough.

Returning home for lunch, I run into the postman, who is leaving the mail in our "mailbox" basket on the porch. He's very friendly. And smart. He carries a bag of dog bones in his satchel, which he gives to every dog that crosses his path. A small gift to ensure that the canines will not hinder his access to the mailboxes. We receive a letter from Madrid, one of the few pieces of mail that isn't an ad. A former Secretary of Aznar's government, whom I have dealt with on several occasions in my work as a journalist, is coming to Manhattan and suggests we have lunch together. It's a good opportunity to go to the city and get an update on what's going on in my country, which is currently experiencing numerous demonstrations against the war in Iraq. A lively discussion is guaranteed because Aznar supports the military campaign. The whole family has been to New York a few times to join the peace protests—truly ingenious events, with marionettes and creative banners. Weapons of mass destruction or not, I don't think people ever learn anything through force. Whatever is imposed on anyone, good or bad, it's always rejected.

History is full of examples. Families too. How many of us believed what our parents told us based on the principle of "Trust me, we are your parents and we know better"? Anyone knows that the lessons your parents try to impose on you, as reasonable as they may be, will be ignored and will not be accepted as valid until you have had the experience yourself. Well, a country is just a family ... with a lot of members. Many years ago, in 1812, my Spanish countrymen banished the evil King Ferdinand VII and proclaimed an exemplary constitution in Cadiz. Then Napoleon Bonaparte had the idea of invading us to make us more cultured through the French encyclopedia. For our own good. But you know what? We told him where to stuff it. We preferred our antiquated ways; at least they were ours. So the people of Madrid took up arms against the French Army with the revolutionary intention to ... restore the obsolete monarchy! Can you believe it? Napoleon had wanted to modernize the country by force. But Spain, which was becoming a leading democracy in Europe, took a step back and was once again immersed in darkness. That's just the way it is. Countries seem to like to develop on their own, and when they are pressured to do so, they tend to do the opposite.

So we're off to New York City for a few days. Via the Internet, Sarah arranged a yearlong house exchange: our house in Madrid for an apartment near Washington Square. It's in a wonderful location. You walk downstairs and find yourself on the sidewalk with the Fiorello LaGuardia sculpture. Apparently, before becoming an airport, LaGuardia was a celebrated mayor. It is the apartment of Ada Ferrer, the head of the Latin American Studies department at NYU, who has gotten a sabbatical year to consult documents at the Madrid Public Library and the Archive of Indies in Seville. With kids, we've had little chance to take advantage of the exchange, so we plan to enjoy the city as much as possible during the school vacation.

We arrive in Washington Square equipped for an overnight stay in the Antarctic. The wind howls, whipping against the buildings, blowing wildly down the streets and increasing the infamous wind chill factor among the pedestrians.

After a risky trajectory from the subway exit, sidestepping sheets of ice, the vision of the light in the doorway brings us more joy than Hansel and Gretel felt when they spotted the little gingerbread house. The apartment building borders the Village and Soho—it's in a great spot, next to the Blue Note. Tonight Manhattan Transfer is playing. We'd like to go, but with three small children, I think not. Relieved, we enter the building in search of a peaceful refuge. But good old New York doesn't do anything halfway. You are either freezing or burning up, and as soon as we greet the doorman, our bodies begin to experience the greenhouse effect. In just a few seconds, we move from freezing to the boiling point. In the elevator, gloves and hats suddenly seem excessive and the frost on our coats begins to thaw. When we open the apartment door, the wave of heat from the radiators nearly finishes us off. Without time to reach the coat rack, sweaters and scarves fall to the floor as we rush to throw the living room windows wide open. In the distance, we can see Houston Street blanketed by snow. A freezing wind ruffles the curtains. The situation borders on the absurd. It's 4°F outside and we are forced to slide up the windows to avoid suffocation. This place is a pizza oven. Leaning out of the window, my face frozen and backside red hot, I am experiencing the exact opposite heat situation of those nights when I grill on the backyard barbecue. We realize we are not the only ones affected by the temperature extremes. In the red brick tower that serves as a residence for NYU professors and in other nearby buildings, all the guillotine-type windows are half-open.

Is it possible that the radiators do not have a thermostat to regulate temperature? It seems ridiculous, but no. In the city that Mayor Bloomberg has tenaciously tried to green with the Million Trees planting initiative and is a member of the C40, the leadership group against climate change sponsored by the Bill Clinton Foundation, there is apparently no one alive who can lower the radiator temperatures below 219°F. Two hundred and 19 degrees! I'm relieved my children have passed the crawling stage so we don't have to worry about them touching the cast iron and burning their hands.

Radiators reached this city before the light bulb went off in Edison's head and he figured out how to light all the apartments with an incandescent wire. At the time, people would use kerosene lamps. Life expectancy was very low. Some clever guy put two and two together and came to the conclusion that people were dying from a toxic cloud. Those were times when scientists thought that the center of the Earth was empty. There was no talk of bacteria or penicillin and many influential men supported the theory. Gas lamps became the national poison and New Yorkers began to keep windows open when they slept to dissipate the toxic smoke. Dying warm and toasty is better than freezing to death. So when heating installers reached urban areas, engineers had to adjust the calculations of the physical reality to the social one. To the numbers established in the tables, they added 30 percent. That was it. New York radiators were calibrated to heat houses with the windows open. No one ever thought differently in those times.

Good night. We take to our beds like Buster Keaton with wool caps pulled down to our eyebrows so that the frozen air of Houston Street, flowing through our open windows, does not wake us up. Tomorrow, if it's clear, we'll go ice-skating in Central Park before seeing the Rockettes at Radio City Music Hall. The lovely theater that Judy Kane, Sarah's aunt, would visit as a young woman while it was being constructed. Her friend's father was one of the engineers responsible for assembling the innovative stage, which can be raised in a feat of hydraulic genius. When it opened in 1940, the world's largest theater not only amazed the art world; its elevator system was so advanced that the U.S. Navy incorporated identical hydraulic systems in its World War II aircraft carriers. During the war, government agents guarded the Radio City Music Hall's basement to protect the Navy's technological advantage.

The Washington Square apartment is full of books, most of them about Cuba. While we have breakfast, I look over a few of them. I am curious because some of my ancestors made a fortune on the island. The inheritance evaporated in 1898 after the Spanish-American

War, which some distinguished Rhinebeck neighbors supported with ships, munitions and large sums of money. Aye, aye, aye ... You get the idea. I find a mention of the Fesser history. They were the first family to liberate slaves on the island ...Wow! This is cool! Except...Wait a minute. It seems that abolition in my family case, rather than being a humanitarian cause, was mostly a layoff. A Havana newspaper's article says that the Fesser slaves were begging my ancestor not to fire them, please, since they wouldn't be able to find another job and their families would starve. Oops! Now I am confused. Confused and overwhelmed. I get an idea of what it must have felt like to be Edison's son because, given all my ancestors' accomplishments, I don't imagine what my generation can do to stand out. It's better to come from nothing and to transform your life into a success than to come from success and turn your life into nothing. Anyway, I decide to take the book and go downstairs to make photocopies to send the scoop to my parents. When I open the door, an enormous cat slips inside. Meeow. It belongs to the neighbor. Good morning. The neighbor asks me about Ada and the girls. I tell her that they are at our house in Madrid and that, as far as I know, they're doing well. Almost all the doors of the apartments that face the long carpeted hallway are wide open or ajar. "What's going on?" "Good morning. I'll get the cat," says the lady as she goes into our apartment in search of the feline. The tiger, actually; it seems New York cats got the same hormones as the turkeys. They are jumbo-sized. Another neighbor steps out carrying a trash bag. He opens the slot on the wall and drops the bag down the chute. Fourteen floors of freefall until it reaches the trash can. The neighbor turns to say hello to someone having a cup of coffee inside another apartment with the door open. Two children run after each other in the hallway. They go into one apartment and then out again. They enter the next apartment and go out again. In the 21st century of our era, in the city of skyscrapers, these people live in the same way as in those in the main square of a little town in the Mediterranean.

We go skating and I only fall twice. I am fascinated by the Christmas show with Santa and the Rockettes. Finally, we decide to visit Chinatown. A friendly man convinces us to go to a small room for a massage. "You get a discount. We consider five people a gloup." "What's a gloup?" asks Julia. "A group," I volunteer, a little embarrassed. "Sorry, but her English is no so good." "Come in, come in," he says, smiling. We go in and fall into a row of massage tables with holes for our heads. We laugh lazily as they crack our bones. When we're about to go, we realize that Julia has fallen fast asleep. "She's adorable," the Chinese man comments. "Come back again and we'll give you the gloup discount." We eat in one of those restaurants where you choose an aquatic specimen from the fish tank. In China, where they eat just about anything with legs except the table, they demand freshness. From the tank straight to the pot. It is an intense experience for our kids to exchange glances with the bass before they catch it ... but they have to admit that it's excellent steamed. As is the serving of tiny snails that we all remove from the shell with the help of a pin. Yum!

The former Spanish Secretary calls and suggests we go to the Oyster Bar below Grand Central Station. Today it is closed. "How about some Ethiopian food?" I suggest. Silence. "Ethiopian?" "Trust me; it's delicious."

Meskerem Restaurant, on the 124th block of MacDougal Street. You wait at the bar drinking a St. George beer, premium lager from Addis Ababa, until a table opens up. If you like spicy food, welcome to paradise. If not, be careful with the beriberi sauce. You pull off pieces of the *injera*, a spongy rye crepe, with your hands and pick up the food from the plates in the manner of tweezers. The lentils with garlic and ginger are delicious. There's lamb with rosemary wine sauce, chicken with boiled egg, and ... spaghetti with tomato. You heard me. Pasta is the legacy from the Italians to their colony of Abyssinia.

Suddenly I notice the pinkie finger on the left hand of my companion is grasping a tiny piece of *injera*. He notices my surprise and tells me that he was brought up in a large family during the time when food shortages were common in Spain. He quickly learned to defend his piece of bread from his siblings. It's become a reflex action that he is incapable of erasing from his hard drive. He can't help it. Some years ago, in Washington, D.C., he went to a formal dinner at the White House with members of the U.S. government. The discussion touched on issues of top security and multi-million dollar business deals. A linen tablecloth and a banquet served by white-gloved waiters. All the while, he was inadvertently holding a piece of bread with his pinky in case the American Secretary of Defense was considering whether to steal it from him.

The subject of war came with dessert. "Spain can't miss this opportunity to be part of history. We made the mistake of staying out of World War II and paid dearly for it with 50 years of isolation. Now we have the opportunity to march, hand-in-hand, with the most powerful nations on Earth and Aznar doesn't want to miss his chance." Ugh! I wonder if Spain's president has been accepted by the leaders of the aforementioned powers as a member of the band, or if he is just serving as president of their fan club. But there's no time for further discussion. The former Spanish Secretary has to go. He'll be in touch. That's what it's like being a politician: there are always people waiting for you.

Since I still have an hour to kill before meeting up with Sarah and the kids, I decide to get a haircut. With the drowsiness brought on by lunch, having my hair washed and the little scalp massage, I'm half asleep. A Japanese woman cuts my hair. From my dreams I hear her ask me if she should even out my eyebrows. I say no thanks. She repeats her question a few minutes later and I again refuse. The third time she brings it up, she catches me off guard and I ask her: "Why, are they too long?" Surprisingly, she says they are. I'm a bit perplexed. Taking advantage of my confusion, she combs them upwards and snips the hairs that stick out. It's the first time anyone has ever done this to me and I start to feel anxious. I feel like the girl who plays with her mother's razor for the first time and then becomes concerned that shaving is going to cause her leg hairs to grow back more quickly. Will I end up with Martin Scorsese eyebrows because of my Japanese hairdresser?

Hair never ceases to amaze as you age. I think the Spanish comedian Riqui López has the best theory on the subject. Bald as a light bulb, he claims that his hair, like beauty, is on the inside. The irrefutable proof of this is that, over time, hair, like water, has started to leak through his different orifices: the ears, the nose…

With respect to hair, the men of Rhinebeck fall into two categories: those who make an appointment at Trendsetters and those who get their hair cut by Gioffi. You can easily tell them apart on the street. One is a modern cut and the other is just your everyday trim. Twenty-two dollars versus $10. I've been to both places, but I like to sit in the Sportsmen Barber Shop on Market Street because it gives me the impression of entering into a film set in the 1950s. Even at the risk of my hair. If you don't catch Gioffi in a good mood, he will take three mis-swipes at your hair and then act as if nothing happened. "Next!"

Today I catch him in a good mood. I am getting spruced up because tonight we are going to the annual Christmas party at Lottchen Shivers and Donald Rothschild's, a yearly anticipated event. Gioffi asks me if I've ever been to Europe. "Come on, Gioffi, you always ask me that. I'm from there, for God's sake." "Oh," he says, "Italian?" "No, Spanish." He's no longer listening. For him, Europe is Italy. His barbershop is lined with flags of all the Italian soccer teams. "People tell me, we have bought European oranges at the supermarket. We have tried Italian prickly pears and they're delicious. I tell them: you've tried nothing of the kind. Don't you realize that they aren't ripe when they pick them, so they don't have the same flavor? Who do they think they are, telling me about fresh fruit?" A customer enters. Gioffi greets him. He's from Oregon. He trains racehorses. He's happy because he won a horse race there although he admits it would be much more satisfying for him to win in New York. Those that do not do well go to the butcher's and the meat is sent to France. "To feed dogs?" asks Gioffi. "What the heck, no!

People eat them in Europe." "Does it pay well?" "Seven cents a pound." "Well, that's not much." "Yeah," he says, "sometimes it's not even worth it. One of my horses just got a limp and instead of sacrificing it, I gave it to the son of an Indian who works for me. The boy is thrilled. Do I have to wait long?" he asks as he flips through a magazine. There are two customers ahead of him. The man from Oregon says he's going to have a cup of coffee and come back later. After he's left, Gioffi tells me he wouldn't live in Oregon for all the wine in the world. It's up there on the border with Canada. "If you think it's cold here, you haven't seen anything yet, buddy. Besides, it borders the sea, you know? The humidity seeps into your bones. Not me. You'd have to be crazy to go to Oregon. Okay, you're done."

Buckets of snow begin to fall. This means tomorrow I'll have to take out the shovel ... again! I finally bought an anti-stick one. I found an old one in the garage, but each time I tried to dump the shoveled snow, it got stuck on the metal. Like when you put your tongue on the flagpole in winter and then can't pull it off. I thought all shovels were alike, but apparently not. There are also ones with special powers like Harry Potter's broom. The new shovel works like an industrial-sized Gillette Fusion Proglide Styler. It leaves the driveway and the path to the front door with a magnificent close shave. I was very excited the first time I had to use it to shovel snow. I was also enthusiastic about the idea of having to climb on the roof. If your roof isn't very slanted, you are advised to remove the snow so that the weight doesn't cause the roof to cave in.

At first it's fun to shovel snow, but when you have to do it day after day, it gets old very quickly. Fortunately, our house is close to the street. In the front, we only have to shovel the driveway, the path to the front door and the stretch of sidewalk that corresponds to our house. In the backyard, we clear a shovel-wide path to be able to reach the grill. The shoveled snow forms white mounds next to the deck door. During our Christmas party, Sarah chills bottles of beer and sparkling wine there. You only need to open the sliding door and grab one when you need a refill.

On Christmas Eve, my mother-in-law, Peggy, loves to attend mass and listen to the beautiful hymns. We accompany her to the Church of the Messiah. After the service, we meet Father Gallagher. Currently, he leads the Episcopal parish but he hails from the competition. In the United States, the best pastors, like the soccer player stars of *La Liga*, occasionally sign up for the other team. Father Gerald Gallagher was ordained at Saint Peter Basilica in Rome. Luis Pérez, the pastor of the Reformed Church of Rhinebeck, comes from the Pentecostal Church. It reminds me of when the soccer player Figo went from Barca to Real Madrid, which stirred quite a controversy.

As a newly ordained Catholic priest, Gallagher was transferred from his first Brooklyn parish for disagreeing with Pope Paul VI's encyclical letter on birth control. His next assignment was to a small African-American parish next to JFK Airport. This turned out to be a real gift. He learned the beauty of a different culture and earned the respect of the people in the community. The concept of celibacy in a culture with African roots didn't mesh, so what happened next was no surprise. Father Gallagher met Joy, a lovely nun who was thinking of leaving the convent. They married, and six years and four children later, he was received as an Episcopal priest. Now he's in Rhinebeck in charge of a beautiful stone church with magnificent stained glass windows. On Sundays at 10:00 a.m., the church is bursting at the seams. Some of his followers confess that they are not believers but go to church anyway because they like his sermons. They can identify with Father Gallagher when he preaches that no one is perfect, that God gave us the power and responsibility to make good moral decisions, and that the Church does not have the authority to make those decisions for us. "I'm here to help out however I can," he says, "but you don't need me to communicate with God. Speak directly to Him." Gerald Gallagher prefers to be called Jerry. He likes it when neighbors drop by for a visit. All are welcome to be part of his parish family. He hopes that whatever draws them to the church will lead them to a closer relationship with God.

In 1980, when Jerry made the decision to be received as an Episcopal priest, he was actually motivated by the same concerns that led to the Reformation in the 16th century. Discovering the philosopher's stone of the Christian schism: that to reach God, you don't need a broker. He didn't believe that there was only one right way to do things, dictated by the Pope, but rather that the Creator could adapt His love to the different ways of life of His children. So Jerry switched from the deductive philosophy of Descartes to the inductive method of Sir Frances Bacon. It was a way to approach faith that became popular in the United States after the Revolutionary War. Free from the tyranny of King George III, the American patriots had no intention of ever again bowing to a distant monarch. They abandoned an authoritarian God and came to know God through the flesh-and-bones Jesus, neighbor and companion of hardship.

Here, the Christmas season ends on December 31st, when we go to dinner at the Kufners' house. The Kufners are a German couple whose friendship we won at a silent auction. Well, sort of. Let me explain. Fifth-grade teachers Chantal DeFile and Catherine Menconeri organize a trip every year for children and their parents to see the whales on the Massachusetts coast. It's an excuse to learn a bit about marine biology and follow the route of the first European settlers in New England. This year I go with Max. We visit a theme park in Plymouth that is a replica of a village of colonists and Wampanoag Indians. At the Plymouth Plantation, all the characters are professional actors who interpret the lives of the former inhabitants. You can go into their houses and talk to them. With the old settlers, I mean, because the actors are always in character. They talk to you as they would have back in 1620. With 1620 ideas and language. I don't know how they keep sane. I walk into one house where a guy was reading a manuscript. I say hello and he asks me to sit down. "Where are you from?" "From Spain," I say. "Oh," he says. "So what role do you think your King, Philip IV, should play in the European wars?" I stare at him, thinking he was mistaken. The European wars? I try to respond: "Well, I guess we'll have to see what happens." A woman comes in to drop off some eggs that her hens lay that morning. I change the subject: "Hey, what would you think if I told you that man had landed on the moon?" "I don't think it's likely," he says, without skipping a beat, "but I suppose it's possible. Given that the planets are separated by water, if someone had a cannon powerful enough to launch toward the star sea, once there, you could swim to the moon. Where did you tell me they had fired the cannon?"

The school organizes a benefit to raise funds for the annual Whale Watch trip. Parents, students and teachers prepare skits to perform on stage and a silent auction is held. People from the community donate goods and services. And sometimes there are unsuspected things like a coupon form: "A boat ride on the Hudson River in our sailboat! Signed: The Kufners." People write down their bids on a sheet of paper. Someone offered $30 for the sailboat ride and we raised the bid to $40. Other people bid $50, so we went up to $60. I don't remember what the final bid was, and anyway it's not important, it's for the kids' education, but we won the boat ride from the Kufners. We were very lucky. Stephanie teaches German literature at Bard College and Gerald works as a neurologist on the other side of the bridge. They share with us the European spontaneity of being able to drop by someone's home unannounced for a glass of wine.

To celebrate the German New Year, Mary, Sarah's sister, and her husband, Manoocher, are joining us. Sarah's brother-in-law is a Kurd and was born in a city called Elam in Iran, near the Iraqi border. He is an economics professor at Allameh Tabatabai University in Tehran, but he's also spending a sabbatical year in Rhinebeck. Manoocher is involved in a microeconomics project. He's one of those people who believe that mathematics doesn't exist, that it resides only in people's imagination. "Economics," he informs me, "works just like a pair of scissors: you need two blades. One is the value of the goods and the other is what consumers are willing to pay for them. They only cut when the two blades are together." Economics does not like perfection because it's impossible to make money in a transparent world. A chaotic, opaque and crisis-ridden environment is the best breeding ground for selling lies to investors for a fat profit.

Today's date means little to Manoocher because Iran uses a different calendar. The Persian calendar should mark the year 2500 or thereabouts, but the Iranian government has updated it with the Islamic calendar. The year Mohammad went from Mecca to Medina is one. In other words, if you want to know what year it is in Tehran, subtract 621 from the Western calendar year and you'll have your answer. In Iran, the New Year coincides with the Spring Equinox. The mullahs wanted to prohibit the celebration because it has no relation to Islam, but they couldn't. It is Iran's most important holiday and the people aren't willing to give it up. One reason for its popularity is that adults give money to the children on that night.

We arrive at the Kufners. The entry hall looks like a shoe warehouse. The vestibule holds several shelves full of shoes, tennis shoes and ski boots. Those who want to can take off their shoes; those who don't can just walk on in. The Christmas tree is adorned with real candles in the traditional German fashion. The candles are from Europe because they have to be just the right size to fit into the special holders that are clipped to the branches. Stephanie suggests a game that she used to play with her siblings when she was a child: to place bets on which candle will be the last one to go out. We all join in. Once all the candles burn out, our hostess replaces them with new ones. She's not afraid of a fire starting because the pine tree is green and anyway, she has a bucket full of water close by, just in case.

If someone peeked in the window, he'd think we were crazy. It seems the Germans celebrate New Year's Eve by jumping from one place to another. So here in the living room, we are all jumping. German tradition dictates that you have to bring in the New Year with your feet in the air. New Year, new life. So let's jump! When the clock strikes midnight, you have to jump. It doesn't matter if you jump on top of a table or on a rug or if you do it in the living room or the kitchen. Besides the Kufners and their three children, Illiana, another enthusiastic German, Boona and some other friends are participating. My kids are happy. Being allowed to climb on the couch and jump around on the tables until their heads hit the light fixture is the closest thing to an action film they have experienced. I finally understand Van Halen: I get up, and nothing gets me down …

When the German ritual is over, and given that 500 years ago, Spain and Germany were the same nation, joined under the rule of the Holy Roman Emperor Charles, I propose that we turn to the Mediterranean ritual, so we eat the grapes I've brought. In Spain, if you want to have good luck during the New Year, you have to eat 12 grapes at midnight. One for each of the 12 bells. You do it in real time—the bell rings and you eat a grape. We decide to cheat so as not to overwhelm the novice participants. We replace the clock with a frying pan and a wooden spoon. To give everyone time to gobble up the grapes, I bang the gong at the rate of once every two seconds. There you go. We now move on to an American tradition: you have to kiss whomever is next to you. People aren't dumb though; they tend to place themselves strategically. Amid the clamor, I locate Manoocher and remind him that it's New Year's Eve, and, following the Iranian tradition, I ask him for some money. He tells me to get lost and turns the conversation to numbers.

There are several mathematical problems that have never been solved. You don't come across geniuses every day. According to Manoocher, the last great mathematician was Cantor. "Cantor?" asks Stephanie, surprised. "You've heard the name?" "Of course, he was German." It seems this guy was so smart that he solved an enigma by saying that the enigma has no possible solution. Solution: there isn't one. How about that? Using this same method, I can think of a couple of things to solve, too. I ask Manoocher if there are still some pending problems in math. He tells me there are, that they are now trying to figure out if there's a number between infinite minor and infinite major, because it seems that all infinites are not alike. Cantor demonstrated this.

It is mathematically proven that a segment of two centimeters and a horizontal line contain the same number of points. However, this changes when we enter the world of decimals. Natural numbers are

130

precise and go from one to infinite. There is nothing between 1 and 2. But in real numbers, there is an infinite succession of numbers between 1 and 2: 1.1, 1.2, 1.3 ... 1.01, 1.02 ... 1.001, 1.002 ... Cantor elegantly proved that the infinite of those real numbers is larger than that of natural numbers. At a banquet, natural numbers represent the number of guests from one to infinite and real numbers the dishes that will be served to each guest. If you begin with the first guest and give him plates 1.1, 1.2 ... you will never reach the second guest. Good thing it's not our party.

The Kufners take a nutshell boat with a tiny, lit candle and place it in a cooler full of water. Along the edges of the cooler, rolled sheets of paper stick out of the water. Each sheet contains a prediction for the New Year. When it's your turn, you swirl the water with your finger so that the boat moves. When it approaches the edge, the candle in the boat ignites one of the pieces of paper. That is your oracle. You have to put out the fire by dunking the paper in the water. Then you read the fortune aloud. Gerald's reads: "Your hair is going to fall out, but we don't know on which part of your body." Manoocher gets: "This year, one of your organs is going to double in size."

New Year's Day is a perfect day to go to the movies. We go to see *Supersize Me*, a documentary about a man who decides to eat only McDonald's hamburgers and it almost kills him, at Upstate Films, the town's art movie theater. It's the same theater where we saw *Bend It Like Beckham* and *Bowling for Columbine*. We see a preview of the new Almodovar movie. The miracle of having a movie theater within walking distance is due to a long-haired, idealistic couple that arrived in town in 1972 aboard a dilapidated VW bus in which they had traversed the U.S. Two movie lovers who couldn't find a spot in the distribution of conventional movie theaters, DeDe and Steve Leiber decided to form a nonprofit organization to bring the diversity of film culture to non-urban settings. So they started to bring foreign pictures ... and a bunch of happy friends who came to visit them in a large school bus, and woke up all the neighbors on Chestnut Street. Subsidies, ticket sales and private donations have made it possible for Rhinebeck to have one of the 100 or so independent movie theaters in the country.

The Leibers love to show foreign films, but it has become increasingly difficult for them. Robert Redford is indirectly at fault. Traditionally, there were two movie markets: the immense one of Hollywood productions and a smaller one, accounting for just six percent of the total, which showed movies made in the rest of the world. The gap is due to the protectionism of the large studios and the American public's dislike of subtitles. The rise of home video signaled the slow death knell for the few subtitled films. At the same time, Robert Redford grabbed the spirit of the Dallas-based USA Film Festival, and moved it to his Utah home. After the Sundance Film Festival was created, quality, low-budget American movies began to be produced. Independent films, and in English to boot. So why would you go to see an art film in Japanese on a small screen when you can see one in your own language? Thus, the showing of these productions has eaten into the already tiny market share of the movies made beyond these shores. By the late '80s American independent films had supplanted foreign language productions. 1989 was the watershed year when Steven Soderberg's film *Sex, Lies, and Videotape* premiered at Sundance and went on to become a major cross-over hit.

"I'm never going to eat another hamburger in my life," says Nico after watching the documentary. We'll see about that. The problem is not consuming hamburgers; it's eating them non-stop. "Okay, okay," he says, "but I'm never eating another one." An attractive dark-haired woman stops us at the front door of the theater. "I'm Natalie," she says. "Are you Spaniards?" "Half and half," we answer. She tells us that her boyfriend is from Malaga and that they live in the area. "Well, then, we'd love to meet him." We exchange phone numbers. We meet Daniel De la Calle the following day. He has come on his bike from Rhinecliff carrying two chorizo sausages. His mother had sent them to him from Spain but he's a vegetarian. He wants to know if we want them. "Are you kidding? Bring them over right away! Max, get the bread!" Daniel would become a great friend.

It snows again. This time in the form of an ice storm. The wet snow sticks to the branches of the trees and immediately freezes, leaving them with a glazed look, as if they'd been caramelized. It's very pretty but dangerous because the branches can break under the weight. Today I agreed to go hiking with my friends Jeff and Tim on Slide Mountain, the highest peak in the Catskills. There's ice on the road and I have to drive slowly and tap the brake constantly. Even so, the car skids a bit. I've never seen so much snow in my life. In our backyard, the kids dig tunnels where they go to play. Incredible. We reach the parking lot. This is where the path to the top of the mountain begins. Time: 4.5 hours. Difficulty: Strenuous. Length: 6.8 miles. Be prepared for magnificent views. Actually, it's just 4,180 feet high, but with so much snow and some snowshoes I put on for the first time in my life, I feel like we are on an adventure in the Tibetan Himalayas. *Tashi delek.*

With snow shoes I can walk easily forward and fall for sure if I try to go backwards. I start to get hot after going up the mountain and decide to take off my gloves. Big mistake. Half a minute later, my fingers are as gray as mousetails. There's a lot of fog and I can't see much beyond the back of the person in front of me. The trees are encased in a half-inch of ice. It looks like a crystal forest. A poignant silence prevails, broken only by the cracking of a branch as it breaks and falls to the ground in pieces. The breathtaking landscape makes time stand still. Before we realize it, we've reached the summit. Well, at least that's what we think. Here we need to apply Cantor's theory, which Manoocher explained to us on New Year's Eve. Mathematicians can precisely solve problems that have an analytical solution. Those with a numeric solution require a series of calculations that have to be resolved by a computer and only in an approximate fashion. We know that the result obtained is the closest we can get, but we don't know exactly how close we are. In other words, if we reach the summit when it is foggy, such as in this case, we'll reach a point where we won't be able to tell if either we are still climbing or if we have started our descent yet. The highest point of the summit is something that cannot be precisely determined, as is not the area of a circle. To calculate it, mathematicians divide the circumference into increasingly small segments. A curved line is the fog in the mathematical world So it's Cantor's fault that Tim, Jeff and I are high up in the Catskills and can't see a thing. We don't know which infinite is greater: our hunger or our thirst.

To resolve the first enigma, I take a bag of figs from my backpack. The sugar in the fruit will do us good. But ... we will have to wait for another day because they are frozen solid. There's no way to get your tooth into one of them. "Jeff, didn't you bring some solar panels?" Tim laughs because he works for Jeff and is the person responsible for installing them. "Okay, we'll try to quench our thirst." Tim takes out his water bottle. Same story. The water has solidified and if we try to lick it ... well, you know what happens. "So, boys, we should head down." "What were we thinking when you suggested going to the mountains at Christmas time?" "Hasn't anybody read John Burroughs?"

As we walk down I remember with a better understanding the stories that Cándida used to tell me about picking olives in her hometown. Spain is to the olive what Colombia is to the coffee bean. The finest olives in the planet are grown in the province of Jaen, where the red clay soil is rich in chalk and retains moisture. The hills of Andalucia get really cold in November and Cándida used to get frostbite on her fingers while picking the olives by hand to avoid bruising the fruit. Today's hike will help me write that scene with more accuracy. If that scene makes the cut. We'll see.

6

January

The main lobby of the American Museum of Natural History is home to the world's tallest freestanding dinosaur mount. A Barosaurus mother rears up to protect its young from the jaws of a mean Allosaurus. A natural reflex. A motherly instinct. A nice gesture that, unfortunately … didn't help much to preserve the species, since dinosaurs are long vanished from the surface of Earth. Oh, well. At least it wasn't our fault. Ironically, the skeleton mom seems to be reading a phrase engraved in the dome above its head that says: "There is a delight in the hardy life of the open." Is this a joke? I don't think so. It is a quote by the 26th President of the United States: Theodore Roosevelt. The New York State Legislature honored the so-called "conservation president" with a memorial rotunda at the American Museum of Natural History and the Barosaurus display is part of it. It's a tribute to the man who placed 230 million acres under federal protection and stated, "The nation behaves well if it treats the natural resources as assets which it must turn over to the next generation increased; and not impaired in value." It's a call for conservation placed directly above an extinct animal. Teddy was one of the first presidents to realize that if no hunting controls were put in place, the only animals that would survive on Union soils would be the stuffed bears that became his namesake.

Unfortunately, ecological awareness came too late for some of the museum's inhabitants, especially for the star of the Hall of North American Mammals: the bison. Taxidermied bison can be observed enclosed in a glass showcase called a diorama, a three-dimensional replica of the prairies created long before all the visual effects we take for granted today. We largely owe this marvel to Carl Akeley, the biologist who revolutionized taxidermy in the early 20th century. Until then, hides were filled with straw and the poor desiccated animals' clumsy shapes did not reflect their true anatomy. In addition, tanning techniques left much to be desired. The gorilla was shaped like a pear. Tanners would quarter the chest, leaving the nipples drooping downward with stuffing visible through the nipple holes. A real shame. Finally, Akeley came up with the bright idea to make clay molds of the animals. Plaster casts could be made from these molds, which were then used to produce a definitive skeleton in paper mache—a light but sturdy mannequin on which the animal's hide fit as snuggly as a slinky dress on Penelope Cruz.

The story of the bison has fascinated me since my visit to the museum. It is intimately related to the lives and customs of the Native Americans I read about when searching for evidence to support John Raucci's barefoot-running theories. But in researching bison, I found a lot more material about their extinction than their moments of glory. As the bison disappeared, so did the people, and vice versa. The most impressive text on bison is William Temple Hornaday's 1889 memoir. As chief taxidermist at the Smithsonian and one of the founders of the conservationist movement, Hornaday dedicated numerous pages to describing the incapacity of politicians to protect buffaloes from massacre.

I am engrossed in reading Hornaday's memoir when I hear the little bells jingle on the front door. *Jingle, jingle* ... I'm at 6408 Montgomery Street, the offices of H.H. Hill Realty—serving northern Dutchess and southern Columbia counties for over 15 years. Assisting in the sale and purchase of Hudson River estates, Millbrook farms, landmark properties, residential land and commercial—both full-time and weekend residences. *Jingle, jingle* ... H.H. Hill Realty: All offerings subject to errors, omissions, price changes and withdrawal without notice. No, I'm not making a bit of extra money on the side selling real estate. I've occupied an empty office to write my screenplay for the movie *Cándida*. Or at least I'm trying to. Screenplays tend to go through some 20 drafts before they're finished.

From downstairs, I hear a voice calling out a greeting without obtaining a response. Everyone must be out to lunch. I hear footsteps on the stairs. The door to my office opens and a smiling face pops in: "Huck?" "He's not here," I say; "he's next door." The man disappears and returns a few minutes later. "No one's there. Can I leave a message?" I stand up and introduce myself: "Hi, I'm his brother-in-law." "Nice to meet you," he says. "How are you?" "I'm okay," I respond, "if we don't go into details." Since I notice he's carrying a large box, I ask him if he needs any help. He shakes his head and I think I hear him say he's from Sony, so I'm guessing he is delivering a new TV. I tell him to leave it with me if he wants. "Should I sign a receipt?" "No," he says. "I don't need to sign?" "No, I didn't say Sony," he says. I realize that it's with a U instead of an O. It's SUNY. "Ah, the State University," I respond, apologizing for my mistake. "So you come from New Paltz. I love Huguenot Street. I'm European and I have a real weakness for stone houses. You know what I mean, don't you?" No, he hasn't got a clue what I'm talking about. But he doesn't lose his composure and gives it another try. "My name is Sunny." "Oh, Sonny," I say. Of course. Sonny. As in "son of." "Hello, Sonny." "Well, my name is actually Sunny. Like the sun. Not Sony, neither Sonny nor SUNY. It's Sunny, and I'm a friend of Huck's."

I thank him for the clarification although I have to admit that Sony, Sonny and Sunny sound identical to me. That's what it's like to be a foreigner here. Once past the initial formalities, and even though I know it's none of my business, my curiosity gets the best of me, and I ask him about the contents of the box. "This package? It's buffalo meat," he says. I almost swallow my gum. "Are you kidding me? Aren't buffalo extinct?" I start in again: "So where did you get that meat?" "From my Texas ranch. Would you like to try it?" he asks. "I'm cooking some tonight." I quickly agree. "Well, tell your wife and go over to Huck's house tonight." "Okay," I say. "We'll bring some wine." He leaves with the box, and I immediately regret my offer. I pray in silence to Bacchus, the Roman god of wine, asking him to help me choose the right type of grape. Cabernet Sauvignon, Merlot or Malbec: Which one goes with a steak from the largest mammal in North America?

* * *

When gay marriage became legal in Spain, the producer of my radio talk show there (*Gomaespuma*, which ran from 1982 to 2007), confessed to me that his boyfriend had proposed marriage during a romantic dinner by saying, "Do you want to marry me and adopt a dog together?" For people who have never had children, a pet can become the receptacle of all their affection. This reality hits home tonight at Huck's house near the Red Hook Country Club, when I meet a lovely couple with a cute Chihuahua. One of the men decorates Manhattan apartments for a living. He apparently has exquisite taste, and celebrities fight over him. Celebrities are a class of clients that, he tells us, there is only one way to handle: once they accept his services, they have to give him the keys and leave. They must abandon the premises and not return until he's finished. It might take him a week or several months to decorate an apartment. Regardless, they cannot return or ask questions or suggest anything until he informs them that he is finished. If not, there's no way he will take them on. They can drive you crazy. His partner is an architect and a true book lover, who claims that libraries are essential for keeping a people free. He is a benefactor of the New York Public Library. He discusses the manuscripts of the poet García Lorca, which are kept in the archives of the Stephen A. Schwarzman Building. He encourages me to go there. I'd love to, but assume that being a Spanish journalist won't be enough to convince them to let me touch them. Just like they wouldn't let an Italian correspondent in Paris take the *Mona Lisa* home for a weekend. But who knows? You have to try everything in life, so why not? We toast for the day when we will look at the poet's manuscript together in New York. And we do so in Spanish since he is of Cuban descent. *Salud!*

The red wine is a Protos, from Ribera Del Duero, with enough body to accompany great emotions. Sarah and I imagine that the buffalo roast will look like the ribs of the Flintstones foot-mobile. The interior designer takes a sip and gives his approval while he looks tenderly at the Chihuahua resting in his lap. The dog is named Pancho after Francisco José Villa, the Mexican revolutionary who fought for the poor, but tonight Pancho is in no mood for revolution. The poor thing is under the weather because he has to undergo an operation in a few days. What's wrong with him? Everything, his worried owners inform us. He has a bad knee, he needs two molars removed and they're going to take advantage of the operation to get him a cheek lift. Didn't you notice how ugly the poor guy is, they ask me, with his droopy face? And Pancho is a glutton. "We've caught him eating from the pâté platter at home on several occasions." *Diiingggg* ... We have no time to respond because the oven timer goes off. Like the bell at the end of class at school, the ring suddenly shifts the conversation away from the dog and we jump without transition into the bison universe. "The meat's done!" cries Sunny. *Habemus buffalum.*

The first thing we notice is that the roast is not as large as we'd expected. While serving up the meat, Sunny, who was Huck's roommate in boarding school, tells us he's returned to the East Coast to attend a course on shamanism. In other words, to delve into the mysteries of the shaman—a word from the Tungu language of Siberia to describe an individual with the capacity to modify reality, or at least the perception of reality of the rest of us mortals). *Right!* I raise my eyebrows at Pancho. He responds by tilting his head. I whisper to Sarah: "Is it just me or are too many things going on at this dinner at once?"

Sunny is learning about the spiritual universe of Native Americans at the Omega Institute outside Rhinebeck. The shamanism lessons explore the Andean worldview's three human levels: the Hanan Pacha or spiritual level, the Cay Pacha or worldly level, and the Ucu Pacha, or ego level. Sunny takes notes in silence.

Omega Institute. Renew your spirit. Create connections. Find meaning and purpose. Thirty years devoted to holistic studies. Courses in spirituality, yoga, meditation, our place in the universe and whatever else is going on over there. Each of Omega's six learning paths is supposed to take you on a journey toward greater fulfillment and a more deeply engaged life. To get there from Rhinebeck, you head south on Route 9G, turn left on Slate Quarry Road, drive about four miles, and then make a right on to Center Road. You take another right at Fiddlers Bridge Road and then the second street on the right, Lake Drive. It's right there—the Omega Center, with more than 100 buildings. On a hill stands its crown jewel: the Omega Center for Sustainable Living, which has one of the top 10 wastewater plants in the world. On a guided tour, Omega CEO Skip Backus will proudly tell you that you can fill up a glass in the toilet and drink it without a problem. Well, not exactly. But he will tell you that the water that Omega's students flush becomes drinkable again after passing through the Eco Machine, a natural filter system that replicates the purification processes that plants and organisms in rivers and lakes carry out every day.

Omega covers 200 acres of woodlands on the former grounds of the former Yiddish Camp Boiberik: gardens; vegetable patches; herbarium; basketball, tennis and volleyball courts; walking paths; a cafeteria specializing in vegetarian meals and a shop offering music, books and imported clothing that could be confused with Halloween costumes. You can have massages, facials, health and nutrition consultations and therapies. There are cabins for retreats and a long pond for swimming or canoeing. More than 23,000 people attend educational programs every year, like a workshop on "Releasing the Grip of Fear," featuring renowned actress and UNICEF ambassador Mia Farrow as one of the speakers.

At Omega, Sunny is learning that the Great Spirit is like a bottle of water that sprinkles a few drops each day. We are the drops, and we must return to the Great Ocean of Life to recast ourselves in it. We are cosmic antennae, but the ego impedes us from receiving spiritual information and sharing it. Jesus Christ and Buddha understood that our spirit is a fiery spark of the Great Fire, so they returned to it. They knew that the world moves through energies—those that heal and those that make us ill. For them, seeing an aura was an everyday thing. Sunny, whose full name is Hugh A. Fitzsimons III, came to Omega to take notes. He is motivated by solid reasons that aren't immediately clear. Hold on for a few more pages.

The bison meat is surprisingly tender and delicious. Rather than a Flintstone-type rib, it looks like a delicate entrée on the menu at Le Petit Bistro in Rhinebeck (the best French restaurant in Hudson Valley; reservations recommended). The piece we taste is dressed only with a bit of olive oil and a couple of garlic cloves. Hugh cooked it at a low temperature. The Hill siblings contribute a side dish of carrots cooked in aged rum and caramelized with homemade maple syrup. "So we're wolfing down a real buffalo, right?" I ask, still amazed. "Yes," says Sunny, it's an authentic grassfed bison from a Texas ranch. A bison ranch in the Southwest? That's right. The image doesn't at all mesh with my memories of *Bonanza*. ("*On this land we put our brand, Cartwright is the naaame, fortune smiled, the day we filed the Ponderosa claaaim … Here in the West, we're livin' the best, Bonanzaaa, if anyone fights any one of us, he's got a fight with me. Bonanzaaaaa … *") Sunny notes my confusion and explains. "When I inherited some land on the Mexican border from my grandfather, I decided to get rid of the cattle. They looked sad. So I went to an auction and bid on a few head of bison." No one says anything, but we are all thinking the same thing: He went to auction off the sad-faced cows only to buy a few bison, like a guy who plans to spend Saturday afternoon at a George Cole auction, and returns with a box of fishing lures.

In nearby Red Hook, George Cole auctions compete in entertainment value with any good show on Broadway. As far as I know, George has yet to auction off a buffalo, but I'm convinced he wouldn't have any problem doing so if he could somehow benefit from it. "Okay, next mammal. Who's got $300 to get it started? Three hundred dollars, going, going, gone!" When George started his business, he was eight years old and had just $5 in his pocket. He got on his bike and went to an auction down the road. At eight o'clock that night, his mother came looking for him. He filled his mother's car three times and still had $2 left. The next day he sold every item to local antique shops and came back with $45. Today he has a great empire. Each time a house changes hands, its contents end up at the auction house. "Come on, you know you want a buffalo. Do I hear one hundred? One twenty-five! One fifty! Two hundred! Sold! Two hundred and fifty dollars, buyer number 27."

All kidding aside, Sunny has quite a story. In 1998, his family, the Fitzsimonses, divided up his grandfather's land. While Sunny chose to raise bison, his father and siblings preferred to stick with cattle and oil. When Sunny explained that he wanted to preserve the land of his ancestors for his grandchildren, his family thought he was nuts. They told him he was playing God with that kind of philosophy. But Sunny shouldered on alone, and tonight he's ecstatic because he managed to persuade the Texas governor to return the wild animal status to bison. For Sunny, this is an honor. Bison were for many years classified as endangered species; once their numbers began to grow, the government kept them in the bureaucratic limbo of exotic animals, like the zebra or the kangaroo. It wasn't fair. Bison are native to Texas, which they inhabited long before settlers. They deserve to be classified as wild animals living in the wild.

Bison in the West again? It's been more than 125 years since the last herd of bison roamed the Great Plains. I'm amazed to learn that these 2,000-pound herbivores have reemerged in the myth of the legendary American West, the Old Frontier. Before the Frenchman LaSalle mistook them for African bovines and branded them as buffaloes, an estimated 60 million to 75 million bison roamed North America. They were the physical and spiritual nourishment of Cochise, Crazy Horse, Geronimo, Red Cloud and Sitting Bull. The Native Americans hunted them in ambushes or by chasing them to the edge of cliffs, where the thrust of the herd caused them to plummet to their deaths. But only a handful were captured until after the Civil War, when thousands of men went west, following the railroad. In just a year and a half, the famous Buffalo Bill had killed 4,000 bisonheads to feed the workers of the Kansas-Pacific Line. Shooting bison from the train windows became a national pastime. They dropped like flies, but no one knew how to take advantage of such easy prey. They used only their tongues, which were pickled and sold in Manhattan restaurants, where they were were considered to be a delicacy. Some hides were exported to England and Russia for aristocrats to use as blankets in their carriages. But the Industrial Revolution changed things. The new engines needed belts, and the production of leather in Argentina was insufficient. Then someone discovered that bison leather was more elastic than that of cow leather. Thousands of unemployed soldiers killed an average of 15 animals a day to obtain $3 per hide. By 1884, bison were scarce. The entirety of the Great Plains was strewn with carcasses coveted only by scavenger birds.

Out of a population of 70 million, only three bison were saved in Texas, on Charles Goodnight's ranch; 50 survived in South Dakota, on Pete Dupree's ranch; and in Montana, two bulls and two females, were rescued by Samuel Walking Coyote, a Pend D'oreille native, from the territory of the Blackfoot. The two mating couples were the origin of the herds inhabiting Yellowstone Park today. That was the end of living in the wild for the bison. Since then, their descendants have remained locked away in protected areas or zoos.

When Sunny inherited the 17,000-acre Shape Ranch in 1998, he had no doubt that he should reopen the space to its ancient residents. The existence of bison in Texas today is a three-century accident compared with the million years the bison populated the same territory. The American buffalo formed part of the landscape and evolved at the same time as its vegetation. Bison have always respected their natural environment because it provides their nourishment. The cow is not privy to this information and therefore degrades the grasslands. It lingers in the area and doesn't leave until it overgrazes it. Bison move with the speed of antelope and carry out a balanced pruning. Shortly after this species was reincorporated into the Shape Ranch, the birds, which need high grasses to nest hidden from predators, began to return to Carrizo Springs. After the birds returned, foxes began to prowl. The circle of life was reestablished. "It seems easy, doesn't it?" said Sunny, aware of the diners' fascination. "Let's see who dares to point out that in Texas, the conquest of the West, with so much blood spilled, was based on a mistaken approach. That, without Indians or bison, our promised land lost its charm, its meaning and its infinite bonanza. Texans will look at you like you were a Martian or something. They don't even believe in buffalo as a business. The idea of eating a bison hamburger sounds worse to them than consuming a chihuahua filet does to you."

Pancho startles at the culinary reference, which he seems to understand. A chill ran down his spine. Poor thing, he's exhausted. It's getting late for everyone and it's almost time to leave. Sunny invites us to visit the ranch. "On January 6, we celebrate the harvest," he says. January 6? Impossible. In Spain, January 6 is Twelfth Night, and a decent Spanish father would never leave his house when the Three Wise Men are supposed to bring presents for his kids. No way. "But we could visit the Alamo," Sunny continues, "and then spend a few days at the ranch." No way. On the other hand, the Three Wise Men are all about Spanish Christmases and we're now in New York, where Santa Claus has just paid a visit. But no, I shouldn't. "If you're interested in shamanism, he insists, you would enjoy talking to my partner, Ted Herrera. He was born in the Coahuiltecan Sacred Land where the peyote grows. He is a member of the Spiritual Elders of Mother Earth and the founder and spiritual leader of the Rio Grande Native American Church. At the ranch, he officiates the sacrificial rites." Of course, the Three Wise Men could leave a rain check for a family activity that we could all enjoy upon my return. "Are you up for it?" "No, I'm sorry. I'd love to, but I can't … "

* * *

It's January 5 and snowing heavily. The storm has caught Huck and me on our way to the Albany airport and the poor visibility forces us to slow down. We cross the river up in Hudson and can barely make out the bridge railing. WAMC, our local National Public Radio station, announces the laws that will go into effect in the New Year. Maine will become the fifth smoke-free state, with smoking prohibited on all of its streets. In New Hampshire, it will be forbidden to imitate the voice of a political candidate on the phone. In ... *bzzz*—a temporary interference erases the name of the state—tongue-piercing at a tattoo parlor is now prohibited, and anyone who wants to have his tongue pierced must go to a dentist's office from now on. In California, driving while watching TV is now a felony thanks to a bill promoted by television stations, which do not want to face civil lawsuits for traffic accidents. That's because if someone entertains himself with a plasma screen in his car and ends up in a crash, he can file a multimillion-dollar lawsuit against program producers for having distracted him. This is something that is beyond absurd anywhere else in the world but entirely within the realm of possibility in the United States. Filing lawsuits has become something of a national pasttime, a lottery in which you actually have a good possibility of hitting the jackpot.

Sometimes it seems as if the word "accident" should be removed from the dictionary. For instance, when Shawn Perkins was hit by lightning in the parking lot of King's Island Amusement Park in Mason, Ohio, he sued the park's owner, Paramount Communications Inc., for neglecting to warn him not to be outside during a thunderstorm. In another ridiculous case, Michelle Knepper of Vancouver, Washington, randomly picked a doctor out of the phone book to perform liposuction. The doctor accepted her as a patient and did the procedure. Well, the result was not so great since ... the doctor happened to be a dermatologist instead of a plastic surgeon! So she filed a suit against the phone company—why not?—and won $1.2 million for herself plus an extra bonus of $375,000 for her poor husband, who was suffering a tremendous "loss of spousal services and companionship." You really have to feel sorry for them.

The parties responsible for America becoming a litigious society are a large group of lawyers who lost their scruples long ago. They advertise on TV, in newspapers, on the New York subway. In English and Spanish. You sense them circling like vultures around hospital emergency room doors, pouncing on each injured person who arrives. "What happened? Do you realize you can get money from this tragedy?" There they are, in the name of justice, convincing you to sue even your father, if necessary, for not providing the education necessary to have avoided the calamity that has currently befallen you. If a driver hits somebody with his car and the breathalyzer shows him to be drunk, and it is proven that he had a beer at your house, be prepared to fork over some money or face a jail term for offering him that beer. Yes, it's that absurd.

For more than 30 years, a prestigious non-governmental organization located in Washington D.C., the Legal Foundation, has fought to control this system of frivolous lawsuits. Its founder, Daniel J. Popeo, claims that the true beneficiaries of this senselessness are personal injury lawyers. After winning the lawsuits, they pocket large sums and the plaintiff takes home only crumbs of the booty. In Madison County, Illinois, for instance, one law firm sued the telephone giant AT&T on behalf of its consumers. The lawyers argued that the company had not announced to its customers that they could buy telephones rather than rent them. They won. The affected customers each received a check ranging from $15 to $40 while the law firm earned $80 million. Given that they are aware of the interests of the supposed defenders of defenseless citizens, you can't help but wonder how judges support the lucrative intentions behind these lawsuits. Here's the answer Popeo offers in an ad for his organization in the *New York Times*: Local judges who hand down sentences depend on donations from the attorneys that file lawsuits to finance their re-election campaigns. In March 2003, for example, a judge ordered Philip Morris to pay $10 billion because he considered that the inscription "low in tar" on its cigarette packages led smokers to think that smoking wasn't harmful. Of the total sum, the magistrate allocated the scandalous figure of $175 million in lawyers' fees. Curiously, the judge who signed the verdict had received 80 percent of the funds for his election campaign from attorneys' donations, including a check for $10,000 from the same law firm that sued the tobacco company. But thanks to the Legal Foundation, the Illinois Supreme Court revoked the sentence two years later, based on the fact that it was the Food and Drug Administration that had authorized the inscription "light" and "low tar" on cigarette packs.

Things being as they are, it doesn't surprise me at all that Danny Shanahan, one of my Rhinebeck neighbors and a cartoonist who is regularly published in *The New Yorker*, lately has been holed up in his study preparing a fat book of jokes about lawyers. I'm afraid he'll have enough material for two volumes. I imagine him observing the snow today from his study window and asking himself where the sleazy lawyers are hiding before they emerge from the fog as soon as the first pedestrian slips. I must confess that the real reason I subscribe to *The New Yorker* is to see the cartoons, even though I pretend I do it to read its profound and long articles. I am especially fond of Danny's cartoon that precisely captured Rudy Giuliani's authoritarian style when he was mayor of the world's business capital. In Danny's cartoon, there's a sign at the entrance to Manhattan warning drivers: "Entering New York City. Beware of the mayor."

Huck turns off the radio. We leave the car in the long-term parking at Albany Airport and take a bus to the terminal. The flight is miraculously on time, despite the snow, and we go through security without incident. There aren't too many people. Here, the Christmas season ends on New Year's Day. We're traveling to the sunny southwest with several retired couples escaping the cold and the possibility of fracturing their hips on their slippery front steps. Goodbye snow, hello dust. See you later, Catskill Mountains; welcome, infinite flatlined horizon.

* * *

At San Antonio Airport, Sunny, the history professor-turned-rancher, greets us with "Welcome to the largest town in the world, strangers." He extends his hand, I hug him and he takes advantage of the proximity to grab my bag and throw it in the air like a lasso. It lands in the back of his "horse," a metallic old nag with four-wheel drive and a flexible body to absorb impact in the case of an accident—in other words, a Ford truck. We get in and click our seatbelts. He revs the engine twice and it roars. Another neigh and we gallop towards the highway that some Texans jokingly call "the NAFTA Superhighway," after the North American Free Trade Agreement. For the map-friendly, it's Interstate 35, the highway that runs from Duluth, Minn., through Chicago to Laredo on the American-Mexican border. We head south, toward Atmahau' Pakma't, the sacred river of the Native Americans, which Americans call the Rio Grande and Mexicans the Rio Bravo. We're heading toward the ranch that the Spanish king granted to the loyal Juan Francisco Lombrano in 1806 to witness the gradual, unstoppable return of the bison to the Great Plains.

We enter San Antonio de Padua. Yes, you got me right: the original name of San Antonio was a little bit longer. Spaniards like to embellish the language and Americans love to trim it as much as possible. For the same reason, the city founded in 1781 with the Spanish name "El Pueblo de Nuestra Señora la Reina de los Ángeles del Río de Porciúncula" is simply known today as L.A. The countryside ends abruptly, as if the landscape we observe from the pickup belongs to two different movies—one of trees and the other of buildings—without enough still shots between them to make a dissolve. The city is home to the 2013 NBA basketball champions, the Spurs, and Huck is interested in the future of some of its players. At the 2013 Atlantic Sun Conference, the western teams were on a winning streak. Any of them could compete equally with the best of the Eastern Conference, even though they have traditionally been inferior. The Spurs have an A-team formed by international figures. The star is Tony Parker, who was raised in France by American parents.

We park. Sunny lives in a residential area where wooden water towers rise high above the houses. We leave the bags to greet his wife, Sarah. She is the daughter of the bishop of the Episcopal Diocese of West Texas, just across the street. Very nice. We'll go to the ranch tomorrow.

Before dinner, we take a walk to the historic fort of *The Alamo*. We walk along streets built following twisted irrigation channels, and it seems easy to get lost. Here, service stations sell the cheapest gas in the U.S. Everything is cowboy-themed. Even the swings that hang from the trees, made of car tires, are in the shape of horses. It's as hot as it looks in a John Ford picture. The horizon is hazy and the air so dense you could take a bite out of it. I haven't gotten a chance to change my clothes, so I'm wearing a turtleneck sweater that's perfect for combating the arctic cold of New York. Sunny tells me not to worry. "Don't you know the saying?" he asks. "If you don't like the weather in Texas, just wait 15 minutes." Forty-five minutes later, we enter a lovely patio in front of the mission where Davy Crockett became a hero. I take off my sweater. It looks like rain.

Here, a new version of the film The Alamo has been recently shot and the most difficult assignment for the producers was to find actors that would fit into the narrow historic uniforms of the 19th century Mexican Army. San Antonio has the second-largest population of overweight people in the United States. Only Detroit beats it. Childhood obesity is a national epidemic. As I flipped through *The New Yorker* on the plane—for the cartoons, of course, because I certainly don't want to put on any intellectual airs—I saw one in which two witches are talking next to a cage full of overweight kids. One laughs and says to the other: "Remember the days when we had to fatten them up?"

The Alamo is a place that imposes respect. The old mission has become a sacred temple of history. But which history? As always, there are different versions for every taste. In 1821, the extensive territory of New Spain (including Texas, Mexico, Central America, and other former Spanish territories in the American Southwest) separated from the Spanish Royal Crown and became the Mexican Empire. After an ephemeral

Catholic monarchy, the federal government gave its governors considerable autonomy. The Mexican state of Texas opened its borders to emigration and began to receive thousands of Americans who, in search of cheap land to start their own cotton farms, settled on the banks of the Brazos River. You see? Migration in this hemisphere began in reverse, from north to south. In 1835, General Antonio López de Santa Anna, warned of the expansionist plans of its northern neighbor and proclaimed the need to control the borders and impede the entry of more Americans. A year later, he marched with his troops to clear out Texas. A handful of brave men decided to defend with their lives the right to keep their lands in Mexico. The battle occurred in the secularized mission of San Antonio de Valero. Thousands of soldiers surrounded the mission, which would go down in history as the Alamo, the name that preceded the hometown of the Spanish soldiers who had guarded it during colonial times: Alamo de Parras. General Santa Anna, in true Napoleonic style, subjected the inhabitants to a brutal three-day siege. Lieutenant Coronel Travis responded to their battle cry, *ni rendicion ni retirada* ("I shall never surrender or retreat"), with a cannon ball. There were 1,600 soldiers against 200. The bloodbath became legend.

It's enough to observe the visitors to the Alamo to confirm that this is a sacred place for many. The people read the signs in silence, as if they were before the tomb of a Sufi prophet in New Delhi. The men who are remembered here were from 28 different states and nations. But what were they really fighting for? "What happened here," an African American man, who actually appears to be homeless, tells me at the entrance, "can be written with a capital H, History, and then seem like a feat; or we can leave it in lowercase letters, and divide it into two words: his story. Think about it. Of his story, we are before the biased interpretation of the facts that the winning party always makes." "Winners?" I ask. "Everyone at the Alamo was killed." "Yes," he says, "but a few days later, Sam Houston arrived [who, in the aforementioned movie, was played by Dennis Quaid] and wiped out Santa Anna's army at the Battle of San Jacinto."

And to commemorate the Battle of San Jacinto, he tells me, every year on April 25, women still dress in yellow and throw flowers to protest all wars.

So Texas declared its independence from Mexico and became a republic until it joined the United States in 1845. "In school, they taught me that the Battle of the Alamo was an international conflict between the obsolete, old-fashioned Mexican rules and the modern, revolutionary U.S. ideals of freedom," the man continues. "But that theory doesn't take into account the fact that Mexico had just abolished slavery and the Texans supporting the rebellion were actually in favor of maintaining free labor for their rich cotton fields." There is a minute of silence, and then he stares at me. "Don't even think about repeating these conclusions out loud."

I thank the nice man for his opinions, wondering how he could be so intelligent yet end up homeless, and say goodbye. Oh boy. Now I'd have to do some research. Why does everybody I keep encountering in this country seem to be giving me homework? Anyway, it actually seems like the conquistadores didn't rely on slaves during their three centuries of control over the Texas territory. The 1792 census listed only a total of 34 blacks and 414 mulattos, some of whom were indeed free men and women. How was this possible? Well, because in Spanish Texas intermarriage among blacks, Indians and Europeans was a daily procedure. Slavery started to flourish when the American settlers crossed the Mississippi River and brought their black workers along with them. Mexico didn't like it and made the importation of slaves illegal in 1830. The slaveholders didn't blink. To evade compliance, they converted their life-term workers to indentured servants. Blacks were forced to sign contracts claiming that they owed money and would work to pay the debt. Well, at least they would try... since the low wages made repayment impossible. Mexico counterattacked. In 1832 the state of Texas passed legislation prohibiting worker contracts from lasting more than ten years. No more loopholes. Then came the battles of the Alamo, San Jacinto ... and by 1836, the enslaved population in the free Republic of Texas was greatly increased and the cotton industry flourished.

So, are all these facts interconnected? Who knows. I remember a scene from the documentary *The Beatles Anthology*. George Harrison and Paul McCartney couldn't agree about the facts of some event they were discussing, so George told Paul: "Man, if you and I, who were in the same place, can't agree on what happened there, just imagine what historians must write about past events they never attended."

We return to Sunny's house to clean up a bit. When I open my bag, I find a note from Baggage Inspection telling me that, in order to protect me and the other passengers, the law demands that the Transport Security Administration physically inspect some suitcases. The TSA appreciates my understanding. If I have any questions, I should call them at the number listed. I do have a question: Why do they always have to open my bag and not the bags of all the people who travel by plane? But I'm not going to bother to call them. I take a shower. There's a party tonight.

Sunny's wife, Sarah, has a friend called Ginger who just turned 50, and they've included us on the guest list for her birthday party. Ginger lives in a shiny new house in a new neighborhood, so new that it looks like a theme park. The Spanish Colonial chalet, is large and very comfortable inside, with a 16th-century Spanish architectural floor plan I so admire. The walls are covered with tapestries and rugs that the owners collect. An earthy red and sky blue Navajo tapestry catches my eye, as does a Persian rug with geometric designs. No artificial dyes were used in these rugs. They are all natural colors. Yellow from saffron. Red from pomegranates. Blue from indigo leaves. Brown from nutshells and grey from the natural color of the wool. Ginger likes to knit in her spare time. Sunny and Sarah give her a bag of buffalo wool, a small offering collected from their ranch. She accepts the gift gratefully but seems a bit confused. Bison have a long way to go before they become part of daily life in Texas. I wonder how bison could not have hides like cows, but have wool like sheep.

We wish Ginger a happy birthday and say hello to her husband, who is an ophthalmologist. They have been very kind to include Huck and me on such a special day, along with their closest friends and family. Everyone admires the multi-tiered cake, which, following current cake trends, reproduces three photos of Ginger in colored sugar. "Too bad it was a surprise party," Ginger says, "because they chose the worst photos in my album; there are several where I look a lot better." She begins to unwrap her birthday gifts. Like in a TV contest, she announces the contents of each package and passes the gifts around so we can observe them and admire how original the birthday cards are. One of the cards says that now she'll have to get used to pronouncing the f word. It appears to refer to the swear word that is censored on television with a beep and in the press is written as f---. But no, this f is the first letter of ... fifty!

Ginger's husband asks us to form a circle and join hands and, with his eyes closed, he gives thanks for a rewarding life, a loving wife and close friendships in a short prayer that ends with "God bless America." We break ranks when the food is served. He has prepared an exceptional buffet: Crab quesadillas, fresh spinach salad with ruby red grapefruit from the Gulf Coast, wild rice with blueberries and nuts. Actually, this rice is more like a cereal that absorbs up to four times its own weight in liquid. It grows in marshes, is crunchy and tastes of hazelnuts. There's salmon that he smoked on their patio. What a guy! And beef marinated in Pequin chile pepper, slow-roasted and served with mushroom sauce. I taste it and almost pass out. Like in the Johnny Cash song, it "went down, down, down and the flames went higher. And it burns, burns, burns, the ring of fire." Clearly, a lot of Texas cooking uses this red pepper, tiny but deadly, which is native to the coast. Except for a Thai variety, this is supposedly the hottest pepper on the planet. Hotter than the cayenne pepper in plant sprays used to ward off bears in Rhinebeck. Coahuila Indians, accustomed to snacking on spicy peppers throughout their lives, eat Pequin chile peppers as we would apples.

At dinner, I meet Kenny, a friendly guy who is fascinated by firearms. "What I love about Texas is that here you always have something to shoot at—doves, wild boar, deer," he tells me. He says he entertains himself by shooting prairie dogs, small rodents that have no use. Looking through his gunsight, he waits until they pop their heads out of the den to blow their brains out. *Bam! Bam!* Another guest wears a t-shirt that says: "You don't need to call 911, this is Texas." For some reason, people here go nuts over guns. When I was studying at the University of Southern California, the film history professor told us that in one of the first movies shown in Texas, a train approached on the screen. When the train was in close up, people in the audience, believing that it was coming at them, began to shoot the image until there were only holes where a movie screen once stood. The desserts arrive. In the line for the cake, I speak with a young woman who is also impressed with the menu. She loves to eat, but not to cook. "Do you know my favorite thing to make for dinner is?" she asks. "No idea," I say. "Reservations!" she responds. Sunny, Sarah, Huck and I leave after coffee. Thanks so much. We have a long trip ahead of us tomorrow. Adventure awaits us.

We get up early and have breakfast at a Tex-Mex restaurant. Coffee with milk and *chilaquiles*: cheese and scrambled eggs in a corn tortilla with salsa and beans. Delicious. A salute to the colors of the Mexican flag: chili, tomato and onion. I order another cup of coffee. Right away, sir. Here, the waiters are very attentive, perfectly attuned to your needs. Fourteen percent of the workforce in Texas is Mexican. The Mexican workers are called *paisanos* and number about a million. Most are concentrated in San Antonio. Austin, the state capital, an hour-and-a-half drive to the north, is the seat of government, university education and Dell Computers. Many people drive there daily to work. A little further to the northwest, the hills rise to form the celebrated Texas Hill Country, where rivers and music are born.

We're on the road. Sunny drives a refrigerator truck and I accompany him in the cabin. His son Patrick follows us with Huck in the pickup. Along the way, we stop to buy a chainsaw to cut wood on the ranch. We're going to cook a bison over mesquite wood. The small hardware store looks like a remote island amid a huge asphalt parking lot.

In Texas, you can use any excuse for being late to work except that you couldn't find a parking space. We purchase the chainsaw that Sunny was told was the world's best: an STIHL 319, made in Germany. The hardware store employee who's waiting on us raves about the chainsaw. It has a grated piston, which guarantees better lubrication so it will last longer. The chainsaw comes with its own thermostat and automatically senses the temperature and relative humidity and adjusts its settings accordingly. It also lies flatter than other chainsaws. So let's buy it then. Sunny also picks up a pair of Gatorline gloves reinforced with aramid fibers, which are used to lengthen the lifespan of tires and bullet-proof vests.

Ever since he abandoned his history books to become a rancher, Sunny has surprised himself by doing things he'd never imagined. We can sacrifice the bison at the ranch, he tells me, but we can't sell the meat until the animal has been inspected by a vet. Once it passes the test, we have two hours to transport it by refrigerator truck to the butcher. *Hoooonk, hooonk.* The trucks we pass greet us by honking their bellowing horns. "It seems I now belong to the truckers' club," Sunny says, amused. *Hooonk, hooonk.* That's a sound that brings many Americans back to their childhood. Here it's common for grandparents to hoist up their grandkids on the side of the road so they can make a downward gesture with their arms, asking truckers to give them a honk. *HOOONK.* ... This time I'm the one to return the greeting to an Alabama trucker by waving my arm from the cabin. I'm loving it.

Sunny, being a former professor, cannot help his pedagogical nature, and points to the landscape. In ancient times, he says, the prickly pear was the king of plants. It is a paddle-shaped cactus where tiny cochineal live. The Spanish conquerors were fascinated by those little bugs. Sunny stops the car and we hop out. Just like in a movie closeup, his boots kick up dust as they hit the ground. We approach one of these majestic plants and are able to see the tiny dots on their branches. Sunny scrapes up a couple of the whitish insects with his knife and shows them to me. Then he pulls out his business card and wipes the insects on them as if he were spreading pâté. Immediately, the card turns a radiant scarlet. Pure red. The color we owe to Mexico. Cochineal red for painting and for dying clothes. Red peppers are used today for dyeing cold cuts and chorizo, which, until the discovery of the Americas were black and appeared rotten. We continue on our way. On both sides of the highway, we see red-tailed hawk nests in the mesquite trees. In the winter, when there are no leaves, it is easier to locate these birds of prey—they hunt like crazy since it's easier to see what moves on the ground. Originally, mesquite grew only on the Gulf Coast, but Spanish livestock ate the seeds and distributed them through their scat as they headed toward the Pacific. Now there is mesquite in abundance throughout the Southwest since cattle are everywhere: the longhorn, intensely colored and with extra long horns; the English Hereford; the Charolais, brought over from France; the Italian Chianina ... everywhere you look, you see cows. The short-haired bovine overran everything and eventually took over the bison's habitat until 1873, when Joseph Glidden came up with the idea of barbwire and disproved the notion that you can't put doors on the prairie. The invention, which you can use today to enclose a square mile for about $400, grants the cowboy the great privilege of being able to determine the best time for inseminating his herd. A four-wired fence, the second wire of which is electrified, today prevents losses due to the friskiness of the enormous Brangus bull, which, used to mount the fragile heifers until literally breaking their backs.

We're on the other side of the Mississippi. This is the land where millions of Americans dream of leaving everything behind to become cowboys some day. A place where the code of honor has more weight than the law. Where sunsets are viewed on horseback, in full-color cinemascope. Where they say a man experiences a real sense of freedom denied to the rest of us mortals. Where restaurants serve mountain oysters—bull testicles—as appetizers. Texas occupies a fourth of the landmass of the United States and which nevertheless has a relatively small population. Where ranchers, far from getting rich, content themselves with not going broke every season. Where annually, some 12 million acres of land are abandoned to erosion. Where a man's word and a handshake were traditionally enough to close a deal—which was as much about honor as the fact that, in the old days, most ranchers didn't know how to read. Where, when Sunny was a boy, no one was allowed to mention the theory of evolution at school. In Texas, it seems that the cows evolved, but man, who was created in God's image, did not need to. According to Jane Kramer in *The Last Cowboy*, the old and far-off West is a corner of the world that is synonymous with paradise for a man or a cow, but a living hell for a woman or a mule. And where, as suggested in *Buffalo for the Broken Heart* by Dan O'Brien, another pioneer in bison-raising, the flame of myth continues to burn because American ranchers, the most honest people on Earth, are incapable of lying to others but constantly deceive themselves.

We cross the Nueces River, where the Mexican-American War began. Texans believed that their border was the Rio Grande whereas Mexicans placed the border some miles north, next to the river we are now crossing. Large gold deposits were discovered in California and President James Polk took advantage of the territorial dispute to declare war on the neighboring country. If he won, California would be his. I ask Sunny about the Texas independence movement that is periodically mentioned in the press. He responds, with irony, that Texas will indeed become independent someday and will divide into two territories: that of "Tex" and that of "Ass."

We drive through the small town of Carrizo Springs, popularly known as Chorizo Springs, given the large Mexican-American population. It is the urban center closest to the ranch. Before mesquite trees grew here, the area was grasslands, which made hunting easier because the animals were in plain sight. From Carrizo, we take the farm road for seven unpaved miles until we finally see the iron goose egg on the gate announcing the entrance to Shape Ranch. The button-like sun begins to slip into the buttonhole of the horizon. A road runner speeds by. People say they bring good luck. They look like skinny, gray chickens with white spots. They are lightning fast. This one has a lizard in its beak. It will most likely pin it to the trunk of a mesquite tree, where it usually establishes its pantry, so that the sun will dry the meat to produce lizard jerky. But the roadrunner isn't the fastest animal in these parts. That honor goes to the drones from the military base nearby. Nonetheless, Sunny says that roadrunners are very fierce. They frequently attack rattlesnakes. "Did I hear you say rattlesnakes?" I ask. "Yeah, there are thousands around here."

If you're out in the wilderness and suddenly feel like Cassius Clay knocked you out, chances are you've been bitten by a rattlesnake. You should immediately apply a tourniquet, but don't make it too tight because you don't want to cut off the blood supply to your extremity, and then eventually loosen it just so you can slow the flow of venom. You should put ice on the bite and rush to the nearest hospital. The old method of making a cut in the wound and sucking the blood usually leads only to serious infections or irreversible gangrene. At any rate, about half the time, the snakes don't have venom in their fangs when they bite you because they've already used it up with other prey. Snakes never voluntarily attack humans. That's precisely why they use the rattle to announce their presence. The rattle on the tail says: "I don't want anything to do with you, so get out of here before it's too late." They only attack people in self-defense, when someone steps on them, or through a miscalculation. That's because snakes can't distinguish prey with their eyes. They have two heat sensors in their heads and when the signs captured by both get crossed, they launch an attack without knowing whether the prey is a mouse, a rabbit or a human. They also sometimes identify their prey through smell. When they stick out their tongue at you and hiss, they are only trying to sniff you. When it gets cold, they burrow in the ground to hibernate. When the sun begins to warm everything, they start to emerge, but they're pretty groggy and weak from hunger, so it's easy to avoid them.

When the bonfire at the ranch that night turns to embers, it's time to have a little snack. I'm in charge of the appetizers. We stopped at HEB on the way down, where Sunny sells his bison meat, to see if the store needed to reorder. With 300 stores throughout Texas and northern Mexico, HEB is the eleventh largest company in the United States, according to *Forbes* magazine, and was established by a Texan by the unfortunate name of Howard E. Butt. At HEB I picked up a '95 Rioja Marques de Cáceres, imported by a distributor in Birmingham, Alabama. And a Torta del Casar—a cake filled with a Spanish creamy sheep cheese that melts in the mouth, which we are finishing off in front of the fire. Tonight's menu is bison hamburgers cooked over mesquite coals, beans and rice with chili. Janelle, the wife of the foreman, Freddy, is cooking.

At Shape Ranch, the bison eat only grass and gain weight in a natural way. They gain little during the winter months, the season when the grass is inactive, but fatten up quickly when the prairie blooms in spring. That happens with cattle too. But fencing changed the course of history. It kept ranchers from moving their cattle freely in search of green pastures. Once it was possible to store maize without rotting, feedlots appeared. A pregnant cow needs about 30 acres of grasslands for herself during the 283 days of her pregnancy. She needs another 12 acres to feed her calf in summer. Taking into account that the calf will need two years to reach the 990 pounds necessary to provide the cuts of meat the market demands, the calculations are easy. It's much cheaper to send the calf to the feedlots when it is between 14 and 18 months old. The consumption of grain produces the white streaks that the consumer expects to see in his steak. In four weeks, the cow is ready for the slaughterhouse. The meat's marbled appearance, which we take as a sign of quality, is actually a degenerative process. Ruminants lack the enzyme to metabolize starch and consuming cereals makes them sick. For that reason, in the U.S., cattle are given some 19 million pounds of antibiotics annually. It is estimated that 95 percent of cattle that go to feedlots are treated with growth hormones. In addition, the grains they eat have been grown with the aid of pesticides. Very appetizing.

The mesquite wood has turned to embers and it's time for the meat patties to go on the grill. Since it is lean, bison meat needs little cooking or turning, just like fish. We finally taste the Thunder Heart hamburgers, which are low in cholesterol, rich in protein and taste like the grasslands. Delicious. In a country where meat travels an average distance of 1,500 miles from ranch to dinner plate, we are enjoying the luxury of tasting an animal that roamed freely just a few yards away. Now it's time for bed. There are no lights nearby and the stars shine brightly in the night sky. They are the same stars observed in Crystal City, a few miles north of here, where the Japanese were kept in prison camps during the Second World War.

Early the next morning, I'm in the ranch kitchen with Sunny's partner, Ted Herrera, who was born in Mirando City, Texas, to Maria Lara, a Tlaxcalteca, Chichimeca and Huichol Indian, and Eduardo Herrera, a Tlaxcalteca, Chichimeca and Coahuiltecan Indian. Tall, with long hair, a thick moustache and a goatee, Ted stares intensely at me from beneath a felt hat adorned with a red ribbon. He is the Tlahtoami (principal speaker) of the Tlaxcalteca and Affiliated Tribes of Texas, and retired in 1998 from his position as a Kelly Air Force Base program manager, where he oversaw the development of policies and procedures that governed over 5,000 aircraft journeymen. In 2000, after a personal journey led him to meet with his people in the foothills of the volcano at the Wirikuta Natural Reserve, he started a partnership with Sunny to raise buffalo for ceremonial and economic purposes. We say hello and immediately begin a conversation.

Sunny once worked as a teacher at the Good Samaritan Center on the West Side of San Antonio. That's where young offenders who have two strikes against them are sent. It is their last chance because a third strike means juvenile detention. When Sunny inherited the ranch, he knew he didn't want to become a cowboy or sell his soul to the multinational oil companies, but he felt lost. A student at the center, Ramón Vázquez, convinced him to meet a *peyotero* he knew. That *peyotero* was Ted, and they quickly became friends. At the very heart of Sunny's venture is the notion that the animal is sacred to many people. This was

160

going to be holy meat from holy animals raised in a holy way. What he did not expect was the unholy drop in live animal prices two weeks after he purchased his foundation herd. But let's get back to Ted first.

Raised as a Mexican near the ocean, in Corpus Christi, Ted tells me he spent his life trying to fit in with Americans. He looked at the shoes his friends at school wore and bought the same ones to imitate them. "I belong," he says, "to the first generation of our indigenous family who graduated from high school." There he played football. It wasn't until high school when a minor wound sent him to a doctor for the first time in his life. Prior to that incident, all his medical needs were taken care of by peyote and other Indian remedies. Going to the doctor was a luxury none of his family had ever enjoyed. In high school, Ted was very athletic, but could never be named captain because that was a privilege reserved for white people or the cotton ranches owners' children.

Slavery ended after the Civil War, and in the late 1800s, the plantations were replaced by smaller cotton ranches, but until the mid-1960s Indian families were still required to work on the cotton ranches with their young children. Ted started doing a man's workday at six years old, working from dawn to dusk in the sweltering fields for less than 50 cents an hour. "I have always perceived," he confesses, "that we were modernday slaves working on a plantation." After finishing school, he went to work for the Department of Defense, from which he retired after 32 years. He says he gained two things from that experience: a good retirement pension and an enormous emptiness inside. He asked himself: "Where is the American dream they tried to sell me?" Before the Treaty of Guadalupe Hidalgo of 1848 his ancestors lived in disputed land, between two rivers. Mexico claimed Nueces River, north of this area, as its border, but the United States wanted to draw the line further south, at the Rio Grande. Texas tribes were victims of Governor Mirabeau B. Lamar's Indian Eradication Policy. In 1847 Ted's ancestors were given a year to decide whether to stay in place or go to Mexico. Most decided to stay in place and became "white citizens" of the United States. "Although our people was never treated as white citizens," Ted tells me, "it was better to be mistaken and mistreated as a Mexican American than to be killed as an Indian." I nod, taking it all in. "So what are we now?" he asks. "Latinos? Americans? Indians?" He says he lost his identify with his people. They called him Teodosio, a name he found difficult to pronounce, while he became Ted to most Anglos. The only thing remaining for him of his culture was medicine. His grandmother and mother used peyote buttons for everything. They worked hard in the German-owned ranches, picking cotton as well as the seeds, from which they extracted a liquid to waterproof cedar and give it a redder color. "I was very young so I used to accidentally cut my feet with the machete," he says. "But I had to keep working, so I put some dirt and spider webs on my wounds and that was it." His family would arrive home exhausted, and his grandmother would give him a cup of peyote tea, which renewed his strength.

After Ted retired, with an impeccable service record, he collapsed into an easy chair and began to dream awake. His dead grandmother would appear in his dreams to beg him to reconnect with his people in Sierra Madre. Confused, Herrera finally decided to travel to Real de Catorce, which was once the richest city in North America thanks to its silver mines. It's hidden in the mountains of San Luis Potosí, 9,000 feet above sea level. To get there, you have to go through a claustrophobic tunnel 1.5 miles long. When Ted finally emerged from the tunnel, he was surprised to discover a tribal community of spectacular beauty. In 2001, *The Mexican*, a comedy, was filmed there with Brad Pitt and Julia Roberts. The film doesn't have many exterior shots, but it did bring the first telephone lines to the area, plus a Jacuzzi specifically requested by the actress. That's where Ted found the sacred lands from which the Huichol collected *híkuri*, known as *peyotl* in the Nahuatl language (the official language of New Spain for 126 years).

In Real, Teodosio Herrera—Ted's real name—felt that he was a member of the Huichol Nation. He was happy for the first time in his life. He discovered that today, most of his people live in the Mexican states of Durango, Jalisco and Zacatecas. From there, they travel the 250 miles that separate them from the sleeping volcano, El Quemado, to leave their offerings and collect their medicine every year. He also learned that the Huichol are not the only ones who go to this peak in search of peyote. There are many backpackers who the Indians refer to as *pulgosos*. These are people who confuse the medicine with the drug. Ted tells me that if you aren't prepared spiritually, taking peyote will only cause nightmares. Peyote is a gift from the gods, to whom thanks should be given. Peyote is our brother, he tells me, like the water, the sun and the rock. Because it has a soul and the inert exists only in our ignorance.

On that pilgrimage to the Native American Mecca, Ted found himself. He felt part of something much larger. He told me he understood that there is a spiritual world to which we all belong: the five-fingered ancestors, the animals and plants. Traditionally, Native Americans learned to connect with that world through initiation rites. When a boy turns 15, he has to spend the night alone in a sacred space, without water or food. He must drink peyote tea and wait to see if the spirit of his protector animal appears. It may be a buffalo, coyote or jaguar. Once the young man has the vision, he can go home again. This is how the young man learns to receive spirits and to never feel fear again. Ted always tells his grandchildren: "Do you think that when I leave this reality I'll stop loving you? No, I'll always be by your side."

Sunny yells that the coffee is ready. "So what did you think about my friend Ted?" he asks. Without giving me a chance to respond, he says: "Now you know why I went to Omega. When I inherited the ranch, I was walking on the property and discovered Native American rock carvings. Then I met Ted and then the bison came and suddenly, everything fell into place." A chill runs up my spine, but since I don't want to get all mystical, I ask him: "How many bison did you buy at the auction?" That was on November 5, 1998. "Two," he tells me. "A two-year old bull and a one-year old bull. They can't be by themselves. They die of a broken heart if they are left alone."

The Longoria brothers, Alfredo, Ataulfo and Gilberto, are trying to get a tractor started outside. They will need it to load the sacrificed animals onto the refrigerator truck. When they finally get it started, they join us. "What's up, man?" The three of them were born in Carrizo Springs, and although they are completely bilingual and speak flawless Spanish, they speak English to each other. Their names have been adapted to English, too—Freddy, Ulfo and Gilbert—to avoid the pronunciation problems poor Teodosio faces. Janelle has prepared breakfast: corn tortillas with bison hump meat. It's a delicacy, tender and flavorful, which falls apart like pulled pork when you take a fork to it; it's Mexican-style barbecue enveloped in a moistened sack and slow-cooked overnight in a pit, buried 12 hours on a bed of coals. Janelle has covered the hole with a corrugated board, placed more coals on top and then put in a pipe to let it breath. The result is amazing. Yum! They cook the head in the same way, Ted tells me, which for him is the most delicious part of the animal. The Huichol man likes to eat meat from the bison's cheeks, tongue and eyes in tacos and he cracks open the skull to eat the brains. He then boils the skull to clean it. Finally, he decorates it with bright colors.

This morning, the coffee is accompanied by *marranitos*, pig-shaped pastries and sweet empanadas filled with sweet potato filling. I stick to the savory dishes, especially hump-meat tacos, with salsa in freshly prepared tortillas. I love them and eat several because I fear I won't be able to have them again for a long time. The banquet is accompanied by a cold beer. The Longoria brothers prefer Netro Light because it is the cheapest at 99 cents. You go to the supermarket, they say, and you always find huge stacks of all the other brands. However, where the Netro should be, there's usually only an empty space. I squeeze a little lemon into the can, add some salt, take a swig and, wow, fabulous! But we have to get going ... the action's about to start.

Before getting into the vehicles, Ted has to purify the participants. We form a circle. Herrera lights a handful of herbs and starts to circle us. He envelops us in a ring of smoke that he blows towards our faces, using a feather as a fan, which he points to the heavens. It is an eagle feather. Other natives use condor, hawk or sparrow hawk feathers. Each tribe uses the feathers of the bird that flies the highest over their lands or the birds that go closest to the creator of the universe, which is the same thing. For Native Americans, feathers are not decorations, but rather antennae to communicate with the spirits. In other words, they are like the satellite dish I use to watch *La Liga* soccer games. (I wonder how Real Madrid did today, by the way.) Herrera raises his hands to the sky, pointing the eagle feather toward the sun, and recites a prayer in the language of his ancestors. He tells them to take the spirits of the bison we are going to sacrifice.

> *Kio ye'n panate'l wemu'k pamesai', ye' ye'n.*
> *Emna' ayema ment nawaso'l ko'p*
> *Emna' ayema ment nawso'l wakate'*
> *Ye-ina'n elia'wa-ite nawi'*
> *Ye-ina'n elia'wa-ite ment mete'l.*
> *Maptama'k emna' ayema' nawi' swahue'l.*
> *Ye'n aneluem apakam nawi hak ye'n kayase'l hak*
> *Emna' mete'l wama'k*

"Creator, it's me," Ted translates for me later, "Rattlesnake in a Hailstorm. Listen to me. You gave medicine to my people. You gave us bison and we lost them. We lost our spirit. Now you have given it back to us and I will lead with my heart towards your spiritual world."

Freddy is in charge of finding the herd. I ask him if I can go with him in his pickup and, together with Blacky, a black dog sporting a t-shirt, we head down the dirt roads of Shape Ranch. The healthy pastures provide food, shelter, hiding places and good spots for the reproduction of dozens of species. We see a white-tailed rabbit, quail, blue jays, a kara-kara eagle, a white hawk, a deer, some scat from wild boar … but there's no sign of our target. Apparently, except during the mating period, when all the bison form a large herd, the bison live in families just like elephants do, making them hard to locate. Since the arrival of the bison, pools have become a paradise for aquatic birds. Freddy tells me that the cattle did not know where to drink. For a cow, being away from a water source for a half a day can mean death. That's why they concentrate around pools, defecating in the water, contaminating it and closing the door to other users. Bison do not always drink in the same place. They travel great distances during the day, and search for springs by scratching the soil with their hooves or digging holes by butting their powerful heads against the soil. Nor do they need to nap under trees. They aren't afraid of temperatures reaching 120°F. Their wool provides insulation against the hard sun, the wind and the nighttime frosts. During the summer, they lose their coats to be cooler and they grow them back in winter to provide warmth. Birds pick up the tangles of wool they shed to make nests and mice use the wool to heat their dens. Bison are not afraid of storms, either. Quite the opposite: they head directly towards them to get past them as soon as possible. Bison always move against the wind in order to smell danger.

The bison can be quite violent. There are two reasons for them fighting. The first is sexual: During the mating periods in late June and early September, the males fight over the females. These squirmishes tend to be more psychological than physical. Like professional poker players, both contenders for a female resort to bluffing. The winner wins without putting its life at too much risk. The second reason for strife is territorial control. A bison needs 25 acres of pasture. Territorial fights are brutal and may end in death. Shape Ranch covers 17,000 acres and has a herd of 300. Sunny could triple the number of heads he has, but he doesn't want to run the risk of being surprised by a drought, which would force him to feed the bison hay or grain. Ranching is simple work, he says, but keeping it simple is a tough job. His goal is to provide grassfed meat, so he doesn't share the philosophy of the big names in ranching, such as Ted Turner, the founder of CNN. Turner is the second-largest private landowner in the U.S. (the first is John Malone, founder of Liberty Media), and owns a fifth of the entire bison population in the United States—55,000 head that graze on two million acres spread across several states, mainly Nebraska, New Mexico and Montana... But Turner's bison are sent to feedlots between the ages of 16 and 24 months to be fattened with corn like cattle before being served up as steaks at the Ted's Montana Grill restaurant chain.

Freddy pulls up next to a pumpjack, which has been extracting about a barrel of oil a day from the subsoil for the past 30 years. It's not a lot, but it helps to pay Sunny's bills. The foreman scans the horizon with his binoculars and at last exclaims: "There they are!" Where? I can't see anything. "Can't you see the heifer?" he says, pointing to some thicket. It takes me a minute to see it because its blond wool is perfect camouflage against the tall yellow grasses. Like in the stereoscopic images of the magic eye, the silhouettes of some 30 creatures appear, about 300 feet away on a hill. They have enormous brown and black heads with tiny eyes. A male lifts its head. It can't see us, but it can smell us. With the wind on their side, they'll always discover you.

On the East Coast, when you purchase land, you are the owner of all of the land. If you dig into the ground and find treasure, it's yours. In the West, however, the Spanish conquerors applied the legislation that was in effect at that time in Spain. The right to property extended only one meter below the surface. From that point until the center of Earth, everything belonged to the king. Mexico did not change these laws after emancipating from Madrid. Neither did the United States once the land was under its jurisdiction. As a result, in what are now the states of Texas, Arizona and Colorado, a single plot of land can have two owners: the owner of the surface area and the other of the minerals beneath it. Not many people know this. Real estate deals have been made in the West without the buyers' knowing that the contract sometimes does not include mineral rights. Initially, this circumstance didn't seem to affect anyone, so there was no reason for concern. The surprise happened when prospecting for oil and natural gas grew rapidly in an effort to avoid depending on foreign energy. Ranchers who own wonderful lands discover that they can't stop oil companies from digging holes in their pastures and erecting oil wells. They destroy the landscape in exchange for nothing. They dry up the springs and poison the aquifers. They arrive with a permit signed by the owners of the subsoil. This authorizes them to operate there, as long as they remain at least 600 feet from the dwelling.

On occasion, the beneficiaries are people who are not even aware that they own the mineral rights. In Tampico, in Tamaulipas State, Mexico, for instance, Joaquín Baldridge received a visit from a stranger several years ago. Joaquín had returned from the port where the captain of a Thai ship had quietly told him that if he helped him find a dog for the crew's supper, he would give him $1,000. However, Joaquín was not in the business of chasing greyhounds, but rather of growing potatoes and raising Brahmin cattle, so he told the stranger in colorful Mexican slang to go to hell. Upon his return to the González Ranch, Joaco was radioed that a gringo was waiting for him in the office. The man was an American oil company executive. According to the visitor, Joaquín's Grandfather Atwood had bought ranches in Texas and later resold them but kept the mineral rights. His grandfather was now dead. Joaquín's father had emigrated to Mexico with his family after World War II and they were never notified of anything. Now the executive told him that a big company wanted to search for oil on a property whose subsoil Joaquín and his siblings were the rightful owners of. "Us?," Joaquín asked, skeptically. "You," the American assured him. Joaquín gave his permission for the subsoil to be mined and today receives 10 percent of the profits from the exploitation of a ranch he's never seen. You can never predict the troubles or surprises the subsoil in the West may have in store for you.

Glug, glug, glug. To produce a barrel of oil, the metallic rod must pump 250 barrels of water. A filter separates the liquids and the black gold drips slowly, like coffee from a coffeemaker, into a tank. It smells of tar. Freddy tells me there is oil everywhere, but it's too expensive to pump because it's so thick. But because of the war in Iraq and all that nasty business, prices skyrocketed, allowing activity at the Texas oil wells to resume in many wells that had been abandoned. Freddy was correct to predict, at the start of the war, that the high price of oil would again make the expensive operation of its extraction profitable. He tells me a story he says he's heard many times: someone returned home and found his house swimming in oil, which had overflowed from the toilet or faucet. For Sunny, who owns the subsoil rights of the Shape Ranch, a daily barrel from each pumpjack means a big check every month. It's not enough to retire to the Bahamas, but it's enough to help pay off his bank loan. However, depending how the bison meat business goes, his hopes to remove the pumpjacks to leave the landscape free of mechanical sounds.

We look for mature bison. Adult males weight 2,000 pounds, twice as much as cows. In the first two years of life, bison use all their nourishment to build an impressive bone structure since their ribs also cover their humps. Beginning at 48 months, they develop their musculature. The hump, which is not a ball of fat like camels have to store water, is the strongest muscle, a necessary crane to hold up the enormous head. Females become fertile at three years and continue to be so throughout their lives. Most live to about 20. We try to attract bulls so that Sunny can shoot them close to the refrigerator truck to make it easier for the Longoria brothers to drag the animals to the truck. Freddy has a trick. He shakes a metal box in which he's placed a handful of alfalfa treats. The bison recognize the sound because the foreman has been training them. It is the ranch's only concession in its non-intervention policy with the animals. One, two, three shakes of the enormous rattle and they come running. The bison are fast and strong. Powerful shoulders allow them to reach a top speed of 30 miles per hour after a couple of strides. Bison can beat horses easily over short distances. They move like a flock of birds. Their hindquarters are light and turn without losing even an ounce of speed in the maneuver. The lead animal commands from a distance. It changes direction and the rest follow. If the leader decides to charge at us, the rest of the herd will follow suit.

We call the others on the cell phone to tell them we've located the herd. Reinforcements soon arrive in the truck. Sunny grips his .44 magnum rifle, the gun Clint Eastwood used in *Dirty Harry*. The bullets have a tremendous impact but do not pass through the animal's body. If they did, the same shot could injure another bison. Sunny gets out of the jeep and approaches the herd. A few yards from his prey, the hunter consults the notes he took at the Omega Institute. Rather than simply slaughtering the bison, Sunny is going to shoot it with the ritual of a sacrament. "The Native Americans," whispers Ted Herrera, who has placed himself beside me to recount the events, "believed that only warriors with a pure heart could hunt bison. Those who were noble with nature and applied the principle of the authentic hunt preserve the two species: that of the hunter and the hunted." The hunt is one of the Seven Generation Decisions. "Haven't you noticed that many Native Americans have seven feathers in their shields?" asks Ted. "They symbolize seven generations. You are the feather in the middle and, before making a decision, you have to remember what the three generations before you did and attempt to visualize how the decision you make will affect the three generations that will follow you. My people never wanted to kill an animal for sport. My grandfather was such a great hunter that he could kill deer while they slept. Those skills are lost." Ted takes a deep breath and continues his story: "If the hunter is capable of reaching a pure decision, the bison will come and deliver its life voluntarily." *Bang!* The shot resounds throughout the valley as the first victim falls. I anxiously await a stampede … but it never occurs. Then I recall a passage from *Buffalo for the Broken Heart*, which claims that wild animals understand better than humans that death forms part of the circle of life. To my amazement, the rest of the bison approach the animal lying motionless on the ground. They smell it; scratch it with their hooves. They stay by its side. Then I realize that the bison do not moo. Rather, they begin to moan in the wind.

If the shot hits the magic spot, three inches below the ear and three inches from the neck, the bison keels over. If you miss, the situation becomes dangerous, as the bison releases adrenaline. You'd better have a handful of bullets at the ready in that case.

This is not actually hunting, since there is no need to track the prey; rather, it is more like a harvest. Like the grape picked for wine, the grass on the prairies varies every year. Depending on the heat, cold, rains or droughts, the meat takes on a special taste every season. *Bang*! *Bang*! *Bang*! Sunny shoots until six bison fall with what seems like mechanical precision, although it is not easy for Sunny. When you feel true respect for an animal, you become emotionally involved. It is a very intense experience. That's why Sunny approaches the bison to ensure they do not require a coup de grace. The surviving bison appear to respect him, too. He walks among them like a bullfighter, looking directly at them.

Ted blesses the fallen animals with sacred water, which he offers to the four cardinal points in honor of the Heavenly Father and Mother Earth. "Creator, Grandfather Bison, you gave power to our people. Thank you, Grandfather Fire, Big Brother Stag, Water Spirit. Thank you." The rest of the herd gradually withdraws as Herrera begins a canticle to notify his ancestors that six new spirits are on their way so they should prepare for their arrival. The blessed water contains peyote. You have to prove that you are at least one-fourth Native American to be considered indigenous. Once you have passed this test, you can request membership from the Native American Church so that they will issue you a membership card. It is the only way to use peyote without the Public Health Department reporting you for the use of hallucinogens. "I belong to the Native Church of the Rio Grande," Ted tells me. "We don't need churches to celebrate our rituals and to respect our traditions. But that's the way things are. In Carrizo Springs, there are many Native Americans and they don't know it or don't want to. They think they're Mexicans and if you tell them otherwise, they will deny it. They become angry and you could get into a fight. No one wants to be Native American." When Teodosio Herrera first met the grandfather of JoAnn, his current wife, who is part Comanche, the old man told him: "I love you, but I asked my granddaughter not to marry you because your skin is dark and you two will have dark children. And because of that, those children will suffer." His advice came from his own struggles as a dark-skinned Indian ... but the couple didn't pay any attention to him.

The vet examines the animals and gives his okay. Gilbert and Ulfo slit the bisons' throats so that their blood can return nutrients to the soil. Then they chain the hind hooves of the first bison to the tractor's mechanical shovel, which slowly lifts the tons of pure muscle into the refrigerator truck. In two hours, the bison will be in the hands of the butcher. In the afternoon, the foreman will return with the hides and heads. The harvest is complete. Now, anyone who tastes the meat will benefit from the proteins that made the Native Americans whose diet was based on bison grow strong and tall. They were much taller than the Spanish conquerors, who were so impressed by the Indians' stature that they brought them along as bodyguards to the conquest of Mexico.

If the animals are sacrificed in winter, their hides serve to make blankets and rugs since there is wool attached to the hides. During the other seasons, since hides lose their wool, boots, gloves or vests are made from them. Motorists love the softness of the *civalo* leather goods, as the Native Americans called the bison. Each hide weighs some 55 pounds and is an inch wide at the level of the hump. Tribal women used to work it until they could fold and sew it. Now it's time to order the work of the bison tanners, which is not easy. Most tanners work with heavy metals whose use is prohibited in almost every country. The skulls are for Ted. After decorating them, he'll sell them for a few thousand dollars at a pow wow celebrated annually in New Mexico. Representatives of over 50 tribes meet at the University Arena campus in Albuquerque. At this annual gathering, traditional enemies, like the Apache and Comanche, are now working together. The challenge is to obtain a larger "drum" than the one used at the previous event. The "drum" at a Pow Wow is a group of several drummers. The more popular the "drum," the more dancers it will attract. The more people who dance, the more people will come join the celebration and contribute to its colorfulness. Native American crafts originated from these offerings. Tradition stipulates that you should offer the best you have, so to make a sacrifice you must give up something of value. If you don't obtain what you've asked for, it is because you did not make a sincere offering and you can't fool the creator. Ted, who grew up eating armadillo meat, which he says is as juicy and tender as pork, makes a good profit selling his decorated skulls. He is happy. In Real de Catorce, he met a shaman who told him: "They cut our branches, they cut our trunk, but they couldn't destroy our roots." Ted makes an effort to transfer the pride of being a Native American to his grandchildren. That includes respect for life and nature. Believing is part of the healing. But he tells me that he doesn't plan to ride a horse like his ancestors did because his Ford is a much better option.

The harvest is carried out without the stress of the slaughterhouse, which tends to darken the meat. The world-renowned doctor of animal science, Temple Grandin, recommended that Sunny sacrifice his animals out in the open. Sunny never thought he'd have to kill his bison. His idea was to buy calves and sell them as adults a couple of years later. But the day Ted Turner stopped buying bison to increase his herd, the market practically crashed and the only solution was to sell meat. It wasn't easy. First he tried in San Antonio, without success. Then he tried at the farmers' market in Austin. Finally, success arrived one afternoon in the form of a telephone call. It was the chef of a restaurant that had dared to serve bison goulash in the Texas capital. A customer had found the remains of a bullet in the stew, he said without pretext. Sunny was mortified, thinking that it was the end of his business. Oh, no, quite the contrary, said the chef, he actually thought it was cool. It proved the meat was real. He wanted to order much more.

Bison meat is pink with yellow fat, which is its natural color. It is sold in stores at double the price of beef. Consumption is still low, but there is an incipient social movement to support organic cultivation, consumption of local products and respect for the philosophy of Native Americans, all of which push bison toward their natural market niche.

Huck and I have to return to the snow back home. We spend a final night in San Antonio. It's time to thank the Fitzsimonses for the trip. We dine at a French restaurant, which, like many French restaurants in America, including one of my favorites in Rhinebeck, is called Le Petit Bistro. At the next table, Tony Parker of the Spurs is enjoying dinner with friends. Tonight I sleep in the room of one of Sunny's children, Patrick. The cork-lined ceiling is covered with posters of actors and singers. What better place for the stars than the ceiling? Watching over me are Jimi Hendrix, the Blues Brothers, Steve McQueen on a motorcycle, Bruce Lee, Guinness Extra Stout, Francisco "Pancho" Villa in a reproduction of an old Wanted Poster offering a $5,000 reward, and a black-haired girl who gives me a naughty smile. I can't keep my eyes open. But wait a minute: Isn't that Natalie Merchant smiling down at me from the cover of her album *Tigerlily*? The same girl who stopped me a few weeks ago in front of Upstate Films, the Rhinebeck movie theater?

In the morning, Sunny drives us to the airport and puts an ice chest next to our bags. "What's that?" The night before, I had mentioned Miguel Ansorena, the chef from Spain's Navarra region, whose skill at the grill is unmatched and who offers the world's best beef steak at the Imanol cider bar in Las Rozas. It's quite an institution in Spain. "It is a gift from the house so that your chef friend can prepare it," Sunny tells me with a smile. "Tell him not to punish it with too high a flame or it will be dry." Grateful, I open the white Styrofoam container to peek inside. It contains several large vacuum-packed pieces, which are frozen hard as rocks. "Thanks, but how will I take them to Madrid?" I ask. "The same way they will go to New York," says Sunny. "When you go, take them out of the freezer and put them back in the cooler with dry ice." "What kind of ice?" "Don't worry, they sell it everywhere." We hug goodbye. Thanks, I tell him, from the heart.

7

February

Today is St. Valentine's Day in Spain; on this side of the pond, they ignore the saintliness of the historic figure for which the holiday is named and just call it Valentine's Day. Besides, in North America, it's more of a celebration of love than of lovers—a subtle difference that enables people who don't have partners to participate in the holiday, thereby exponentially increasing its commercial potential.

Our children celebrate it at school. Each kid takes handmade cards to class bearing friendly messages for their classmates: "You're my best friend. I love being with you." "You're so hot!" For Sarah and me, the children have prepared some more conventional cards at school. The teachers managed to get them to the mailbox on time because they arrived last night. For this reason, we have three different versions of "I love you a lot" stuck on our refrigerator. We open the refrigerator door, grab a bottle of *cava*, close the door, verify that the love notes are still there, and go out whistling.

It is dark out by the time we reach Delmar's party. Here the temperature drops drastically as soon as the sun sets and the car tires crunch as they advance down the snowy roads, as if we were driving over pieces of stale bread. We park and suddenly realize that the only condition imposed by the host to attend his Valentine's Day dinner was to wear something red. Oops. Too late. The only thing we've got at hand is the cap to a red marker we keep in the glove box. Feeling like a nerd, I put it in my shirt pocket. Oh well, let's go in.

Delmar Hendricks looks like the man he is—a nice guy. He is now a consultant for Lincoln Center in New York, but for many years he handled 700 performances per season as a booking director for both the Avery Fisher Hall and the Alice Tulley Hall. Absolutely passionate about theater and opera, Delmar has added a new appreciation to his life in the country: the joy of gardening. It's a shame it's so late because the little red lights decorating the trees do not give off enough light for us to enjoy the splendid flowerbed, fish ponds and many sculptures scattered over the hillside. We greet the other guests. Some men wear carnations in their lapels. John Corcoran, creator of one of the works of art that adorn the property, is wearing a red hat with large earmuffs which, he explains, his grandfather used to wear while foxhunting. His wife, Liza Macrae, a landscape artist who combines native flowers with the skill of an Impressionist painter to create gardens, talks with Rachel Simon, John's friend since their student days in the art department of the experimental Goddard College. Rachel designs elegant lamps for her own company, Lights Up. Her mother, a writer who works at a cultural institution in New York City, gives her passes for the shows she can't attend, but since Rachel spends a lot of time in China, every now and then I get passed a ticket to an interesting event. In other words, Rachel is my very own Foreign Press Center.

Thanks to this pecking order, I recently had the enormous fortune to meet at City College the man who enjoyed a reputation of having the highest credibility in the United States for more than half a century: CBS Evening News anchorman Walter Cronkite, the very one who always ended the program with his famous "and that's the way it is." He was celebrated for his re-transmission of the Apollo 11 moon landing, his visit to Vietnam and his excellent interviews on the Watergate scandal. He learned how to slow down his speech until he managed a deliberate form of expression that made him wildly popular in the 1960s and 1970s. Cronkite spoke on television at the studied pace of 124 words per minute. That's slow compared with the 165 words the average American pronounces per minute during a normal conversation.

I began as a radio reporter in Madrid under Jesús Hermida, a great journalist who had been a TV correspondent in New York for many years and who greatly admired Cronkite. Hermida always commented on how generous Cronkite was with his staff, so I was determined to emulate the feats of the man from Missouri some day. One winter afternoon, at the time that I was chief editor of the Antena 3 Radio nightly news program, Pilar, the office secretary, told me that her father was coming for a visit that afternoon. Pilar's father was a very humble, slight man who wore a beret pulled down to his eyebrows. He had traveled from a remote Galician village to verify the modest professional successes of his daughter in the capital. I suggested to Hermida that he lend Pilar his office during her father's visit so that he could return to his village a proud man. He agreed and the secretary sat in the old man's leather chair. Already impressed that his daughter would work in such a large, luxurious office, the old man's eyes widened like saucers when he saw Spain's most famous TV personality, Jesús Hermida, enter and address his daughter in the following terms: "Do you have an assignment for me, Pilar? I'm at your service." Pilar, somewhat embarrassed, shook her head and proceeded to introduce the television star to her father. The handshake was worthy of a World Press Photo award, and the villager's expression suggested that he was anxious to get back home to tell the whole town about it.

Bonjour! Philippe Labeau, Rachel's husband, is 100 percent French when it comes to eating and drinking wine, but pure American when it comes to defending the opportunities this nation offers. "If I'd stayed in Paris, I would have been buried in shit," he told me once over a bottle of Rioja, whose qualities he found difficult to recognize given that it wasn't from France. "A guy like me, without money and lousy at school, would only be able to work in a factory in France. Here, though… just look at me." "I'm trying," I protest. "I look at you … but where?" Philippe has one eye that veers to the side, like Marty Feldman's in *The Young Frankenstein*. "You're going to drive me nuts if you don't look at the eye that doesn't wander, dammit!" he says. I ignore the wandering eye and that's it, problem solved. You see? Just ask and you'll learn the answer. As women suggest to us all the time, it's always better to ask. The three Wise Men wouldn't have lost their way to Bethlehem if they had stopped for a minute to ask for directions. "Get down off your camel, Mr. Balthasar, pose a simple question and the three of you will make it on time." But no, and now we have to sing the carol till the Twelfth Night of Christmas.

In Brooklyn, Philippe has his own Video Assist Company for the movies. He learned how to operate the equipment, decided to buy some, and now has constant work on shoots, especially for television ads. It seems that the fascination for filming an ad in Manhattan is alive and well. Every week, some foreign ad agency arrives to town. He works only a couple of days a week. "I travel, meet some interesting people, earn some money. I have a house in Brooklyn and a weekend house in this Hudson Valley paradise. What more could I ask for?" I suggest another glass of Spanish wine. "Oh, *non, non, non.* No way, man, let me open a bottle of Bordeaux. You know what I mean, right?"

Our children love Philippe because he's one of the few adults who addresses them without trying to be courteous. He swears and teases them mercilessly. Of course it helps that he is naturally warm and friendly, not to mention the fact that he lets them shoot paintballs with his rifle, gives them firecrackers to bury in the sand and make cans fly through the air and gives them bling resembling the garish jewelry that rappers wear.

Delmar! At last we spot the host of the party in the kitchen. We say hello and thank him for the invitation. We are amazed by everything he has prepared for the occasion. Triple red. The first dish is a tomato soup topped with a cloud of sour cream. Excellent. A beef stew is the main course, followed by a chocolate cake topped with raspberries. Finger-licking good. The red crystal glasses for the white wine are in keeping with the party's color scheme.

Carrying our plates as we wander around Delmar's home, I get the sensation that we are on a private visit to a modern art museum. Many of the pieces in his collection are associated with his years heading up the poster and print program at Lincoln Center. But let's rewind a little. The actual home of the Metropolitan Opera, the New York City Ballet and the New York Philharmonic Orchestra opened in 1962. Four years later, Hendricks got an offer to be the house manager. It was only six weeks after Delmar staged his last Broadway show: Maine, with Angela Lansbury. By then, Lincoln Center only had the concert hall rented by the Philharmonic but it was better money and a tempting challenge, so Hendricks moved to 10 Lincoln Center Plaza. And it didn't take him too long to realize that the artists prefer to play that venue because they don't have to deal with the subway vibrations of Carnegie Hall!

But two big stars in music particularly liked working in Avery Fisher Hall: the Spanish guitar player Andrés Segovia and the Polish pianist Artur Rubinstein. When Rubenstein chose to celebrate his 80th birthday on that stage, Lincoln Center decided to honor the occasion. Before the concert, Delmar went up to Mr. Rubinstein's dressing room—a level above the stage—and accompanied him at the elevator down to the stage where they were alone for a moment. There, the booking director presented him with a geode, one of those marvelous stones with a beautiful interior. Rubinstein said, "Thank you very much, Mr. Hendricks. I guess it's better to have a stone given to you before the performance, than one thrown at you after it." Then he looked back at his Steinway piano tuner (a buddy who traveled with him everywhere) and asked him: "What are we playing now?" The tuner told him and he said, "Oh, yes," and started to hum. "Tee too teee, tee tee tah ... okay!" And off he went to meet his public. That was his way of remembering.

During this time period Delmar met a magnificent philanthropist called Vera List and, with her help, he headed up a new poster and print program. When you think about Lincoln Center, the first thing that comes to mind is a cultural center whose stages have been graced by some of the best in the business, but Delmar also focused on the creativity of the programs and posters announcing their performances. Vera and her husband were among the first people that Mr. Rockefeller called asking for contribution for the Lincoln Center in the late 1950s. The Lists had a lot of cash at that point because they had just sold their company: BVD underwear. So, with Vera's inspiration, Delmar jumped into the visual arts. He went to visit galleries and began to hire top artists to design the billboards. The results of this initiative—undertaken by the likes of Helen Frankenthaler, Robert Motherwell and Gerhard Richter—are on exhibit in the Lincoln Center gallery. It is definitely worth a visit although few people know about it because it is hidden in the basement of Lincoln Center.

Delmar began his career in the theater as a stage manager. For 10 years he worked on tours and Broadway and Off-Broadway shows. And he had a blast. He recalls bringing actors like Ginger Rogers and Ben Johnson to an enormous outdoor theater in Atlanta. The stars, then in their fifties, were not as famous as they had been in their twenties, but they still had big enough names to fill thousands of seats. "We had to have a certain percentage of actors who belonged to the union," he explains. "And because of that equity requirement, during the summer stocks I often had to play parts for the smaller companies. Just to fill the gaps." And he loved it although, he modestly admits, amid laughter, that he wasn't any good. We insist that he couldn't have been that bad. Another guest points out that acting well depend on one's taste... He lowers his voice to a whisper and says, "I don't know if you know that Andrew Lloyd Weber had to pay $1 million to a certain female actor so she wouldn't play Sunset Boulevard on Broadway! She played the lead role in London and had it stipulated in her contract that she would also do the New York production. But Weber hated her so Glenn Close played the part on Broadway." Wow. Apparently, the mysterious actress was the one who did *Evita*; so some of us launch into the familiar chorus: "Don't cry for me Argentinaaa..."

On this evening of love, the main topic of discussion among the guests at the table is the French government's decision to forbid the use of Muslim head coverings in public schools. Opinions differ. We talk about the dangers of mixing the divine with the human, of the role of religions in military conflicts. I recall the special reports I broadcast from Sarajevo after the fratricide there. The testimonies I heard there filled me with indignation. An Orthodox Christian recalled that during his childhood, the priest forbade him to play with certain children because they were Muslim. On the other side, a Bosnian mullah made the same comment, but in reverse, telling Muslim children not to get involved with any kids whose parents had not embraced Islam.

* * *

Today is the third Wednesday of the month and the municipal truck assigned to pick up cardboard passes by first thing in the morning. It's time to put the collapsed boxes in a pile next to the sidewalk. It is truly astounding how much trash this society generates. There is more packaging than actual goods.

Jumping on an empty printer box in an attempt to eliminate one of its three dimensions for recycling, I spot my brother Javier engaged in a similar operation two houses down. He shouts out to ask me if I've got a flashlight. I tell him I do, but I want to know what he needs it for. "Just bring it." I complete the box-squishing and go over to his house to see what he wants. Javier has just moved here with his wife, Piluca, and their three kids to work on the *Cándida* script with me. It's our third movie together, the first one I'm directing. We were collaborating via the Internet, which was not very efficient. I prefer much better human interaction than machines. Like the bumper sticker that says: "Sometimes when the Internet doesn't work I talk to my family ... and they seem to be nice people." When Javier came for a visit to discuss a scene, Sarah encouraged him to move here for a few months and found him a rental house down the street from ours. So we're neighbors now. The corner of Parsonage and Chestnut Streets is Rhinebeck's Spanish Harlem. "I have to show you something," he says, excitedly. I grab the flashlight and we go down to the basement. Shelves are overflowing with rusty tools, cogs, unidentifiable utensils, car parts, broken lamps, tiles, a box of ball bearings ... it is a junkman's sanctuary. "That's not what I wanted to show you," he says. He removes a piece of plywood from the floor to uncover a 3-foot-wide hole. He tells me to point the flashlight toward it. "What the hell?" I jump in. It's not too deep. I kneel down and see a little passage heading south. I go in with the flashlight, walking several yards before it ends suddenly. "That's it, it's over." "Could it be an air chamber?" my brother asks. "I don't know, it's very strange. Really weird."

A few days later, I see Valerie Kilmer, the village clerk, and I take advantage of the encounter to ask her if she knows the owner of the house my brother is renting. "Sort of," she responds. "I went to school with him." "Would you know by any chance why in hell he has a tunnel in his basement?" "A tunnel?" "That's what it looks like. A big hole that could be used to hide something." Valerie shrugs her shoulders. Just as I'm about to head through the door of the Town Hall, I hear her mumble something under her breath: "Maybe it was a stop of the Underground Railroad." I turn around. "An underground railroad?" I ask. "The tunnels through which the slaves escaped," she says. "As far as I know, we had three stops in Rhinebeck: one on Livingston Street, another on East Market and a third on Oak Street."

* * *

On the bicentenary of the founding of the United States, February was declared official Black History Month. It is an opportunity to recognize the enormous contribution of 13 percent of the population to this country's development. The initial idea came from Carter Woodson, who in 1912 became the first black man to earn a degree from Harvard University. Woodson launched Black History Month to commemorate the birth, in February 1818, of Frederick Douglass, the lion of Anacostia, an American Abolitionist of impressive intellect. Years later February would also mark the beginning of a new uprising by the descendants of the slaves.

On February 1, 1960, four students from North Carolina Agricultural and Technical State University in Greensboro made history. They sat at the counter of a Woolworth's cafeteria and asked for a menu. They received no response. Only whites were served at the tables and counters; African Americans had to order and consume their food standing up. The four remained seated for hours, which turned into days, waiting to be served. It was the call that launched the Civil Rights Movement. The possibility that a candidate of African American origin would one day occupy the White House was simply unthinkable at the time. On the second day, other people joined the original four until there were 27. By the third day, they numbered 300; on the fourth day, 1,000 black youth demanded to be served by the bewildered white waiters. And the South exploded. Massive protests were organized in 54 cities of the nine states with the largest African-American populations. The rest is history.

African Americans who want to know more about their origins take advantage of February to make pilgrimages to Africa. On the West Coast of Africa, the homeland of the millions of the people who would work the fields in the United States, there are two sanctuaries that must be seen: Gorée Island in Senegal and the town of Mandinka in Gambia, where the main character of *Roots*, Kunta Kinte, grew up. ...

African Americans' reencounters with their relatives on the other side of the Atlantic tend to be difficult. During these painful journeys, many visitors reproach the locals and may even accuse them of being traitors. "Why did your father sell mine?"

The Egyptians invented slavery some 1,500 years before the Christian era. In need of manual labor to build their funerary monuments to the pharaohs, they made expeditions to northern Sudan in search of muscular Nubian laborers. The Roman Empire inherited this custom from Egypt. However, Egypt did not want to give up the business so Egyptians acted as intermediaries between Europeans and slave traders in the continent's interior for centuries. In the seventh century the expansion of the Koran doctrine and the search for gold and salt led caravans to

Central Africa, which would bring back more prisoners to the slave trade centers of the East Coast.

The balance of power in the slave market shifted with the Portuguese invention of the caravel; an upgraded version of an Arab boat, called a *carib*, that could sail against the wind. Thanks to this new ship, Portugal was able to move the slave market to the West Coast, sidestepping the Egyptian middle man. This was the root of the modern conflict between the West and the Arab world.

The House of Slaves and its Door of No Return is a memorial to the Atlantic slave trade on Gorée Island in Senegal. Those who rebelled were kept in punishment cells to persuade them to change their minds. These windowless, suffocating, humid rooms were filled will recalcitrant prisoners for weeks on end. Joseph N'Diaye, the guardian of the museum, which was declared a UNESCO World Heritage Site in 1978, still recalls Nelson Mandela's bitter tears during his official visit there when he was the president of South Africa. Mandela had spent a few moments in silence in the dark cell and when he emerged, tears filled his eyes. "It reminded me a lot of my cell in the Robben Island prison," Mandela confessed.

When the Portuguese reached Gorée's harbor in 1444, they found a peaceful fishing community. Less than two miles across from the Dakar coast, the Lebou, skilled mariners, took their *pirogues* to sea in search of fish. The Lebou, hired today by their desperate, impoverished neighbors in Sub-Saharan Africa to take them by fishing boat to Spanish beaches, the entry port to Europe, can interpret the ocean by the color of its tides. The waters turn black when schools of squid predominate; blue due to the presence of tuna and sardine; green when sea bass are present; and yellow when sharks are lying in wait. At the time of the Portuguese arrival, no one suspected that the ocean foam could also turn red. But it did ... with the blood of the thousands who refused to be taken as slaves and as a result, were slaughtered, their bodies thrown off a cliff.

In 1510, after hearing about the weak native laborers who had died from exhaustion in the fields of the Americas, the spanish king authorized the deportation of Africans to its overseas colonies.

The Portuguese, Dutch, English and French all hired inhabitants of the West African coast to find victims among the more backward groups of the African bush. "Why did your father sell mine?" Slavery came to the U.S. coast in 1619. A Dutch ship, *Man of Warre*, sold 20 black men to the settlers of Jamestown, Virginia. This was a year before the *Mayflower* would dock in Massachusetts. The Yoruba of Nigeria—whom American plantation owners coveted as studs—and the well-built Mandinka laborers suffered the greatest losses. The Europeans had done the math and knew that for every 200 men shipped, just 60 would arrive in good condition to the markets. More than 6 million people died during the ocean crossings.

* * *

In February, Rhinebeck schools celebrate Black History Month with special activities. The local paper announces a conference for fourth- and fifth-graders on the Underground Railroad and the Freedom Quilts. I recall Valerie's words at Rhinebeck Town Hall and my enthusiasm grows. Ms. Trish Chambers will give the presentation wearing clothes from the Civil War period. The announcement acknowledges the generosity of the donations to the Town Museum, which made the event possible. I call Max's teacher to ask her if I can go. Mrs. Menconeri agrees. Yeah!

The kids applaud loudly when Ms. Chambers, from Poughquag, New York, appears on stage dressed in clothes from the period and accompanied by a young actor. She explains that she is dressed just like her countrywomen during the years before the Civil War. "Southern residents had access to textiles from Europe," she explains, "but we didn't. Northern inhabitants had to work hard for a living. I've decorated my hat with paper flowers and feathers from native bird species. The dress

I'm wearing is dark, with small drawings. It's a trick we use to hide stains and burns from the coal stoves since these are our only clothes. My companion, as you can see, is in full color. In effect: brown pants, flowery vest and black jacket. There are no clothing stores where we come from. He had to travel to have a suit made. It is very elegant, but clothes get worn out. Today, trying to dress his best, he had to combine the pants with the jacket from another suit."

Ms. Chambers tells us that the name Underground Railroad originated from the story of Tice Davids, a Kentucky slave who escaped from a plantation in 1831 and reached the Ohio River. His master was hot on his trail and finally caught up with him as he swam in the river. Just as he was about to reach him by boat, the sound of a bell distracted him for a minute. When he turned around again to look for his prey, the man had disappeared. The bewildered master told his friends that the slave must have fled through an underground road. The feat was widely repeated and "underground road" was soon used to describe all mysterious escapes. Later, with the arrival of the railroad and the fascination that invention inspired, the organization became known as the Underground Railroad and those who led it called themselves conductors.

The conductors advised the fugitives on how to move from one stop to another. They protected them and sent coded messages to the next conductor to alert him of the fugitive's arrival. "Uncle Tom says that if the roads are not too bad, you can expect the wool bales by tomorrow. Send them on to market to test the price; there's no additional charge." In other words: "Some slaves will arrive tomorrow morning and they should be sent on to the next stop because there are no signs of danger."

On the Hudson River, the slave boats docked at the ports of Kingston on the west side and Poughkeepsie on the east. From there, the human merchandise was taken to the market on Catherine Street. In 1790, there were 420 slaves in Rhinebeck. The largest slaveholder, Henry Livingston, had three. Like the rest of the states on the East Coast, in New York, slaves were treated with more decency than in the South.

Many of them ate at the same table as their masters and few suffered the aberration of being sold or separated from their families. Soon the people in the Hudson Valley joined the secret escape system that opened the doors to freedom in Canada.

In the basement at 12 Livingston Street, there is a 6-foot tunnel lined in stone with a wood-beamed ceiling. Inside the tunnel coins from 1810, a gold crucifix and old bottles and cases of alcohol were found. The gallery leads north to what was an open lot with a small church on it in the early 19th century. From Rhinebeck, the fugitives went to Millbrook or Pawling and from there to Albany and then on to Syracuse. They then traveled to Rochester and finally, to Canada.

The first challenge the Abolitionists had to face was to overcome the language barrier. Africans didn't know how to read or write since they had been denied an education by law to avoid uprisings. Besides that, slaves of numerous ethnic groups lived together but could barely communicate with one another. The second major problem was that slaves were not familiar with the stars in the night sky. The African peoples traditionally got their bearings from the sun, which was useless for the escaping expats since they had to remain hidden during daylight hours. The problem was further compounded by a third stumbling block: the lack of familiarity with the lands the slaves had to cross to reach freedom. The solution was to send secret messages to the slaves on the plantations so that they could make a mental map of their escape route.

In an effort to infiltrate the plantations, Underground Railroad conductors and Abolitionists traveled to the south. Perhaps the best known was Peg Leg Joe, who risked his life going from plantation to plantation to teach the slaves to sing a gospel song called "The Drinking Gourd." The music, which was permitted by the guards of the work fields during the most difficult farm work, proved an excellent way to secretly communicate instructions for the mass escape plan. The "drinkin' gou'd," a hollowed out gourd used in the plantations of rural America as a water dipper, had exactly the same shape as the Big Dipper star formation.

At the end of the handle was the North Star, aligned with the Earth's axis, which appears fixed in position, constantly pointing to the North Pole. The point of reference used by mariners during their voyages was finally within the reach of a people that had never paid much attention to celestial signs. The information spread like wildfire among the slaves as they plowed the land, attended church or gathered in their huts.

From Mississippi to Carolina, the slaves sang, "Follow the Drinking Gourd," to one another. The song was a complete manual for escaping the tyranny. "When the sun come back, When the firs' quail call, Then the time is come, Foller the drinking gourd."

On December 21, the winter solstice, the sun begins to rise a bit higher in the sky each day. That was Peg Leg Joe's sign. The escape had to take place in winter, for reasons we'll get to in a minute. If someone got confused while looking at the sky, the sound of the quails as they migrated south over the fields during the coldest season of the year would clear up any doubts. The second verse served to encourage the slaves: "The riva's bank am a very good road, The dead trees show the way, Lef' foot, peg foot goin' on, Foller the drinkin' gou'd." The chorus was: "Oh, Foller the drinkin' gou'd. For the Ole Man say, Foller the drinkin' gou'd. Foller the drinkin' gou'd." These lyrics were a call to the hundreds of thousands of black people who were forced to work near the Tombigbee River in Alabama and Mississippi. On overcast nights, when the clouds covered the stars, the river served as a point of reference for the journey north. In addition, Peg Leg Joe had used charcoal or mud to draw a left human foot and a round spot in place of the right foot on the trees as a sign to the escapees that they were on the right path. The song went on to explain that at the end of the river, another would appear, the Tennessee River, which they should also follow. The song ends with the arrival to the banks of the great Ohio River, which had to be crossed to reach the Promised Land. "Oooh, folleeeeeer the driiiinkin gouuuuuuud."

The average journey from the work fields to salvation on the banks of the Ohio River lasted a bit more than a year. Slaves had to flee in late

December so they could reach the river in winter, when it was frozen solid and they could cross it on foot. The slaves, who came from the African bush, didn't know how to swim. Although hundreds of Underground Railroad collaborators sporadically patrolled the river in search of new Tice Davids to hide from the masters chasing them, they also looked for bounty hunters in the area.

Peg Leg Joe was not the only one to camouflage secret messages in the songs sung on the plantations. Anyone with a good gospel music collection may be surprised after analyzing the lyrics. The continual reference to the house of God and home is code for a free country where the slaves can feel as if they were in heaven. Famous gospel songs like "The Gospel Train's a'Comin'" and "Swing Low, Sweet Chariot" directly describe the Underground Railroad and their conductors. In the former, the lyrics speak of a train that is arriving which has room for many more and that makes several stops along the way. In the latter, one verse says: "I looked over Jordan, and what did I see, Comin' for to carry me home, A band of angels comin' after me. Coooomin' fooor to carry meee hooome." It is a lovely tribute to the town of Ripley, located on a hill on the banks of the Ohio River, from which the Abolitionists would help the fugitives cross the river.

* * *

In the events room at Chancellor Livingston Elementary School, Ms. Trish Chambers shows the children a drawing on a blackboard. "Do you know what this is?" she asks. "It is a traditional blanket made from rags that the slaves patched together. Do you know what it's called?" "I do, I do!" several students enthusiastically respond. Ms. Chambers picks the boy in the green sweater sitting in the second row. "A quilt!" "Yes, it's a quilt." Max turns around, seemingly wondering why in the world his father is there. But when I ask him about it later, he tells me it doesn't make the slightest bit of difference to him.

Besides slaves, the Southern plantations had another person who, although she wasn't beaten and got to sleep in a comfortable bed, worked as hard as a mule or a slave: the master's wife. She was responsible for making all the clothes for everyone living on the premises—white and black. She had to complete this task along with other chores that slaves were not permitted to perform, such as going through the mail, for example. In the United States, the women's movement had yet to begin and women at the time did not have it easy. They had to give birth to their children in the living room since the master of the house would not allow the physician to enter the private rooms upstairs. When the couple visited a photographer to immortalize themselves in separate portraits, to save money, the wife's photo was made from the negative-plate previously used to photograph her husband. That is why on the mantle above the fireplace at Poplar Grove, a peanut plantation in North Carolina, the lovely woman of the house looks like the bearded lady at the Ringling Brothers' Circus. It wasn't that women were more masculine at the time. It was just that their husbands' negative superimposed the men's moustaches over their delicate features.

The only fun the wives of the plantation masters had within their golden prisons occurred on Saturday afternoons in the form of a dance. They would push the living and dining room furniture aside to make room for a dance floor and a live orchestra. Unfortunately, in keeping with the strict Methodist doctrine, the party had to end at midnight. However, since those ladies were not willing to give up the only entertainment God granted them on this Earth, they would often order a slave to move back the hands of the clock as midnight approached in an attempt to extend the party for a couple of hours more.

Given that plantations had a minimum of 20 slaves, it is no surprise that the woman of the house did not have enough time to sew decent clothes for everyone. Curiously, in Africa, men are generally responsible for sewing, but the European tradition imported to the Americas imposed its rules and the women taught their female slaves to sew. Not out of charity but out of self-interest. The slaves' dressmaking services brought in some extra income to the plantation. Women would rent out the services of the Africans to relatives or friends, and in the operation, the seamstresses enjoyed more freedom of movement. To keep up appearances, the women would lend the slaves their own clothes or give them permission to accept tips. In this way, several women were able to buy their freedom in exchange for the money received for their labor outside of the plantation.

On the plantation, these slaves devoted their limited free time to making blankets for their families. They worked on them in the evenings, robbing themselves of valuable hours of sleep after an exhausting workday, or during their free afternoons on Sundays. They would join pieces of rag to a cord made from strips of tobacco or flour sacks. The quilt designs faithfully reflected their tribal traditions. Although quite varied, the quilts had no closed lines because the slaves did not want to attract bad spirits that, according to their beliefs, would attach themselves to the rectilinear roots of the trees. Once the quilts were finished, they were briefly spread out on the roofs of the shacks for good luck. Where everyone could see them. This practice soon became such a familiar sight, such a mysterious "black thing," that it did not seem strange to the masters. The Underground Railroad conductors knew this and decided to take advantage of the opportunity.

Ms. Chambers tells the kids that the quilts served as secret maps. They gave instructions and warned of dangers using a set of symbols familiar to the ethnic groups of Western Africa. They were hung in the plantations and the Underground Railroad stations leading to Canada. Each quilt would have a single symbol to decipher. The abolitionists tried to make it as easy as possible for the fugitives. A red square in the center of an icon that depicted a hut meant heat: come in, you're welcome. When the square was dark, it meant that they were in a safe place but that they should not attempt to come today.

Ms. Chambers uses a pointer to call attention to several geometric shapes, each with its own name and explanation. She says that one is called "drunk's path" because of the zigzagging lines. "Do you see them?" "Yes!!" "It is a sign to the slaves that they should leave the marked path because there are bounty hunters in the area. One of the recommended tricks was to temporarily go in the other direction since a black man heading South was never a cause for suspicion. This is the bear's claw," she says. According to Ms. Chambers, this meant that the slaves should seek refuge in the mountains and, once there, should follow the path of a bear as it will lead to food and water. "Who knows what this is?" "I do, I do!!" "An hourglass." "It could be, but it isn't. It symbolizes a bowtie. It means that it is time to disguise oneself, time to change out of slave's clothes." She goes on to explain the plaiting of the Irish chain stitch, which represents chains. Slaves escaped by yanking their chains from the wall, but they could not break the shackles binding their hands and feet. This symbol told them that there was someone nearby they could trust, no doubt an ironsmith, who could help remove the shackles. Ms. Chambers introduces a dozen more drawings: a boat, geese, a flower wreath. She ends by asking for a big round of applause for her companion, the boy wearing the brown pants with a red flowered vest. Time's up, kids. The students line up to return their classrooms.

On the half-mile drive home from Max's school, Natalie Merchant's "Motherland" comes on the radio. The melody exudes a sadness that seeps into the bones. It is quite poignant. Daniel De la Calle told me that Natalie was doing a photo shoot for the album cover on the banks of the Hudson on the morning of September 11, 2001, when she was surprised to see an American Airlines plane flying almost level with the water. It was the plane that would hit the first World Trade Center tower just minutes later. The terrorists followed the river to reach Manhattan. The gaping wound that brutal impact left in the hearts of millions of Americans is reflected in each note of the song. "Motherland, cradle me. Close my eyes. Lullaby me to sleep. Keep me safe. Lie with me. Stay beside me. Don't go, don't you goooo ... " I turn up the volume. "Motherland" helps me to imagine the immense sadness of the Mandinka warriors chained in the holds of the Dutch ships en route to the New World. "Motherland" is good for any sadness. Natalie didn't compose it thinking of the Twin Towers, but it fits the tremendous sorrow that followed the attack. But while "Motherland" beautifully reflects sadness, it simultaneously offers a glimmer of hope. "Cradle me. Lullaby me to sleep." Like a child who has had a nightmare and is desperately calling for her mother. In other words, sadness is mixed with hope, with the possibility that the mother will appear and "Keep me safe. Lie with me." I suddenly think about the movie scene in which the main character is destroyed because he can't be with the woman he loves. I can't wait to call my brother Javier and make him listen to Natalie Merchant's song. "Motherland" fits perfectly with the sense of emptiness and the desire to find love again. Great works of art are for everyone. I hope I can get the rights to the song for *Cándida* because music is the most important part of a movie. Music without images can work, but no one wants images without music.

March

Sarah's excited voice wakes me up. "He's here! Guillermo, get up! The guy with the camera is in front of the house again!" I hesitate a bit before reacting. I have a hard time waking up and, besides, we got to bed late after a night of noshing on American buffalo ribs. Given the generosity of Sunny, who gave us two huge pieces of meat, we decided to keep one in the freezer to take to Spain and enjoy the other one at home with friends. The exquisite preparation was in the hands of a high-ranking individual from the CIA. Not the espionage CIA, where we think we may also have a friend (we are highly suspect of someone who frequently travels to the Middle East), but rather the CIA located 10.7 miles south of here: the Culinary Institute of America. It is a nonprofit culinary college where any visitor who enjoys food can have a near orgasmic experience. Located on a beautiful property overlooking the Hudson, in a majestic building that formerly housed a Jesuit novitiate, the CIA offers degree programs on Culinary Arts and Baking and Pastry Arts. It is the West Point of chef schools and is run much like a military academy—with order, cleanliness, efficiency. Every day, nearly 3,000 students follow the instructions of 130 chefs who, representing 16 countries with specially interesting culinary traditions, teach classes and manage five restaurants open to the public on the campus. The classrooms look much like the set of a TV cooking show and can be seen through the windows in the hallway. In one of the kitchens, the students prepare rhubarb pies. There has been a growing interest in using local produce in the kitchens to support Hudson Valley suppliers. American chefs have always idolized French cuisine, but in my opinion, French sauces are too rich: because they were invented to disguise the stench of the rotten fish and poultry that was delivered by coach to the Louvre Palace. Now the American chefs are taking a fresh look at their own resources and learning the art of eating the landscape. The privilege of surviving on the bounty that their surroundings provided. That's why the Mediterranean diet is so tasteful ... and so difficult to export: because cooking, in a country like Spain or Portugal, consists mainly of knowing how to choose a good product at the market. If you get a fresh fish, all you need to do is sauté it in the pan. Do you want a good salad? Peel and slice an orange and just add a little bit of paprika, black olives and red onion and a splash of olive oil. It's idiot proof.

Charlie Rascoll, the chef who dared to cook a bison at home last night, teaches Mediterranean cooking at the CIA. He has traveled to Spain many times and knows every ingredient, every original name of every wine. "Did you bring my thermometer?" he anxiously asks his wife, Debbie Howe, as he checks the oven. "Of course," she says, knowing that her husband would be terribly upset if he couldn't use his thermometer to check the inside temperature of the meat. When they go out, she always sticks it in her purse. Chefs have the same problem as doctors: friends are always making them work. "Would you mind taking a look at this bump on my neck?" they ask. "Would you mind just tasting this soup? Does it have enough salt?" That's why doctors always carry a stethoscope in the glove box of their car and chefs always have a meat thermometer handy. Although if you're going to compare, doctors get the bad end of the deal because chefs generally have the opportunity to enjoy what they prepare but doctors normally don't consume their patients.

But let's rewind to last night. ... Standing in front of the stove, I'm approached by Charlie, who whispers in my ear, "The secret is butter." I look at him a bit confused; for a moment, I think he might just be a member of the other CIA and he's speaking to me in code. "The secret to

196

what?" I ask. "To the flavor of your meat, dummy," he responds, making me think of the other great defender of the fatty portion of milk: Julia Child. Charlie decided to approach the buffalo meat as a piece of game rather than beef. The butter was used in place of the bacon with which game used to be wrapped. He opens the oven door just a bit and sticks the thermometer into the roast. The red line on the metal thermometer begins to rise and stops at exactly 135°F. "Perfect!" he says. It smells delicious. He removes the roast from the oven and prepares a sauce made with the butter mixed with the dripping juices. He adds a few spring onions and begins to reduce the mixture over low heat. "Charlie, what would have happened if you'd left your thermometer at home?" I ask, curious. "I would have just used my hands," he says, shrugging his shoulders. "No way!" "No, seriously, don't you know the trick?" He asks me to extend my right hand and then grabs my index finger. "Relax your arm!" he says as he shakes my hand to loosen it up. "Much better." Then, as if he were a ventriloquist act in Vegas and I were his dummy, he guides my index finger to my face and uses it to push my cheek intermittently. As if he were repeatedly ringing a doorbell. "Can you feel it?" he asks. "How could I not?" It's a very strange sensation, being attacked by part of your own body. The terrible case of the kamikaze finger. "Pay attention," he says in a professorial tone, "because the feel of the cheek is the feel of rare meat." He then leads my finger to my chin. "A bit tougher, am I right?" I agree, testing it to prove he's right. "Yes, it's exactly what a steak should feel like if you've been asked to cook it medium rare." Finally, he pushes my finger against the tip of my nose; a texture tougher than the previous ones. "And this is what well done feels like."

But now it's morning and the "photo guy" has returned and is taking out his camera again! I run downstairs in my camouflage pajamas that the Three Wise Men brought me while I was away. I spot the enemy car parked on the other side of the street and can make out the profile of an individual leaning out of the window. My blood is boiling. I open the front door and run out into the street like a wounded lion towards the car. As I run, I thank the lucky stars that my culture hasn't accustomed me to keep weapons at home because in my desperate situation, who knows what I would have been capable of. It's been six months since his first mysterious appearance and, ever since, I've dreamed of confronting him and marching him before the authorities. Our kids raised the first voice of alarm one day when Sarah and I returned from the office of our vet, Dr. Tumolo, our beagle Lola's best friend. They told us there was a man who had been snooping around the garage while we were away and taking pictures from the street. "Who was it?" "We don't know. Did you ask him what he wanted?" "There wasn't enough time," said Max. "When the guy saw me running toward the car, he took off." Well, my oldest son didn't exactly use the term "take off" to refer to the way the individual fled. He used a Spanish phrase that, when translated into English, means "get the hell out of here while throwing Communion wafers," which, believe it or not, is a very offensive thing to say in my country.

A few weeks after the first photo guy scare, the spy was spotted again. This time, he was located inside a car parked along the sidewalk. The man was taking photos. The information provided by Adriana, a friend who was taking care of the kids for a few hours, led us to seek an answer to a question that had begun to seriously intrigue us. Perhaps he wasn't taking pictures of our house, but rather the street, in preparation for some public works. Perhaps he was a city employee who wanted to document the century-old trees previously marked with a red X. But no. When he appeared again, it was clear that the camera was pointed directly at our yard, our house and its inhabitants. It occurred to me that it could be some misguided paparazzi that mistakenly thought that my private life would somehow interest the gossip circles in Spain. It didn't make much sense, but since the sensationalist press is widely popular, I thought that maybe, faced with the disproportionate demand for famous people, the paparazzi had opted to enlarge its list of victims to include us, the SKP, or Semi-Known-People. But then a close encounter of the third kind occurred ("*Papá*, come home, the weird guy is here again") and we discarded the possibility of a reporter for obvious reasons. The paparazzi can be bothersome, but they don't tend to be so moronic as to waste their valuable time taking photographs of a garage with a basketball hoop on it.

At the Rhinebeck Town Hall Sarah was told that the administrators were not planning any works in the area that could involve the photographic documentation performed by the individual described. Sometimes, they explained, they do take photos of properties to include the new homes and recalculate taxes, but they weren't doing so at the time. I began to go down the list of probabilities in my head and became increasingly worried with each new turn of the screw. Is he a violent man? In Spain there were a handful of journalists who had been threatened by ETA, the Basque terrorist organization. In my professional environment, we lived among colleagues who had gotten used to the uncomfortable routine of putting up with the constant presence of bodyguards or police officers. In recent months on our radio program, we had begun to launch severe criticism against the intolerant criminals. Since this coincided time-wise with a strange episode near my home, I couldn't help but put two and two together. Early one morning as I was walking out of my house on the way to the radio station, a car passed by and then quickly went into reverse. Intuition told me to jump out of the way and go back inside. I heard the screeching of tires and when I looked outside, I saw the car turn around at the end of the street, drive into the wrong lane and jump the median. I scribbled down the license plate. When I mentioned the incident to the head of security at the radio, his expression was worrying. For days after that, he personally came to pick me up and we did all sorts of things to mix up our routes and avoid red lights. After a week of uncertainty, he went to see me and patted me on the back. "It's over." "Really?" "You don't have to worry; we found the car." "What was it?" "Nothing, it was something else. It doesn't have anything to do with what we suspected." I don't think I'd ever felt more relieved in my whole life. Now, however, considering the irrationality of terrorism, I'm starting to wonder if the mysterious photographer is planning an unpleasant surprise for my family. I urgently needed to hear the voice of a reasonable person telling me I am just imagining things, that I should just calm down and not give too much importance to the presence of the Third Man.

The occasion presents itself during dinner with Sarah's step-brother, Bruce Howe, and his wife, Joan. She is a smart cookie. She started a successful travel agency in Red Hook, Star Travel, and since the business is slowing down because of people's access to Internet, she is considering switching to wedding planning. We think it is a great idea—certainly, there are plenty of scenic sites to get married in this valley. Bruce offers me another glass of wine and I talk to him about the incident with the mysterious stalker. "We have a friend here from the FBI," he says, "you should talk to him." "Great, thanks." So we talk to the guy, who is sitting across from us. "Do you have small children?" he asks Sarah and me. "Three," we say. "Oh!" His side of the table falls silent while ours grows increasingly alarmed. "Why did you ask us about our children?" "Well, that could be a reason. Perhaps the guy is a pervert planning to kidnap them." Arggghhh!

And that's the only reason why today, March 20, 2003, the date chosen by President Bush to launch his multilateral invasion of Iraq, I am desperately running toward the mysterious car where a man has just snapped another picture. My first reaction is to note the license plate and type of vehicle in case the suspect flees again. Dressed in my Christmas camouflage pajamas, I reach the car out of breath. The man is taking notes in a notebook that I rip out of his hands. "What the hell are you doing? I'm calling the police!" "Go ahead, this is public property and I can have the right to take any photos I want." I confront him: "This is the sixth time you've come to my house and I want you to tell me what's going on right this minute!" "Okay, but just calm down." I take a long look at the guy. He's a grandfatherly type with blue eyes that look at me with a panicked expression. He seems like he's about to cry. I soon get the feeling that I've really messed up this time. "This…well, I'm a bit nervous, but… could you tell me what you're doing?" "I'm an actuary." "An actuary?"

"Yes, I earn a few bucks working for the bank." "So?" "Your house was sold in the last year and the bank has commissioned me to determine if the sales prices of Rhinebeck homes coincide with real market prices. I take photos, calculate the square footage and make comparisons." "Oh," I mumble. I feel like a complete idiot in the middle of the street in my bellicose pajamas, which lack pockets to stick my hands into to give the impression that I'm relaxed. I'm also in my bare feet standing in a puddle of freezing water. *Mierda!*

I apologize and ask for his card to prove his identity. He opens his jacket and takes out a card. "Here you go," he says, kindly. "Don't you think you should be wearing shoes when it's 34°F outside? You'll catch pneumonia." "Oh, sure," I say. "Thanks for the advice." *Vroom, vroom . ...* How absurd, like when a friend's cat jumps on your lap and you're not sure whether to pet it or push it away. I watched as Kenneth drives off, the menace that for months had planned an attack on the peaceful Spanish family living temporarily on Parsonage Street, as he headed toward a bank office.

Sarah and I laugh, relieved, about the innocent encounter. No paparazzi or Mafia or twisted pedophiles. Goodbye, anxiety. Hello, feeling of guilt for having almost caused a poor guy who could pass for Santa Claus at Macy's to have a stroke. As I'm showering, I'm trying to think how I could compensate my victim for the unpleasant episode. I get dressed and before picking up my brother, I go over to Samuel's and buy a box of chocolates. Ira Gutner, the owner, has hung a sign out front, which has the name of the shop and a drawing of a chessboard. There are several stores with hanging signs, but Samuel's is special. It's 100 percent natural, untreated Spanish cedar. So, probably every year he has to turn the sign around to balance the effects of the sun, and every five years, he has to sand it down and repaint the letters. At Samuel's I write a long note to Kenneth, recounting the story that ended with the disagreeable encounter. "Dear Kenneth, you can't imagine how sorry I am..." I end by inviting him over for a glass of wine anytime he likes. I head over to the post office to send him the box of chocolates: $20 for chocolate and $3 for stamps. I don't know if Kenneth will try the chocolate or throw it in the trash, perhaps suspecting that the crazy guy wearing a mercenary outfit who stands barefoot in freezing puddles has contaminated the chocolate with anthrax.

I arrive at the office of H.H. Hill Realty and turn on the computer. I've got loads of ideas scribbled on pieces of paper scattered on my heavy mahogany desk with three locking drawers. It cost me 40 bucks at a second-hand furniture shop in Kingston … plus a cracking noise at the level of my third vertebra when I lugged it up to Huck's second-floor real estate office with my brother-in-law, Manoocher. I keep thinking about Kenneth and can't concentrate. I imagine him being unable to do his actuary calculations due to the assault he suffered in broad daylight. That's something the tax system cannot permit. Updating information is necessary to be able to charge taxpayers more. Taxes are charged here in proportion to a property value, which varies depending on how the owner uses his property and which year that the property title changed hands the last time. But there's more. Not all square feet are equally taxed. A room with a built-in closet pays more than one without one. That's why you see so many George Cole auctions with armoires. And a room without heating pays less than one with it. That's why some screened-in porches become summer living rooms.

The Kenneths of the world must be on the alert while they patrol the streets, camera in hand. Keep a watchful eye. They know where they have to look. Rules are there to be broken. By simply letting the grass grow in a corner of a yard and then harvesting a couple of bales of hay, some clever neighbor can transform his buildable land into a special tax-exempt agricultural zone. *Riiiing.* I have a call. Is it Kenneth? No, it's Sarah. "The Kufners have invited us to do some iceboating," she says. "Hurry up. Stephanie is waiting at the lawyer's office next to the bagel shop. Grab the camera because they're going to give you permission to take photos from the bridge." "Really? Great! I'm heading out the door."

Early in the month, the Hudson River began to freeze, to transform into a solid white block—a glacial costume that offers the best conditions in the past 20 years for practicing boating on solid water. It's a success attributable to constant cold temperatures without rain to wrinkle the surface. The result: so-called black ice, smooth and transparent, which the absence of wind has kept free of bubbles and other imperfections. Like the glass-bottomed boats tourists take to admire the coral reefs in the Caribbean, on the river and especially on small lakes and ponds, skaters can look beneath their feet at the turtles and fish lethargically going about their hibernation. Sailing fans have asked the authorities who control river navigation to keep the icebreakers out of Rhinecliff Bay. The request was accepted, leaving a skating rink more than half a mile across. The rink extends to the open canal next to the Kingston side, which enables the passage of cargo ships and oil tankers traveling to Albany. A tiny line in a massive glacier where it seems water never flowed. It looks like the North Pole. We've begun to break cold temperature records, with an average daily low temperature of 25°F. The signal boxes of the railroad tracks froze, halting connections with New York and New Jersey. There are not enough plumbers what with all the burst pipes, crack, crack, like the skin of roasted chestnuts, because of the freeze.

I reach the law office located next to the bagel shop. My stomach starts to growl when I smell the toasted bagels next door. I realize that I forgot to eat breakfast, what with all the excitement of having resolved the case of the mystery photographer. Bagels. Is there anything more New York than a Sunday morning at the kitchen table perusing the infinite sections of the *New York Times* with a cup of coffee in hand and a well-toasted bagel with cream cheese on the plate in front of you? I doubt it, except perhaps with the addition of a plate of smoked salmon with lemon, onion, capers and a hardboiled egg. Oh, and a strong Bloody Mary with a piece of celery sticking out of it.

Stephanie Kufner sees me through the window and gestures me to come in. It's goodbye to my sopressata di campo bagel. There's no time for munching. "*Guten morgen.* This is my attorney." "Hello, nice to meet you." "Can I see your I.D.?" "Okay." "I have just signed a paper that notifies that I know you well and that you are an excellent person. You are nice, aren't you?" "Yes, and very clean too," I say. "You will need this piece of paper to get permission from the bridge authorities to take photos of the river from above." "Thank you." "We're off," says Stephanie, "I'll go with you because I want to take pictures of my boys iceboating." "Let's go."

The Kingston-Rhinecliff Bridge actually links the old capital of New York with Rhinebeck, but its name refers to the original ferry route that joined the two banks a bit further south. It is a steel structure measuring 7,800 feet with two 30-foot traffic lanes. In the center, where this engineering wonder reaches its highest altitude, a U.S. flag flies 240 feet above the Hudson. The flag serves to guide the drivers above and the boaters below on the speed and direction of the wind. Sadly, several people have chosen to end their lives here. Hans Boehm, one of the most enthusiastic human beings I've ever met, almost fell into the water when he tried to stop somebody from jumping off the bridge. It was around 5:00 p.m. Hans was returning home from his job at the Benedictine Hospital in Kingston, where he managed the inpatient psychiatric unit, when he saw an individual standing in front of his car and appearing very agitated. Cars were stopping in both lanes trying to pass the car. Oh, man. Hans recognized the guy as somebody he grew up with, and sensing that something was terribly amiss, he rolled down his window and yelled the man's name. He was trying to catch the man's attention and distract him from what he was obviously considering. The man turned his head, looked at Hans, and alerted by his presence, bolted towards the railing. Damn! Hans sprung out of his car and raced after him. The man was already climbing over the railing by the time Hans grabbed him from his side. Life froze for a couple of seconds. Not a single word transpired between them. And then the moment was over and the man, who was about 6'3" and 180 lbs., was pulling Hans's feet off the ground. Hey! Hans let go of the man's hand and then … the man was gone.

For a remarkably long time, Hans sat on the curb staring off into the horizon. It was very odd. All sorts of people showed up to deal with the man's car, but nobody ever questioned what he was doing there. Only after he finally stood up did anyone ask about him. "Are you fine, sir?" "Yeah, I guess so," he replied, walking to his car. He got in and drove home. From there he called his medical director at the Benedictine Hospital to tell him what just transpired. The man on the bridge had been one of their patients. Hans felt horrible. The doctor came over and sat down with him for a couple of hours. Hans had grown up with the man's brother. But for some reason he couldn't get in contact with the family. He figured they would be probably very upset with him due to the psychiatric service he had provided. Deep in his heart Hans had known that the man was in very bad shape, but still … he could not stop questioning why he had called out his name on the bridge. Had that been a good idea or had it triggered the fatal ending? Could he have done something differently? Hans was traumatized.

The night before the funeral Hans got a call from his former classmate, the man's brother. "Hans? Man, I just heard that you were the guy on the bridge!" "Yes, I'm so sorry…" "We knew there was somebody at the bridge that tried to stop him, but we had no idea it was you. Why didn't you call us?" "Well, I didn't know what to do," Hans said, almost choking. "I figured out you guys wouldn't want to talk to me for the rest of your lives." "No, man. You have to come over and be part of the service. We're feeling horrible for you right now. We can't imagine what you have been going through. Please, please, please, come to the service tomorrow and let us know what happened. Nobody is angry. We want to hold you, man." The relief that Hans felt was just unbelievable. He attended the service and afterwards sat in his friend's family room answering all sorts of questions. At the end, the minister, hoping to relieve Hans from any guilt that he could still be carrying, graciously said: "Listen, there is a reason why you were there. We call it divine intervention." What that devastated family did for Hans was very sweet, difficult and tremendously generous.

It added a very peaceful and loving touch to a difficult episode. That emotional event has never left Hans entirely, and he still misses that guy.

I heard this story, deeply moved, from Hans himself at a party he had organized at the end of summer. Hans had invited several people to eat the oysters he had collected from the rocks at Cape Cod during his two-week vacation. They were all from Wellfleet Bay. There, it is common to entertain oneself at dawn by combing the sand with large rakes in search of giant clams. They are used to prepare traditional clam chowder and are also steamed and covered in a typical sauce of butter, garlic and parsley.

Hans loves oysters. Taking advantage of the low tide, he puts on a steel mesh glove and heads out with his tool belt to wrench mollusks from the cliffs. He has a mason's hammer, an oyster knife and a 3-inch iron ring used to stop any oyster that passes through from ending in his basket. Since they tend to clump together, the first job is to separate them. He can't take clusters or he could risk losing his license. Removing oysters one by one makes more room to breathe for the remaining ones, and is the way the *oysta* diggers give back to the community. It is a dangerous job, given that their heavily striated shells are very likely to make some nasty cuts. That's a risk that in Cape Cod is worth it when you have a good day and return with 100 oysters in your bucket. Hans brought a bucket full of oysters to Rhinebeck and another two overflowing with seawater. He froze the salt water in the freezer he has in his garage. Nothing special. Here, a lot of people hunt, so they need industrial-sized freezers to keep the butchered deer or the plucked turkeys, as well as 15 quarts of Breyer's vanilla ice cream, bags of doggie treats, trays of hamburger meat, pizzas, Chinese dumplings, chicken wings, lemonade concentrate … and many other things which, should the valley be declared to be in a state of emergency, the families could survive on for a couple of years.

From the time Hans left the Cape to the day of the party, he made sure that the Wellfleet oysters felt right at home. He changed their water daily by melting some of the gallons of seawater he brought with him. When the great day finally arrived, he offered us a terrific banquet.

Installed next to a tree trunk that serves as a counter, I couldn't believe how many he could open with a shucking knife. It's a tough and risky exercise. Mediterraneans know all about it. During the Christmas season, the Spanish emergency rooms receive hundreds of individuals who have cut a finger with an Iberian ham knife; a similar proportion of the French are treated for having stuck a shucking knife in their palm. Hans's knife was procured at the kitchen utensils store of his brother-in-law Richard. The one with the bike. Another crazy outdoorsy type. The three Curthoys sisters have chosen to share their lives with men more enamored of the field than poppies. Nola chose Tim, who takes advantage of every summer to canoe on the lakes of the Adirondacks, camping in mountainsides overrun with brown bears. Her sister Tricia is married to Richard and Cathy lives with Hans who, incapable of sitting still, has made a backpack golf bag to carry three golf clubs. The basics: a wood, an iron and a putter. He gets up at dawn to be the first one on the green at the Red Hook golf course. He plays 18 holes at full speed. Following the ball in the air in real time. It's a way to keep in shape, finish the round and still get to his job in Kingston on time.

The Wellfleet oysters were as delicious unadorned as they were with a few drops of lemon or bathed in a red horseradish sauce. Tender, juicy, creamy and excellent. Hans noted my gastronomic enthusiasm, for which reason he took a break from his oyster-shucking duties to show me his tomato crop. "You have to see them; they're wonderful." It was chilly and Mars shone clearly in the night sky. Next to the garage, a group played a game to see who would be the first to hammer a nail into a wooden peg. Their laughter was contagious. "They are heirloom tomatoes," Hans said. "They look like bell peppers," I commented. "Well, they're tomatoes. Smell them." Indeed they were. Just your regular tomato was pale, deformed and fragrant, until they were genetically manipulated by man, who made them round, colored and insipid. Hans sliced one open. Its pinkish exterior revealed a blood-red interior. He'd bought some coyote urine, which he'd sprayed on the fence to keep the deer away. So far, it seemed to be working.

I was fascinated by the tomatoes. I asked Hans how to get some heirloom seeds and when he thought the best time for planting was. The seed part was easy. Just type "heirloom" in the search engine, he told me, "and 20 addresses where you can send away for them will pop up. You have to plant them on President's Day. It's a rule of thumb." "What do you mean by a rule of thumb?" "A custom. Things you have to do, period. The expression originated in England during the time when a husband was allowed to hit his wife with a ruler, as long as its width did not exceed that of a thumb." "You're joking, right, Hans?" "Who knows; that's just what they say."

Anyway, I followed the planting rule to the letter. So, on the third Monday of February, the day on which the birthdays of Washington and Lincoln are celebrated and Americans have an excuse to take a long weekend, I ventured into the world of horticulture. I almost lost a few fingers in the process. The ground was frozen from the surface till the magma and the hoe bounced in my hand as if I were trying to penetrate an armadillo's shell. I had to literally use a hammer and pick to break the soil and make a few holes in which to put my tomato seeds. Covering them up was quite a feat. It was more like doing a jigsaw puzzle than planting, as I had to search for little frozen pieces that would fit in the holes created by the hammer claw. I had always imagined planting as an activity done in a straw hat in the sunshine. But I did it. Or, more precisely, I thought I'd done it. It would be months before I realized that my efforts were in vain. The seeds died from exposure to the cold. Hans forgot the minor detail that I'm a city boy and failed to tell me that while you do in fact plant seeds on President's Day, you do so in yogurt containers inside the house. All that about planting them in the ground comes much later, when the potted plants begin to flourish and the first warm days beckon you to transplant them to the definitive garden. In other words, at the end of May. "Oh oooh, I'm an allieeeen, I'm a legal allieeen, I'm a Spanish man in New Yooork…"

Now I'm in the middle of the Kingston-Rhinecliff Bridge, which has spent 45 years at the service of the community. I'm recalling how

Hans became teary-eyed when he remembered how he wasn't able to keep a man from jumping into the troubled waters. There is a sign on the railing that reads: When there is no hope, there is help. This is a last-ditch effort of the National Suicide Prevention Lifeline to save a life. 1-800-273-TALK. I get goose bumps thinking about the desperation of those who come here and of the deep wounds they leave, after jumping into the void, in the lives of loved ones. The worst thing about suicide is not for those who've gone, but rather for those left behind. The flag flutters, perfectly horizontal; a good omen for sailors. An agent of the New York State Bridge Authority has driven Stephanie and me in a truck with blinking lights from the tollbooth. He parked at the curb and told us he'd wait for us in the truck until we were finished taking photographs. "No rush. Don't hurry on my account," he said, kindly. The panoramic view of the Hudson transformed into a block of ice is quite impressive. It is a three-dimensional *Ice Age* without the need for bi-colored 3-D glasses. The only thing missing is a saber-toothed squirrel trying to store his prized acorn in Tivoli Bay. The avalanche could extend for miles into New York City.

"Hey, guys!" Gerald Kufner waves his arms at us from far below. "Helloooo, Kufi!" I think I can spot Sarah, too, or at least her green parka because she's covered up to her eyebrows to protect herself from the 5°F weather. She's standing next to a bonfire that someone has lit in the middle of the river. It's so cold that the fire doesn't even make a pond beneath the firewood.

Click. Click. Click. This may be the last time I take out my old Cannon, with 36-exposure Kodak 400 film. *Click. Click.* The digital world has consumed the analogical one. Kodak was one of the three best-known brands on the planet, along with Coca-Cola, and the Real Madrid soccer team, but I fear it will have to fight hard not to be on the list of extinct species, together with Pan Am, TWA and Woolworths. *Click. Click.* I photograph the rhythmic, choreographed movements of ice boating. There are the catamarans, gliding like skaters on the long runners installed on their rudders. True historical relics that come out of hiding every now and then. Stephanie points them out to me. *The Vixen*, which belonged to John A. Roosevelt, the president's uncle. *Rip Van Winkle*, which still belongs to the Livingston Family. Most are over a hundred years old. Mahogany masts crowned with sails. *Click. Click. Click.* That's enough. We head down towards the ice.

We reach the river through Rokeby, a 43-room stucco house on 420 rolling acres overlooking the Hudson. It is located in Barrytown, a place where time stopped in 1959, when the railroad discontinued passenger service. Owner Ricky Aldrich gives access to anyone requesting it. Ricky, a great conversationalist, is a friend of the Kufners and continues to live in the great family manor (that is, paying its exorbitant property taxes) because he rents out the adjacent buildings, which were converted into apartments for Bard College students. The young people bring them to life.

Two hundred years ago, New York was the resident state of practically all U.S. multimillionaires. From their impressive homes, they arrived to the city aboard their luxurious wooden yachts, or attached their private cars to the trains that stopped at the halts of their residences. Those were different times and different fortunes. After income taxes were imposed, most of the properties were sold or handed over to the government.

Some heirs, unable to manage the upkeep on their ancestors' legacy but still wanting to conserve the family assets, shed some of the property. They may sell the main residence with most of the land and reserve the coach houses, the maids' quarters or the laundry building to make them into homes. At any rate, these architectural works are more beautiful and larger than most modern homes. Some people also agree to donate their properties to the people of the United States, which enables them to use the homes for family celebrations on certain dates, or even to continue living in a small enclosed area of them. Others have sold them to private citizens. Brokers who got rich on the stock market in the late 1990s, young people who made a killing on the Internet before the bubble burst or celebrities or successful photographers and writers who can fork over several million dollars without a problem. Gore Vidal lived at Edgewater for 15 years before he went into voluntary exile in Italy. According to his autobiography, he always regretted the decision:

> I sometimes wonder if I should have given it up. The dream always starts in the same way. I have just bought the house back from the man I sold it to. Before I cross the railroad tracks to the house, I stop to say hello to Mr. Navins. He is postmaster and storekeeper in a one-room cabin opposite the small Barrytown station house. Though long dead, he is very much alive in my dream. "Always thought you'd come back," he says.

Thanks to Cynthia Moyer, the first designated picture frame conservator at the Metropolitan Museum of Art, Sarah and I had the chance to visit Edgewater. Just like Joanne Woodward and Paul Newman did many times before. It doesn't surprise me that Gore Vidal missed it. Poor Gore. Its beauty rivals that of Tara, the mansion in *Gone with the Wind*. Inside, an octagonal library illuminated by a skylight is the focal point of the house. It has 24-foot-high ceilings where Vidal may have written and rewritten the script for *Ben-Hur*. I write a couple of lines for my *Cándida* screenplay in my notebook, hoping that the place would give me luck. Outside, a two-story porch with six enormous white Doric columns surrounded by weeping willows faces a meadow that reaches the river after 54 yards.

Near the Village of Tivoli, there is an architectural gem with a For Sale sign on it: Callendar House, at the end of Dock Road, the former home of American Express founder Johnston R. Livingston. They are asking $10 million. Just another day of shopping. "It will sell," my brother-in-law Huck informs me. "Probably for $7 million, but it will sell." Is it the money? The beauty of this valley and its proximity to the global business capital attracts fortunes from around the world. These woods hide illustrious surnames in other currencies. We actually had dinner at Callendar House recently, to celebrate the Jewish holiday, Purim. Its tenants, however, are not what you would expect. We met

Steve and Linda Levine soon after arriving in the United States because their daughter, Grace, went to nursery school with Julia. Steven, as his wife likes to call him, is an artist with a solid academic background and extraordinary talent. Rather than painting on canvas, he sculpts architecture and landscapes. He has devoted his life to buying historic homes in poor condition, or practically in ruins, and returning them to their former glory, even improving on them. The Levines buy a property and live there while Steve works to return the building to its original form. He doesn't fix houses; he restores them. When he's finished, he sells the restored property and moves on to the next one. Steven is my only nomadic friend.

The Levines began with small properties but their business soon grew since Steve does such a good job. Currently, he resides in a castle, like Capitan Haddok in the Tintin series, which in taxes alone must consume some $70,000 a year. He will soon hand it over to a movie star and seek out another incredible place to live in while he restores it and we will again be invited to dinner to enjoy it. Thanks to their constant moving, like on a real Monopoly board where all the pieces are friends, we have the privilege of enjoying the most incredible places in the whole valley. At this Tivoli manor, a pair of architectural pearls from the drawing board of the mythic Stanford White are being erected. Marquetry coach houses in a stream bed frequented by deer. The deer are lovely but no one wants them. They eat the flowers and carry the tick that spreads the dreaded rheumatic Lyme disease. During hunting season, the owners of the mansions usually let the local townspeople hunt on their properties. A fellow hunter once told me that the photographer Annie Liebowitz, who is a neighbor, hires an expert archer to discreetly and quietly eliminate the pests.

Also at the Purim dinner were the Dorins, Jay and Lisa, and Karen and Carlos Valle. We are celebrating the time when the Jews who lived in Persia were saved from extermination. A story recounted in the Biblical Book of Esther that is read in synagogues on the 14th day of the Hebrew month of Adar, which falls just a bit before Easter. Each time the text mentions the name of the bad guy, Haman, the faithful respond to the rabbi by booing, foot-stomping and rattling their noisemakers. Haman. Boooo! Jay admits that he doesn't remember the holy story very well. "We Jews celebrate something every 15 days," he tells me jokingly, "and it's hard to keep up." However, "any excuse to eat is a good one," he adds. "We Jews love to eat. When you get up in the morning, the first thing they ask you is: 'Have you had good sex?' 'Yeah, so now let's eat.' Sex and food are the two main things that have sustained my people," he says. Steve opens a bottle of wine and surprises me by saying he wants to practice his Spanish. "You know Spanish?" "A word I learned when I was little and I want to know if I'm still pronouncing it correctly." "So what is it?" "*Al-bon-di-gas*," he says. *Albóndigas*? I can't believe it. Meatballs? What type of Spanish teacher taught Steve to say meatballs instead of "hello" or "goodbye"? "Excellent pronunciation," I tell him.

Carlos, who is a psychiatrist and, curiously, Hans' boss at Benedictine Hospital in Kingston, is Peruvian. He's brought a bottle of pisco. "Oh, great," I tell him. "I love pisco sours." "Good," says Steve, "because you have to make them." Me? You want me to make the pisco sours when the closest thing to a cocktail I've made in my life was mixing rum and Coke to make a Cuba Libre? In the kitchen, I discreetly open the pisco and note that the back label has instructions for preparing pisco sour. Thank goodness. Pisco sour: three shots of pisco and two of simple syrup. If you don't have simple syrup, don't panic because, according to the label, it's made by dissolving two tablespoons of sugar in a glass of water. Add an egg white, a few ice cubes and into the blender it goes. The mixture starts to foam. A good sign. Pour the mixture into some glasses and, delicious! "Steve, do you want to try it?" "*Al-bón-di-gas*," he says. In other words, yes.

We chat with Karen about intercultural marriages. She tells us that her mother, a petite woman from New York City, ended up in a Mormon cemetery because her father, who was not a practicing Mormon, was from a family who followed the prophet Joseph Smith, the man who said that an angel appeared to him in Manchester, New York, and gave him a book written in ancient Egyptian and some special glasses so he could translate it into English. The writings revealed that the promised people of Israel had crossed the Atlantic in a canoe. Engaged in a fratricide struggle in the New World, the bad guys killed the good ones and God, as punishment, turned all the survivors into Indians and black people. In the late 1800s, according to the founder of the Church of Latter Day Saints, God personally asked Smith, through his special envoy, the angel Moroni, to take charge of redeeming the lost people and to convince them to return to the fold. Karen's paternal ancestors arrived from Europe and formed part of the Hand Cart Migration that led many Mormons from the East Coast to Utah. Her great-great-grandfather was in charge of making whisky for one of Brigham Young's wives. At the time, firewater was not considered alcohol, but a medicine to settle an upset stomach. With those paternal roots, together with the Catholic roots of her Peruvian husband and the agnosticism of both, Karen confessed that the closest they'd come to imparting religious teachings to their children was to recount the story of the Easter Bunny.

On the evening of Purim, a biblical moon shone in the sky, high-lighting the tri-dimensionality of the blue-gray clouds. The columns of thick smoke from the three fireplaces heating the Callendar rooms rose toward those clouds. Lisa Henderling mentions an article she'd read in the newspaper that said that thanks to super telescopes, astronomers had begun to travel back in time. They do not actually observe the stars but rather the light emanating from them. Consequently, if they can locate an object that took some 470 million years to travel the distance that separates the telescope from the star's point of origin, they are observing the Big Bang in real time. Sarah says she had read that, too, and that in Baltimore, astronomers have taken a photo that is just a stone's throw from the origin of the universe. Amazing.

Now, the same frozen river we observed that night at the Levines' house is full of life in the light of day. Several young people skate over the iced surface, propelled by a towel that they make into a sail. The gusts of wind push them to dizzying speeds. Apparently it rained some yesterday.

The water spread uniformly over the surface of the river, evening out every lump and hole. The cold night has smoothed out the ground, making ideal conditions for ice skates. Dozens of cars with New Jersey plates are parked on the bank. Capital of New Jersey? Trenton. New Jersey is the country's most ethnically and religiously diverse state. Only New York has more Jews and only Michigan has more Muslims. In New Jersey, ice boating is widely popular. It is a fiercely competitive sport with New Jersey residents' eternal rivals on this side of the river. They have come for the rematch. New Jersey inhabitants want to challenge those of the Hudson Valley to a regatta. Only once were they actually able to compete and on that occasion, the New York team won.

This type of competition is usually celebrated by following an equilateral triangle drawn on the ice. Each side has to measure a minimum of a mile and two of them must face the wind. A 40-foot iceboat carries six or seven sailors. On a day like today, the crew would have to lie down on the windward sides to keep their balance and try to reduce the friction in leeward sailing. Here on the Hudson, they travel very fast. The 20-mile circuit has been completed in less than 48 minutes. The speed record was 72 miles per hour. However, the large old boats can reach up to 105 miles an hour if the wind is right.

I see many more boats than I expected. The single-seat fiberglass catamarans measure 16 feet and float well on the water, which is why they can also be easily adapted to thin layers of ice.

Gerald Kufner, also known as Kufi, motions me over to his iceboat for a spin. I help him push off the boat. We then tumble onto the padded wooden plank and head out towards the horizon. Watch out for the boom he warns me, don't even think about raising your head. What with the excitement of the moment and the concern about becoming headless like the famous Sleepy Hollow horseman, I get in a position that doesn't give me a good view of the horizon. I try to improve my view and, lo and behold, the boom smacks me in the temple. It actually just brushes against me, making my hair stand up as if I'd seen Gioffi at

Sportsmen. We start to gain speed. The wood creaks and groans like the Columbia space shuttle taking off from Cape Canaveral. When it turns, we seem to be on a rocking horse; one of the runners lifts 3 feet off the ice. I wonder if we'll capsize. No. Gerald is an expert sailor so I'm safe with him. We reach the *Jack Frost*, a tropical wood beauty that belonged to president Franklin D. Roosevelt. We make a half turn. We seem to be flying. How fast are we going? Some 30 miles per hour. Only 30? I could have sworn we were going 200. We stop. It was fun. Gerald will now take out Sarah, and Stephanie will photograph this historic moment.

When my wife returns, we head towards the bonfire. In the distance, I can see a Christmas tree standing in the middle of the ice. It even has decorations. The bullfighter Rafael "The Rooster" said it best: "It takes all kinds of people." Someone offers us a cigarette and a sip from a bottle of brandy. Chocolate cookie? No, thanks. There is everything here. It looks like the IGA of Red Hook. More and more people join us. We are lucky enough to meet some of the nuts who love this unusual sport practiced assiduously by people born between the 45th and 50th parallels. Someone covers my eyes from behind. "A wonderful day for a spin on the river with boat runners," a man says in a child's voice. "Who are you?" "*Al-bón-di-gas!*" he responds.

* * *

I usually go out on a bike with Steve. Nothing too fast. Slowly, that's the best way to enjoy the view. We often go up 308 and turn left on Pilgrims Road. Rhinebeck sits above the river, but once we begin to climb, the valley view is spectacular. In springtime, Steve looks for turtles to draw in the lakes flanking Cedar Heights. We go down by Oriole Mills, crossing horse farms with white fences on green pastures. I feel like one of Enid Blyton's Famous Five when they stopped to drink fresh milk at an English farm. Steve is familiar with every house, every rock along the way. He tells me he was born on the other side of the river. "It's another world," he says.

The landscape of the western bank is completely different: pure mountains. The frontier. Everything is more enclosed. You grow up without seeing your neighbor and that sensation makes people different from those of this open valley. Salva, an accounting assistant who works in Kingston, has told me that he manages the accounts of millionaire clients who have never crossed the Hudson. Who've never traveled to New York. I mention this to Steve and he says something that makes me think: "Imagine the river as an immense mass of water that separates two worlds," he says. "When I was a boy, there were no bridges that crossed it, only ferries, which were neither frequent nor pleasant to ride. Today there are bridges, but some people still feel the psychological separation of the river." Steve has a fond memory of the first time he crossed the Hudson from Newburgh to Beacon with a handful of friends on a ferry in the 1950s. At the time, the DIA museum was a cardboard box factory for Nabisco cookies. Its enormous red neon sign, the only relic from the past, burned the retinas of the inhabitants of the western bank every night. Steve and his friends didn't know what they would find in Beacon. Would people speak the same language? Back then, crossing the Hudson was like traveling to the moon.

In the 1960s, several of the historic buildings of the Hudson Valley towns were torn down, including large homes next to the river, to make room for modern buildings that were never constructed. Both Beacon and Newburgh lost much of their historic architecture. It was an age of supposed splendor in which the vintage lost all its value and simply became old. In Poughkeepsie, the Nelson House, the classy hotel owned by Emmet Coughlan and Walter Averill that had hosted an inn since the days of the American Revolution, was dynamited. Right across from the Bardavon Theater, the Nelson House opened on May 19, 1876. Franklin D. Roosevelt gave a memorable speech from its main balcony, and the White House staff worked out of there when the President returned home to Hyde Park. It was just a jewel where customers could find any luxury. An obligated stop between Albany and New York at the time when a car trip to the capital could easily take 24 hours. But in the early 1960s no one valued being located right downtown; open the door, take a few steps and you could go down Main Mall Row. With middle-class Americans' access to car travel, a revolutionary concept took root: motor hotels. Motels were on the outskirts of the cities (so you could avoid traffic jams) and had ultramodern rooms with the latest televisions and mini-bars. Best of all, you could almost reach your room without having to get out of your car! Goodbye to the Nelson House's white-gloved waiters.

When plans were made to modernize the cities of Upstate New York, the idea was to import manual labor from the South. Many African Americans came here to build that dream. But the economic crisis caught up with them and created pockets of poverty in cities that were incapable of absorbing such a large unemployed population all at once. In the 1970s, Poughkeepsie tried to revive its downtown by turning Main Street into a pedestrian shopping area, but the city lost the war against suburban malls. In 1981, the closure of Luckey Platt & Company was the definitive blow to the local economy. For most of the 20th century, Luckey Platt was a major retail destination for the entire Hudson Valley. It was ahead of its time in charging a fixed price for every item in the store, and Sarah's mother, Peggy, lived those glory days as the person in charge of mail and telephone orders. She also had a daily radio program at WKIP, Mon-Fri 7:30 am to 8:00 am, in which she played the character Luckey Lucy and announced promotions interspersed with music. That was a little before *Imus in the Morning*. You see? I have a professional connection with my mother-in-law.

Until the 1920s, buildings had to meet only building codes. That was it. Then came the idea to divide the town into different zones: business district, recreational district, shopping district, residential district … you name it. Each one had its own building rules. The advantages and disadvantages of this system could be more or less contested but, according to Ted Fink, a member of the American Institute of Certified Planners and a nature lover who was thinking like a planner before he was 10 and ended up earning a Master's degree in urban planning and policy, zoning was upheld by the U.S. Supreme Court because it viewed apartments and industry next to single-family houses as a public nuisance. Or, as the Court stated, "like a pig in the parlor instead of the barnyard." So then, preventing poor immigrants from invading wealthy residential neighborhoods became one of the reasons why zoning caught on in the Hudson Valley and across the nation. It was relatively simple—prepare a map of the districts to lay out where the zones would be. One community could then cut and paste what another had done, property values would be stabilized, and the city fathers were happy. These codes are what impede entrepreneurs of the cities like Poughkeepsie from starting up businesses that would benefit the local population and create jobs. The current struggle is to overcome these constraints and obtain a permit to open a food store in a residential area, for example, so that people can walk to the store to buy potatoes and milk. Or to open a restaurant in an industrial area so that the yearly one million tourists visiting the Walkway over the Hudson, an abandoned railroad bridge turned into a pedestrian park, can stop and get something to eat. In other words: get back to traditional urban planning. Instead of 300 pages of regulations, a three-page flyer with buildings codes based on architecture and landscaping would be enough.

But that's the future. In the past, Steve had an uncle named Joe, whose parents pressured him to study medicine. Joe disappeared one day and telephoned them from Nairobi six months later. He was staying at a cousin's house there, but after a few weeks, he bid him farewell and began to wander. He took nothing with him. He owned nothing that could be robbed, and he had nothing with which to rob anyone else with. He traveled some 100 miles until he reached a small village. The local villagers accepted him and he formed part of the Massai tribe for two and half years. Back in New York, they'd given him up for dead and held a funeral for him. ... As an unknown poet wrote, "Life is but a stopping place. A pause in what's to be. A resting place along the road ... to sweet eternity ... We'll claim a great reward ... and find an everlasting peace together with the Lord. Amen." But two and half years later he returned by foot to Nairobi and telephoned his family again. Hallelujah!

His parents immediately flew to Kenya in search of their prodigal son: "He's alive, he's alive!" They begged him to go back with them. But Uncle Joe didn't want to. He continued to travel north. He was in Egypt. He crossed the sea and made it all the way to Norway. Without knowing it, Uncle Joe had traveled in just a couple of months the route that would take *homo sapiens* millions of years to complete.

In Oslo he married a Norwegian woman and together they returned to the United States. They separated shortly thereafter. When Steve asked his uncle why they had divorced, his answer left no doubt: "When we met, she didn't know English and I didn't know Norwegian. We liked each other, but when we could actually communicate, we realized we didn't have anything in common." Later, against all family advice, he invested his savings in a building in a rough neighborhood in Newburgh. Joe went to collect the rent on his apartments carrying a tribal club from the Kenyan village where he had lived … and the tenants religiously paid their rent.

I could fill a couple of books with Steve's and Jay's stories. I could even write another one using the anecdotes in which both participated. Their last adventure was a recent trip to Jamaica to escape the New York winter. They were crossing a stream when an eight-foot-tall guy appeared with a machete. He demanded all their money and of course they immediately handed over everything they had. The guy put it in his pocket and turned away. Before his figure disappeared on the horizon, Jay decided to shout out to him: "Excuse me, mister, couldn't we get a receipt?" Without waiting for a reply, they took off (or, as the Spanish would say, they started to get the hell out of there while throwing Communion wafers).

Steve and I also frequently cross the border to the west to go hiking in Shawangunk Ridge State Forest. This was historically hostile territory, with many battles between settlers and Native Americans. A mountain range formed of the rock that until the 1800s was used in all mills in America. A conglomeration that when cut in the shape of a wheel maintains the pitted texture perfect for milling grain. The paths are lined with blueberries. In spring, hundreds of birds perch on the shrubs to gather the fruit, and beneath them, Timber rattlesnakes silently await their prey. If you're not careful, they can confuse your hand with a bird and bite you. So, if you see any, slowly walk away. Don't try to pet the snake or kiss its head (yes, there are idiots who have done that). The good news is that the rattlesnakes do not have venom in their fangs 40 percent of the time because they've just bitten someone or something else.

At High Point, there is a panoramic view that takes your breath away. The point has an official marker dated 1943, which certifies that it is the highest point of the ridge. It also carries a warning that anyone who destroys the marker will be fined $250. But it doesn't tell you the altitude. Oops. Somebody forgot that little detail. In other words, I can't tell you how high we've climbed. From here you can see Watchtower Farms, the huge experimental farm of happiness that the Jehovah's Witnesses established in the Wallkill countryside. It looks like Emerald City amid the savannah. It has everything you would expect in a city, including a print shop that produces 5,000 pocket Bibles daily. On the Shawangunk cliffs, there are caves that have ice year round. Green moss growing on the rocks filters the waterfalls. Native tribes in the area gave the place its name. Shawangunk means "smoke in the mountains," most likely because the ridge is always enveloped in a mysterious fog. The view was a source of inspiration to the master painters who built the tiny village of Cragsmoor, whose stately residences are today mostly ghostly ruins among the weeds, and formed the heart of the Hudson River School in the mid-19th century.

Sometimes we stop in Ellenville on our way back from hiking. The city was prosperous when the channel that joined Pennsylvania and Albany passed through its downtown, but the railroad made water channels obsolete. Later, its biggest source of wealth was closed: the television antenna factory. Tax pressures forced the owners to move the factory to North Carolina until the satellite finally buried the little business it had left. Today, the scant possibilities for a job in the area are written clearly on an enormous sign for marine recruitment on the way into town. Steve still has several friends here. In a restaurant with an Irish name run by a

Belgian chef, we ask about Mickey. They call him on the phone and inform us that he'll come in half an hour. While we wait, we enjoy an aged beef fillet that the chef hung for 23 days to give it the wild flavor of game.

Mickey is a personal friend of the Ellenville banker who took Steve under his wing when he entered the world of business. Steve was twenty-something and had just escaped the Vietnam draft by faking insanity. He stripped naked and dressed in translucent trash bags. They arrested him for public exposure. With that record, the army didn't want him. Plastic-wrapped balls were not appropriate for a soldier in the middle of the jungle. So Steve traveled around the world with the banker. Luxury hotels. First-class airline seats. "A conservative type, but a fighter and with principles," Steve remarks. They were at a casino in the Bahamas on a winning streak one night when the banker suddenly asked the croupier: "Why aren't there any locals in this room?" "Those are the rules, sir," the employee had answered. "Is that so? And who made those stupid rules? If you want to be three times more successful, you should enable the local population to benefit from the casino. And you'll see how doing that benefits you." He left in disgust.

Another time, Steve was having lunch and the banker asked him: "How much money have you earned today?" "Two hundred dollars, why?" "Well ... I've earned $55 million." He would say anything. When Mickey arrives, he tells us that he is very disappointed with their mutual banker friend. "Why is that?" "He went to Florida to live out his remaining years. He's not interested in me anymore," he says. "He only wants to be with his billionaire golfing buddies." "That's not true," says Steve. "I know he comes back every now and then and takes you out to dinner." Mickey lowers his head and doesn't say anything, but it's obvious that the kindly gesture isn't enough for him. He's 88 years old, wears a red plaid shirt and a light blue baseball cap. For his generation, friendship means something else, and it's not measured in money.

Mickey forms part of a history that is disappearing: that of World War II veterans. He was stationed in Belgium and states that Hitler would have won the war if he'd paid attention to the advice of his generals. He says that the American army greatly respected the German army. He tells us that in Belgium, many Americans died of hypothermia. The Germans were perfectly equipped and the Americans froze. It's that simple, he says, adding that at the end of the war, the focus was on fuel. That gas was the main concern of the Allies: to make sure the fuel supply to German tanks was cut off.

Mickey complains that he got a traffic ticket because of us. For speeding. For not having told him in advance that we were coming and thus forcing him to rush over here. He says that the public coffers are so low that the police don't forgive even a mile over the speed limit. "They need our money." Previously, there had been a gentlemen's agreement of 10 miles between the speed limit on the sign and what the car's odometer said. If the sign said 55, you weren't stopped unless you were going over 65. "Now," he says, "a police car with its siren on will pursue you for going 56." But Mickey has driven with worse enemies than this on his tail. In Europe, he was General Patton's driver, and many of his ideas about the war were informed by what he heard behind the wheel. I ask him about his boss, the man whose soldiers captured more enemy prisoners, and liberated more territory, in less time than any other army in history. He tells us that Patton greatly respected the Germans but detested the Russians. Americans just couldn't get along with the Russians. It just wasn't possible.

* * *

March is a month of transition in Rhinebeck. After nonstop rain for days on end, the view has changed completely. The ice has melted and the Hudson flows slowly but steadily like the tongue of a glacier. It gives the impression that the Earth is moving. It is said that this month appears like a lion but leaves like a lamb. But you never know. With the arrival of the first thaws you finally get the feeling that the long winter has ended. Tulips and daffodils growing in grass hollows in the ice fields help convince you of this. But then you'll be caught off-guard by a snowstorm.

It is possible. At any rate, March is the sweetest month of the year in the valley because the sap returns to the trunks of the sugar maples and it's time to prepare syrup. The Native Americans noticed this phenomenon because they watched the squirrels licking the bark of the trees. They deserve credit for guessing this because the raw sap tastes dreadful, not sweet at all.

The bounty of the harvest each year is determined by meteorological conditions since the combination of cold nights and mild days is what makes the sap gush. You have to pay close attention to nature because the toothsome solution only flows generously during a brief six-week period. If you tap the tree too early you won't get anything; if you wait too long, the liquid will be scarce and bitter. The glory days begin when, by mid-morning, the sun raises the thermometer up to the 40s. Warm days allow the roots to collect water from the soil again and produce the sap that will bleed through the holes you drill in the bark.

Trees don't have hearts to pump blood through the body like animals do. The rising of the sap from the roots to the top leaves, 140 feet above the ground, is a miracle that science has yet to explain convincingly. The experts talk of surface tension, of the difference between the atmospheric and soil pressure ... but no one knows what runs the capillary circuit that brings life to tree cells. The circulatory system has been identified, though. Like human beings, trees have veins and arteries. The florema consists of conduits, which, beginning in the roots, transport the sap to nourish the plant, depending on the needs of the moment.

Now let me introduce you to the auxins. They are the plant hormones that coordinate the growth of a tree. Auxins are true data collection centers. In nature life moves according to the air temperature, and auxins are the ones who read the thermometer and tell the tree what to do according to the weather conditions. When it gets cold, the tree is forced to reduce the machinery. It has to make a slow transition before complete stupor sets in. Mandatory hibernation occurs since the frozen ground impedes the flow of nutrients. Winter passes and the first signs of spring appear. The startup occurs with great caution. The auxins check the outside temperature according to protocol. One warm day isn't enough. Two or three warm days in a row is something to consider. If the temperature averages 40 degrees or more, at midday the ground thaws and the roots are able to drink water with nutrients again. The tree is ready to start sending up sap to awaken the buds. Spring is here! Yahoo. But, wait a minute! The thermometer drops to 30°F again at night. "What's going on?" the auxins wonder. "Should we awaken the tree, or should we let it hibernate a little longer?" At midday the warm weather tells the auxins it's time to sprout, but at dawn the cold weather tells them to hold on. The data is very confusing, but like companies during a crisis, they have to make a decision. Well, let's consider the chain of facts. The tree could definitely produce sap and send it up to the canopy. If it does that, then the buds will bloom. But if it gets cold again and the terrain freezes ... no more sap will be produced and the baby leaves will die of hunger. On the other hand, if the tree waits too long, other plants will steal the nutrients from the ground that the maple needs to have a decent diet ... Bummer! What to do? So the auxins take the middle ground. They advise the maple to deliver a huge stream of extra-sugary sap to fatten up the baby leaves in case they have to shut down the production for several days.

New England benefits from this temperature confusion that makes sugar maple sap gush several times during the transition weeks between winter and spring. That is also the harvest window of opportunity in New York. Once the weather stabilizes, the sap will flow constantly, but in a much smaller quantity and of a much lesser quality. The tree leaves are not babies anymore. The danger of freezing nights is over, so there is no more need to produce "formula" sap—the extra-sugary sap that makes the best maple syrup in the world.

Syrup production is serious business at the Hills' sugar shack. It is a wonderful excuse to spend some time outdoors and to receive visits from friends who want to know about liquid gold production. In previous months, Huck has been engaged in collecting firewood. You have to burn a lot of it during the evaporation process, and any time an acquaintance loses a tree in a storm, my brother-in-law is right there to haul off the remains in his Toyota. The first thing is to tap the trees.

We look for maples with a diameter of at least 10 inches at the height of our chests, or that are at least 30 years old, which is the same thing. The idea is to bore holes with a manual drill, fitted with an 8-millimeter bit, which looks like it was used by Dr. Frankenstein to trepanate skulls. You can make one hole in young trees and two or three in the older ones. Huck teaches me. Too many holes in a weak tree can kill it. Too few in a leafy tree is a waste. Never try to tap an old hole and never make a new hole too close to an old one. This, it seems, is like insulin injections for diabetics; you have to keep changing locations to avoid overusing the veins. At approximately a palm's width from the knot that marks the wound from last year, I start drilling. Wow! It's much harder than I expected. You have to push hard. By the end of the day, I fear I'll have calluses on my fingers and blisters on the palm of my hand from pushing the drill so hard. "Guillermo, wait." "What?" "Tilt the bit up a little to facilitate the dripping of the sap." "Oh."

So the first hole is done. An inch and a half deep. I take the metal spile and with the hammer, *tap, tap, tap*, I push it into the hole. Great. On the spile, I hang the sap bucket with a hook and put on its lid to keep out bugs and everything else you sweep off country porches. We do this in tree after tree, until we've made holes in all of them. "No, not that one!" shouts Huck. "Why not?" "Look up and notice the dry leaves stuck to the branches." "So?" "Compare them to the leaves of one of the trees we've made holes in and you'll see the difference." Oh, he's right; they're different. This isn't a sugar maple, but a silver maple. Similar, but it doesn't produce syrup. Sugar maples have leaves with more rounded tips. Got it.

When the sap emerges, you have to empty the buckets before they overflow and much of the harvest drips to the ground. A healthy maple can produce 10 gallons per hole. So every morning before heading to the office, at lunchtime and in the afternoon before returning home, we take a spin to see how the collection is going. Every time we find a full bucket, we empty it into a big plastic container that we later take to the sugar shack. It's not a good idea to leave the sap in the buckets overnight because if it freezes, it will lose its desirable properties and you'll have to throw the top frozen layer out.

Once the first 100 gallons have been collected, the production process begins. John Corcoran helps set up the burner and is responsible for the cooking. John has to constantly watch the temperature of the liquid because there is no way to know when it turns into syrup just by looking at it. Its characteristic amber color only appears after it cools. In the boiler, it has the pale color of murky water. Physics dictates that it will be ready for bottling when it reaches seven degrees above the boiling point of water. If John left it any longer, it would turn into sugar. If he removes it too soon, we'd have only insipid liquid. Midpoint is when the maple cream appears: a molasses-like substance the consistency of peanut butter.

Boiling sap in the sugar shack requires a very generous flame to reach high temperatures. The sap is piped from the outside tank to the enormous pan-like evaporator that is heated with firewood from below. The evaporator is divided, like a maze, by walls that channel the liquid on a concentric path that ends in a tap. On the final stretch, John carefully notes the temperature and releases the syrup when the mercury reaches the desired line. Outside, by turns, we are reducing the logs into a reasonable size so they will fit into the mouth of the burner. Here, everyone knows how to wield an ax. The slowest idiot in town has cut firewood hundreds of times. I have to learn how to grab the handle in the right position, to calculate the distance and to maximize the impact so as not to lose strength by the third strike. By the second day, I've got it down pat and I view it as a healthy form of exercise. Clearly, the gym is an invention of the urban dweller. Ash wood splits like an open book. Locust is a bit harder. There's no one alive that can split an elm when you hit a knot. Considering that to obtain a gallon of syrup we need to boil 40 gallons of sap (and evaporate 39), the most frequently repeated phrase is that of the celebrated Groucho Marx in the train sequence of *Go West*: "Bring wood!"

Let's take a look at that elm trunk that resists the ax. John studies it. He places it on the ground. He looks at it again. One clean blow and he splits it in two. No knots or bumps. John Corcoran is used to working with heavy tools and to handling, cutting, sawing and pounding big pieces of iron. He's a sculptor. A creator of practical sculptures. He likes for his work to be used so he makes chairs, tables, clocks and coat racks. "Conceptual art is too much for me," he says one morning as we drive to New York in his beaten-up Volvo. "What do you mean?" "I prefer that my things have a direct connection with people. Something you can sit on, let's say, while you fight with your husband. But they are still sculptures." "Should we stop for coffee?" We stop. I get out and notice the bald tires on the asphalt. I instinctively kick a tire. "You think this car will hold up?" "Of course it will."

The reason we reach the World Financial Center with the chassis of his old Volvo nearly dragging on the ground is that we are transporting three heavy steel plates, of 275 lbs. each, in the trunk through the snow. At six in the morning, we pick up the material from a warehouse in Kingston that looks like a set for the musical *Oliver!*. We then pick up his assistant, Jonah, and head out. The *Wall Street Journal* had selected one of John's designs for a monument in tribute to Daniel Pearl, the reporter who was kidnapped and murdered by Al-Qaeda in Pakistan. John took the work seriously. He hung a photo of Daniel on the wall of his Tivoli studio for inspiration. While he made pencil drawings in his sketchbook, he looked at Daniel, that violin virtuoso who radiated vitality and spoke five languages, including Farsi, Hindi and Spanish. Then John decided to also put up a portrait of his father—the Corcoran he never met. He was a *Science Illustrated* photographer who died in a car accident when John was still in his mother's womb. John produced three solid plates that project light with fiber optics focused on inscriptions on the wall. John said that the steel, when touched (touch it and you'll see) transmitted strength and sadness. The light helps alleviate the sorrow.

Images of Pearl's murder were broadcast around the world in February 2002. In addition to the unfortunate death of a reporter, repeated over and over, the news shook up the U.S. press because it demonstrated a definitive shift in the concept of the war reporter. The parties engaged in a conflict no longer view the media as neutral observers, but rather as a strategic element to be used to their advantage. Daniel Pearl, who was investigating the Pakistani connection of Richard Reid, the man who tried to blow up a passenger jet with explosives hidden in his shoes, never thought he was going to die. If he had, he would not have risked his life just before turning 39 and with his wife pregnant with their first child. He would have taken precautions. Calling a meeting at a restaurant in downtown Karachi did not seem too risky. He just fell victim to an ambush and the United States lost a man who, through his celebrated "Middle Column" in the *Wall Street Journal*, tried to make American readers understand that other cultures and other ways of viewing the world exist.

The three of us carried the steel up to the ninth floor of the building on Liberty Street, where the *Wall Street Journal* offices are located. We set about installing them. They didn't fit because the floor was not level. We forced them in ... by pounding on them. With difficulty, *tap, tap, tap,* they eventually fit. At the end of the exhausting day, we went down to the street for a cigarette. Nine floors, two security checkpoints, the frigid air. It's not worth it. No wonder no one smokes in New York.

"The installation looks good," I tell John. I am clearly moved. "Do you really like it?" "Of course. A lot." I decide to write an article about it for *El Pais*. "Do you think I could talk to one of Pearl's colleagues?" "It's worth a try," he says.

The reporter who answers my questions is named Robert Frank. Everything he says reveals a sincere admiration for his fallen colleague, so much so that he infects me with it and I feel deep sadness for not having had the opportunity to meet Danny Pearl. In all his travels, Frank tells me, Danny was willing to adapt to the local cultures. In restaurants, he asked for the most exotic dishes and was interested in the seasoning. He knew the current jokes and always had his violin handy to improvise a fusion of blues with any type of music he came across. He never forgot that there were human beings behind the news.

John Corcoran's sculpture [three solid metal plates that project light on the inscriptions on the wall] symbolizes the light that the reporter shone in his search for the truth and that terror could not darken. To the contrary, thanks to the scholarships that today bear his name, Pakistani journalists have the opportunity to travel to the United States and work in the mythical Dow Jones building together with Danny's former colleagues at the *Wall Street Journal*. The funds originate from the money raised at more than 100 concerts last October 10, his birthday, given by musician friends who organized musical events in 17 countries. Pearl's memory still shines in the most cosmopolitan city of the planet, which is where it should be. Robert Frank confesses to me that Danny Pearl's memorial sculpture motivates him to go to work each morning.

The thermometer reaches 219°F. At the end of the labyrinthine pan, when the sap has reached the optimal temperature that indicates a sugar concentration of 66 percent, John opens the faucet and lets a stream flow over the cheesecloth that filters the mineral elements before the syrup drips into a bucket. Occasionally, the mixture bubbles and threatens to flood the sugar shack. John relies on an old trick. A drop of milk in the evaporator and the rebellious sap calms down.

The kids come by after school. We pick up a ladle of snow and pour some maple syrup on it. It crystallizes. They love it. Julia and Phebe, John and Liza's daughter, demand another round. Some friends show up with a bottle of vodka. "So that the work will seem easier," they say. Great. Vodka and syrup. Yum.

After six weeks of harvest and the four or five intermittent days on the calendar devoted to the boiling, it's now time for bottling. We've collected 1,800 gallons of sap, which, divided by 40, produced 46 gallons of syrup. Fortunately, I've brought my gloves. The first thing is to heat the syrup in a big cooking pot with the aid of a propane tank, to kill the bacteria. Hot syrup will also help to seal the glass bottles better. Properly bottled, homemade maple syrup will last a year in the pantry. But if you're not careful, it won't last more than a few minutes on the breakfast table. "Nico, there's a pool of syrup on your plate!" "But I love it, *Papá*."

9

April

"Okay, here's a question: so what's the capital of Ohio?" "Columbus."
"Of Louisiana?" "Baton Rouge." "And of Oklahoma?" ... "Not a clue."
At breakfast I ask my children to drill me on the state capitals to see if
I've finally learned them. We use some plastic map placemats Sarah and
I bought at a museum shop during a moment of responsible parenting.
The theory of providing learning materials sounds wonderful but
in reality, once again, it is something else all together. The kids think
that school teaches them enough so in the end, I'm the only one who
made the investment worth it. "California?" "Sacramento." "Florida?"
"Tallahassee." "What about Oklahoma, *Papá*?" "I don't have a clue, Julia."
"Oklahoma City." That was such an easy one.

The kids go to school at 7:30 a.m. When they come downstairs
with their backpacks ready, the toaster begins to spit out English
muffins. Sometimes, if a miracle occurs and we are all neatly combed
in time and we all have both of our shoes tied and we've found the
book that mysteriously disappeared, which just had to be around here
somewhere, because "I swear I left it right here yesterday," and then it
just casually appears under the bed, "I have no idea how, *Papá*, because
I left it right here"—if all of the circumstances come together which,
as I said, depend more on the will of God Almighty than on the
Fessers' capabilities as a family, well, then we have the luxury of
cutting some croissants in half, caramelizing them with a pinch of

sugar in a skillet, pressing them down with a spatula and serving them with butter and red currant jam. Yummm ...

The milk is really fresh. In this valley the grass grows even in your sneakers if you leave them outside overnight. However, in contrast to the popular belief, the most important thing for producing milk is not pasture but access to water. Almost in the same proportion as maple syrup, a cow needs to drink 30 gallons of water to produce just one of milk. New York and Wisconsin are the states with the most abundant supplies of this precious liquid. It is said that nearby Salt Point owes its name to the fact that at this road crossing, ranchers used to feed their cows salt to make them thirstier, to make them drink more, and therefore to produce some extra quarts of milk.

Unfortunately, though, many farms in the valley have been abandoned and their fields have fallen into the hands of housing developers. That's because the heavy milk regulations granted to the big companies who lobby in Washington, make it almost impossible for a local farmer to make a profit producing milk. The money is in the distribution. Period. Only some local farms, like Ronnybrook, which is situated in Ancramdale on land where the Osofsky family has raised Holstein cows for 70 years, have dared to take the plunge into packaging and selling under its own brand milk (and ice cream), and they are thriving. And Ronnybrook would do even better if the authorities allowed the dairy to make its own cheese. But again, health regulations are sometimes too exaggerated. To give you an example, there are rumors that the 4H booth, where everybody lines up to buy a milkshake at the annual Dutchess County fair, may be forced to close ... due to its proximity to the cow stables. Hello? Doesn't the milkshake come from those same cows' milk? On the other hand, Red Hook has a smart program to save farms. The town buys the land development rights from the farmers, providing them with extra money to do business, and preserving the beautiful land from developers—which avoids the construction of new buildings that would bring more people to the community and, eventually, increase the school taxes.

After breakfast, in the immaculate silence of Rhinebeck streets, a slight noise can be heard in the distance. Sarah sharpens her senses, like the cowboys who can sense a stampede. She sounds the voice of alarm: "Come on everybody, you're gonna be late!" The school bus is just about to turn the corner and it's time to make a dash for the bus stop. Sarah yells her warning in English and the children, who have just told me the capital of Oregon is Salem, change from the language of Cervantes to that of Shakespeare to respond to their mother. Julia says, "Okay, Mommy." Nico asks, "What?" and Max looks at us, yawns and protests, "But we still have five minutes!" Welcome to a bilingual home. These are some lucky kids. Our children, without any additional effort, came with the dual system installed. *Adiós! A pasarlo bien.* Have a good day!

In this country there are 215 million people over the age of five who use only English to communicate at home. My family belongs to the group of 47 million residents who speak a second language. I am not referring to the absolute number of immigrants; that's another story. I am alluding, based on Census data, to the percentage of immigrants or direct descendants of immigrants who regularly speak to their children in their native language. This figure has grown exponentially in the past few decades. Until recently, parents didn't want to pass on the stigma of being a foreigner to their children, and with the intention of keeping them from facing problems of xenophobia, they buried their language in the memory chest. Today, to speak another language is viewed well socially and the idea prevails that you can be an American and also belong to another culture. To give you an example: Antonio Banderas's daughter will speak Spanish as well as he does, whereas Carly Simon's grandmother from Valencia did not even teach her granddaughter to count to three: *uno, dos, tres.* However, transferring your linguistic heritage to your offspring demands some extra effort that I can understand not everyone is willing or able to provide. It is also a drag for the children, who definitely don't want to cope with weird-speaking parents. Sometimes if you speak to them in your language, which they obviously understand, they will answer you in English. Maybe to avoid embarrassment; or maybe it's simply easier for them. I understand, but excuse me, I don't necessarily want to have foreign kids either. That's the way it is to raise bilingual kids—sometimes difficult for everyone but worth it in the end.

Listen, it goes beyond the language. Children don't generally like strange elements that differentiate them from their peers. The tenor José Manuel Zapata, who is performing at the Met, spent last weekend with us. Sunday morning, he began to sing "O Sole Mio" in the backyard. While he did so, Julia looked all around with a terrified expression to see if any friend of hers was witnessing the spectacle. When Zapata finished, she pulled on my shirt tail to make me bend down and then whispered in my ear: "*Papá*, why can't you just have normal friends?"

But anyway, if you venture into the fascinating world of two languages, which definitely offer two different cultural positions for facing life and, therefore, a wide margin of tolerance, it is wise to establish some guidelines to avoid problems. The first rule speech therapists recommend is to not mix languages. Each phrase should begin and end in the same language. Either, *niño, súbete al coche* or "Kid, get in the car." But no *súbete al car niño* or *get into the coche, kid*. The second golden rule is to decide on the precise occasions for using the two languages. For example: always use English with Mom and Spanish with *Papá*, and when a third person arrives, everyone speaks the best-understood language. The kids tend to be as clever as foxes in this regard, and it's not easy to fool them. If a Spanish friend shows up and speaks to them in English, they notice his accent and jump right into Spanish.

For example, Steve Mosto's father, Adolfo, born in Santiago de Chile, never spoke Spanish to his son. Not a word. "We are Americans and in this house we speak English" settled the question. Also, it didn't help that his mother, a purebred New Yorker, did not understand a word of his father's native language. The only times Steve and his sister Joanne remember having heard their father in original version, without subtitles, was when Adolfo lost his temper or when his family called from the highlands. This doesn't surprise me because, regardless of how well you know another language, you will always rely on your native one for two specific occasions: when angry and while counting.

Steve grew up without ever having noticed that his father was a foreigner. Until the first day of college, that is. When his parents said goodbye to him on the Rutgers campus, another student he'd just met blurted out: "Wow, that's some accent your dad has!" His response was: "Really?" Steve truly didn't know what he was talking about. "Surely," he thinks now, "it must have been a mixture of a natural defense mechanism that denied the evidence and the national ignorance we sometimes demonstrate." But what is certain is that Steve did not realize he belonged to a minority group until the Small Business Administration informed him in 2001 that he had the right to tax breaks. They gave him the benefits established by New York City to favor disadvantaged groups because he was born in Paramonga, Peru, where his father worked as an engineer at a sugar plant. He seized the opportunity to position his company in a highly competitive world, that of steam; a universe I am determined to discover, which is why I'm now on the train in the company of my younger brother, Javier, who has offered to take some pictures of the steam action.

Sarah drops us off at the Rhinecliff station, which until recently was considered a small hamlet of Rhinebeck and today is a desired enclave where a modest house with a view of the river could sell for $1 million. Things have changed. People used to call the inhabitants of Rhinecliff "River Rats." It was largely populated by servants for the estates of the rich families; such as the Astor and Delano estates. There lived the personal maid to the first Mrs. Vincent Astor, the coachman, and many others. Originally Rhinecliff began mostly because of the construction of the railroad. The Italians were the Mexicans of that era. Cheap labor. Hard work. Peggy's friend, Molly Thompson's father, was a good example. Pascuale "Patsy" Della Cella came straight from Italy, never lost his accent, and worked hard to become the superintendent responsible for impeccably maintaining the train line between Rhinebeck and Hudson.

He lived in Rhinecliff. His wife came from Hudson, where her Italian mother ran the numbers. The place was known for its brothels. Molly remembers as a little girl climbing up a fence and watching the men going into the houses. When Sarah's father, Harry H. Hill, Jr., was suffering from ulcerative colitis, Patsy hired him. Harry was in Harvard business school but he was so sick that he took a term off. His doctor told him, get out in the fresh air and do some physical labor. So he worked on the railroad. Hammering ties. And when Harry died, a group of four men came to the house. Peggy had no idea who they were. They said they had worked on the railroad with Harry and they just wanted to come and pay their respects. In the pantry of 6484 Montgomery Street, the Hill-Howe house, there is a memory of that time: a black metal lunch box with H.H. Hill scratched in it. But let me tell you a little bit about my wife's father.

Harry had a severe case of ulcerative colitis when he was 15 years old that remained with him. He never went to class at the University of Virginia without an extra pair of underpants hidden among the books in his briefcase. For that reason, he didn't qualify for active duty during World War II; which almost broke his heart. Every year he would go up to Albany and take the entrance test, and every year he would fail it—for the Army, the Navy, the Marines, the Air Force, the Coast Guards ... even the American Field Service wouldn't take him on as an ambulance driver. So everybody joined up ... but him.

Harry was devastated because 4F people, those who were found to be unfit for military service after formal examination by the Entrance Processing Command, were really vilified and looked down upon. Finally, he talked to the editor of the local paper who advised him: "Harry, don't give it a thought. Get yourself educated so that you can make a better world when the war is over." And off he went to business school at Harvard and then law school at Yale. Right after he graduated, he went to work for the government as an attorney and was stationed in Europe. His assignment was to investigate what the Nazis had done with the Dutch diamonds. In the course of his job, which consisted largely of interrogating German industrialists, Harry traveled through France, Belgium, Austria, England and Germany, where he attended the Nuremberg Trials. Six months later, when his work was finished, he saw Jimmy Byrnes, the American Secretary of State, walked right up to him, and said: "I understand you're going home. I'd like to get a ride on your plane." Harry was invited on board President Truman's personal plane, nicknamed the Sacred Cow. His return from Europe made big news in the *Rhinebeck Gazette* and the *Poughkeepsie Journal* editions of January 31, 1946.

After that, Harry Hill, Jr. felt relieved and glad that he had finally done his bit for his country. There are pictures of him at the American Legion where everybody else is in uniform but he is in a business suit. However, the veterans accepted him because he too had done his part. In May 1946 Harry opened a law office at 13 Montgomery Street, in an historical building that he purchased from the Wager family. He started with just one employee: an old lady who was a family friend and knew some secretarial work. In no time he was surpassing the lawyers in Poughkeepsie when it came to big verdicts. He gained tremendous respect among the insurance companies because he was honest, truthful … and successful. They always wanted to settle with Harry. They never wanted to go to trial.

Harry had a number of legal assistants as his practice grew. The fifth and last one was Bob Marvin, whose many children I have met through the years. Bob remembers my wife's father as a man who was always full of energy and enthusiasm. "He was a funny man," he's told me. "Once he spent a week jumping from the table on the office to the floor. When I asked him what was all that about, Harry told me, 'Well, I'm going to jump soon from an airplane and I need to practice!'"

Harry worked for Redfield Vose, a very wealthy man who wrote the insurance policies for the A&P Co., the largest U.S. food retailer until 1975. Vose had his own plane and his own yacht, and Harry got to know him because he was a friend of Vose's private pilot. They became pals and Vose took Harry to Alaska to investigate A&P's canneries and fisheries.

Then Vose got interested in buying left over DC-3s after World War II in any part of the world and Vose sent Harry off to find them. So the Rhinebeck lawyer went to Hong Kong, found an abandoned plane, and got in touch with Vose. "Where are you?" the insurance man inquired. "In Hong Kong," Harry happily replied. "What?!! Get out of there right now; it's too dangerous! Forget about the DC-3!" "All right," Harry said, "but since you don't want it, do you mind if I buy it for myself?" "Do what you want, but just get out of there!" "Okay." So Harry borrowed money from banks, his mother and a few other people, and got that plane home filled with things he had bought in Hong Kong: rugs, furniture ... After that he went back to his practice but the DC-3 episode was always in the back of his mind. Then Vose called and said, "I want you to go back for more planes. I'll pay your way." So Harry took his wife Peggy with him and off they went on an international airplane shopping spree.

To make a long story short, Harry ended up buying six planes for himself, which he leased to North Central Airways, a commuter airline in Chicago. They couldn't use jets because they only needed to cover short distances, but those propeller planes worked beautifully. Ultimately, he sold the planes to that company—all but one, which he kept. And the family took one trip to Florida. Soon after that, Harry arranged a golfing trip and invited 30 friends from Rhinebeck. Peggy was dropped off at the halfway point, in Richmond, Virginia, where she visited a friend, and the group of Rhinebeck men continued on flying to St. Augustine, Florida for a whole week of playing golf with the boys under the blue sky. But the very next morning Harry suffered a heart attack in the breakfast lounge and died. The terrible news traveled fast to Rhinebeck, but Peggy couldn't get home by plane to her five children because the weather was atrocious. She had to return by train—a journey that seemed endless.

Bob Marvin, by then an associate of Harry's, took over the practice. I can't tell you the number of people of that generation who still stop Sarah on the street to regale her with a new anecdote about her father, and quite often with watery eyes. He was a character who touched many souls, and a lot of people truly miss him. I am so sorry my wife didn't get the opportunity to know him well.

Javier and I take Amtrak. The trip passes by the third and last stretch of the 315-mile-long river that begins on lands claimed by both Iroquois and Algonquian. It is an impressive river that has tides three feet high every 12 hours. The stream advances at an average of one mile per day but the combination of islands and bends, added to the effect of lunar attraction, speeds up the current in some stretches to several miles per hour, creating whirlpools that put the odds firmly against a swimmer being able to stay afloat. The Hudson flows at sea level from Troy, the city of the mythical butcher Samuel Wilson, the Uncle Sam who supplied U.S. troops during war against the British in 1812. The salty ocean waters penetrate more than 70 miles of the upper river, creating an estuary. The natives called the Hudson *Mah-hea-kun-tuck*, the river that flows in two directions. In this habitat, freshwater fish co-exist with oyster beds and abundant marine creatures.

An eagle circles obsessively above us. They have returned. The DDT farmers used against pests in the 1960s turned eagle eggs soft and they broke before hatching. The species was on the verge of extinction. In 1972, the use of DDT was prohibited. The half-life of DDT in the soil is 23 years. The danger has passed. Now you can see dozens of nests close to the Rondout waters, near the town of Wawarsing. The eagles swoop down to catch rainbow trout in their claws and consume them in the treetops.

Things have improved tremendously. Back in the 1960s in Newburgh, Steve Levine used to go down to the river with friends after school. There was a small waterway called Murderers Creek. Two miles upstream was the DuPont factory and others dumping carcinogens, paint, Benzine … all kinds of chemicals into the water. Downstream, before the Hudson, a mill dyed felt for pool tables and all sort of things. So, they would go out there on a Tuesday and the water would be orange. Thursday it'd be purple. Saturday it'd be green. Steve and his peers played a game in which they had to guess which color the river would be that morning.

Besides the dye, they also had raw sewage running into the Hudson. So they had to navigate among human drops, chemicals and dye. Directly across from Newburgh, in Beacon, there was also a battery factory. That site has long been closed, but to this day, it's still a hot spot for all the Cadmium that was involved in the battery making process. "Maybe that's the reason why," Steve told me once, laughing, "I look this way. Hee, hee."

In the early 1980s Steve bought a warehouse in Newburgh to start a clothing business. It was a former tile manufacturing plant and it was packed with electrical transformers—six of them, each the size of a car and full of PCBs. The substance used as a conductor, that companies like GE dumped into the Hudson—a good coolant, but very dangerous for the environment. When he bought the plant he walked down to the river and the rocks were all green and purple and white. It kind of looked like a gold mine. The rocks of the cliff had been marbleized because they dumped the entire mineral excess over them while they were still hot and they melted and covered the whole shore. It was bizarre. And it is still there. It's never going to break.

Not too long ago the Hudson River was disgusting. It was slimy, filthy, smelly and oily. Not any more. In the late 70s the environmental movement started to clean it up. At the same time a lot of industries closed down and moved South because of cheaper labor. DuPont said, goodbye, we're out of here. So did Texaco, Nabisco and many more. Good news for the water, but really bad news for the employees.

In April, the buds of the trees timidly reproduce the landscape in a pale, pointillist version of autumn. There are red buds of chestnut, the brown of the red oaks, the yellow-green of weeping willows, which contrast with the little white flowers of the dogwood, the yellow of the dried oak leaves and the green of the pine trees. It's amazing what you can learn about nature by living in it. There's nothing like going to Rome to understand the Romans. I know things now that I would never have imagined occupying part of my hard drive. For example, I recently learned that a sheep is capable of memorizing between 20 and 30 human faces. After that, it will see you, but it won't know you; therefore, it will think you're a vet and will take off running. Another thing: if you want to identify the males in a flock of geese, you need only notice which ones are missing feathers, because they have plucked one another during their fights for the females.

On the train I open the notebook that I'm bringing to take notes. A piece of paper falls from the pages. My brother grabs it from the floor and looks at it with curiosity. "What is this?" "An invoice," I reply. "Are you renting your house from the church?" "Yes, we are," I answer him with a smirk. "But I thought you guys owned it." "Well, we thought so too." "What do you mean?" "Oh, it's a legal nightmare. The Old English system found its way to the New World."

I've learned this piece of history through Buddy Rogers, the soft-spoken man who takes care of the Reformed Church on South Street. I went to pay him a visit and we sat on a table full of old maps and some yellow documents dated more than 200 years ago. "In Rhinebeck," Rogers volunteered to me, "there lived a wealthy landowner whose name was Henry Beekman, a New York City merchant. In 1697 Beekman secured from the English crown, through the colony's governor, a vast parcel of land from which the village and town of Rhinebeck were created. With the arrival of Dutch and German settlers fleeing the wars and famine of continental Europe there arose a desire to establish Lutheran and Reformed Dutch churches. Beekman was of the Reformed faith and by a deed dated August 26, 1730, granted two parcels of land to the newly formed congregation of Palatines coming from Kingston:

"The first consisting of two acres to be used for the building of a church and a cemetery and the other parcel consisting of forty four acres which "tract shall be employed to the benefit and behoof of the church forever...and in neglected whereof...contrary to what it is intended to be granted for...land to revoline its property to the said Henry Beekman his heirs and assigns, as if such instrument as these presents had never been made."

Uh-oh. Good old Henry introduced in his deed a funny stipulation: the church could only use his land to generate resources for the congregation. Not to sell it. Otherwise, it will reverse to the Beekman heirs. Okay. What kind of resources? Lumber, stone and oil if they were lucky enough to discover it … but that miracle did not happen. The Palatines were also supposed to take sap from the pine trees and use it to make varnish for the British navy, but it didn't work out either. The sap quality was not good. So what was next? Years went by with the land just sitting there and the church needed money. To get around the problem, about 1792 they divided Beekman's property into 134 lots with the idea of leasing them in perpetuity to people willing to build a house. The initial price was $12 a year. Unfortunately, the demand wasn't as great as the reverend expected, so the lots were put out to bid. They sold, I mean they leased, but some for a sum as low as 50 cents a year. In any case, at the time the whole operation made a decent amount of money for the church: $850.

The problem is that, more than two centuries later, the Rhinebeck Reformed Church keeps collecting annually the same amount of money for the land lease: $850. That's peanuts for the congregation. To be honest, a pain in the neck because of the time consumed and the expense of collecting the rent surpassed its profits. The church would love to end this chapter of history. Sell all the lots at once, make some money and move forward. The house owners would love to end the nonsense of sending a 50 cents check in an envelope with a stamp that is worth more than the included payment. Nobody is happy with the system. Not even the banks. Only a few years ago they wouldn't even take mortgages on these properties. You know, bankers are very square-minded and they don't like to loan money to owners who actually don't own their own houses. Go figure. Thank God eventually somebody came up with a temporary solution. Now, in order to get a mortgage the house owner has to pay in advance all the church rent for the term of the mortgage. If the lot has a rent of $1 a year and the mortgage last 30 years, the buyer will have to give $30 to Buddy Rogers before he or she gets approved by the bank.

Other churches in the state of New York have experienced similar situations, but none of them had the unique revision clause that Beekman wrote in his deed. Rhinebeck has the exclusivity in this legal nightmare. Buddy pointed out to me that if the church stops the leases, which pretty much means stopping using the land to generate income for the church, the land will go back to Henry Beekman heirs—and there are thousands of Livingstons in the U.S. somehow related to the original owner.

So, the astronauts went to the Moon, but I will have to keep paying the Reformed Church a ridiculous check for the rest of my life. Really? Rogers surprised me with an answer. He tells me that back in the 1960s Sarah's father explained to him that the only way the church could legally get out from under it was with a special act of estate legislation. "But," as Harry pointed out, "the kicker comes in: to prepare the necessary paperwork to be considered by a State legislator would have cost a minimum of $50,000 in fees. A quantity out of proportion for the church's modest budget then, and still an unaffordable amount today." "Any other solution?" Yes, Harry Hill Jr. suggested a much cheaper one: "Get a law school taking it on as a class project. It will be a fascinating challenge for the students, don't you think?" Hello, Columbia! ... Fordham? Is anybody in Syracuse or Albany listening to me? I hope so. Actually, probably the problem could be fixed today in a classroom as a school project. All it will take is a bunch of teenagers tracking with patience on their computers all the Beekman living heirs. Why? Getting the heirs to give up their rights on Henry's will would set free the church and allow Buddy to sell the property once and for all. Amen.

As soon as we leave the Rhinecliff station, the tracks cross the private train stops of the great mansions. That of the Mills, the Vanderbilts and the Roosevelts ... Grand homes belonging to illustrious names of course, but ... to live in one of them, to spend your life in one of them, that of Sam Hall stands out above the rest. Sam is possibly the man with the fastest reflexes in the entire valley, the screenwriter known for his work in daytime soap operas like *Dark Shadows*. He lives in a wonder among wonders. It is the only mansion facing southeast, and therefore has light year-round. Not a minor detail considering the long New York winters. It has large rooms and a terrace in the attic (unlike most of the mansions, where the attic is divided into tiny rooms for the service staff), where you can sip a dry Martini as you witness a sunset that will force you to pinch yourself every afternoon to confirm that you're not dreaming.

We pass through Beacon, named for the bonfires that were lit on the hilltops to warn the patriots of the arrival of the British armada. The Americans placed massive iron chains here to impede the advance of the British fleet.

Javier points to the Military Academy at West Point. In this location, the Catskill Aqueduct crosses under the river. It is a civil engineering work comparable to the Suez Canal. There are 133 miles of pipes to carry from the mountains the 1.8 billion gallons of water that are consumed daily in the Greater New York area. A height difference of 985 feet between the reservoir and the water's final destination gives the water enough energy to reach up to a building's sixth floor without being pumped.

"Croton-Harmon. Croton-Harmon," the conductor announced. Here, the diesel engines of the train stop and the train hooks up to the electric system. Yonkers, Nyack and the Tappan Zee, where the Hudson widens so much it resembles the open ocean. George Washington Bridge, one of the world's largest hanging structures, the Harlem Bridge, and finally, the city. Here we come, New York. "Start spreading the news. It's up to youuu, New York, New Yoooork..."

10

May

On July 18, 2007, a tremendous explosion shook the windows of Grand Central Station. Frightened travelers who looked out toward the street saw a terrifying column of smoke rising above the nearby Chrysler Building. It was 6:00 p.m. There were rumors of a second terrorist attack in New York City and telephone lines went dead. Panic spread. At the intersection of Lexington Avenue and 41st Street, a 400-foot steam geyser spewed a mixture of asphalt, cement and metal, which descended over the streets of Midtown Manhattan as if it were a new Biblical plague. The geyser roared like Niagara Falls, and thousands of people who had just finished their workday ran through the streets. But not everyone got away. A tow truck was lifted 12 feet by the escaping gas and its two occupants were scalded over 80 percent of their bodies by the 400°F steam. A block away, a 51-year-old woman died of a heart attack. Three firemen and a police officer were seriously injured as they tried to save lives. The rest of the people ran and ran, abandoning purses and briefcases amid the panic. Many lost their shoes during their desperate escape. The streets were deserted, with people's personal effects littering the sidewalks, like the photograms of the Warsaw ghetto that Polanski portrayed in his movie *The Pianist*.

Inside the area cordoned off by police, a 40 feet by 30 feet crater spewed orange flames that made the mud boil like volcanic lava. On the radio, a city hall spokesperson warned that the huge crater could expand since cracks indicated the collapse of the entire affected area. The horrific spectacle lasted a couple of hours. Finally, Mayor Michael Bloomberg called a press conference to announce that Al Qaeda had nothing to do with the explosion. That was the first sigh of relief. What was it then? A failure in the city infrastructure. Specifically, in the steam system. Steam? The media immediately focused on Con Edison. But it was not company policy to offer details. "We are investigating the accident," they said. Con Edison President Kevin Burke indicated that the explosion might have been triggered by the downpour in the city that morning. The rain seeping into the ground after the storm could have caused the steam to condense, he said, which just confused journalists. "What is he talking about? The rain caused an explosion? What should we write in the headlines?"

The hope of obtaining a coherent explanation about what happened in Midtown came from a modest office at 23 W. 36th Street, the headquarters of Mosto Technologies Inc. After an endless string of calls and emails, a public relations agency managed to locate Steve Mosto. "Could you explain to the press what happened?" "Yes." "Wonderful!" They contacted him early on July 19, assigned him a personal assistant, Tina, and at midday called him to a downtown hotel for a press conference. They urged him to dress nicely. In light of the solemnity of the occasion, Steve appeared in an impeccable wool suit. Unfortunately, the insufferable heat of the New York summer caused him to sweat profusely. Uh-oh. The PR director yelled in desperation: "Tinaaaaaaa!" The assistant ran downstairs to buy a new shirt for Mr. Mosto. They also gave him a razor, shaving cream and aftershave lotion. He was given precise instructions: "Hurry up and get ready, please, because the media are becoming restless in the conference room." "No problem." A few minutes later, the Steam King was ready and walked down the hall to the conference room. It was his moment of glory. "Make sure, Mr. Mosto, that your answers are brief and concise," Tina reminded him before opening the door. "Don't worry, Tina," Steve replied. "Remember you don't have to respond to everything they ask. Understood?" "Okay." "Be careful because the press will try to make you name a guilty party; just stick to recounting the facts. Got it?" "Got it, Tina." "And don't make your answers too long. Is that clear?" "Yes, yes ... " The door opened and just as Tina had predicted, all the major media outlets had come: Fox, ABC, CBS, the *New York Times*, *Daily News*, *New York Post*, NPR, Crain's ... "Tina?" "Yes?" "I need to tell you something." "What is it, Mr. Mosto?" "This is so cool!"

That afternoon, journalists at last got an idea about what had occurred. Although just as Tina had predicted, Steve had to make like a bullfighter and dodge the bull. Far from the objectivity our profession prescribes, some journalists ceaselessly insisted that Steve should accuse Con Edison so they could open their news programs and articles with that. He was disgusted to witness how a Peabody Award winner tried to wear him down to the point where Steve would have said something that wasn't true. "So, Mr. Mosto, according to you, the accident could have been avoided, correct?" "Well, preventive measures can always be increased but ... " "I see, but technically, you would say that Con Edison is responsible for what happened, isn't that right?" "Look, Con Ed is responsible for distributing steam, but we are talking about an accident which..." and, a few hours later, that same interviewer appeared on television: "You heard it yourselves, the steam expert seems to point to Con Ed as the party directly responsible for the tragic occurrence. Investigators will have the next word. Now, on to sports."

It took Steve, three days and two nights to satiate the New York media's hunger for pipes and pressure gauges. Question, answer. Question, answer. Finally, the telephone stopped ringing and the privilege of being on the front page reverted back to the usual heroes. But Steve's vast knowledge about safety reached the ears of the municipal authorities. City Hall invited him to advise the commission that was preparing an investigation associated with the July 18 explosion. Steve took the floor and explained to the advisors how the system worked and the probable causes of the fatal accident. He answered many questions and helped develop initiatives for preventing more accidents in the future.

Overnight, he became New York's steam expert. Steam Man, the man responsible for developing the new safety measures the city is adopting.

But my story takes places four and a half years before the events described above. May 2003. The 24-inch underground steam pipe installed in 1924 near Grand Central Terminal had yet to explode. "Hi, Steve." "Hi, guys." The engineer who wants to be a guitar hero in his next life smiles at us. He's just about to take us on a tour beneath Manhattan. He's going to show us where the steam that emanates from manholes comes from. We are enthusiastic. "Are you ready?" "You bet." "Okay, let's move on."

It's pleasant outside and like any sensitive person who visits New York on a spring day, we wish we lived here. Under the light of the May sun, the streets of Manhattan look like a scene from a Woody Allen movie. We walk up Sixth Avenue where the hot dog vendors are serving the first hungry office workers of the afternoon. The smell of sauerkraut wafts above the sidewalks. We head towards Rockefeller Center. We are not going to climb 850 feet to reach the Top of the Rock observation deck in the Art Deco building. No. We'll be travelling in the opposite direction: towards the center of the Earth.

The thermometer reads 55°F outside. We decide to do a little loop and cross Fifth Avenue to admire the Public Library building up close. The library supposedly holds the Spanish poet García Lorca manuscript that Pancho José's owner urged me to check out. At the front door of the magnificent building, we observe the stone lions: Strength and Patience. Mayor LaGuardia gave them their nicknames because he believed that New Yorkers exhibited those two traits during the Great Depression. At 44th Street, we spot our first steam leak. Hurray! I point it out to Steve. "I'm sorry to say that it isn't a steam leak," he informs us. "What?" Next to the zebra crossing, a nine-foot orange plastic chimney belches white smoke. "Well, that sure seems like steam to me," Javier says. "It is indeed," Steve confirms. "Wait a minute," I jump into the conversation, trying to keep my cool. "Let's try to work this out: so it is steam escaping from somewhere, but it's not a steam leak. I see."

Manhattan is built on a rock bed, which makes it hard to dig trenches in the ground. Thus, all utility companies take advantage of the "six-feet-under" channels to lay their pipes. The water pipes run above those of steam and when the former suffer a leak, the water drips down on a pipe which has a temperature of 338°F. "What you get is steam," Steve tells me, enjoying my amazement, but it's not from a leak in the heating system, but rather a leak in the water conduction. The drinking water boils as soon as it touches the hot pipe. Transformed into steam, it seeks the first grate it can find to escape outside. Manhattan sidewalks offer 3,000 grates to choose from. When one of these leaks is detected, authorities place a chimney on it to ensure that pedestrians don't get burned. The chimneys are orange cylinders with white reflective tape that fit over thick plastic funnels. Technically, this type of leak is known as lazy steam and does not pose significant risk. To identify it, navy blue tape is placed on the top of the chimney. New York's steam loop is fed from seven steam plants; three of which are also used to produce electricity. These plants run on gas during the warm months and diesel during the cold winter months since the former does not burn well at low temperatures.

The beauty is that, thanks to a free transportation called pressure, the steam flows from the plant to the houses through the pipes without needing to be pumped. The speed will be determined by the width of the pipes. The wider the pipe, the less friction the steam would have to support and the faster it will travel. With a very narrow pipe, the steam would lose force and stop before reaching the buildings. With an exaggerated wide pipe, the steam would effortlessly climb to the top of the Chrysler Building. So ... you got it. The width of New York's underground steam pipelines was determined by compromising between the ideal width and the cost of iron.

Fisssssss! We came around another white geyser. This is definitely a more virulent leakage. Steve estimates that it's at green alert level: a steam trap malfunctioned. "Wow," I say, alarmed. "That doesn't sound good. Shouldn't we ask for help?" Tinaaaaaaa!

As the steam advances through the pipes, it leaves a liquid trail, just like snails do. That water is technically known as condensate and it must be eliminated at all costs if we are to avoid the consequences of the fearful water hammer. *Boom*!! The term "water hammer" refers to the disaster occurring when a watery mass hits the walls of a pipe at full speed, like the battering ram that was used in ancient times to strike the castle gates. "Steve…?" "Yes?" "There won't be an explosion here, will there?" "No, we're safe," he assures me. It's all so confusing. Let me see if I can clear this up.

The condensate circulates at the bottom of the pipe while the steam, which weighs less and moves more quickly, occupies the top part. Traps are installed at the bottom of the pipes to drain the excess liquid. The condensate, like the train that advances without the conductor in action movies, tends to slow when the land is flat. Engineers know this and lay the pipes at a three-percent decline to force the condensed water towards the traps.

Pipes leave the manufacturing plant with a diameter of 30 inches, and enter the buildings with a section of 12. The joints are narrow only in the upper part of the pipe because, if they used concentric reducers, the condensate would remain trapped at the bottom of the funnel-shaped joint, like salmon in river dams, and could not jump to the narrower pipe of the next stretch. So it won't reach the trap.

Properly functioning steam traps open to release condensate and automatically close when steam is present. However, if the mechanism fails and the condensate starts to accumulate, the valves self-destruct, opening the traps completely, and the steam emerges in the light. *Fissssss*!!!! At $25 per thousand pounds, Con Ed loses a bundle. "Oh, well," says Steve Mosto. "Better to lose money than human lives."

At last we reach Rockefeller Center, the largest private building project ever undertaken in modern times. If you look up and observe the facades of the skyscrapers, you can easily spot the mechanical floors. They are dark because those floors have no windows. A machine room in the basement suffices for traditional buildings, but the towers need to distribute them throughout their structure to achieve greater energy efficiency. For every 10 floors of housing, skyscrapers have to devote one floor for equipment. This coincides with the structural need to connect the central pillar with the external weight-bearing walls. The problem is solved by filling in some floors with iron triangles, which make it impossible to inhabit the space but which can house some machinery. This solution explains the mysterious disappearance of the 13th floor in many elevators.

We can no longer see the sun by the time we reach 1251 Avenue of the Americas, the Exxon building, flanked by buildings over 500 feet tall. It is the second-highest building in the complex: 750 feet divided into 54 stories. Con Edison is responsible for maintaining the steam piping up to the meters located at the building's entrances. Once past the private property wall, responsibility for installation and maintenance, including possible leaks, falls exclusively on property owners. Steve found this out shortly after returning from his musical adventure in Tennessee. He learned that the pipelines were more than 100 years old and sprung lots of leaks. Technicians served the needs outside but no one was responsible for maintaining them inside the buildings. The astronomical price of NY property had forced multinationals to move south in search of more affordable headquarters. They took all their qualified employees with them. By the mid-1990s, there wasn't a single steam engineer in Manhattan. In 1997, Mosto Technologies Inc. was born. Steve based his business strategy on a simple objective: help major real estate complexes save money on their steam bills.

The Twin Towers were his best customers. The World Trade Center required hundreds of thousands of dollars in repairs annually. Initially, they asked Steve for periodic checkups and a few new parts. The installation of new equipment, where the real money was, was beyond Mosto's capabilities. Any company that wants to undertake reforms in a New York City building has to be bonded for $10 million, which for him would have meant a payout of some $50,000 annually. Impossible. Forget it. But the Port Authority of New York and New Jersey, the agency that owned the famous towers, trusted him and let him know it: "We trust you, Mosto." "But I don't have any insurance," he told them. "It doesn't matter. You provide the materials and the workers and we'll cover you under our policy. Just don't make any mistakes. If you cause us problems, we'll make you pay through the nose." "Got it."

He was given an extraordinary opportunity: a $500,000 budget that persuaded him to put most of his eggs in one basket. Who could have predicted the tragedy of 9/11? In 1993, the World Trade Center had suffered a terrorist attack in which six people died. One of them could easily have been Mosto. As an employee of a service company, he made regular visits to the same basement where the explosion had blown a 100-foot hole in the reinforced concrete. But that was a long time ago and now the future looked bright. The project consisted of replacing an obsolete valve, Old Bertha. To install the new parts and machinery, Mosto faced the difficult task of demolishing a 50-foot wall, which, paradoxically, would collapse on its own just a few months later.

After the attacks, Steve's business took a nosedive. Together with the understandable sense of anxiety he shared with fellow citizens, Mosto had the personal misfortune of having lost 40 percent of his income in one fell swoop. The remaining 60 percent would decrease by more than half in the weeks that followed. The world was obsessed with safety, concerned about the possibility of new attacks, and no one was thinking about investing a cent in repairs. Through no fault of his own, he was billing only a third of his previous income. The unexpected blow put Mosto Technologies Inc. dangerously close to declaring Chapter 11.

Steve had to act quickly. He requested a meeting with Joe Szabo, engineering manager of Rockefeller Center, to try to convince him: "Joe, you need me." In 2001, the complex had a steam bill of nearly $2 million. Steve offered to gradually reduce costs by locating internal leaks in the system. "I'm a steam buster, Joe." "What exactly are you proposing, Steve?" "I only ask for a percentage of what I manage to save you." Szabo listened with interest and decided to give him an opportunity. "Okay." The first year, Mosto Technologies reduced the Con Edison bill by $50,000. Gradually, he learned how to work more efficiently and six seasons later, the annual savings at the Rockefeller Center approached $200,000 annually.

We go down to the basement of the complex, which is like the engine room of a ship. The heat is unbearable, but Steve is happy here, like the Phantom of the Opera in the bowels of the theater. "How do you like that, men?" he asks, smiling. "It's pretty, isn't it?" Thick yellow pipes bring down the steam that comes from the street at a speed of 100 feet per second. "Don't touch them," Steve warns Javier who is getting close to take a picture. "We're talking 374°F." The steam travels up through the building's 54 floors, it is thanked for services rendered, and sent down the drain without a second thought. Con Ed doesn't accept returns and millions of gallons of water are lost. Water that is more than 1,000 times purer than the water that comes out of the faucet because the evaporation process eliminates all minerals. Any bottling company reading this chapter?

Click. Click. Javier keeps taking pictures and I keep asking questions. The steam circulating above the condensate cools and condenses, reducing its volume by 1,700 times. This action produces a void that violently suctions the water, causing it to hit the roof of the pipe. *Clang!* That's the familiar sound that we've all heard in the radiators at home. After the clang, the water bounces, forming a wave that advances down the pipe. More steam arrives and once again, when it floats over the water, it condenses adding liquid to the pond and causing a new clang. The wave keeps growing like a tsunami. *Clang, clang, clang,* until the water completely plugs the pipe, forcing the steam that comes at full speed from behind to shoot the condensate out like a cannon ball. This water bullet eventually collides with the steam ahead of it, and expands, building up pressure 10 times higher than the pipes can withstand. *Boom!* The result will be a tremendous explosion that could cause the building collapse. Voilà, the water hammer!

July 18, 2007, the intensity of the storm that hit New York in the early morning overwhelmed the suction capacity of the drains of the sewer system. At Lexington Avenue and 41st Street, the pipeline section flooded. The rainwater started to cool the metal walls of the steam pipes, producing a large amount of condensate inside. There was still hope: 800 feet away, there were two traps. But both failed. The condensate brought with it the remains of a powerful industrial adhesive, epoxy, which had been used recently to seal a leak in a joint. The epoxy blocked the trap's opening mechanisms. The rest is history.

Click. My brother Javier's camera is digital but he added the mechanical sound to give the illusion of snapping pictures. In the middle of the basement, we stumble across some giant fans driven, like the wheels on a boat, by steam pressure. Since the windows of this gigantic buildings in New York could not be opened, the law mandates that at least 15 percent of the air must be fresh air to maintain healthy ventilation. During cold weather, the steam heats the air that is transported with the force of the fans to the grates of apartments and offices. In summer, the process is inverted: the steam is used to compress a gas called 134A that absorbs heat as it expands.

This ingenious system, conceived in 1924, is still used today in the basement of the Rockefeller Center, but with 21st-century smart technology. Before a sophisticated control panel, the supervisor decides how long the building will be connected to the Con Ed network to avoid the peak hour of 7:00 a.m., when it has to compete with the demands of 2,000 other buildings in the city. When we return to the daylight, Steve suggests another adventure: a visit to Ground Zero to meet his friend Dennis Malopolski. We accept his offer.

* * *

The work to clear the debris has advanced considerably, but the site still produces quite an impression: the enormous black hole gives me goose bumps. Here the Twin Towers were erected, the crown jewels of the Port Authority.

"Hi, Dennis." Steve introduces us to Dennis Malopolski, the mechanics supervisor who was responsible for the complex energy network that provided power to the World Trade Center—the customer that received one of the highest bills for steam consumption in the whole city. Only the United Nations and Peter Cooper Village, the residential development on the banks of the East River, paid more. By replacing the system's obsolete steam traps alone, Steve was able to save the WTC a million dollars the first year. "Wow," my brother says. "No wonder they're so nice to you." Steve smiles. *Click.*

Next to the offices, a Memory Room has been set up. It is a place where the families of victims can go when they need to. Malopolski invites us to go in. I feel a chill down my spine. It's full of portraits. Many of them are young people. Recent graduates with brilliant careers ahead of them. Twenty-something-year-olds that worked for the world's leading financial firms. The best of the best. Dennis breaks the silence. "I lost 75 friends all at once that day," he says. "Seventy-five." I get a lump in my throat. "I was luckier than they were," he says, sobbing, "because I was able to escape by boat." There are many dedications, poems, keepsakes. "If tears could build a stairway, and memories were a lane, I'd walk right up to heaven and bring you back home again." Some parents have left a biography of their son. Unopened presents, stuffed animals, good-luck charms are stored here. It's called the Family Observatory. It has a splendid bay window that overlooks Ground Zero, from where you can observe the progress of the works.

We climb into a van, with Dennis at the wheel. He drives us to the underground parking and we cross the esplanade where the new Freedom Tower is planned. You can guess the location of the fallen buildings by the 5-inch steel pillars sticking out every 10 feet, the shadows casting their silhouettes on the ground. The World Trade Center had 116 floors, six of them below ground. It had the largest refrigeration system in the universe, whose only remaining testimony are four huge pipes: two blue pipes for Tower One and two green ones for Tower Two. The pipes have walls five feet thick. Through them, after the process of steam cooling, the overheated water was discharged into the river. I can't help but imagine the fish in the Hudson surprised by the flood of warmth and the fishermen taking the stripers out of the water already pre-cooked. I come with this idea because I'm a sympathizer of Trout Unlimited. I get the annual calendar, the car sticker, and all that. Dennis corrects me: "Actually, it wasn't so bad. The maximum temperature of the water from the WTC heating system that was discharged into the river was 90°F." A nice warm hot tub.

In the remains of the parking lot, the fireproofing material marks the spot where the reinforced steel structure was. It is a type of gray foam produced by mixing cement and a soft rock called vermiculite. Dennis tells us that the beams were designed to withstand a four-hour-long domestic fire before the steel would overheat. He says that when the plane hit the building, it caused the effect of a snow plow. It pushed everything in its path into the corner, creating a flashpoint where the fire took on impressive proportions.

We go into the tunnel. "What is this?" "It's an old train tunnel that was incorporated into the WTC structure to give access to delivery trucks." A tunnel that leads us ... to an underground station built in 1908? I feel like the Goonies when they discovered the lost caves. On the other side of the wall sits the safe of the Swiss Bank, where gold and silver bars worth $200 million were recovered. The safe walls are five feet thick. It required a week of work, with heavy machinery, to get inside it. Lives are lost but money remains. In the 1970s, the abandoned station was turned into a storage center. The tunnel that trains used in 1905 to cross beneath the Hudson still remains. Wait a minute. Hasn't anyone ever told Stephen King about this? An armor-plated chamber containing $200 million in gold ingots and a hidden tunnel that connects to the Jersey waterfront without raising suspicion? What more could you ask for? What was Spiderman doing in the movie hanging from the window of the 100th floor when the real intrigue is actually 65 feet below ground?

We head upstairs. Onlookers gather on the other side of the fences. Ground Zero has already become a powerful magnet for attracting crowds. "When the reconstruction is finished," says Malopolski with a sigh, "we'll be the largest tourist attraction in the city. We'll be number one. I say that with pride, because it will be a New York tribute to our people fallen in combat." We hug goodbye. It's hard to believe, but 50,000 people worked till very recently in the space before our eyes. The entire population of a city like Sarasota, Florida. And nobody is here anymore.

* * *

The emotions stirred by the visit make us silent on the train ride home. "Do you want to work a bit on the script?" "Nah, I don't think so." "*Candida* is supposed to be a comedy, right?" "Right." "Then … forget it." "Okay." Down the aisle I spot the head of my neighbor Al DeCotiis. He likes to play the electric guitar and sometimes I hear him practicing while walking Lola around the block. And yes, this friendly low-key guy founded one of the top marketing research firms in the US: Phoenix Marketing International. Al researches what the market demands are for many big companies. If a TV network is going to launch a new show, they call Al to do a study on what the audience would like to watch. If a car manufacturer is upgrading a car model, they contact Al to figure out which gadgets would appeal to the young drivers. And so on. So Al knows what's going on in America. "After so much research, what's your conclusion about the States, Al?" I asked him once. "Well, it seems that we now live in a country with no purpose," he replied. "Wow!"

Gradually, the magnificent nature bursting from the riverbanks reminds us that life is always much more powerful than death. No matter how much you cut the grass on the ground, the roots remain below and the plant will re-sprout with more force after pruning. I know that Al is confident that we'll find our path again. We should be confident. We must overcome.

11

June

I'm planting peonies in the yard. This is the second time I've attempted it. The first was last week, after which I accidently mowed them down with the lawn mower. I don't know what it is about that diabolical contraption, but after starting the engine, it transmits an insatiable desire to devour any vegetation in my path. It must be genetic. Once we gave my father an electric saw for Father's Day, *rrrmm, rrrrm* … and if my mother hadn't stopped him, he would have transformed all of our backyard trees into bonsais. For some reason, it is every man's dream to have a gift certificate for Conway's Lawn & Power Equipment. The aforementioned peonies come from Locust Grove, Samuel Morse's estate in Poughkeepsie. The house of the inventor of the famous code … dot, dot, dot, dash, dash, dash … is now a museum and its shop sells cuttings of the original peonies planted in its gardens in 1898. What a year—the same one as that of the Spanish-American War. Hopefully, more than a century later, these white flowers will serve as a symbol of peace at my house.

I'm not the only one working in the yard on this sunny morning. It's Memorial Day, when many people put their hands in the soil. Americans share the true passion of Thomas Jefferson, who wrote at Monticello: "No occupation is as delightful to me as the culture of the earth, and no culture comparable to that of the garden."

Peas are the first to be planted because they aren't afraid of frosts and they have to be ready for the 4th of July menu. Then come lettuces, broccoli, brussel sprouts, kale and potatoes. The rest of the vegetables have to wait until the ground gets warmer. At the Phantom Gardener, where a sign warns you that "all unattended kids will allegedly be given an espresso and a free puppy," Norbert Lazar teaches a workshop with useful tips for beginners. To prepare a plot for gardening, for instance, you should plant wheat grass. It will kill the rest of the weeds. Let it grow, not too tall though, and then cut it down. Build raised planting beds to make weeding easier and allow roots to grow downward instead of spreading out. Ideal for nice long carrots, raised beds will provide you extra room to grow more plants. Every two weeks, sow a new row of lettuce, arugula and romaine seeds and label them so you can have continuous harvests. Potatoes and beans are complimentary since they tend to repel the other's enemy beetle. Carrots and basil love tomatoes. Interplant squash, beans and corn. Squash leaves provide shade to the bean seedlings, which will later grow wrapped around the corn stalks. Green beans will have provided abundant nitrogen to the soil by the time they are ready for harvest. Finally, Norbert gives us two very special pieces of advice. First, a well-kept secret: a gardener's best tool is the Japanese Hori Hori weeding knife. And, of course, Norbert's most important lesson: "The fact that you *can* doesn't necessarily mean that you *should*." If the plant you want is going to kill a local species, the Phantom Gardener won't sell it to you.

Sarah and I walk to the school. Today are the elections for three members of the school board and the annual school budget. At the last minute, an unexpected candidate has joined the race. During the electoral campaign, he hung a sign at the intersection of South Parsonage and the street that leads to the school. It's a board painted with an arrow pointing the way to exercise the right to vote. The sign thanks voters for their participation in the election and, curiously, includes his name in large block letters. Some neighbors are against propagandizing in front of the school and they show their displeasure with comments launched from their car windows. The new candidate is unfazed. He sits in a folding chair next to the highway, greeting people on their way to the polls. Good morning. We pass by him, following on foot the same route Sarah or I take by car every morning at 7:10 a.m. to drop off Max at middle school. From the house, we have to cross Market Street, where there is always a traffic jam at the intersection. Fortunately, for every three or four cars heading down, there is always a nice driver who stops to let us cross even though there is no obligation to do so. These little things make getting up early much more pleasant. We pass to the south side of town and go by the minipark. On the east side of the street, there is a traffic sign that always catches my eye. It's white and has a silhouette in the shape of a large duck followed by four ducklings. It reads, "Watch out for ducks."

To the west lies Crystal Lake, with houses nestled among the trees near the shore. There was a time when, during the long winters, ice was harvested from these waters and stored in warehouses to be used during the summer. In the late 19th century, the United States managed to cut from its frozen waters 25 million tons of ice annually, which was shipped from Boston to Japan, China, the islands of Southeast Asia, South America, the Caribbean and occasionally, even some Mediterranean port. In this way, the frozen rivers and lakes of northern regions provided work to thousands of people who otherwise would have been unemployed during the winter months. It was a much larger industry than you would think— in 1886, ice exports produced revenues comparable to those obtained by the sale of cotton or grains.

When the average temperature reached 10°F, the lake surface would freeze in a few days. A week later, when the ice sheet thickened to the three inches needed to withstand the weight of a person, the sinking technique was used. Workers waited for the first snowfall, which usually left a white blanket two or three fingers deep over the ice layer. Then the men would make inch-sized holes three feet apart in the ice. The water underneath would filter through the cavities, and the snow would sink in it. This cold soup froze, forming part of the initial ice block. This process would be repeated several times until the block reached the ideal width of 15 inches. Ice blocks had to be at least 12 inches across if they were destined for national consumption and 20 inches if they were going to be exported since half of their volume melted during shipping.

Once the desired solidity was achieved they brought in huge draft horses to drag the blades that shaved the mounds of snow joined to the ice. Then heavy steel plates were used to smooth out the bumps and clear impurities from the surface. Mounted on a type of plow, workers would mark the lines. Parallel lines three feet apart. The operation was repeated until the ice resembled a huge chessboard. The blade was replaced with a shovel with six knives. Guided by the lines, the men would cut the blocks to a depth near the water. Goodbye horsepower. Now it was time for manual tools: saws, tridents and shovels. As they were separated, the first blocks floated down the water canal to the warehouse.

The ice house was located next to the bank. It had a double wooden wall filled with sawdust. Workers pushed in the blocks with harpoons. Some had to stand in the frozen waist-high water as a steam-powered conveyor belt lifted the blocks to the hangar. There they were piled on top of each other and the spaces between them were filled with sawdust or tree bark until an immense block the size of a church was formed.

In the summer of 1900, the ice man visited Rhinebeck homes twice a week. Those were the days when shelves were hung from the ceiling to keep rodents away from the food. Iceboxes, small cabinets with a zinc-lined interior and a drawer below to catch the melted water, would revolutionize the household economy by offering the incredible possibility of preserving foods. Milk could be consumed fresh in August, solid butter was served at the table, lettuce leaves remained crunchy and the meat didn't smell rotten.

"Boys go to college to get more knowledge; girls go to Jupiter to get stupider." Max repeats this little verse sleepily from the back seat on his way to school. The saying is all the rage among six-graders. Of course the girls in the class reverse the order and send the boys to that gaseous planet to get stupider. I am amused by the sayings my three kids pick up at school because, curiously, they are similar to those I exchanged with my own school buddies when I was young. I suppose all civilizations share those types of reactions when we begin to discover life. Lately, Julia has been fascinated by two trick questions: "Guess what." "What?" "A chicken butt." "Guess where." "Where?" "In your underwear." As for Nico, he was at the height of scientific discovery, enthralled with household experiments. After accepting some bets, he showed us that an ice cube wrapped in aluminum foil would melt before one wrapped in a kitchen towel.

We arrive at Bulkeley Middle School each morning by driving up a one-way hill that crosses the parking lot where the high school students park their cars. The first time we visited the school it was for open house in September.

The teachers explained the Golden Opportunity to us, previously known as the Golden Ruler in reference to the yellow color of the wood with which teachers slapped your hands. Thank God times have changed and punishment has now become an opportunity. "Your kids can stay after class," they told us, "to work with teachers if they need help." I was tempted to ask them: "Could I come, too?" It's difficult to imagine how lost a parent is when his kids ask for help on homework from another culture. I don't mean due to the lack of historical or geographic references, which you can always look up. It's that they do division differently here! In Spain, we put the quotient under the denominator, while in America, they place it above the dividend. And forget about subtraction. "*Papá*, how much is 27 minus 9?" Nobody takes anything in English. Instead, they borrow. In other words, you don't subtract and carry the one; you carry the one and then subtract. Jeez.

The teachers also talked about other opportunities of a green color. This is done so that the kids can earn a bit of cash so they won't have to depend on their parents for every whim. These are lessons in the value of money and spending it responsibly. On Wednesday, the high school soccer team is playing a home game. Max is the ball runner. He runs like a hare after every ball that falls afield and earns $10 a week for his effort. Not bad for an 11-year-old.

"Hi, how are you?" It's Susanne Callahan. She has a German mother, Irish American father, and was born in Rhinebeck. She speaks impeccable Spanish. Five years in high school with a Spanish teacher enabled her to master it. Just like Fred Woods, John Marvin, Vicky Norena, Richard Steers, Frank Mazzarella, and many others. Every year, there is a new batch of graduates with a surprisingly broad knowledge of the language of the country where I was born. The person directly responsible for this extraordinary result is named Tony Orza, born in the Bronx, in an Italian-American neighborhood where several dialects (Neapolitan, Calabrian, Sicilian) of southern Italy were spoken. In the 1960s a new wave of immigration (mainly from Puerto Rico) began to move into the neighborhood. As the demographic make-up began to change, many Italian Americans chose to move to the suburbs. Those were the days in New York when Puerto Ricans were derogatively called roach killers, because they wore pointed shoes that could easily reach the bugs in the corners. *West Side Story* material, my friends.

Tony grew up studying Latin, first at school and then with the Jesuits at Fordham University. When he was a sophomore in high school, he decided to study Spanish. His teacher was a lively Italian American who made the course fascinating. Later, he had a professor from Zaragoza, Julián Lamas, who taught at Marist College in Poughkeepsie for many years. Orza discovered a new Spanish, with the *zeta*, very different from what he was used to hearing on the subway from the mouths of the Latinos who returned home complaining: *mucho trabajo, poco dinero* (too much work, not enough money.) Inspired by these two dedicated teachers Tony decided to major in Spanish and become a Spanish teacher, thereby destroying his mother's dream of him becoming a doctor or a lawyer. His father, a hardworking truck driver, almost had a heart attack when Tony decided to pursue a degree in Spanish philology. "What kind of a job can you get with that degree?"

In 1967, thanks to the money his mother had secretly saved up over the years, he was able to go abroad to study in Spain. He spent six months in Santander, another six in Madrid and three in Salamanca. There he kissed his first girlfriend beneath the Roman bridge and ever since, the idea of Castile has been associated with happiness in his mind. Upon his return, he got his first job as a teaching assistant at SUNY Buffalo. Part of the assistantship involved taking summer courses in Spanish Literature at the University of Salamanca, where his professor for Contemporary Spanish Theatre was the famous playwright Alfonso Sastre. When he returned home, he rejoined his department to teach Spanish and, in later years, Tony would use Sastre's plays in the Advance Placement Spanish Course at Rhinebeck High School. Then 1970 came. The United States had become deeply involved in the Vietnam War. Nixon was being pressured because only African Americans and the poorest citizens were sent to the front. A lottery system had to be invented to recruit young people. Government officials put the birthdates, day and month, in a rotating drum and the destinations in another. One morning while he was teaching class, one of his students asked him innocently: "When is your birthday, Mr. Orza?" Tony responded: "November 22." "Oh," replied the student casually, "then you won't have to correct any more tests. You got number 9." The student showed him the newspaper: he would be drafted soon!

That Sunday, Tony, who didn't often attend Mass, went to church. A letter was read in which the Catholic Bishops of America demanded the right of any Catholic to become a conscientious objector. In those days, only Jehovah's Witnesses and Quakers were granted the status of conscientious objectors based solely on their religious beliefs, without consideration for ethical or personal motivations of any type. In the meantime, Tony received the letter from the Department of Defense to report for a physical. He passed. The possibilities for his future were reduced to three: embrace the army, flee to Canada or request a position as a translator for the army, which would at least keep him from having to go to Vietnam. He went to Canada, but could only stand being a fugitive for one day. What he saw there just wasn't for him. He didn't want to live in exile, like an outcast, far from his family and friends without knowing when he could return. He chose the third option and filled out the application form for the Army Language School. Among the multiple options offered, he chose Portuguese as his preferred language and Brazil as his chosen country. The test could not have been easier. They gave him a sheet with vocabulary words in an African language unknown to him. Each word had an English translation beside it and they asked him to make sentences with all of them. As simple as proving that he could distinguish a verb from a pronoun or an adjective. After passing the test, he received a certificate of acceptance in the mail, although with a few modifications. On the original form Tony Orza had filled out, someone had scratched out the boxes corresponding to Portuguese and Brazil and instead marked Xs in those of Laotian and Monterrey, California.

He went to complain to the military: "You want me to learn Laotian so that you can send me into the villages that you're going to bomb to promise the people there that we will bring medicine and food. In other words, I'll be the first to be hit by enemy fire." "Well," the military officer replied, "we all have to sacrifice something for our country." "In that case," Tony responded, "sacrifice your son." He left the building. He sought help from the offices that the Catholic Youth Fellowship had opened on Lafayette Street in order to facilitate the granting of conscientious objector status to Catholics. With a pile of letters of recommendation from priests and professors, and after having responded to numerous questions about his religious beliefs on the form, he turned in the application. A year passed, which he spent teaching Spanish at the SUNY campus at Stone Ridge. In January, the answer finally arrived. He was granted an exemption of military service on the condition that his job would be in the interest of the national welfare. He thought that his devotion to teaching would fit the bill, but the response was negative. No, the army did not consider education a service in the public interest. Okay. He could work in a hospital, prison or center for the mentally ill. They had no intention of making things easy for him. But he looked for a job anyway. Through the director of the language department at Ulster Community College, he found a job as an orderly at Kingston Hospital. He worked from 3:00 to midnight for $75 per week. Tony was responsible for bringing the dead to the hospital morgue and shaving the patients who were scheduled for surgery. In 1971, the group of attendants at the hospital in the former capital of New York State boasted some of the best-educated workers in the country. Not surprising given that practically all of them were liberal professionals who wanted to escape the draft.

Besides working as an orderly at Kingston hospital, Tony found a part-time position as a Spanish teacher in the Onteora School District. It was in Boiceville, a small town west of Woodstock. High school Spanish teacher Domingo Lagos was a former Jesuit who hired him immediately after confirming his mastery of and passion for the Spanish language. Every morning, he taught three classes before heading to the hospital. After 12 months of orderly service he received a letter from the hospital stating that he no longer would be required to finish the 24-month period of his contract. They didn't need him anymore. Just like that. He quickly said goodbye to his hospital duties and began looking for a full-time teaching position.

One morning, while in midtown Manhattan searching for work, in the shadow of the Allied Chemical Building, from whose roof the metal ball descends each January 1 to announce the arrival of the New Year, Tony came across a newsstand that sold newspapers from around the United States. As he paged through the Kingston paper, *The Daily Freeman*, he spotted a small ad for a Spanish teacher for a school in Dutchess County. And it was a permanent job! The ad didn't say which town it was since applicants had to be filtered through an agency first. Without a second thought, he grabbed the phone and began to call all the schools in the county. "Red Hook High School? Are you looking for a Spanish teacher?" "No." "Wappingers Falls?" "Nope." "Millbrook?" "Sorry." After receiving dozens of negatives, he contacted the principal of the school in Rhinebeck: "What's that?" "Oh, yes, that's us." "Aha!" "Well ... if you're really so interested, you should come immediately." When he showed up in Rhinebeck for the interview, the principal called the French teacher, whose son Tony had taught at Onteora High School. The teacher enthusiastically recommended him and the principal offered him a contract. "You have to teach four Spanish courses and one French course." "French?" "Yes." "But I don't *parle* French. I only studied French for a year at college. I don't speak the language." "It doesn't matter," the principal said. "I'm sure you'll figure something out. Sign here."

At the time, Rhinebeck had already adopted a curriculum that differed from the rest of U.S. schools with regard to languages. In 1972, French and German were considered difficult languages in the United States, which lent prestige to those who decided to study them. Spanish was stigmatized as an easy language whose classrooms were filled with the less able students. In his new job, Tony Orza was driven by a tremendous vocation, similar to a religious calling, to change the status quo for good. As he unpacked his bags, he made the promise to himself that each and every student would leave the course speaking fluent Spanish. To this end, he developed two golden rules. The first: a half hour of homework every day (weekends included). "If I can correct all your tests in one night," he told them, "you certainly can spend half an hour on homework every day." He accepted no excuses. The students needed structure, some rules and discipline. From the start, he didn't allow them to speak a word of English in class. "You can say anything you want, as long as you say it in Spanish." In order not to waste important classroom time, the students always found their daily worksheets on their desks when they walked into the classroom. As far as the second rule goes, Tony realized from the start that his students, especially in the eighth-grade beginning class, needed to learn and have fun at the same time. In his classes, Tony used Spanish pop music, movies, and stories he made up himself about one Benito Pecho de Granito, a guy who spent his mornings lifting weights to impress the neighborhood girls.

The summer trips to Spain began soon thereafter every other July. At first, he brought together students from three schools: Kingston, Red Hook and Rhinebeck, to be able to fill the spaces. A few years later, he couldn't even process the huge number of applications from his own school. He met his wife on his first trip in 1973. She had gone as a Spanish teacher chaperone from Kingston High School. She's accompanied him on every trip since, so much so that their daughter once asked: "Mom, Dad, we're Spaniards, right?" "No, why do you ask?" "I just thought since we go to Spain every year we must have some grandparents there or something … "

For students learning Spanish, the trip to Spain confirms the concepts they have been learning about at school. It is not a question of learning a language, but rather of understanding the possibilities that speaking one offers. What Tony Orza has been able to achieve with these students is close to miraculous. Get ready to be blown away. Those in the fourth year of Spanish take the Advanced Placement Exam administered by Princeton University. Nationally, 70,000 students take the exam. The highest grade is five. The average obtained by Rhinebeck students is 4.5, consistently placing them at the top of the list of schools. I mentioned that one day to Emilio Casinnello, the Spanish Consul General in New York. "I think Orza should be awarded the Spanish Civil Merit Medal. From his classroom, he's done a lot to promote our language and our country." But Casinnello was going back to Spain soon and my proposal evaporated in the halls of his official residence on the East Side.

"You have to meet Tony, Emilio," I insisted again to the Spanish Consul General during a visit he and his wife made to Rhinebeck. They were coming to spend the weekend and Sarah told me she was going to buy some flowers to make the house more inviting. Half an hour later she called me: "Are the Casinnellos there yet?" "No." "As soon as they arrive, bring them to my parents' house. We're having a wedding." A wedding? What wedding? To make a long story short, on her way home Sarah passed by the Town Hall and saw a lot of cars parked. She went to take a peek inside. There was a public meeting. Okay. On her way out she noticed a groom and a bride standing in the hallway. Willy Sanchez, the justice who was going to marry them, approached my wife: "Would you mind being a witness for a wedding? This couple needs a witness." Thinking that it wouldn't take much time, Sarah agreed. But then, when Willy was introducing her to the bride, Sarah suggested a better plan: "I think I might have a more adequate place for the occasion. Why not come to my parents' house and get married there?" Two telephone calls followed. The first to Sarah's mother: "Are you okay with hosting a wedding now? Stick the two bottles of the champagne that we kept from our wedding in the freezer." The second to me: "She is such a beautiful bride! She can't get married in a court room. She's from Canada and her family won't be here. Let's be her family and make this a little more special." "Okay."

* * *

An hour later, the wedding took place in Peggy and Bud's living room. The bride and groom were both very nice. They had come to renovate the Rhinecliff Hotel, an institution well known for its wild parties, and transform it into a weekend destination for New Yorkers. The Spanish Consul General and his wife, Mr. and Mrs. Casinnello, acted as witnesses of the ceremony too. Julia and Makenzie were both flower girls. Mrs. Casinnello was amazed: "I can't believe it, I just can't believe it. Why on earth did your wife take those people to her parents' house?" "What if they're criminals?" "Well, if they are," I said, jokingly, "the judge will arrest them because he just collected all their personal data." They brought with them a photographer who made a complete portfolio of images of the couple—next to the piano, going down the staircase, on the porch. We felt very fortunate to meet Willy Sánchez, a judge with a heart of gold. He is a man determined to give a second chance to kids who, for some reason, had stepped across the fine red line of legality. Well, Willy was given a second chance too, you know. When he first arrived to Rhinebeck, he was not dressed in a robe at Town Hall, but rather enrolled in a rehabilitation program for teenagers on Holy Cross on Riverside. That's why he was perfectly aware that it's possible to leave hell if someone is kind enough to show you the exit. "If you do get out, don't slam the door on those behind you."

"You have to think about Tony Orza," I insisted that night to the Spanish Consul General as we sat before a plate of soft shell crabs at 40 West, the superb restaurant that today is called The Local. "Yes, yes," he said, "I'll see what I can do." "Thank you," I said. "And now, back to business: shouldn't we order more soft shell crabs? They are amazing." "Be my guest."

Speaking of celebrations, not everything about teaching has been a bed of roses for Tony. According to the Spanish teacher, school education has shifted to what he calls "touchy-feely teaching." "It seems like the teacher has to reward students for their progress, regardless of whether it is minimal or even non-existent." Tony is aware that during the first days of class, his demanding, looming presence strikes fear in the hearts of his students. But as his 104-year-old Italian grandmother tells him: "Better they cry than you, Tony." After the first acid test, the kids usually relax and Tony doesn't remember a single instance where he had to raise his voice to ask them to sit down or be quiet.

"But the tables have turned," he says, sighing. He remembers when he began in 1972. During hallway duty he had asked the kids to hurry back to class. One of them, to waste time, made believe he had to use the bathroom. He went to the bathroom to pretend to wash his hands and then walked to the class as slowly as possible. Tony gave him a pat on the back and said, "Let's get going," encouraging him to speed up. The student turned around and punched him in the chest. Tony knew he had to react to maintain his authority and pushed the student's arms away to defend himself. The principal appeared. "What happened? I can't believe it! Mr. Orza, I'm so sorry you had to be involved in such a disagreeable incident." He defended the teacher and suggested he take the day off. Tony opted to stay. The next day Tony was informed by the teacher's union that he could press charges. Tony refused to do so.

In 2003, Tony gave his students a text to translate. One student used an Internet translator to save time but he hadn't realized that his brother had changed the Spanish to French to do his own homework. He turned in his paper with a smirk on his face. Wait, this is in French.

The kid apologized, saying that it was his brother's homework. We must have gotten our papers mixed up. But Tony let him know that he wasn't falling for it. "It's in French but it's not your brother's homework because these are the phrases I gave you in English." So he called his mother to inform her that her son had been cheating. The woman showed her claws. How dare you call my son a cheater! Tony told her the evidence was overwhelming and that he couldn't think of another word to describe what the student had done. The mother defended her son and informed Tony that he had not sent any note specifically informing students that using an Internet translator was prohibited. She called the principal, who sided with the mother to avoid conflict.

Another time he was explaining the verb *dejar* in class. Indefinite preterite. In the middle of the lesson, he decided to ask: *¿Quién se dejó la ropa en el coche de María?* (Who left their clothes in Maria's car?). The next morning, the principal called Tony into his office. "It's inappropriate to make sexual references in your lessons." "Sex?" He defended himself by saying that he only meant to refer to an ordinary item, such as clothing, to capture the students' interest in class. "Sorry, but I have to open a file on this." "What's going on?" In Tony Orza's 30 years' of experience, he had never altered his teaching method. Neither had the teenagers changed; they shared the same problems and worries as those from the previous year. So, what then? "The change had occurred in the system," he says, "which, suddenly, had become incapable of understanding the significance of clothing left in a car in the middle of a Spanish lesson."

The first serious problem came with a joke. Tony had always used humor in his lessons. "The kids are 13, 14 … 17! I can't tell them the story of Little Red Riding Hood," he says. "It's not a case of going too far; I wouldn't even know how to do that. It's just to teach more effectively. I think students can tolerate a few jokes, which, in any case, are not nearly as racy as the ones they tell during recess." The Latin teacher, who is Jewish, had told a joke during lunch which Tony thought was funny.

"It was in no way anti-Semitic," he explains. "The proof was that the Latin teacher couldn't stop laughing. I thought it would be a good idea to tell the students in class. A Jew and a Chinese man are traveling by train. The Jew says: 'I don't like the Chinese.' The Chinese man asks: 'And why not?' 'Because they bombed Pearl Harbor.' 'Oh, no,' the Chinese man responds, 'that was the Japanese.' 'Well,' says the Jew, 'what's the difference, Chinese, Japanese, they're all the same.' After a few minutes of silence, the Chinese man responds. 'I don't like the Jews,' he says. 'You don't say, and why not?' 'Because they sank the *Titanic*.' 'Oh, no, the Jews didn't sink the *Titanic*. It was an iceberg.' The Chinese man shrugs and says: 'Iceberg, Spielberg, they're all the same to me.'" The class burst out laughing. Everyone was smiling except for the principal, who was visiting the classroom that day. Since the principal didn't speak Spanish, Tony asked a student to translate the joke. He thought the principal would be impressed to see how a 13-year-old girl was able to understand a joke in another language and easily translate it into English. But as soon as she had finished, the principal's face turned to stone and Tony was called into his office. "I can't allow Chinese and Japanese citizens to be insulted at this institution," he said. "And much less for you to make fun of the Jews." At the time, Orza was unaware that he was adding insult to injury. Just a few days earlier, a Jewish student had been eating matzo when a bully threatened her: "I'm going to kill you." Naturally, that terrible incident had frightened her and she reported it. The principal, concerned about the implications of such a severe decision, decided against expelling the bully. The Jewish student's mother threatened to sue the school for not taking action and now, thanks to Tony's little joke, the administration feared that the warning would become a reality. So Tony became the fall guy.

The school sent a report to the district superintendent. "I've heard a lot about you, Mr. Orza. I can't go anywhere in this valley without hearing what a wonderful Spanish teacher you are," said the superintendent, somewhat ironically. He then opened the folder containing Tony's file and showed him the list of incidents, including that of the clothing left in Maria's car. I must congratulate you, Mr. Orza. You are one of our best teachers. Anyone can plainly see your achievements listed on this service sheet. Excellent. However, I have to fine you $1,000." "A thousand dollars? Do you know what a language teacher makes?" For 10 months, he had $100 deducted from his salary. "I had to pay through the nose," Tony explains, "just because no one dare reprimand a racist student, everyone else lost their right to have a sense of humor at school." That principal has since left the Rhinebeck School district.

Next was the incident about the singer Paloma San Basilio. Tony wanted to explain the meaning of the word *desnudo* (nude) and since you had to leave English in the hall before entering the classroom, some students didn't understand what he was talking about. So he used one of the singer's album covers. On it, Paloma is in a pool with her head above the water. He propped the album on the blackboard. "Who swims nude in the water?" he had asked in Spanish. A student quickly responded: "Paloma." Laughter and more questions followed. He thought the lesson was over. To the contrary, it had just begun. A religiously devout student filed a formal complaint. Tony Orza was back in the principal's office. A new file and a second visit to the district superintendent's office. "Well, well, let's see what we have here. How's it going, Mr. Orza? I see you're determined to become a repeat offender. I have to send you to therapy. I hope six sessions are enough to rehabilitate you."

The psychologists repeatedly asked him: "But how could you know whether Paloma was naked under the water? What makes you think about nude bodies, Mr. Orza? How are your sexual relations with your wife?" "Okay, that's enough!" Tony got up and spoke his mind to the psychologist. "I didn't come here to talk about my wife. I came here to discuss education. You are before the victim of a witch hunt, not some dirty old man. Make no mistake about it." The psychologist was at a loss for words. He was one of those people who speaks in monosyllables—"Oh, yes, oh, no"—incapable of appeasing the Spanish teacher's extreme embarrassment about having to attend sensitivity sessions.

What was going on? He didn't think he had crossed the line and he didn't let his students cross it, either. One day they practiced different meanings of the qualitative adjective *buena*. When used in reference to a woman, buena could mean "good" or "attractive." One student wanted to be funny. Teacher, he asked him: "Is your wife buena?" A few laughs and then silence. Tony responded: "Yes, she's as good as your mother. She visits the sick and helps people." More laughter. After class, the teacher heard how the rest of the class made fun of the student, saying that Mr. Orza had outsmarted him. He was really going to pay for it this time. "Mr. Orza, under no circumstances should a student in your class feel he has the right to ask you about the sexual habits of your wife." "How can I control what a student says?" Orza wondered. The file stated that his wife was the subject of a sexual discussion in class. "My poor wife," said Tony. "She's the most modest women in the whole valley." But she's not the only one. His daughter is also on the list. He showed the class a photo of his daughter when she turned 23 and proudly exclaimed how pretty she was. The psychologist said: "Tony, do you think it's appropriate to use your daughter as a sex symbol in class?" "Look, I'm a father and I think my daughter is the most beautiful woman in the world. Like most fathers. Nothing more, can't you understand that?" "Oh, yes, oh, no."

Working as a teacher nowadays is no easy task. The governor of Missouri has asked teachers to unscrew one of every three light bulbs to be able to pay the electric bill. In Oklahoma, some teachers volunteer to drive buses, scrub floors and cook in the cafeterias to compensate for budget cuts that have forced them to dismiss staff. In Oregon, teachers have given up 15 days of salary. In several districts of Colorado, school weeks have been reduced to four days. Throughout the United States, neighbors bake pies to raise funds to avoid losing a music teacher or a special education teacher, frequently the first two staff members to get laid off. Nevertheless, this does not deter the men and women who remain standing next to the blackboard out of a love for what they do. What does discourage them is discovering that the system no longer supports them. Many teachers want to turn 55 so they can retire. Tony Orza is 60 and cannot imagine the day when he will have to pass his baton on to the next person. Who will continue his mission? "Who will withstand the flood of complaints that rain down every time the Catholic religion is mentioned too often in class?" he tells them. "I mention it so that the students can understand Europe, and Spain is in Europe so they have to know about Catholicism. I tell them about the Santos Inocentes celebration and about how when we visit the cathedral in Ávila and see the statue of the Romans laying the sword on newborns, the students will know what they are seeing. One student accused me of playing too many songs that mentioned the Virgin Mary. But, girl, it's about culture. If I take you to Seville to see the Macarena procession, you'll get goosebumps, even if you aren't a believer." "Macarena? Aaaaaaah, Maaaaacarena." "Oh! No, the song is something else."

Outside the school, the sun shines. "Any idea how the voting is going?" "Not a clue." We run into Gina Fox, who is returning from exercising her right to vote. She enthusiastically tells us about the two morel mushrooms she found this morning and then consumed for breakfast, sautéed in butter. The talk turns to the new candidate. I am surprised that he can campaign on voting day so I ask Gina about it. "You can," she explains, "as long as you remain at least 100 feet away from the table." Apparently the man showed up early that morning with a tape measure to find the exact spot. "Will he be elected?" "I don't know." We continue walking as I try to wheedle out of Gina where she found the mushrooms. She is not going for it.

Gina had taken me to look for morels last week. Someplace in the woods. I found an abandoned bicycle tire, black with yellow lengthwise stripes. But when I approached, it moved. It uncoiled itself and before my eyes the meter-long ribbon snake (which looked more like it measured a mile), slithered away. But nothing happened. It looked at me disapprovingly and went on its way to the stream to lay some two dozen eggs because it's that time of year. Goodbye. Before I could regain my composure, another incident of greater intensity occurred. I played the lead in a scene from Alfred Hitchcock's *The Birds*. Specifically, I played the role of my favorite actress, Tippi Hedren. I was looking for mushrooms among some shrubs when I came across a blue jay's nest. Beautiful, with all the eggs carefully arranged. Suddenly, the mother bird appeared from nowhere and pecked at my head. I crouched down but she grazed me, screeching like a crazed pigeon. Shaken up by the pecking, I ran off while the bird flew over me a couple more times. When I escaped from the radius of her protection zone, the mother blue jay continued to nervously jump from branch to branch, threateningly observing my movements. I told her, "You had better watch it or I'll squeeze you so that you'll turn into a common raven." She must have understood my threat because she stopped screeching. Without the need to study biology, these birds know perfectly well that their blue coloring is not from pigment but rather from the effect of the light refracting off the internal structure of their feathers. By squeezing them, you mess up the geometry and it's goodbye to the party dress of the mascot of the Toronto baseball team.

In Missouri, where Gina is from, they recommend looking for morels in thickets where deer hide. Unfortunately, for this very reason, the ticks are also on the attack there. They have a pair of pincers that they move continually until a living being passes by, at which time they hook onto them. It could be a deer, a human, a dog or a raccoon. It's all the same to them. A tick never knows what its mode of transportation will be; it rides on a coyote or on a man with a law degree with the same ease. Since they transmit the dreadful Lyme disease, you have to be extremely careful.

The delicious mushrooms supposedly grow among ferns. We were looking for them close to the dry elms, next to the old oaks and underneath the hickories, some hairy trees that look like a throwback from the *Lord of the Rings*. But no luck. Morels need specific temperature and humidity conditions to grow. Otherwise they don't appear. When they do have the right circumstances, they sprout quickly, like popcorn in a pan. When you do spot them, it's best to pick them and put them in your basket immediately. They won't grow any bigger because if you give them a few extra days of life in the field, you run the risk that another mushroom hunter will pick them first. Animals won't touch them, but men will kill for them. At Belvedere, a former manor with magnificent views of the river that had been transformed into a hotel, "They would have bought them on the spot," says Gina. Debbie Rodriguez grew up in that lovely house. Her father ran a fat farm there. According to Hector, Debbie's husband, "He invented the best business in the world: people paid a lot of money to drink water and eat practically nothing." "Good morning." "Good morning!" Returning from the school, we again come across the new candidate greeting voters, who barely respond.

* * *

We will know the result of the election tonight, but in the meantime, everybody is doing mental calculations to figure out if the school budget will pass or not, which actually (I mean the fact of doing calculations) makes a lot of sense in a rural community like Rhinebeck. The word calculation comes from the Latin *calculis*, which means rock, and refers to the pebbles that the first farmers collected to count their livestock. For each sheep that went to pasture, one rock was placed in the pile. For each sheep that returned to the stable, one rock was removed from the pile. When the number of sheep and rocks coincided, it meant none was missing. Hopefully, no votes are going to be missed tonight either, so the new school budget will be approved, and Rhinebeck High School will get greater facilities for our children.

Whatever other news happens today in the rest of the country, we can count on getting a summary of it on CBS's *60 Minutes* next Sunday. The news magazine is an oasis of prime-quality journalism in the middle of an informational desert when it comes to real news. More than 100 million Americans watch the show's trademark ticking clock at least once a year. If you mention *60 Minutes* in a conversation, inevitably someone will tell you that they grew up with it. It's the oldest television news show in American history and the most successful. Its quality of journalism has always been very high, and it still sets the standard for what journalism should be. In the television world everybody seems to be concerned about statistics: What does the audience want? More consumer news? More health news? More good news? CBS figured that what the audience really wanted was to be informed. Period. As a result, *60 Minutes* never went through a time of reimagining itself. And it keeps bringing truth in a smart way.

Don Hewitt, the show's original executive producer and its creator, modeled the show on *Life* magazine. In 1968 he looked at the latest issue of the magazine and realized it had the perfect format to follow for a news show. The cover story was on Martin Luther King and the Civil Rights Movement—just the kind of story for *60 Minutes*. Inside the magazine was a great piece on NASA and its next trip to the Moon. "We'll do that story too!" And then, at the end of the magazine, there was Jackie Kennedy and a picture of what was in her closet, including her shoes. Hewitt decided to do that story too because he knew American women would love it.

Hewitt's idea was to have a mix of news content. That's still the case, and that's what you'll hear if you visit the *60 Minutes* headquarters at 555 West 57th Street (off 11th Avenue). Bill Owens, the show's current executive editor with whom I had the chance to meet once, has to be conscious of the mix of the three stories as he prepares each episode. He must include something for everybody, from an economics professor who wants to see what's happening in the global market to a young student who wants to see a story on digital media. The mix is the secret formula of the house.

The show's original reporters—Mike Wallace and Ed Bradley—were as famous as any American movie star or sports star, so when they left the program, people thought that the show was really in trouble. But the next executive producer, Jeff Fager, made sure that the show was going to keep the original format.

To cast new correspondents has been pretty tricky. Reporters for *60 Minutes* must be curious about what's going on in the world and be able to smell out a story anywhere on the planet. They also have to be very good interviewers. Therefore, they must be excellent listeners, with plenty of curiosity about every little thing. But, as Don Hewitt used to say, "The only thing people need to know about *60 Minutes* is that our reporters can tell a story." That's very different from and much simpler than an average news report. "Imagine sitting at the dinner table with someone who is able to captivate you with a great anecdote that keeps your interest," Bill Owens suggested during our informal meeting. "At the end of the night you comment to your wife, 'Man, it was great! What an interesting person!' That's sort of what we're going for. Obviously, the stories have to be news, but the key is in the way you tell them. We want them to be engaging. Our reporters have to be excellent storytellers."

The *60 Minutes* journalists have a large budget and travel all over the world. They go out to shoot and then work with an editor to write and cut the footage, which can take weeks or even months. Finally they show the first draft to Owens and CBS News Chairman Jeff Fager in the screening room. In that chamber will also be a woman known as "the police." She has a book of transcripts of every interview that has been conducted. And she has read everything that happened in these interviews to make sure that nothing is taken out of context and that poor editing has not been done. After the first screening, the group discusses the story's subject. Fager and Owens raise various narrative points and ask questions. Owens might say: "Boy, that interviewee is fantastic, but why did you present him without letting us know where he comes from?" Changes are made, and the story gets better. To make the cut for *60 Minutes*, besides telling the truth, the episode has to be enticing. Even controversial investigations into corporations that advertise on the program are welcomed. That's happened before, and unhappy sponsors have pulled their ads. But, as Bill Owens confessed to me, "*60 Minutes* has got nothing but its reputation." Good for them.

12

July

James Lewis Smithson was born in France in 1765, the product of the illegitimate union between the Duke of Northumberland, Sir Hugh Smithson, and his lover, Elizabeth Hungerford Macie. That's why he was named Jacques Louis Macie. He inherited a considerable fortune from his mother, the widow of a wealthy man related to the royal family. After studying at Oxford University, he carried out several studies in chemistry, mineralogy and geology and was elected a member of the Royal Society of London. He traveled throughout Europe, exchanging knowledge with the most renowned scientists of the time. At the end of his days, Smithson, who had never crossed the Atlantic, stated in his will that all his assets were to be removed from the United Kingdom and placed at the disposition of the U.S. Congress. This was Smithson's personal vengeance against the rigidity of the British system, which denied him the right to use his father's last name. The document explained that, in order to access the money, the U.S. Congress had to allocate every last cent to the creation of an institution that would serve to foster knowledge among humankind ... and disseminate his last name among the English tourists. The members of Congress agreed. Today, the Smithsonian Institution in Washington, D.C., is the largest museum complex in the world.

Sarah took me there for a visit because she had done an internship in the framing department of the American Art Museum one semester and had fond memories of that time. We first stopped at the National

Gallery, attracted by a curious exhibit entitled "Helga's Pictures." It consisted of innumerable portraits of the same German woman who wore a languid expression and posed (often nude) in different beautiful landscapes. The artist, Andrew Wyeth, seems to have spent half of his life surreptitiously drawing his neighbor Helga (keeping it from his wife, his art dealer and the rest of humanity) but after his death the secret was exposed. He must have had lots of closets in his studio because the Helga painting collection was extremely prolific. Or maybe he had a huge basement, like everybody does in the Rhinebeck area, since underground property doesn't get taxed.

Next step was the building in the Greek classical style that houses the Smithsonian American Art Museum. There it hangs: Edward Hopper's *People in the Sun*. "Oh!" William Johnson's *Young Man in a Vest*. "Bravo!" And Rockwell Kent's *Snow Fields*. "Wow!" But also, to my surprise, there we found the fascinating Indian Gallery with the works of illustrator George Catlin.

In his own words, Catlin was an explorer who was "determined to record for posterity the manners and customs of the Native American population before they disappear forever." Part adventurer, part anthropologist, he traveled tirelessly, following the trail opened by Lewis and Clark, The Smithsonian collection includes the works from his 1830-36 expedition, in which Catlin visited 50 tribes living west of the Mississippi River.

The Indian Gallery features portraits of chiefs, warriors, women and medicine men, who observe you impassively from the canvas, as if waiting for you to pose them a question so they could let you know their true history. Particularly noteworthy is the portrait of the Blackfoot tribe's chief, whose melancholy expression seems to foretell what would later happen to his people. There are dozens of portraits that convey the Indians' legendary spirit as well as their grandeur, and, surprisingly enough, several of them break away from stereotypes. For example, next to the grandiloquent profile of White Cloud there is an unassuming Sioux who responds to the unflattering name of Egghead.

However, when John Raucci points me to a copy of the greatly expanded fourth edition (London 1870) of *Shut Your Mouth and Save Your Life*, with 29 illustrations by the author, it doesn't occur to me to associate this book about Native Americans with the visit that Sarah and I paid to the Smithsonian.

Raucci tells me that his second son, David, began to train on the varsity athletic team of the Red Hook high school at 14, but just a month after he started racing, he came down with pneumonia. The doctors diagnosed asthma and he had to learn how to live glued to an inhaler. Worried about his son's condition, Raucci began to think about what could have affected the respiratory system of a young man who was apparently as healthy as a horse. He reviewed the training methods but found nothing unusual. David approached the races with the same technique as all other runners in the world: 45 breaths per minute, inhaling through the mouth. "Then I read *Shut Your Mouth and Save Your Life* and learned about the Native Americans' sacred formula, which they adhered to throughout their lives: nasal breathing." Raucci cross-checked that information with the professional experience of some world-renowned sports gurus and came up with an idea. At the International World Sports event in Seoul, when David Raucci won first place, he was breathing through his nose at a rate of 15 inhalations per minute.

I turn the pages of *Shut your Mouth and Save Your Life* with the respect one should show for ancient writings. The cute drawing of a baby on page 18 suddenly brings me back to the Smithsonian The baby is swathed in a cloth decorated with geometric figures tied against a small board on which his back rested. With his head on a pillow, the infant is smiling at the little bells and bright objects that hang from a circular handle that stretches across his field of vision. It's rather like an Iron Age version of Fisher-Price's Minnie's Twinkling Tea Party Play Gym sold at Toys "R" Us.

I go back to the cover. Uh huh! I read "...written by George Catlin," and realize that the author is the same intriguing man whose paintings captivated me at the Indian Gallery. "Enjoy it," says Raucci, "I have to go." "Cool, John. Thanks, we'll talk soon." Then I turn back to the book. What is this? I take a deep breath through the nose and delve into the book.

> ... I have visited 150 Tribes, containing more than two millions of souls... infant mortality is practically unknown among the Indians ... All Savage infants are reared in cribs with the head bowed a little forward when they sleep, which prevents the mouth from falling open; thus establishing the early habit of breathing through the nostrils ... the healthy condition and physical perfection of those people, in their primitive state, contrast with the deplorable mortality, the numerous diseases and deformities, in civilized communities ...

Well, let me Google something. Okay, I'm back. The Holy Scriptures state that man was created to live 70 years ... and in Catlin's time, only one in four Englishmen reached adulthood. No wonder he was in shock after realizing that the natives lived much longer. Hmmmm ... I keep reading: "*H'doo-a, h'doo-a, won-cha-doo-ats. Straighten the bush and you will have a straight tree.*" "*H'doo-a ... papá.*"

"*H'doo-a papa?*" "What's the phone number to call Spain, *Papá?*" Oh, wait a minute, it's the voice of my daughter, whose five-year-old stature makes her shorter than the kitchen counter where I'm sitting, absorbed in my reading. "Sorry, Julia, I thought I was hearing an internal voice speaking in a Native American language." I finally look around the counter. She rolls her eyes. "What do you need, sweetie?" "The number for Spain?" "What number?" "The one for Madrid, to call Marcita." "Oh, I see." Julia wants to talk to her babysitter because she misses her. I look at the clock and decide it's too late to make a call to Europe. "Marcita is already in bed; you can call her tomorrow, Julia." She agrees, but asks me to write the number on a piece of paper anyway. "Why do you want it if you're not going to use it?" "Because I do." Something smells fishy to me so I deliberately leave off the international codes and write only the nine-digit Madrid phone number. If she tries to call, she will get that robotic voice that has so often driven me to distraction: "Your call cannot be completed as dialed. Please, hang up and try again." "Here you go, Julia, now let me work." She disappears upstairs and I return to my reading.

Raucci has told me that some Native Americans took the regenerative properties of nighttime nasal breathing so seriously that they would sow the lips of newborns closed to keep them from breathing through their mouths. Other tribes, it seems, trained young people to take in a mouthful of water and then made them run long distances without spitting out the liquid. Besides impeding them from breathing incorrectly, the water kept the body hydrated during prolonged exercise.

"*Papá?*" "What now, Julia?" My daughter returns with a suspiciously innocent smile. "Hey, *Papá*, if I lock myself in the upstairs bathroom, could you hear what I'm saying from here?" "No." "Okay." She runs off. You don't have to be too smart to imagine what she's up to. The bathroom has a phone on the wall next to the toilette seat. Before the invention of the cellphone—the technological advance that has banned taxi drivers from talking to their clients because they enter and leave the cab glued to their phones—Americans had already created the need to receive calls in the most unusual places. Yes, our house has a phone in the bathroom. So close to the toilet paper that one day I almost clean myself with the handset. America the beautiful is also the country of comfort. Even for changing a light bulb from the light fixture on the ceiling they have an invention. There is a long pole with a suction cup on the end, called the Roughneck, which expertly grasps the bulb and removes it in three easy twists of the handle.

Boom! I hear the bathroom door slam shut. Nothing serious. I'm concentrating on ancient history at the moment and can't be bothered to deal with my kid's mischievousness. "Good luck with your conference call from the bathroom," I think. "No one will answer because you're missing the international code of 011 and the 34 to connect you with Spain.

Uh-oh. Your call cannot be completed as dialed. Please hang up and try again, Julia. Ha, ha."

In principle, it does not seem too farfetched to start with the premise that, under normal conditions—and Raucci considers practicing sports to be a natural activity—it is much healthier to breathe through the nose. First, the little hairs in the nasal passage filter the air, preventing a lot of dust and impurities from entering the body, some of them so irritating that we are forced to immediately sneeze them out, at a rate of 60 miles per hour. In addition, our nose is equipped with a natural thermostat. It heats the air in winter and cools it in summer, constantly adjusting it to the ideal temperature for the lungs. But there's more. The interior walls of the nasal passages curve in the shape of a shell. It is not in vain that ear, nose and throat doctors refer to them as turbinated bones, for their capacity to push the air to the bottom of the lungs. Doing so, the air will find a larger number of capillaries willing to absorb the oxygen.

The ambitious human body works with two different nervous systems: the sympathetic system (which goes into operation only during emergency situations) and the parasympathetic system, which allows us to function efficiently following the parameters of a relaxed state of mind. The blood vessels associated with the emergency system are situated in the upper part of the lungs whereas those related to normal breathing activity are grouped in the lower area. By definition, the act of breathing through the mouth is an action reserved for extreme situations. This is very useful when you have only two choices: flight or fight. By breathing through the mouth, we send the air to the upper part of the chest and activate the sympathetic system. In other words, we put our body into a state of alert. When we are face to face with something frightening— say, a tiger—panic causes us to take rapid mouthfuls of air to provoke hyperventilation. The generation of stress is a resource that segregates enzymes capable of making us run faster than normal or to swing wilder punches than we would under typical circumstances. It puts us in a state of tension that can save our life when faced with a difficult situation.

It's as if, during red alert, all the cells in the body are donating their energy to those that require a double dose to be able to remove you from danger. This should happen only for an instant, as a last resort to deal with a desperate situation. Anything but death. However, if we force the body into a state of stress for too long, its chemical reactions begin to destroy it.

If we breathe through the nose, we send air to the lower part of the rib cage, activating the parasympathetic nerves and calming the body, even when engaged in vigorous activity. Using the mouth, we transform what should be a pleasant pastime into a personal challenge, and as a result of this anti-natural decision, injuries are more likely to occur. "The human body," Raucci has repeated to me on several occasions, "is not made to use as if we are facing a life or death situation every minute." This was beautifully explained by Dr. John Douillard, the director of Player Development of the New Jersey Nets, when he said that professional football players live to an average age of 56 due in part to the enormous adrenaline rushes to which they are subjected during every training and at every game.

According to Raucci, most trainers teach their runners to breathe through the mouth, based on the false premise that when they take in more air, their bodies will absorb more oxygen and they will be able to run faster. "But this is a mistake." "Is it?" I ask. "Yes. To run faster, you don't need to breathe in more air but rather to make better use of the air you do take in. The fact that the nasal passages are smaller than the enormous orifice in the middle of our face is no mere coincidence. Breathing in small doses allows oxygen to remain in the lungs longer, facilitating its absorption in the blood."

The phone rings. "Hello?" A deep, unfamiliar voice asks: "Hill residence?" We have a telephone contract in Sarah's name, so I answer in the affirmative. "Are you Mr. Hill?" asks the voice. I say I'm not. He asks me who I am then. "I'm the owner of the house," I tell him, and he responds, surprised, with "But didn't you just say this was the Hill residence?" A silly conversation ensues. I'm in no mood to give any explanations to this guy. But he asks me to identify myself. He tells me he received a call from this number. I give him my name and suggest that it might have been a mistake. He then asks me if there's a problem at my home. I say, "No, there isn't; thanks, anyway," and hang up. So who was that guy? I finally figure it out: it must be the man who has to come and fix the dishwasher. I probably misunderstood him and told him to get lost by mistake. He'll call Sarah again. The phone is the worst enemy of a foreigner since you can't see the lips or guess the intentions of your interlocutor.

Back to George Catlin. To use a metaphor, carbon dioxide is the shovel that throws the oxygen coal into the furnace of the muscles. When we breathe naturally through the nose, we exhale less carbon dioxide than we process, which allows the body to keep the necessary reserve in the blood to recover the energy expended during exercise.

When athletes become fatigued, many are obsessed with the need to take in more air and to breathe through the mouth more rapidly. It is true that they take in more oxygen, but also, without being aware of it, they exhale all of their carbon dioxide reserve, which leaves their capillaries saturated with oxygen that has no way to reach the cells. The results are disastrous: instead of recovering and gaining the peak speed they expected, these athletes are slowly reducing their energy production and perpetuating the state of fatigue. Confused, they face an apparent paradox: the situation worsens as they take in more air. The other runners pass them and before they reach the finish line, they feel their legs have definitively abandoned them.

When oxygen is incapable of reaching the muscles because of a lack of carbon dioxide, the tissues become restless. They have two choices: to die or to get nourishment from something that was not originally destined for their consumption. It's a desperate situation, like the Andean tragedy *Alive*, where a group of plane crash survivors were forced to consume human meat to survive. With rapid mouth breathing, the cells have no choice but to activate the anaerobic system, an emergency mechanism known as breathing without oxygen or anaerobic breathing, which is pretty much the fermentation process that living beings used to use many million years ago. When the human body implements this process, instead of oxygen, it burns sugar, and it has the side effect of producing lactic acid. Definitely not a muscle's best friend. In fact, the same scenario occurs on a grand scale when we die: since no oxygen is entering the body, anaerobic breathing immediately takes over and the lactic acid begins to accumulate in the muscles, producing the stiffening of the skin Chris Chestney has seen many times. The rigor mortis.

According to the Norwegian runner Ingrid Kristiansen, who beat the world record on five occasions, one minute of exercise without oxygen consumes the same amount of energy as 13 minutes of aerobic effort. A runner may be surprised that after a taxing workout, he runs slower than before.

In that sense, former Olympic champion Peter Snell gives conferences around the world to spread the word that running slower makes you faster. There's no trick involved. It is known that human muscles contain a genetic mix of slow and fast fibers. Both types produce the same amount of strength when contracting, although the rapid ones obtain it first. This has led to the widespread belief that short and long distance runners each develop only one type of muscle, which is the one most useful for their sport. New Zealand's best athlete claims that this is an urban legend. Snell believes that when we run slowly, we begin to use our slow-fiber muscles but that as we continue running, we switch to the rapid-fiber muscles even though we are still running at a slow pace. Thus, our fast muscles are well-exercised during a consistent training without sprints. Training slow means a faster peak in short races.

This is similar to what his trainer, the renowned Arthur Lydiard, proposed. Lydiard claimed that to increase speed, you had to increase muscular strength based on resistance exercises. He was convinced that if a reasonable effort was demanded of the body, it would always respond. An individual who practices no sport has a capillary for each muscle cell whereas another who trains moderately can easily have three or four blood vessels in the same cell. The more we familiarize the body with the race, the more capillaries it will create so that the blood can help the athlete better practice his sport. Apparently, Lydiard was not concerned with his pupils running faster; but rather that they knew how to access their inherit capacity for running. It was not a question of excelling, but rather of taking advantage of the best you had. Nothing more, nothing less.

The doorbell rings, which is highly unusual. Normally, neighbors just stick their head in the door and shout out, "Hello!" But not this time; now they are ringing the doorbell. "Okay, I'm coming!" I walk towards the door breathing slowly, taking in air through the nose. But it doesn't last too long. Suddenly I'm hyperventilating. I exude lactic acid and am beginning to feel the rigor mortis set in. I hope you will treat me nicely, Chris Chestney. Man, I've just opened the door and it's a police officer!

"Good afternoon." A blue-uniformed officer in sunglasses asks me if I live here, what my name is and why my last name isn't Hill. I tell him and he writes everything down in a notebook. He asks me if he can come in. I tell him he can, but he doesn't. He stands in the doorway, staring at me with a strange expression on his face. Perhaps they have a regulation that they should only enter if you tell them they can't. I don't know; at this point I'm too confused to formulate theories. "What's going on?" "It seems we received a 911 call from this address." "Oh, I get it." The puzzle pieces fall into place. I explain that I have a small daughter who was trying to call Madrid and that, since my city begins with the number 91, she probably dialed 911 by mistake. "So you have a daughter?" "Yes, sir." "How old is she?" "Five. Well, four actually. I mean, almost five." "So your four-year-old daughter calls Spain by herself?" "No ... well, maybe ... " "Is your wife home?" "I don't know." "You don't know?" "It's just that I'm working and I don't know if she's returned. Sarah! No, I don't think she's back yet. Saraaaaaaaaaaaaaaaah! Nope, she's not home." "What about your daughter?" "What about my daughter?" "Is she okay?" "Fine, what do you mean?" "Would you mind calling her so I can see her?" "Of course. Julia!" No answer. "Juliaaaa!" She still doesn't respond. "Juliaaaaaaaaaaaaaaaa!" She must be up in her room. I

290

point to the stairs. I notice that the policeman seems to regret not having come in for a look around. I tell him I'll get Julia. The officer tells me he prefers to wait outside in the car and for me to take my daughter outside. I go upstairs but can't find her anywhere. Not upstairs or downstairs, not even in the basement. I go out to the garage. The policeman is watching me. It's not looking good for me and the shadow of suspicion is weighing on my back so heavily that my legs are starting to buckle. I find Julia's coat next to the basketball hoop, and although right before promising me she wasn't going to call Madrid she also assured me she wouldn't go out to the street without telling me, I'm assuming she has gone to her cousins' house. Just what I needed. ... A cold sweat runs down my back. I approach the patrol car to tell the officer that she must have gone out. ""Your four-year-old daughter has gone out? "Well, not far, just down the street," I say, pointing to the house Javier and Piluca have rented. I see, says the policeman. "I'll just go and get her and bring her here." "Okay."

Julia is not at my brother's house. Javi, my little nephew, who is a year younger than Julia, informs me that he hasn't seen her all day. Now I'm the one who starts to worry. When the policeman sees me return alone, he gets out of his patrol car. "So according to you, your four-year-old daughter called 911..." "Yes, I think so." "And you're sure she dialed the wrong number, right?" "Yes, I think so." "However, your four-year-old daughter is not here..." The air is thick with tension. "No, wait, maybe she's hiding in the house." "Why would your daughter hide?" I envision myself handcuffed and shackled. With the policeman at my heels, I go inside and start to search for Julia in every room. Under the beds, in the bathtub, behind the refrigerator, in the closets. "Julia?" I see a lump resembling my daughter in a corner of her bedroom closet. I pull back the clothes on hangers and find her cowering in the corner. She's sobbing. "What's the matter, honey?" She looks down and presses herself against the back wall. "Here she is!" I shout to the policeman on the stair landing. "Okay, Julia, come out of the closet. Everything will be okay." "I don't want to come out." "Come to *Pápa*." "No!" I extend my hand to her, but she screams. "What's going on?" asks the policeman. I want to die, that's what's going on. As simple as that. Anyone witnessing this scene would come to the same mistaken conclusion: that I torture my daughter physically and psychologically and that she took refuge in the closet while she waited for her guardian angel to come to her aid. A perfect *Criminal Minds* script. "Julia, come out for a minute to tell the policeman there's no problem."

"What's going on up there?" I'm just about to offer up my wrists, go down the stairs with my head down and turn myself in. Any explanation coming from my mouth will sound like an excuse worse than the previous one. Finally, a thin little voice coming from behind the shirts saves me. Between whimpers, she confesses: "I wanted to talk to Marcia." "Okay, no problem. Come on out."

Julia had called Madrid, area code 91, but mistakenly dialed the number 1 twice, which put her in touch with emergency services. When she heard the voice on the other end of the line, she hung up. Then when she saw from her window that a policeman was approaching the door, she ran to hide in her closet.

We finally go downstairs. "Everything's fine, honey." The policeman confirms that she is alive, that she isn't running away from me and that I don't seem to be hiding any razorblades like the barber of Fleet Street. He closes his notebook. Case solved. "Thanks, sorry for the trouble." "Don't worry," he says, "these things happen much more often than you would think. Poor Julia got the fright of her life."

By now it's nighttime. I recount the unfortunate incident to Sarah as we sit in front of the fireplace and we laugh. She goes upstairs to make sure that Julia is doing okay. "Poor little mouse," I hear Sarah tell her. The anxiousness that you have when you see your child suffering brings me back to John Raucci and the will that led him as a father to find a solution for his son David, when he was diagnosed with asthma. I take another look at the cover of Catlin's book and remember a phrase that the Red Hook trainer often repeats: "No animal breathes through its mouth.

Look at the galloping horse," he says. "His nostrils flare, but the teeth remain closed. As a result of their continual observation of nature, Native Americans had guessed that nasal breathing was better." David began to practice nasal breathing. Slowly, deeply and toward the diaphragm. Within a few weeks, he was able to stop using his inhaler and never had another asthma attack.

In the summer of 2002, all the runners Raucci trained switched to nasal breathing. They followed John Douillard's maxim: "The faster you run, the slower you should breathe to facilitate the body's assimilation of oxygen." They began to breathe slower to run faster. Although the boys at first felt they were suffocating and Raucci had to reduce the intensity of the training, after two weeks they all experienced the pleasant sensation of improving their performance and recovering more quickly after the strenuous exercises. That same year, the Red Hook track team classified for the state championships for the first time. In 2004, they won the bronze medal, beating their own record by 17 seconds. Give, and it shall be given.

13

August (One Year Later)

DeFile's first name is probably the most common one in English: John. I was never sure where to put the *h*—Jhon?—until someone told me that the name originates from the Hebrew name Johan. This revelation brought a sense of joy since learning languages is similar to a driver's test in that all theories are useless if you don't later validate your knowledge by practicing. Spanish speakers tend to choke on the Anglo-Saxon *j* in John. They frequently switch to the Spanish pronunciation of *j* and thus transform the name into a yawn. Sarah, who was my English teacher, helped me identify a sound similar to the English *j* in Spanish. We found it by changing the *j* for *ch*. *Ch*...ohn. Believe it or not, it works. I spend the afternoon practicing all of the *j* words in the dictionary—*Ch...udge, ch... oke, Ch...ackknife*—while I pack my suitcase for a fishing trip to Alaska with my friend John DeFile.

John grew up in an apartment on the top floor of Rhinebeck's American Legion Hall, on Mill Street. His paternal ancestors hailed from Italy while his maternal side was Polish Christian. But John's more recent family history, however, took place in the City of Hudson, about half an hour drive north of here. There, his immigrant great-grandfather worked on the railroad, saving up to open up some pool halls, amid whose tables John's parents met. In 1961, the couple turned down factory jobs, the only work opportunity available at the time in Hudson, America's former whaling capital. Instead, John's parents moved to Rhinebeck so that his father could become the manager of the Legion Hall. The family lived upstairs in exchange for running the kitchen and bar downstairs, so growing up, John was constantly surrounded by rough men who came in to drink and chat with friends or to play pool or poker. John was allowed to go downstairs to greet the regulars. He especially remembers a big guy named Clint, who tended to be a poor judge of his tolerance for alcohol. Clint's extreme passion for football would grow with each drink, and soon he would be tackling the chairs or charging at the jukebox to illustrate the most famous plays. Every now and then, a local fight broke out. Nothing too serious that couldn't be forgotten next Sunday over the usual Legion's dinner that the vets and their families shared.

Last May, we watched the Memorial Day parade from the Tigges' yard on Chestnut Street. The Tigges took advantage of the occasion to invite friends over for a barbecue. We sat next to the curb in the folding canvas chairs that we all use to watch our kids' sporting events from the sidelines. Every year, the American Legion Firing Squad salutes the honored dead. The people of Rhinebeck wildly applaud the Cadillac convertibles that transport the honorable aging veterans, who, in turn, salute their fellow citizens.

The most poignant moment of the parade came when the Gold Star Mothers of fallen soldiers marched past. Emotion gripped everyone and even the sugar maples seemed to bow their branches before those women, who managed to smile at the spectators. They demonstrated supreme dignity in the face of the painful loss of a son, which Steven Spielberg portrayed better than anyone in *Saving Private Ryan*. The Gold Star Mothers were followed by the high school band. The sound of the teenagers merrily playing their wind instruments—which, incidentally were introduced to New Orleans by Spanish soldiers stationed there when Louisiana was part of New Spain (1764-1803) and contributed to the creation of jazz—helped ease the sadness that we all felt from witnessing the bereaved mothers who had marched before them. The volunteers from the fire department then made an appearance and the kids loudly begged them to turn on the red trucks' sirens. *Whee yooo...* And the firefighters stopped for a minute to have their pictures taken with their smaller fans. Sarah's cousin, Paul Kane, who used to live across the street, handed out soft drinks to the parade watchers from an improvised stand at the main intersection. "Hey," Paul says, winking an eye at me. "You have to keep with your Rhinebeck tradition even if you sell your house and move to Red Hook." Next came the children's baseball teams. Parents tried to identify their kids beneath their blue caps. Hey, Max! They look so cute.

Violin teacher Carol Schaad, marched behind the Little League teams. She makes incredible progress with her students. Nico attends her class after school and can now play recognizable melodies. Like the Pied Piper, Carol was followed by a group of kids who played *Green Grows the Laurel,* the battle cry of the Union armies during the war with Mexico. The Mexican soldiers—who didn't understand English—hung on to the first two words of the song—"green grows"which for them sounded like "gringos," and in 1846 their derogatory term for their northern neighbors was invented. "Horses!" Julia shouted, extremely excited while pointing at the horsemen that appeared riding those beautiful equines that can be spotted on many farms along the road. And finally at the very end came a pony with a sign hanging from its neck that read: The End.

John DeFile fondly remembers listening as veterans recounted their battle stories in the Legion's cantina, which still serves customers just a stone's throw away from the majestic Beekman Arms, America's oldest operating inn. The vets always found someone willing to listen attentively, he says. The Legion continues to attract clientele because wars keep producing more veterans, but today's vets tend to show up alone and spend only a short time at the bar. John believes that is because ever since Vietnam, no one has been sure what the necessary parameters are for defining a hero.

The first thing John's father taught him was how to use a fishing rod. The competition at the Landsman Kill had been established just before John was born. Every April, local business people and private individuals donated money to buy 1,000 trout for the kids to catch in the kill. The fish would be released into the water on a Saturday and a three-week fishing context would begin the next day Sunday, after a communal breakfast at the Legion. Catches were limited to five fish per day and the prize went to the fisherman who caught the biggest fish.

First name: John. Last name: DeFile. Age: two years. John's father woke him up at 5:00 a.m. one day, brandishing the fishing license. The boy leapt out of bed. They shared some pancakes with maple syrup with the other competitors in the Legion downstairs and at 8:00, after the kitchen was cleaned up, went off to Landsman Kill. John caught two trout that day and became a lifelong fan of the sport. The geography of the area has made it easy for him. Living next to the Hudson River, surrounded by lakes, streams and ponds, is a luxury for a fisherman. John says he could practically cast his line without having to leave his yard. In springtime, he caught trout; in summer, he caught catfish and sunnies. He made his first big catch when he was nine. Like so many Americans, his family took advantage of Easter vacations to escape the terrible cold assailing the northern United States. On San Martin Island, his father rented a boat to venture into the emerald seas of the Caribbean. The waves reached nine feet, and both John and his brother were seasick. But it was worth it. On the other end of the fishing line, a barracuda measuring over three feet was awaiting him. The rest is history.

Sunday, August 5. The adventure that will take me all the way to Alaska begins at 4:00 a.m. My brother-in-law, Peter Hill, an immigration lawyer in Atlanta ("I don't make much money but I help a lot of people," he told me once), is one of those guys who always has a fishing rod in the trunk of his car just in case he spots a pond. Peter, is the one that has convinced me to accompany him on an eight-day trip through the remote waters of the Kisaralik River in … Alaska? I signed up without thinking twice. Six of us are going on the trip. Peter was the first one to be convinced by his cousin Bob Kowal, who is even more passionate than he is about the art of fishing. Not only does Bob travel with fishing gear in his trunk, but he always carries a spool of nylon thread and a hook in his jacket pocket in case he comes across a puddle on his walks. Peter's friend Don, from Atlanta, his Rhinebeck buddy, Jeff Decker and John DeFile, have decided to join the adventure. I am the last guy to join in. I'm a fishing fan, but I also have serious limitations inherent to starting out in the sport at an advanced age. "Don't worry," Peter says to console me, "you'd have to be a real klutz not to catch something in Alaska." "Don't underestimate my clumsiness," I tell him.

It's exactly 4:00 a.m. when Jeff Decker comes to pick me up. Sarah wakes me up and I walk out like a zombie. We stayed too late last night for dinner at the home of Virginia Farias, the extraordinary woman who heads the kitchen at Astor Home in Rhinebeck. Vicky is the personification of the American Dream. She arrived from the Free and Sovereign State of Morelos, Mexico, three weeks before her 16th birthday, without knowing a word of English. At first she lived with friends in the Bronx and later had two children she wound up raising on her own. She cleaned houses during the day and attended English classes for immigrants at the local church in the evenings. Then she started working for Nicole Vidor, a lovely woman who moved to Rhinebeck in the 1980s and opened the Montgomery Street boutique Workers and Dreamers. Vicky was offered a chance to come along as part of the Vidor family package ... so off she and her children went. She lived in a garage apartment on Nicole's property until eventually she bought a car. Then she rented her own apartment, lived independently in this country for the first time, and started to work for other people in the area.

Huck met Vicky through the Vidors. When my mother-in law, Peggy, was looking for help because the good old German Edith had retired and left her, Huck got Vicky to come work for her. Vicky was able to get her green card. Then she married Adolfo, a friendly Mexican pastry chef with whom she had two more kids. The apartment that they rented was on the second floor of a family home in Stanfordville, but soon after the wedding, they were able to move to the first floor for a reduced rate because Vicky took care of the yard. When the owner of the house moved to California and wanted to sell, Vicky and Adolfo couldn't come up with the down payment, so Nicole's husband, Quentin, along with Peggy and Huck, helped them. Now Vicky owns a white house in a green meadow with a stream running through it. She keeps chickens and her ducks, a large vegetable garden, a flower garden, a pig, dogs and a litter of cats … and she lives in paradise. Her Mexican friends in New York City love to come to her place. Who wouldn't?

Originally, Vicky and Adolfo had 14 acres, but they sold off eight of them and in no time paid back the loan for their down payment. When the tenants in the upstairs apartment moved out, they connected it to the downstairs and now it's all one house—a great place where there is always an excuse to hold a party. Last night Vicky and Adolfo celebrated the birthday of the second daughter, Claudia. Under a tent decorated with Western motifs, they served fajitas; beans with bacon, onion, tomato and cilantro; rice in an enormous bowl; plenty of tortillas and cans of beer. The band Constelacion Musical played "Que viva la quinceañera y arriba las mujeres!" ("Hurray to the 15th-birthday girl, and up with women!") and made us all dance a cumbia. Every single Mexican that we know in the Hudson Valley was there. In short, we had a blast, and now it's hard to get back to real life. But Jeff is waiting outside in the car so I need to hurry. "Hello, Ch … eff." "Hi, Mo." "How's it going?" "I'm good, buddy." For Jeff, getting up at four in the morning is part of his daily routine. He has a family business, Decker and Son, whose logo has an image of the yellow backhoe he operates. At 5 am every day, he's already moving gravel or digging holes. Yesterday he fell asleep at 6 pm in front of the TV watching a game of golf, he tells me. Tiger Woods was leading, as usual, but he didn't see the end because at 8:30 Janet, his wife, suggested he go to bed.

We reach John's house in no time and transfer the backpacks from Jeff's car to a van from his moving business. It's difficult to drive through this part of the valley without seeing a DeFile Transportation vehicle. In

1968, John's father learned that the school needed a car and driver to take a special needs child to a center in Poughkeepsie. Federal law mandates that school districts must provide special needs children with the best education specific to their challenges that can be found in the area. Public schools must cover all costs, including transportation. DeFile made an offer and it was accepted. That's how he started his small business with two trucks. In 1982, John took over and won the bid for new routes. The public bid organizers give the school sealed envelopes containing bids with the price per person per day. The lowest bidder usually gets the job. John now has 18 vehicles and transports Rhinebeck special needs children to 15 different schools.

Drivers on staff are mostly retired individuals who make a little extra money working an average of 20 hours per week. They all come recommended by an acquaintance. John doesn't like to place want ads in the paper because he doesn't want to have to deal with weirdoes. In a country where photos of missing children are printed on milk cartons, John can't afford the luxury of leaving the kids in the hands of strangers. By law, each driver must pass a drug test and undergo an FBI background check. Drug testing has become common over the past 10 years. In 1987, 20 percent of companies required urine tests; today 80 percent do, especially in the South. This procedure is actually only useful for detecting whether the job candidate has smoked marijuana. Evidence of marijuana use remains in the body for several weeks, whereas signs of heroin and cocaine use disappear in three days. Alcoholism can also be missed since the body flushes out all traces of consumption in a few hours. The only way to prove a job candidate's alcohol addiction would be to look to see if he has empty liquor bottles under his bed.

After being hired by DeFile Transportation, drivers attend a special 30-hour school transportation course. Then the daily routine awaits them. Early in the morning, they pick up the children in front of their homes. Between 2:00 and 3:30 p.m., parents wait for them in the same spot, entrusting the drivers to return their children happy and healthy.

John also has a yellow school bus, but mostly he has vans. They are all required to pass inspection every six months. When John goes to fill up at local gas stations, he is greeted warmly given that he consumes some 2,300 gallons of gas every month. "Hi, Ch … ohn." "Hi, G."

We drive down several empty county roads, and we get on the New Jersey Turnpike. We drive through the late, great actor James Gandolfini's turf. On our right, we pass Satriale's, the butcher shop featured in *The Sopranos*, which will be knocked down to build some condos. It is said that the Mafia hide in these residential neighborhoods, just a stone's throw from Manhattan, camouflaged among the upper middle-class, so as not to call the attention of federal agents. There's no traffic. Newark Airport: We arrive two and a half hours before the flight. Perfect. We've got loads of time. John takes the van to the long-term parking. Jeff and I wait in line at the Alaska Airlines counter. When it's our turn, we are told that the first flight will take us to Seattle, Washington, and that while we are indeed booked on an Alaska Airlines flight, it is actually operated by Continental. "Okay, so?" "Well, if you want to land on the West Coast this afternoon, you've got to rush to the next terminal." "What?" "Run to Continental if you don't want to miss the plane." "Argh!!!" Dragging our heavy knapsacks, we rush out of the terminal, our hearts pounding.

Somehow we make it from Terminal A to Terminal C. The line looks endless, but it moves quickly. Finally, it's our turn. "Yes," they tell us, "if you hurry, you can make the flight." The staff member didn't even give me the stub for my suitcase. "If I were you, sir, I wouldn't worry about such a small thing. Run!" We gallop to the security checkpoint. We are up against Homeland Security. Another interminable line. "Please, sir, we're going to miss our flight." The officer sits down. "Then you should have come earlier." We have no choice but to wait. We finally get through and resume our race. As luck would have it, our boarding gate is C83, the last one of all. Great. We run down three long hallways whose ends seem to keep moving further away from us. C 83, there it is. Wow, at least people are still boarding. We did it! "Not so fast. You can't board."

"Why not?" "The flight is closed." "But there are still people boarding…" "Right, but your seats have been assigned to passengers on the waiting list. Those are the rules of civil aviation. Ten minutes before boarding, if you don't show at the gate, you lose your seat." The airline employee is very sorry.

An epic begins the outcome of which we cannot guess. The waiting lists for all flights to Seattle are full and there doesn't seem to be even the remotest possibility that we will make the cut. Dawn breaks. Time stops in the airport and the minutes stretch out uncomfortably, like they did for Tom Hanks in *The Terminal*. By mid-morning, we have the impression that tomorrow's expedition to the Kisaralik River towards the glaciers will begin without us and that we'll have to keep conjugating in the imperfect future tense our dream of fishing in Alaska. We go from "I can't believe it" to "How could we have been so stupid?" "It's over." "Wait a minute." "What?" "Why don't we try to change tickets?" "There's no space left." "We don't know that." "There's no hope for the waiting list with the number of people ahead of us, but nobody said anything about the possibility of buying those seats before they are distributed." They look at me as if I were a Martian. We'll try. John calls his wife, Chantal, who checks all the possibilities from her home computer. Calls come and go between them. At last we get a confirmation: she bought two new tickets to Seattle. "Perfect." "Not exactly, there's only one problem." "What?" "I can't go." "Excuse me?" Alaska Airlines has accepted my friends' flight changes, but my flight was booked through Continental and that airline is sold out. "But it's the same plane!" "That's just the way it is." I knew it. In a last desperate attempt, I call Alaska Airlines to see if they have another ticket left. They do. Wonderful. It's the last one and it costs a fortune. But the alternative is to miss the whole trip, so I pay up. Or I should say, I try to pay. They won't accept my Visa card. It needs to have an address in the United States and my card has a Madrid address on it. John lends me his credit card. Your payment has been … accepted. Yahoo!!! In the middle of Terminal C, I shout with joy the same word David Filo and Jerry Yang shouted at Stanford when they came up with their famous Internet browser.

Such is my happiness at being able to board that, boarding pass in hand, I ask the flight attendant if I can give her a hug in appreciation. She says yes, and I give her a bear hug. Twenty-seven hours, six beers and a Wendy's chicken sandwich after leaving Rhinebeck, we land in Anchorage and I step on Alaskan soil for the first time. New York is four hours ahead of Alaska, and here it's 3:00 a.m. At 6:00 a.m., the plane leaves for Bethel, Alaska. Our plane is a Boeing 737-400 with a fuselage as white as snow and the face of an Eskimo drawn in dark blue on its tail. Inside, a black panel divides the plane in two. From the cabin to Row 14 is reserved for cargo. Rows 15 to 27 seat passengers in two parallel rows of three seats across. A young flight attendant with Native American features picks up the microphone. "Are you an Eskimo?" I ask her. No, she's Mexican, from Monterrey. Six percent of Alaska's residents are Latinos and the Spanish culture has left some footprints since Salvador Fidalgo, a Catalan sailor, passed through the area in 1790 and founded the town of Cordova. Also Valdez, the deepwater port and oil-shipping terminal for the Alaska pipeline, got its name from a Spanish Secretary of Defense. As the plane takes off, the flight attendant entertains the travelers. "Let's see," she says into the microphone, "the first person that can tell me what type of drinks we serve on board will win a pin with the company logo." "Pepsi?" "No, sorry." A young girl calls out, "Coca Cola Classic, Diet Coke and Sprite." "Right. An Alaska Airlines pin for the young lady."

From the air, the 370 miles that separate Anchorage from Bethel reveal a spectacular landscape—that of White Fang. The immenseness of it all transports me back to my childhood, when I used to watch a TV series based on Jack London's *Call of the Wild* about the Klondike Gold Rush. I see the tongue of a huge glacier, then the enormous mountains, the highest in the United States, and finally the endless tundra—a table crisscrossed by fjords and several rivers and dotted with gigantic Spruce trees. Today the sun will shine for 16 hours and 39 minutes. Its presence has begun to shorten some five minutes per day, seven times faster than in the latitude of my Mediterranean homeland. Soon the Arctic Circle will be immersed in complete darkness for nine months. That's Alaska for you: a million square miles and a population of 620,000. Alaska's surface area is the size of Mediterranean Europe: Portugal, Spain, France and Italy combined. It's a territory so vast that students from the fishing village of Seldovia, on the Kenai Peninsula, have to travel an hour and a half by boat, five hours by bus and 70 minutes in a small plane every time they attend a school basketball game against students from Bethel. And they don't even have the worst of it: the distance separating the rival schools in the communities of Unalaska and Barrow must travel even further than the distance between Boston and Miami. In Alaska, distances take on a whole new dimension. So do temperatures. Here, sports events are not cancelled unless the thermometer dips below 15°F.

We fly over Matanuska Valley, where it takes an average of 50 days to grow lettuce from a seedling, much less than the 80 days required in the fertile fields of California. Paradoxically, this piece of sunlight-drenched land holds several agricultural records. It has produced 19-lb. carrots and a 138-lb. world record cabbage. Most vegetables, like 90 percent of the food, have to be imported, but there is a small open-field farm operation in the north where the long sunlight hours of summer produce amazing results. It's an Alaskan hop-skip-and-jump to where 1.2 million barrels of oil are extracted daily—black gold that travels from Prudhoe Bay to Valdez through an 800-mile pipeline, which is elevated so as not to interfere with the migration of the long antlered caribou.

At last we spot Bethel. It's located in the Yukon Delta, the largest naturally protected area in the United States. Seven thousand souls live in what was traditionally a winter home of the Yupik People. Prior to the intrusion of Europeans the area had two large communal houses: a residence for men and boys, which was also used for community events such as storytelling; and another residence, connected by tunnels to the first, for women, girls and boys under age five. The men taught their sons to build kayaks and hunt. The women, who were responsible for making household utensils with feathers, leather and skins, gave sewing and cooking classes to the girls. Once a year for a six-week period, the men and women switched houses. During that time, the men taught the girls survival skills, hunting and tool-making, and the women instructed the boys on how to cure skins with their own saliva and make their own parkas with bone needles and thread made from caribou nerve fibers.

The Yupik have slanted eyes; brown skin; flat noses; broad faces; straight, jet-black hair and compact bodies. It gets so cold in these lands that it is rumored that local inhabitants learn to talk almost without opening their mouths. The native language uses a lot of K's. Russians established trade here shortly after the Bering Expedition in 1741, when they became fascinated by the quality of the otter skins. The Russians learned Yupik, developed an alphabet into which they translated the Russian Orthodox Bible and taught the locals to read it. They neither imposed their own language nor treated the Yupik like a savage people. With the transfer of the territory to the United States in 1867, the new residents demanded that the native population become Christian and get biblical names. Not surprisingly, today most Yupik men are named Bob.

The airport runway in Bethel is full of potholes. *Clunk, clunk, clunk.* It's the first time I've experienced turbulence in a plane with wheels on the ground. The road that takes us to the town consists of a mudflat. The nose of a car that fell into a ditch is sticking out. I imagine this spot at night and remember that I read somewhere that Bethel is the U.S. city with the highest percentage of sex crimes. You can't buy alcohol here—or to be more specific, it is not sold here. This is legally a swampy county. Although the sale of alcohol is forbidden, its consumption is permitted. You just have to order it from a liquor store in Anchorage, the transportation hub for the whole state, and have it sent to you. That's just what Peter Hill did. He bought wine in Georgia and brought it with him to liven up the meals on the trip. To facilitate boat transport, he put the wine in some plastic bags similar to those used for blood transfusions. It's not the only drink we have in the arsenal. John brought a bottle of vodka and I brought Nicaraguan rum. Flor de Caña, the best.

Beneath the thin surface of the Bethel tundra, the subsoil is permanently frozen. Because it's impossible to dig there, pipes are laid on top of the streets. The urban landscape looks a bit grimy. Junk and broken furniture litter the yards. It's impossible to bury trash and taking it out of Alaska is too expensive. Besides, in a place where supplies are hard to come by, everything that can be reused is saved. We take another road that leads us to the lake's shore. Welcome to the B&B operated by Papa Bear Adventures—$60 a night—where a hot shower and a clean towel will await us on the day we return from our adventure. It's quite a luxury considering that the water gets distributed in cistern trucks and is also rationed. Papa Bear serves us as the base camp; it's a safe place to leave the urban man's clothes, documentation and money. Our float-equipped aircraft will take off from the nearby Kuskokwim River. Alaska is such a wild, remote territory that you need air or boat transport to get from one town to another. There are no highways. Well, more precisely, here the highways are rivers. There are 3,600 of them, of which 1,500 can be navigated.

A cup of coffee helps when making introductions. There are nine members in our party: six fishermen and three guides. I say hello to Marty Decker, owner and lead guide of Frontier River Guides, with whom I've been exchanging emails in recent months: "Dear Guillermo, you haven't sent the signed document that absolves me of responsibility in the case a bear eats you." "Dear Marty, I did send it to you." "Dear Guillermo, But I didn't get it." "Dear Marty, Well, I'll send it again." "The person signing this contract agrees to assume all risks inherent to a journey down a remote river in potentially dangerous conditions, what with whirlpools, rapids and waterfalls, as well as possible run-ins with wild animals, plus the possibility of fractures, burns, cuts, hypothermia and lightning strikes, which may result in injury or loss of life. Frontier River Guides assumes no responsibility in the event of these occurrences. Amen." "Dear Guillermo, I've just received the signed document." "Dear Marty, Great. Since a second copy should be arriving soon, you can keep both and thus have my legal exemption in case the bear decides to bite me twice." The Marty of the emails takes shape as the rain pelts against the windowpanes of our refuge. He's a leathery guy, with a hard look about him and a deep, melodious voice that instills a sense of calm. He gives each of us a huge waterproof bag in which we have to put our belongings. "What doesn't fit, doesn't travel." He also gives us each a little dry bag in which to keep our fishing equipment and a canteen. These last two items come with clips to fasten them to the boat. Marty tells us we need to start putting on our fisherman outfits because we're leaving right away.

The fisherman's attire is quite simple: long underwear (both top and bottoms), warm socks and a flannel shirt. And of course chest waders, which are like overalls for anyone who wants to feel like one of the Maclean brothers in *A River Runs Through It*. Today, they are made of breathable fabric and end in some neoprene socks. The waders are held up with suspenders, but for safety reasons, as in a plane, you have to fasten your belt. Waders fit very loose. It almost feels like wearing a big plastic bag.

If you stumble in the river and fall in without your wading belt tied, the waders will rapidly fill with water transforming you into a human balloon, and making it nearly impossible for you to climb out of the water. Horrible ending. To avoid slipping, the soles of the boots are lined with felt. You also need a parka in case it rains. And on top of that, a vest with all the fishing paraphernalia you'll need. Plus, if it's sunny, a cap. If it's cold, some gloves. And if you want to look cool, some polarized sunglasses.

Marty tells us that because of the load on the float plane, he'll have to take us two at a time. We should decide who goes first. Jeff pulls out a deck of cards and proposes that we play for the highest card. Okay. A three of spades. A seven of hearts. A five of diamonds. My turn. I can't believe it: I got the jack of clubs. I win. The second winner is John DeFile. This doesn't surprise me. John likes to gamble. He goes to Las Vegas once a year, Atlantic City two or three times and never misses the Thursday night poker game in Rhinebeck. Texas Hold 'Em Poker, of course—five cards in the middle of the table and two in our hands. This is the game that has eclipsed more traditional poker, as a result of the popular broadcasts of the world championships. The rules are simple; the combinations plentiful and the bets unlimited.

DeFile and I take the first one-hour flight, 37 miles southeast in a 1957 DeHavalland BEAVER. Average fuel consumption: 20 gallons an hour. Boris, the Russian pilot, does not seem very friendly. Perhaps he is bitterly recalling when all of this belonged to his country. Who knows? He tells us to put on headsets and through a little microphone attached to his helmet gives us instructions to follow in case of an accident. The roar of the engine impedes us from communicating any other way. Apparently, as I will find an hour later, Boris makes it very clear that we should only talk to him in case of emergency, so as not to distract him during the flight. I don't know whether it's his thick Russian accent or my over-enthusiasm about being part of such a cool experience, but unfortunately, I understand the opposite. I actually believe that Boris is begging us to keep on talking to entertain him during the trip. Like when you travel at night in the pilot seat of a car and the driver wants you to chat with him to keep him from falling asleep at the wheel. In fact, I take my erroneous mission of keeping him alert very seriously, and since I can't think of anything else to say, I ask a series of stupid questions: Boris, how fast are we traveling?" "Are we almost there, Boris?" "How high are we flying again? He doesn't answer me. Surely he must be thinking, "Shut up, dumbass. Look out the window and see for yourself." The plane's radio plays the *Concierto de Aranjuez*, a composition for classical guitar and orchestra by the Spanish composer Joaquín Rodrigo. Written in 1939, its success established Rodrigo's reputation as one of the most significant Spanish composers of the 20th century. I can't think of anything better than listening to this master piece of beauty while flying over the infinite esplanade of tundra on which the herds of caribou look like grains of pepper on a plate of rice. They are the first cousins of Santa Claus's reindeer. They gaze upward when they hear the BEAVER, whose propellers are 600 feet above their antlers. Among the earth colors, the little mauve and rose flowers of the fireweed serve as a natural thermometer that announces the start of the brutal winter. The green stalk fills with buds in spring and blooms from the soil upwards. The number of flower buds remaining tells you how much longer the good weather will last because the fireweed invariably ends its cycle just before the first snows. It usually snows in early September, but sometimes a snowstorm hits in mid-August. I can't come with more questions for Boris, so to keep my entertaining mission I tell him that I was lucky enough to have met the composer of the music we are listening to, Joaquín Rodrigo. Not content with this explanation, I expand on it and tell him that Rodrigo and I were neighbors in Madrid and that he used to come out for a walk and sit in our backyard to rest in the sun. "Cool uh?" But Boris, stone-faced, doesn't respond. John looks at me, amazed. "What the hell are you doing, man? Tighten your lips!"

The plane glides onto the shore of Kisaralik Lake, 1,600 feet above sea level, in the foothills of the Kuskokwim Mountains. This mountain range, 250 miles long and 50 miles wide, is dotted with snow-capped peaks. To the right, Gravel Mountain emerges. To the left, gold mining exploration is taking place. Some men have set up a small camp in a location where they suspect volcanic activity deposited sediments of the precious metal 100 million years ago. They want to use helicopters to make holes in the ground using 800-foot bits. The native Akiak community is fighting them. For many years, the Akiak didn't even allow anyone to put up a hunting cabin in the wildlife reserve, and now they've opened their doors to miners who will destroy the landscape. The state justifies this by promising to distribute the wealth among inhabitants. But this should be taken with a grain of salt. Every year, Alaska residents receive dividend checks totaling some $2,000.

It's drizzling and the wind is blowing. We see a red fox. Marty and one of his assistants, Zach, ready the inflatable rafts on the lakeshore. They are Aire brand, 13 feet by 6 feet, with a tubular seamless bottom, made of Ferrari Precontrain PVC. While we wait for the others, John

310

and I cast our lines. The bait is a little peach-colored pearl resembling a salmon egg. My first grayling bites. Look at that dorsal fin! It resembles a miniature swordfish without the saber. This looks promising.

Finally we head downriver. Eighty-five miles on the Kisaralik, a river whose difficult access has preserved its surroundings intact. Three rafts, a guide and two fishermen in each raft. Before boarding, Marty reminds us that we shouldn't put food or anything that has a scent in the tents. "No toothpaste or deodorant. Got it? All belongings have to spend the night in a hermetically-sealed bag 60 feet from the camp. We don't want to attract any bears." "And if one shows up without an appointment?" "We'll get to that. First: stay together. They rarely attack a group of three. Forget about going for a solitary walk. If a bear appears, the three of us should stick together like a giant creature with six eyes." "Yeah, I nod confidently, and stare at him fiercely." "Actually," Marty corrects me, "staring at a bear is a sign of aggression. Best not to engage eyes with one. You should raise your knapsacks over your heads to gain height and unfold your sweaters to make you look bigger. It's important to look larger to scare them off. If despite these measures, the animal begins to growl and paw at the ground, the situation has turned potentially dangerous. Back away! And if the bear makes contact … the only solution is to drop to the ground, cover your head with your hands and play dead." And then, as CBS reporter Edward R. Murrow used to say, good night and good luck.

This advice would have been a good reason to turn around and ask our Russian friend some more questions (Do these planes need much maintenance, Boris, old buddy?) … if it were not for the heavy artillery protecting us. Marty has a Marlin lever action rifle slung over his shoulder, which shoots 45-70 cartridges. The 45 refers to the bullets' caliber. It's really big, the same diameter as the Winchester 458 magnum rifle used to hunt elephants, with a bore diameter the size of my thumb. The number 70 refers to 1870, the year in which the cartridge was officially accepted by the Armed Forces. The Marlin is not a sports gun. One shot in a grizzly bear's shoulder is enough to knock it down.

"It's best to kneel to shoot," Marty explains. "First, this position lets you control the rifle better, especially if you're nervous. Second, if you miss and the beast attacks you, you can always roll to try to avoid the mortal blow."

We leave at 5:00 p.m. Two guys accompany Marty as summer fishing guides: Zach and Pat. Peter and I will share the first trip with Zach Johnson, an enthusiastic redhead who normally lives in an Indian tepee with his girlfriend Chrissi. He is a mountaineering guide on Mt. McKinley in the winter season. He has climbed that mountain four times. At 20,327 feet, it's the highest peak in North America. He tells me that Alaska has the best powder snow on Earth. The only problem is that you have to ski at night ... in the dark. Here, the big sport is cross-country skiing and each school has its own team. Anchorage, where the most prestigious annual international competition is held, has 250 miles of cross-country trails: the Tour. A duck pedals furiously in front of our boat. It's a Merganser. It swims past three minks that have decided to go for a dip. Arctic terns fly overhead. These birds have the longest migration in the animal kingdom. They live in the North Pole and summer in Tierra del Fuego in Chile. Quite a commute.

Before we depart we prepare some sandwiches. Pat explains what we should do if we fall into the water: "Try to grab the boat by the rope surrounding it. If that fails, just let yourself float on your back, feet-first to be able to push away the rocks. If you lead the way with your head, your skull runs the risk of being crushed like a walnut in a nutcracker." As you can imagine, all these explanations greatly calm my mind.

We will use a technique called fly-fishing. Is there any other? Those who have had the opportunity to try it say they will never go back to traditional casting. Fly-fishing began because the trout's favorite dish, the mayfly, did not attach well to the hook and when it came into contact with water it appeared dead, which made the fish reject it. So someone decided to put a fake fly on the hook, which would sit on top of the water and survive many castings. The Macedonians were already catching trout with artificial insects in the second century. The first fishing rods were 18 feet long, more than double the length of modern-day ones. They consisted of a pole with the bait hung on a string tied to the end. Fly-fishing technology has evolved, but the idea is basically the same: place a small, lightweight bait in the fish's mouth. Flexible rods and heavy lines are used to guide the hook with whip-like movement towards the objective. Since the sound of such a heavy line splashing on the water could scare the prey, a thin thread, called a leader, is attached to the end to create a nearly invisible connection between the whip and the fly.

You have to land the fly next to the finny prey and pay attention because the fish will open its mouth, catch the bait and close it. In just seconds, it will realize that it is not a live organism and will open its mouth again to spit it out. Before that happens, you have to give a quick tug to hook its lips. If you take too long, it will have spit out the fly. If you tug too soon, you'll remove the bait before the fish has a chance to close its mouth.

All baits are called flies because initially they all looked like dipterous insects, but now flies look like anything fish like to eat: frogs, eggs, tadpoles, mice, moths, crabs, leeches. The same technique works for the small trout in the Rhinebeck Landsman Kill and the submarine-sized king salmon in Alaska. The river guide Tomás Gil taught me how to fish on the Curueño River. Tomás has a fishing rod with teeth marks on it because in his hometown on the León Mountains, Spain, the water goes down the canyons and forms ponds that you have to cross with the rod in your mouth. Normally, you throw the fly several yards in front of the spot where you think there may be a fish, upriver, at a 45-degree angle. The heavy line stays to the left of the prey and the fine thread skips and descends toward the fish's mouth at a constant speed, dragged by the current.

The best thing about fishing is that it provides a wonderful opportunity to interpret what occurs in nature. Fly larvae spend the year submerged in the river water, growing beneath the rocks. When the larvae hatch, a process lasting between one and two days, the nymphs go to the surface. There, after their wings are dry, the males fertilize the females and fly to land. The females remain in the water to lay their eggs. They live two or three days and when they drown, the current takes them. When the trout emerge to the surface to eat, fishing reaches its maximum level of excitement because man and beast come head to head in a battle of intelligence. Fish, depending on the days, hours and instincts, could be looking either for nymphs, the yummy flies that are depositing eggs on the surface or for the dead ones dragged downriver by the current. The fisherman has to guess what is occurring to offer the right imitation menu as bait.

When the fish are hungry, they hold in water that is out to the main current, behind the rocks and at the edges of eddies, so as to conserve energy; then they move like a rocket when they see the current bringing food their direction, so they can grab it before another fish does. When they rest, they seek shelter next to the shore in the shade of a tree or bush since they have no sunglasses. Our fishing on the Kisaralik is catch-and-release. The hook doesn't have a point on it and the fish are returned to the water after they are caught. Marty tells us to remove the hook and release them with a quick twist of the wrist. "If you have no choice but to grab the fish," he says, "wet your hands first to avoid removing the mucous covering its body. If the fish loses this protective covering, it will catch an infection and die for sure."

My vest looks like a fishing sampler, with all sorts of gadgets hanging from it. Some are essential; others just a whim. The world of fishing offers thousands of optional gizmos. Zach tells us: "You know you're a resident Alaskan and a real fisherman when you call Cabela's— the outdoor recreation retailer based in Nebraska—more often than you phone your parents."

The first stretch of the river passes through a gorge. The current increases notably as several creeks descending from the mountains merge into the main river. The vegetation is of the Alpine tundra. Near the shore, a few weeping willows make their appearance. The crystalline wa-

314

ter takes on a bluish hue. Two hours later, we look for a place to camp. Marty chooses one of the gravel beaches amid the bushes. It is drizzling. The three guides unload the boats and set up camp. Ultra-light Moss-brand two-man tents. The rest of us continue fishing, as we're not sure how to help. It won't take long to learn.

Pat purifies the river water with a flashlight-like device that trans-forms salt, sodium chlorite, into chloride dioxide. This will prevent Giar-diasis, which is caused by a parasite that destroys the intestines. Pat fills the purification device with water, adds a pinch of salt, shakes it 10 times and presses a button that triggers the chemical reaction. Soon we have homemade chlorine to put in our canteens. In the meantime, Zach digs a latrine and leaves the shovel next to it so that the person using the site can cover the result with sand. We have to burn the toilet paper with a lighter. Peter and Bob have brought a fly-tying kit and start to make their own flies. They take out orange yarn, red thread and Marabou feathers harvested from turkeys. The trick is to know how to take advantage of them. They roll the thread on the hook to form the body and then tie on a feather to simulate wings. They don't have to be perfect. Zach mentions that polar bear and beaver fur are perfect for making flies because they float well. At 9:00 p.m., Marty, who has learned our names, calls us to dinner: Don, Bob, Jeff, Pete, John ... Gioremo!

We get up at 6:30 the next morning. It's foggy and windy. We have breakfast: coffee, oatmeal porridge and bacon. The food travels in a large cooler containing three 8-lb. blocks of ice in Marty's boat. We have to ration it and I feel everyone staring at me when I pick up the milk bot-tle, watching to see how much I use. "You think I'm going to drink it all?" The tables fold and the tabletops roll up. They are wooden slats covered in plastic which, when unrolled, fit tautly on the tables. The aluminum legs are screwed in. The conversation turns to the snoring of my brother-in-law, Peter, who shared my tent. Everyone complains about it. I don't mind because I'm a heavy sleeper but I did witness the racket when I got up to go to the bathroom. For a minute, I thought a bear had gotten into

Peter's sleeping bag. Bob says it looks like rain. "How so?" "When you can see the underside of the leaves of the trees, he explains, it means it will probably rain. The temperature change makes the air rise and the leaves turn over." Wow. We collect our gear. We are in the boats by 11:30.

We're heading downriver. We descend an average of 15 feet every half-mile and the current moves fast. Here we catch Dolly Varden fish, which everyone calls Dolly Parton. Jeff and John are catching nonstop. Every time they get a fish, they start singing: "Well, hello, Dolly, I said hello, Dolly, It's so nice to have you back where you belong ... " I haven't caught even one. "What weight are you using, Guermino?" I show Pat what I'm using. "You'll never catch a Dolly with that. You need more weight. The Dolly is at the bottom. You know what a weight is good for? So that your fly will descend to the level where the fish that you want to catch swim. Look over the side, calculate how deep the water is here and put this tin weight on your line at that distance. Here." "Thanks." "To catch a Dolly, you need to hear the sound of the weight hitting the river bottom." "Hey, Pat, I got a bite!" "See? It's a beautiful fish." It begins to rain. It doesn't matter, though: "Hello, Dolly, I said hello, Dolly ... "

We see a black wolf on top of a hill. "Hey, Pat, isn't that a bear over there?" "Yes, it is—a female bear climbing the slope with her cub."

We stop to look through our binoculars. She's quite far away. It's better that way—females are the most dangerous. Sixty percent of humans who die from Grizzly attacks are killed by a mother protecting her cubs. Normally, bear cubs come in pairs, like socks, and only weigh a little more than one pound each at birth. Delightful teddy bears that become 1,000-lb. predators standing 12 feet tall. They run like the old mopeds at 34 miles per hour. Brown bears are distinguished by the large hump on their shoulders—pure muscle that serves to dig with the claws in the ground. They are fairly uniform with fur color that light makes look like they're graying. The word for gray in Old English was grisly.

We stop to eat a roast beef sandwich and cherries. The cherries are deliciously sweet, perfectly ripe. I am about to spit the pit into the water, returning an organic material to the Earth, but Marty's gesture makes me swallow it instead. *Gulp*. "You can't throw cherry pits in the river because the trout mistake them for salmon eggs and choke." Of course, I wasn't even thinking about that. "Zach, where did you say the trash can was again?"

At Mile 15, the river enters the Kuskokwim Mountain range through a deep canyon. Alder, birch and spruce trees appear in the landscape. We have to be prepared to get a bit wet: we're going into the rapids that plunge into waterfalls. Zach tells us to hold on tight to the raft. We handle the first five-foot jump with dignity. Cool. Category 3 rapids overcome. What lies ahead looks a bit more challenging. A 15-foot drop. "Go ahead, Zach, we're not up to it." Mr. Tarzan stays on board and the rest of us portage our fishing tackle along the shore to avoid danger. On the other side of the rocky drop-off, we spot a pool with more salmon than water. They jump like dolphins, insistently, trying to cross the eight feet that separates them from the high stretch of the river. Marty says it's the first time he's seen red Sockeye so far upriver. It must be an effect of climate change. There's also silver Coho. The smallest ones measure 20 inches and are 10 lbs. of pure muscle.

I take out the pollywog Bob gave me. It's a fly that looks like a little mouse. He made it himself with the orange rubber earplugs they gave him on the Alaska Airlines flight. He slit them open with a knife and slid a No. 4 salmon hook into the cut. After gluing the pieces back together, he sewed a bit of red Marabou feather on the shank of the hook, imitating the tail of the rodent and presto! The real ones are made of deer hide dyed pink. They are cast a bit in front of the salmon and dragged slowly, like mice trying to cross the river. The salmon take off like torpedoes after it. I catch one, and reel it in. Yes! I just caught the first salmon of my life! It pulls strongly, jumping and swimming at full speed in the opposite direction. The fly line burns my fingers. The fish takes off again. We struggle for a while. I finally reel it to shore. You know, John, I need a picture of this moment. I hand him my camera. I grab the salmon with my hands. I know I'm not supposed to but it's just for a second and...."Hurry up, it's getting away from me." *Click*. "Got it?" "Yeah." I look. The photo is blurry. There wasn't enough light and the flash didn't go off. I look like I'm holding a piece of bologna. Great.

At 7:00 a.m., the sky clears and a gorgeous sun appears. I leave the tent. Ours is set up 60 feet from the rest of the camp thanks to Peter's snoring. We're like a government in exile. Today I'm going to travel with John in Pat's boat. We spot a large caribou near the riverbank, a parka squirrel and a bald eagle. We catch seven or eight grayling and, finally, a rainbow trout. It flips and squirms in the air, shaking its head. It fights like a champion, but I reel it in. It measures 15 inches. I want to cry for joy. This time I have to get a good photo. Just as I'm about to bring the trout up to the boat to take its picture, I hear Marty say from the next boat over: "Gulermo?" I smile and release the trout from the hook and let it take off upriver. "Well, it wasn't big enough to merit a photo anyway," says Pat in an attempt to console me. "Last year, we caught one that was 29 inches on the Kenai River. It weighed so much we couldn't even lift it."

We occasionally see the enormous king salmon, with white markings on their backs, waiting for the arrival of death. These 45-lb. red torpedoes have returned to lay eggs in their birthplace after having lived in the ocean for three to five years. The bear eat fresh fish but when the grizzlies grow old and their strength begins to fail them, they hold their breath, go underwater and gorge on these moribund salmon. You have to cast to the kings with a sinking line because they rest deep in the river. It's no easy task. The only way to catch them is to place the fly pattern directly in front of them. Tremendously aggressive, their instinct incites them to defend themselves against being bothered. The trout, dolly and grayling hold behind the king salmon, in the hopes that the skirmish with some rock or the spat with another salmon will cause them to release some eggs. These transparent sacks turn yellow-, pink- or peach-colored once released into the water.

The open season for king salmon has closed, since they are actively spawning. We look for the red and silver salmon that arrived later and swim upriver at an average of 30 miles per day. It is somewhat less in land distance given that the water highway is lengthened by the endless curves. Initially, in the mountains, the river moves in a straight line but on the tundra it becomes more sinuous in its route. The river's meandering path serves as a natural brake to ensure that the current does not reach a speed incompatible with life. They also create natural flooding spots in the river to avoid major natural disasters down the stream.

We have to watch for dangers during the trip. The worst are from the sweepers, spruce trees that lean over the river. If you don't duck, they can knock you out of the boat. Getting wet is the least of your problems because, with the help of a life jacket, you will eventually make it back in the boat. The worst thing is to break an arm or a leg in the middle of the wilderness, where there isn't much you can do. The second threat is a log-jam, which is called a "water braid" here, caused by fallen trees that block the current. We set up camp next to the one Marty has named Kizzam after the magical incantation, due to the incredible fishing there.

So far, I've gotten the impression that our expedition has produced a strange involution toward the monkey. We haven't shaved or taken a shower and we happily burp and spit. What's going on here? Of course this is a very macho experience. But I want to get cleaned up. I ask John for some shampoo because his is biodegradable, and he decides to wash in the river, too. The rest decline—too cold, they say. We approach the water and stick our feet in: it's freezing. Besides, since we're heading south, the rocks are starting to grow moss on them, which makes them very slippery. Splashhh. I disappear underwater and reemerge, pulled by the current, 60 feet downriver. I see John's panicked expression. Relieved, he says: "Hey, I didn't think I'd see you again." Washing your hair with shampoo after five days is blissful.

As the light fades, there are more mosquitoes than air. They are also tiny insects called no-see-ums that you can't see unless they come in a swarm. Marty says that you're lucky if you breathe in Alaska without the insects filling your lungs. We have dinner under a mosquito net. Kind of like a portable screened-in porch. We enjoy the salmon caught during the day. Couldn't be fresher. Marty sautéed it with butter, black pepper and cinnamon. It's delicious. Peter's white wine is a perfect accompaniment to the fish.

We go to bed. At 1:15 a.m., Pat wakes us to announce that the Northern Lights have appeared in the sky. I get out of my tent and find myself witnessing the Aurora Borealis. Fifty miles above our heads, the electrical particles that form solar wind, attracted by the magnetic field of the North Pole, clash with the wispy gases of the ionosphere. There is some light, like that of moonlit nights, because the sun hasn't fully set. The color contrasts are greater when the background is completely dark, but I don't care. Despite the twilight, the show is spectacular. I'm amazed by the ghostly shapes that the light reflections have drawn in the sky, which is tinted a pale green.

Today we'll go into the boreal forest. There are many beaver lodges, numerous bear tracks and lots of bear excrement and remains of devoured salmon. The main river now splits into several small channels. You have to know how to choose the good one. The guides are struggling to avoid the logjams and sweepers. We stop on a beach to walk a bit. We follow a path opened by a bear through the bushes. Marty leads with his rifle, Pat comes at the end with his shotgun. We have to crouch through a tunnel opened by a grizzly among the bushes. We wade through a small back channel with a rapid current. The water is not much above our knees but the current is powerful. We all grab a partner to offer more resistance. I go with Jeff, who is a strong guy. We move slowly, hooked at the elbow like in folk dancing. "To prevent the water from carrying you off," Jeff instructs me, "You should crouch down a bit to lower the center of gravity." "Thank you." "See, I don't need to squat though," continues Jeff, laughing, "since my behind came low enough from the factory." We spend a few tense minutes dragging our feet through the gravel, but we eventually make it across.

Bear tracks are everywhere. We cross a small island again following a narrow path and, at the end of the walk, protected amid the trees, we see an earthly paradise before us. It's an 18-foot-wide stream that is a foot and a half deep. It looks like glass and is chockfull of fish. It's a piece of nature in its virgin state where it's possible that no other human has ever cast his shadow. We gape before the master lesson in natural sciences. The dog salmon, named for their fierce fangs, make craters in the gravel with their powerful tails. The olive green females, which have brown sides with irregular red stripes, lay eggs in the bottom of the nests. The males approach to fertilize the eggs, which they later bury by moving the sand and gravel again. Once hidden, they are dragged a few feet by the current and then anchor themselves, watching for possible predators while they await death. Occasionally, they turn over to bite the trout and dolly who, taking advantage of any distraction, try to lunch on the fishes' future offspring.

Pat points out the rainbow trout beneath the shade of a tree. I put an orange-colored egg on my line and cast it three feet in front of the spawning salmon. The fly settles naturally in the water. Tick. It dredges and travels quickly along the river without any strange tension that could scare my prey. The trout think that my egg just escaped from the salmon and jump like springs after it. It's mine. After some pirouettes and several escape attempts, I reel one in. It's green with bluish speckles and a pink band along its side. It has black spots and a yellowish splotch. A tap on the hook and it's free. It pulls itself together for a few seconds before disappearing. I catch eight more. I cast; they bite. Pat cannot enjoy the moment. His mission today is to carry his 12-gauge Mossberg shotgun in the case of any encounters with *orsus horribilis*. He left his fishing rod at camp. For someone so passionate about fishing, this situation can corrode the spirit. I hand him my 9-weight Orvis fly rod and he grabs it as if it were a canteen in the middle of the desert. He catches a few fish and then hands the rod back to me. After catching more than 20 fish, I stop counting. This has never happened to me before. If these were the streams of the Guadarrama Highlands, where I spent many afternoons with my friend Alfonso del Alamo, things would be different. "Why can't I catch any?" I complained, frustrated after several trout got away.

321

"Because they're really smart," Alfonso said. They learn that the fly that lands on the water and doesn't move will hurt their mouth. They don't eat it. They only tap it with their snouts. Tomás Gil once told me that in the rivers of León, the trout swim with only one fin because under the other they carry a catalogue of the artificial flies to consult which type are being cast to discard them from the day's menu.

You can calculate a fish's age by its size. Large trout can be between 15 and 20 years old. A 20-inch grayling has had a half-century in the water. There's no lack of food. In September, Alaskan rainbow trout look like footballs after two consecutive months of feasting on everything, including caviar. The ecosystem recovers when the egg-laying season ends. The trout will seek out deep pools to retire to for the winter, where they can wait for the last bits of salmon flesh to settle. They will have to pay attention so they don't miss them. The river doesn't give you a second chance. Fisherman can take advantage of the situation.

Marty has chosen the four largest Dolly for dinner that night. I think they're the most of beautiful fish. The male has a gray back and two blue lines and red spots on its sides. The underbelly is pinkish and the fins match the spots. The orange bottom lip is larger than the top lip to form a powerful pincers that perfectly fit in the groove on the snout. The females are more refined looking. The stripes are purple on a pink background and they have a white underbelly. Peter asks me to take a picture of the one he just caught. He wants to hang it on the wall of his office in Atlanta. Previously, you had to send it to the taxidermist to preserve the skin and mount it like a trophy. Now he takes the measurements, takes photos to identify the colors and returns it to the river. Specialized artists can make an exact copy in resin.

Marty kills the fish chosen for dinner by hitting their heads with a rock. *Boom, boom, boom.* All done. Quickly, so they don't suffer. Zach cuts their arteries to drain the blood and guts them. Pat looks for a stick to spear them. I'm responsible for the transport. Back in the rafts, I don't need to wade through the swift back channel of the river: my happiness helps me float on the water.

Zach expertly fillets the Dolly Varden. Their flesh is orange like that of salmon. The Yupik make jerky with this Arctic fish. They have 10 times the caloric and nutritional value of energy bars. While the rest of us sit around the table to share some wine and crackers with cheese, the good Bob Kowal continues fishing. He lives for fishing. He thinks about nothing else. Is there anything else? I'm convinced his soul is in the shape of a sardine. "I caught a 25-inch trout!" he shouts. John responds that he doesn't believe him. Bob repeats that it is huge. "Look. Come and see how I reel it in to shore." John agrees, but he takes a tape measure with him. Halfway there, we hear Bob's enthusiasm start to wane. "It looked bigger in the water," he confesses, "But it is still over 20 inches." John uses the tape measure and announces the result: "Fifteen!" Our laughter echoes throughout the valley.

That night around the bonfire, we finish off the rum and John hands out some cigars he brought to celebrate the end of the expedition. It seems like a goodbye party. Marty plays the blues on his harmonica. He apologizes because he hasn't practiced for two years, but he does a great job. He remembers that his father once took him to Madrid to hear flamenco music. We talk about music. Flamenco and blues mesh wonderfully. Both genres perceive the music as a conversation and both lyrics are laments ripped from the soul. I promise to send Marty a CD of the gypsy guitarist Raimundo Amador playing with BB King, the album *Lágrimas Negras* by the Cuban pianist Bebo Valdes and the flamenco singer Diego Cigala and *Soulerías* by Pitingo, the emergent artist with whom I'm hoping to record a Julio Iglesias song for the *Cándida* film soundtrack. But that's not important right now…

I came to Alaska to fish because I'd been told that the waters melting from its glaciers produced the same phenomenon that the first Spanish conquerors described with respect to the rivers of the Americas: they were so full of life that the fish overflowed onto the shores. It's just that, surprisingly, in addition to the splendid fishing and wilderness experience, I've come across the fascinating biography of the father of Marty Decker, the man who led our expedition. These things are bound to happen. Let's see: if you spend 12 hours in a rubber raft with the same person, you're not going to spend the whole time talking about the stone fly. I took advantage of the occasion to ask Marty about Alaska ... and his father's story came out.

Rubin Decker was a successful musician in the 1950s. Trained as a professional violist, he was a member of the Metro-Goldwyn-Mayer film orchestra in Hollywood on the 1950s. But Senator McCarthy accused him of belonging to the Communist party. In just 24 hours, Rubin's life flipped upside down. He wouldn't turn anyone else in, so he lost his job at MGM. The government closed its doors on him. The only chance to support his family was to accept a teaching position in Fairbanks, Alaska, where no one else wanted to go. Where it is often colder outside than inside the fridge and has the most abrupt temperature changes on the planet: lows of 65 degrees below zero in winter and highs of 90 degrees in summer. Marty was only eight when he was transplanted from his native California to the permafrost and ice, but he learned to love them. He loved the summer, too. After he finishes each school year as a high school teacher in Anchorage, he works as a river guide to be able to enjoy the natural environment he loves. But let's rewind a bit.

When Rubin retired, and incidentally separated from his wife, he decided he wanted to travel. He thought about southern Spain because he loved the Spanish guitar—and the same *Concierto de Aranjuez* that, coincidentally, played in Boris's plane as we flew over the glaciers. In the summer of 1980 Rubin arrived in Andalusia and moved to Tarifa, on the Strait of Gibraltar. Tuna and windsurf paradise. Right across from Morocco. Marty was back home in college when he got in touch with the United States Consulate in Seville because his father had stopped contacting him. Rubin had pneumonia. With little money and no Spanish, Marty traveled to Seville. Some miles south, he found his father very ill and took him to the hospital in the city … where he died a few days later. Marty didn't know what to do. He didn't speak Spanish, had no money for the funeral and, on top of everything else, his father was Jewish, which meant he should have been buried following a specific ritual. He didn't know if anyone was familiar with it in Seville. He sought the assistance of the American Consulate. "Don't worry, since your father was a World War II veteran, the consulate will take care of everything." But they buried him quickly and without ceremony in the Jewish cemetery in Seville. Marty recalls a small section enclosed by a railing within a larger cemetery. "What about the tombstone?" "Don't worry, the American consulate will take care of it." "It's just that I have to return to the university and I haven't got any money for…" "Don't worry, just go home." Rubin Decker had the right to a dignified burial. He spent the war in a B25 bomber as a radio operator and a mid-ship turret machine-gunner. We've checked the dates. He has the right to be buried with honors. There's no problem."

Twenty-five years later, I arrive in Bethel, meet Marty, ask him about his life and he tells me: "I have no idea if they ever put a tombstone on my father's grave … He used to take me to marches to protest the discrimination of African Americans and to peace marches during the Vietnam War. Those last protests led to his being fired from his teaching job at the University of Alaska in the 1960s. I would have loved to have the money to purchase him a tombstone that paid homage to his defense of human rights." "Well," I tell him, "you've still got time to do it." "I don't know." He is disenchanted. "What do you mean?" "I'm not even sure my father is still in that cemetery."

Perhaps I could find out upon my return to Spain. "Would you do that?" "Of course I will," I tell him.

14

September (One Year Later)

September 1, an old woman with an immutable smile is driving at a constant speed of 12 miles per hour by our front yard when suddenly the engine sputters and the old Oldsmobile dies on the corner of Chestnut Street. She turns the key. The battery works ... but the car doesn't start. I approach to offer my help. "I hope you didn't run out of gas." "Noooo ... I've got more than enough," she says softly. "I just put in $7 worth." Her response reminds me of a story I have recently heard at the gas station. The employees were talking about a tiny old lady, whom they referred to as Hurricane Hannah, and saying that when they see her drive up, they make a bet on how many gallons she'll put in her tank. Two? Three? Never more than five.

The blue Cutlass Ciera doesn't budge. "It must be the heat," she says. "Yes," I agree. I offer her a glass of water, iced tea, lemonade. "Nothing, thanks. Don't worry." I look at the odometer. It reads 193,000 miles. "It seems like a lot of miles for a car," I say. "Oh, nonsense!" she replies. "It actually has a lot more; I once reset the odometer."

Aye yai yai. Another failed attempt to start the car.

Tin-tin-tin-tin-tin... Tin tin, tin tin... Suddenly I hear the notes of the "Blue Danube Waltz" from the loudspeaker that announces the arrival of Mr. Ding-A-Ling, the ice cream truck. Iván, the ice cream man, is Ecuadorean and complains that he doesn't sell much. It seems that the sales he makes from a couple of summer camps are the only thing that saves him. "Would you like a Sponge Bob?" he asks. "No thanks, Iván." I ask Hannah if she would like a popsicle. No. She's on a diet. A diet? I look at her closely. She's a tiny woman, with toothpick-like legs encased in compression stockings.

I explain the situation to Mr. Ding-A-Ling and he offers to help out. Iván opens the hood and looks for signs of overheating but finds none. He asks Hannah to turn the ignition and step on the gas. She does so, but it isn't enough. "Ask her to step out of the car for a minute so I can try it," he says. I tell Hannah, "The ice cream man says he could help you more if you got out of the car for a minute and let him take over." "Oh, no, no. Impossible." She wouldn't leave the car even if a tornado hit. She has a cane on the passenger seat. I have no doubt she'd use it if we tried to remove her from her seat.

My brother Javier shows up. "Ma'am, wouldn't you like to come in for a minute? No? Should we call the mechanic?" "Absolutely not." "Can't I bring you a cold beverage?" "No, thanks."

"What's your name?" "Mary." "What a lovely name." "Yes." So Hurricane Hannah is actually Mary. Aye yai yai. I observe the worry in her clear blue eyes. She seems so fragile. As the moments pass, those eyes reveal her growing concern that she'll have to face the reality of not driving a car for a while.

Some neighborhood kids appear. She smiles at them. "Everyone in town knows me," she says. "I have no doubt about that." "They call me grandma. They see me pass by often because I go a lot of places." I know that's true because my children told me that the kids call her Mid-Road Millie. Aye yai yai. The engine definitely won't start. A summer storm is approaching; it's almost 6:00 p.m. and in five minutes the Foxes are going to pick us up to go to the Buckwheat Zydeco concert. "Are you sure you don't want to come inside?"

Ted Fox represents Buckwheat Zydeco, an American accordionist who plays Zydeco, the music that's typical of southern Louisiana swamplands, and his band. Ted is the author of the book

Showtime at the Apollo, a must-read for anyone who loves black music. It's exciting to talk to him about African American rhythms. In his youth, Ted drove his car from New York to Lafayette, deep in Louisiana, in search of small Zydeco clubs, whose music made him feel alive. All of the patrons were African-American except for him, a Yankee who had spent hours behind the wheel for the sole purpose of listening to their music. Everyone bought him drinks. Give my white friend another glass! He was working on another book, *In The Groove*, about the legendary men of the music industry, and had just interviewed Chris Blackwell—the founder of Island Records and the man who introduced Bob Marley's reggae to the world. So Ted decided to send a cassette recording of Buckwheat to him. "Mr. Blackwell, you have to hear this music. It's incredible." Chris called Ted on his return from his famous studio in the Bahamas, Compass Point. He was busy with Steve Winwood. One night at 2:00 in the morning, after an exhausting session, they played the Buckwheat Zydeco tape and came back to life. Chris told Ted, "I want to do a deal for five albums and for you to be the producer and Buck's manager. How's that?"

Ted was passionate about black music and popular culture, but the call caught him off guard. He wondered how a Jewish New Yorker could help a Creole artist from Louisiana like Buckwheat. "Journalists are always the best managers," Blackwell had told him. "Look what Jon Landau did with Bruce Springsteen. Writers are used to analyzing how things should go and why they should be done. You all have a salesman inside you, especially a freelancer like you, and you contribute knowledge that many great singers need." Ted recalled an old saying: "He who represents himself has a fool for a client." Buckwheat was enthusiastic about the idea. Ted looked again towards his mentor, Gerald Wexler, the New York Jewish journalist who popularized soul and invented rhythm and blues on his record label, Atlantic Records, and accepted the challenge. Like Ted, Jerry was not a musician, did not play an instrument and could not read music. But he had a knack for bringing out the best in others. "If necessary," the Atlantic Records magician once told Ted, "I'll dance in the studio so that my artist can understand the feeling I want the music to convey."

Buckwheat is playing tonight in Pawling, NY, and the Foxes are going to show up in a minute to take us all to the concert. "Should we go inside, Mary?" "No, I'm fine here." "Okay, but I think there's going to be a downpour." "Rain?" The thought of raindrops suddenly puts Mary on alert. With the agility of Halle Berry in *Catwoman*, she grabs her cane, hooks the end onto the handle of the passenger window and quickly rolls it up. *Cric-cric-cric.* "The glass is hermetically sealed. My son is a mechanic.Maybe I should call him." "Sure, no problem." I bring our phone and dial the number she dictates to me. I talk to her friendly daughter-in-law, who seems a bit nervous. I give her the exact coordinates for the rescue operation. It begins to rain. Mary keeps trying to start the car. Aye yai yai. She looks tiny in her vehicle.

By the time Mary's daughter-in-law shows up, it's pouring rain. "C'mon, let me take you home." Mary seems determined to remain at the wheel, like the captain of a sinking ship, but eventually she opens the door and gets out. Very slowly. Sheltered beneath the umbrella her daughter-in-law gave her, she gets into the other car. As they drive off, she doesn't take her blue eyes off the blue Oldsmobile that remains defenseless in the middle of Chestnut Street. Her eyes speak volumes. She's probably asking herself the difficult question that people ultimately have to ask themselves when they get older: "Will I ever drive again?"

* * *

I finally find a gap to drive to Stanfordville and say goodbye to my friend Kermit Love before I move back to Spain. Kermit has just turned 86 and is in excellent shape. He still swims laps in his outdoor pool, which is surrounded by plants so that it looks like a natural pond in the middle of a meadow. Kermit is lucky that his faithful partner of many years, Christopher Lyle, is always there to lend a hand. When he calls out

Christopheeeeeer!, the New Zealander comes running to see how he can help the old man with the long white beard, who New York taxi drivers call Santa Claus. Love, the great puppeteer, has the same name as Jim Henson's famous frog puppet. It was a mere twist of professional fate that brought the father of the Muppet Show and Kermit together in the 1960s and whose explosive mix would result in Sesame Street.

Kermit first transferred to television—in the form of puppets—the knowledge of set design that he had gained from his successful time working with Broadway theaters and the Metropolitan Ballet. He increased the size of the puppets, placing them in large outfits that hid the puppeteers beneath them and took advantage of his own hands in the process. He discarded the latex foam he had formally used, which can produce ugly seams, and came out with an innovative material for the Muppets' faces. Since then, puppeteers all over the world use reticulated foam, which is sold in flexible blocks that are cut into thin slices for the AC filters, enabling them to carve puppets in the manner of sculptures, sew their ears and noses on without leaving marks and apply makeup to their faces as if they were flesh and blood characters.

Big Bird was the creature that made Kermit Love most famous, earning him even more than the successful Snuggle Bear puppet he created for the popular Snuggle Fabric Softener commercials. The yellow hen that traveled to Mao's China in 1973 has been a cultural reference for several generations of kids in the United States and many other countries. His charm, apart from the personality given to him by Carroll Spinney, the person inside, lay in a couple of tricks. Kermit painted the edges of Big Bird's feathers a darker yellow to create the sensation of volume in front of the camera. He also attached some loose feathers to fall off during the show to make the character seem more real. I first learned about Kermit back in 1992. One afternoon in the middle of a dental checkup in Rhinebeck, my dentist, Dr. Spitzer, asked me what I'd been up to. Of course he knew that with my mouth open and stuffed with cotton balls, it would be difficult for me to answer. "I wat to maze a pupetz pogram," I tried to explain. "Oh," he said. "We have a client here who makes puppets. His name is Kermit. He'll be here this afternoon. I'll ask him if he would mind you giving him a call." I got the green light to call Kermit Love the next day without a clear idea about who he was. "Hello?" He listened attentively, sighed and said: "Look, Mr. Fesser, I'm very busy. On Tuesday at 8:00 a.m., I'm going on the train to New York. If you ride with me, you have an hour and 40 minutes to explain exactly what you want from me. I'll be happy to listen." Then he hung up.

By the time I boarded the Metro-North train in Poughkeepsie the next day, I had already learned that Kermit Love was the god of TV puppets. I easily spotted him on the platform, introduced myself somewhat timidly and during the train ride along the Hudson spoke nervously of my desire to create a TV show for an adult audience in Spain based on the characters of my radio show *Gomaespuma*. He listened without comment, nodding occasionally. When we reached Grand Central Station, I felt very bad. I was just about to say goodbye to Kermit when he asked me if I was in a hurry. I told him I wasn't and he asked me to accompany him to his studio, an immense loft near NYU. The studio walls were lined with shelves filled with white plastic boxes. Kermit asked one of his assistants to take down two boxes with Muppets in them. "Put on the puppets," he told me, "and show me what you would do on TV with them." "What?" My tongue was tied in knots. I don't remember what I did or said. I acted for a few minutes, completely desperate. "That's enough," he said. "I like your spirit; we can improve your technique later. When are we going to Spain to put this thing together?"

A month later Kermit was in Madrid. He originally came to do consulting work for a week because that's what our budget could cover, then he volunteered to stay for a month. He showed us how to work standing up, with the camera elevated to about 6.5 feet. That way you can't notice that the characters don't have legs. It makes it easy for them to run in and out, turn, and so on. He told us we should create the illusion that they walked, sat, breathed. He also taught us that it is always best, whenever possible, to keep the camera close. Longer lenses flatten the puppets. Use a wide-angle lens so you can highlight the three-dimensionality of the puppet's face. The eyes are mainly what bring a puppet to life. The puppet's hand appears bigger as it moves towards the lens, and smaller as it moves away, increasing the comic effect. He taught us how to synchronize our voices with the puppets' mouths. "You don't have to match every syllable," he said, "but you do need to coincide with key syllables, especially at the beginning and end of each sentence. It's best to keep the hands still, using them only to make some important point. Limit movement to express great feeling." He taught our artists how to make the faces. During those weeks of work in the studio, I discovered the real Kermit, the one who insisted that life is just an illusion, and who was always willing to add a dose of illusion to life.

But today, during my visit to his home, Kermit seems worried. Profits from Big Bird toys, clothing and video games have dropped dramatically and Barney, the purple and green dinosaur, has cornered the market. The Children's Television workshop commissioned a marketing study to find out what's going on. "Guess what they found?" Kermit asks me. We sit. Christopher is also with us, along with five or six or 20 dogs—I don't really know how many they have—which run around the kitchen table. "They've discovered that Barney tells kids what their parents never do because they're never home: 'I love you.' And the kids eat it up."

* * *

The final stretch of our American adventure seems to focus on episodes with broken-down cars. First that of Mary, whose Oldsmobile Cutlass Ciera was finally taken away by a tow truck, and now our own car. We're at home packing our bags for the second time to go back to Spain. Yesterday we tried to do the same thing. Peggy has again lent us her Lincoln Continental so that the bags will fit in the trunk. Raucci was busy so we called Bruno, another good friend, to take us to the airport and bring the car back to Rhinebeck. The road was flooded just before the Bronx. We were distracted by the story of Bruno's cousin, who drives a mail truck. He is assigned the route between Albany and Hartford, and normally takes 40 or 50 mailbags in his truck. On December 22 there was a terrible storm, but he had to get the mail out. The wind made the cabin of his truck sway and there was no way to pull over because snow banks lined the sides of the road. When he finally reached Hartford and opened the back, there was only one mailbag with only one letter inside. "Oh no," he said. "I've risked my life for just one letter: I certainly hope it's the bearer of good news."

We were just 20 miles from the airport and had plenty of time. But the traffic suddenly stopped. "What's going on?" Our lane was flooded. Torrential rains had burst the banks of the Hutchinson River, which flows parallel to the parkway of the same name for five miles. The cars all had to drive in the right lane to avoid the puddle. When it was our turn, the water had risen four inches. "Bruno?" "I think we can make it." The engine of the Honda in front of us stalled. The water level continued to rise. We were terrified. Our engine also stalled. On our right, a waterfall flowed down the hillside towards the highway. In just 20 seconds, we went from driving on land to navigating in the water. The water starting seeping into the car, submerging our feet. The children screamed and climbed on top of the backseat. Sarah and I opened the electric windows—thank God they still worked—and dove into what was fast becoming a lake. The car was floating in waist-high water. Inside the car, the electrical system failed. Now we couldn't have opened the windows, through which our three terrified children watched us. Sarah and I managed to push the Lincoln out of the floodwater and then up onto dry road, out of danger. We opened the doors and let the water rush out as if we had rescued an old submarine. The kids got out. Poor Bruno stepped out of the car shaking his head, still unable to take in what had just happened.

I suddenly remembered the passports and airline tickets. For some strange reason, I still hadn't accepted the fact that we were definitely going to miss the flight to Spain—maybe because everything happened so fast, or perhaps because I wanted to believe that the car was going to start and the water hadn't affected our suitcases. The envelope containing the tickets and documents was soaking wet. The passport visa stamps had faded. The tickets were stuck together in one big lump. While I was laying them out on the hood in the hope that the sun would dry them, I heard Sarah call me. "I'm coming," I said, without looking. She shouted again. "Okay, I'm coming!" What could be more important at that moment than drying the passports to be able to take our flight back? A life, that's what. It's a lot more important to save a life. I reacted too late—she'd done everything herself. She had just pulled a child from a car that was trapped in the middle of the floodwater. The car was almost completely submerged. The driver had gotten out with one of his children but needed help to grab the other, who was still in the vehicle, screaming.

At last the state troopers came. Just like in *E. T.*, they gave us each a little yellow blanket. "This is the second time this has happened today," they told us. "Every time there's a storm we have the same problem in the same place." Really? Hello! Didn't it occur to anybody to put a drain beneath the highway for when the Hutchinson overflows? A fireman lent us his cell phone to call Iberia Airlines and we were able to change our tickets so that we could call the tow truck and get a taxi home. We had to order two cars because we had so many bags and six passengers—the five in the family and Bruno—and we didn't fit in one, according to the Jamaican taxi driver who answered the call. He ordered reinforcements on the radio and his Haitian colleague turned up shortly thereafter. You have to pay for the pickup and drop-off, $150 each way. "It doesn't matter," I said. "Our health is what's important." So $300 later, we were home again with our soaking wet luggage. The kids and I had traveled with the Jamaican driver, who described the wonders of his homeland during the drive. He lived with his wife and son in a room he rented in The Bronx for $900 a month. Max confessed that, except for missing the flight to Madrid, the adventure was so cool. Nico became very serious. "Are you crazy?" he said. "*Papá*, you're such a loser." "Why do you say that?" "Because you didn't let me swim in the lake on the highway and I really wanted to." "Wow. People are drowning, cars floating, firemen intervening … and you want to sun yourself after taking a dip in the flooded road?"

The car was totaled. We learned too late that when the engine gets wet, you shouldn't try to start it because water enters the system and destroys it. You have to leave it for a few days to dry and then it apparently starts with no problem. If only we'd listened more often to *Car Talk*…Given my nervous state, I also forgot to ask the taxi drivers for a receipt, so the travel insurance will not reimburse this loser the $300 taxi fare.

But that was yesterday. Now we're immersed in our second attempt to fly to Spain. Sarah is fed up with washing and drying all our clothes to try to get the smell of mud out. My father-in-law, Bud, helps me secure with duct tape the bags that don't completely close. Once, twice, three times around? Bud has the same problem with duct tape that I have with the lawn mower—it's hard for him to stop. A few days ago he was helping me pack up some books that I had decided to ship. "Bud, have you got some scissors? Bud, have you got some pliers? Bud, you wouldn't happen to have one of those adhesive box labels, would you?" Bud has everything in his cellar, where he's set up a carving workshop "in the duck chamber," as Sarah's cousin, John Wallin, likes to call it.

After retiring from IBM, Bud Howe attended a two-week intensive carving course and returned home obsessed by wooden birds. He has hand-carved a pair of red cardinals on a snowy trunk. A blue jay perched on a branch. Three tiny sparrows with their beaks open, waiting for their mother to return. And dozens of incredibly detailed ducks. A mallard with a green head and yellow beak. A multicolored mandarin with very fine feathers. And a red-crested pochard. His latest creations are so realistic that it seems like they will flutter their wings and fly off the shelf. This would not have bothered Bud since he would know how to track them up in the sky. Yes, this man did his bit to make the whole nation look up at the stars at the same time.

Clarence K. "Bud" Howe grew up in Randolph, Kansas, a town with a population of 400 on a farm with orchards and animals, much like that inhabited by Dorothy and her dog Toto in *The Wizard of Oz*. But one morning, something more terrible than a tornado hit. National Guard engineers came and told everyone they had to evacuate so that they could build an artificial lake on their properties to contain the floods triggered by the frequent rise of the Big Blue River. In 1960, New Randolph was founded. The community received compensation. Authorities relocated the newly built houses and flooded the old town. When the last shingle disappeared beneath the water of the Turtle Creek Dam in 1963, Bud's mother sank into a depression from which she never completely recovered.

Before then, life had been pleasant. Bud's father managed a warehouse of construction materials and his mother taught classes in a one-room schoolhouse. The Howes raised chickens, had horses and other animals and harvested vegetables and grains from the fields. Bud was the second child and the oldest boy. As soon as he returned from school each day, he had chores to do. "Go and kill two chickens, Bud. Give the cows some water, Bud." Thus, when he enlisted to fight on the European front, he knew that his parents and siblings wouldn't go hungry during the war.

He was 17. The Japanese had bombed Pearl Harbor and, like most young American men, Bud wanted to fight on the front. He didn't go overseas, though. He was placed in the rearguard and spent the next five years in several Naval Stations around the country in charge of the radar system. In one of those facilities he met his future wife, who also served in the Navy, and together they returned to her hometown: Poughkeepsie, New York. The International Business Machines Corporation—IBM— soon hired him.

During World War II, IBM had put its resources at the disposition of the Truman Administration to manufacture weapons. The president accepted the offer and IBM received several commissions. In Poughkeepsie, a rifle assembly plant was established to that end. IBM sold the rifles to the army for a tiny profit, which was used to help female workers who lost their husbands in battle. Once the war was over, weapons were no longer produced and some of the company's commercial products were transferred to that plant. The Automatic Controlled Sequence Calculator, known as the Mark I, had just been manufactured successfully after six years of joint research with Harvard University. It was the world's first automatic calculator: 50 feet by 8 feet and weighing five tons. It took a second to add, six seconds to multiply and 12 seconds to divide. A true wonder. The company needed technical staff to develop the production, so thanks to his experience with radars, Bud was hired.

Soon IBM began to incorporate electronic components and created its first huge computer, the 701, based on vacuum tube technology. At the time, Bud headed the division that manufactured punch card machines, the old 24s, and electronic card readers, the old 26s. Back in those days, memory was stored outside the computer on data punch cards. One morning, his boss turned up at his office: "Howe, the data cards are too expensive. You've got to make them at least 20 percent cheaper. Let me know when you've done that." To the executive's surprise, Bud brought all his people together and quickly told his superior they had found a way to reduce costs from $100 to $80. The man from Kansas had a special gift for leading teams.

Top management took note and asked him to lead the top secret Semi-Automatic Ground Environment Project, or SAGE, a gigantic computer for the Air Force, illuminated by a light of 58,000 vacuum tubes, which would revolutionize civil aviation traffic control. The United States feared an attack by the Soviet Union and needed to bolster its anti-air defense system. It commissioned the Massachusetts Institute of Technology, MIT, to design a computerized network of control centers that would cover the whole United States. In 1955, IBM opened a small plant in Kingston, across the river from Poughkeepsie, to manufacture the necessary equipment, and Bud moved to the new office Poughkeepsie remained dedicated to the business of revolutionary electric typewriters. Bud took the model proposed by MIT and asked his engineers to analyze it and transform it into reality.

Twenty-two air control centers were built throughout the country. Along with the military intelligence information provided by radar, ships and air squadrons, they processed information from airports and the National Weather Service. The first center began operations in New York in 1958. The last one opened in Sioux City in 1961. The bulletproof, windowless buildings of reinforced concrete contained a 275-ton computer, occupying a space of 12,000 square feet, which processed radar information at a rate of 65,000 calculations per second and sent it directly to the Combat Operations Center in Cheyenne. From there, the military could send fighter-bomber jets to the sighting zone or give the order to launch a missile against the target identified.

By that time, Bud had managed to bring together IBM's best 50 engineers on his team. He had the ability to discover the potential in people and to put them on the path to success, and all his employees adored him. Everyone called him Bud, with the exception of his loyal secretary, who always referred to him as Mr. Howe. Management sent him to several training courses to increase his knowledge of electrical engineering and even offered to pay for his university studies, but he refused. It was too late for him, he thought. He had wanted to go back to college after the war with the GI program, but his father-in-law discouraged him. "Get to work and earn some money, son. Forget about books. Don't waste your time, Bud. Get real. Get a job, son." It was a decision that he would regret for the rest of his life. In the corporate system, no one without a university degree can serve on an executive board. Despite that handicap, Bud became general manager of the Kingston plant, responsible for 7,000 employees. He had common sense, which, had he gone to college, would have likely landed him in the president's chair. But it was not to be. He would resignedly joke that some PhDs who couldn't even drive on a rainy day without going straight into the puddles served on the board.

Technology advanced. IBM invented the printed circuit board and Bud sent his people to the University of Pennsylvania to study how to take advantage of it. The solution lay in etching the cables in fiberglass because other materials disintegrated at the etching temperature. They developed some chips that were very small at the time: 2" x 10." Memory boards started at 96K and reached156K in the company's heyday. At the time, to obtain 16 megabytes, you needed a computer the size of the James Farley Post Office Building in New York City (which famously bears the inscription: *Neither snow nor rain nor heat nor gloom of night stays these couriers from the swift completion of their appointed rounds*). You would also need the entirety of Penn Station to store the cooling equipment for that computer.

One morning in 1959, the company vice-president went to Bud's office. "Who normally replaces you, Bud?" "What do you mean?" "If you don't show up for work, who is responsible for this mess?" Bud gave him the name of a co-worker. "Okay," the VP said. "Call him and hand me the phone. Hello? I'm the company vice-president. I'm calling to tell you that after four this afternoon, Bud won't be returning to the office. You take over. Goodbye and thanks. Bud, I'll expect you tomorrow, Saturday, at 8:00 a.m. sharp in my office. You should also cancel any plans you have for Sunday and Monday. You're going to be very busy."

The following day, they flew to Langley Field, Virginia, home of the Manned Spacecraft Center. "Welcome to the Mercury Project," Chris Kraft, the center's director, told Bud. "President Eisenhower wants an American pilot to enter orbit. We have the basic technology: the experimental missile launches in the desert of White Sands, New Mexico, have reached heights beyond the atmosphere. We have to win the space race against the Russians."

McDonnell Aircraft had agreed to build three spacecraft in 10 months and the Army said it would construct the proper launch pads, but they needed IBM's help to implement the TAGIS—the worldwide Tracking and Ground Instrumentation System—to follow the rockets' trajectory after they disappeared from sight. The Western Electric Company was awarded the contract and needed to establish a partnership with IBM to design, build and program the necessary computer equipment. Not only was it necessary to monitor the capsules during their orbit, but also to be able to establish constant communication with their occupants. In the months preceding the first U.S. space missions, IBM engineers had to identify thousands of hypothetical problems that could arise during the space flight, come up with a solution to each one and program all of them into the computer hard drive. This would make the Mercury Project the biggest mathematical challenge ever undertaken by a machine.

Two days later, Bud returned to Kingston. "They've given us an impossible mission," he told the board. "A year to create something that no one knows how to make. We'll have to work day and night. On weekends, too. I'm going to need more people." "Exactly how many, Bud?" "A lot, 50 or even 100 engineers." "You've got them." So Bud began to lead the spectacular tracking project which years later would enable astronaut Jim Lovell— "Houston, we have a problem"—to return to Earth alive, and to be able to take a shower at 6484 Montgomery Street in Rhinebeck. The astronaut came to give a speech at IBM's Kingston headquarters and afterwards Bud invited him to have a drink at the house. Well, he felt confortable enough to decide to take a shower in the bathroom that belonged to Sarah. My wife, then a little girl, was so impressed that she made a resolution: she'd never clean that bathtub again. She wasn't going to take a shower anymore so the premises would remain as Lovell had left them.

Cape Canaveral, February 20, 1962: Mercury Friendship 7, a cone-shaped living space no larger than a truck cabin, is mounted on the giant Atlas Launch Vehicle 3B, ready for takeoff. The rocket and the spacecraft together measure 94 feet. Four, three, two, one, blast off! Fuel 103, 101. Oxygen 78, 100. Amps 25. Cabin pressure 58. "Roger, over and out. The route is correct."

IBM had developed a revolutionary system whose effectiveness was about to be tested. At the Mercury Control Center in Cape Canaveral, next to the launch pad, a computer received all the information via radio signal from the spacecraft before countdown. It was a 7090 model: six metal filing cabinets the size of those old gray office filing cabinets, which were interconnected to increase memory storage. Each had the capacity of an audiotape hard drive that could record 300 bits per inch. If the parameters sent from the launch pad and from the spacecraft coincided with those that the computer had programmed as optimal, and if the communication and data computation system also worked property, the launch would be ordered. Zero! There was a huge fireball and the spacecraft began to lift. When the rocket separated two inches from the launch pad, the space tracking system designed by Bud's engineers was activated. All the data collected in real time by the 7090 from that moment on at Cape Canaveral traveled north via 1,120 miles of high-speed cable to two other powerful data processors at the Goddard Space Flight Center in Maryland.

The two 7090 transistorized computers had to decipher all the information they received. First, the parameters sent from the Cape Canaveral launch station as soon as take off was completed: altitude, velocity, apogee, perigee, inclination, orbit capacity, eccentricity and period. During the first 30 seconds, the machines had to determine whether the Mercury capsule had taken off at the estimated inclination angle and whether it was in the correct position and flying at an adequate speed to be able to safely enter orbit. They had to cross-check the real data arriving from Florida against the millions of pre-assigned instructions that had been recorded on the hard drives. If the two information sources coincided, one of the 7090s sent the Mercury Control Center a signal that was translated into a green light with the word GO on it. Otherwise, the sign read NO GO and the mission had to be aborted. In that case, the Goddard computers had to quickly choose the best point of impact in the ocean, provide the speed and position vectors, and calculate the precise instant in which the air controller would have to activate the rescue missile attached to the spacecraft, at the top of the 16-foot metal launch tower. When it did so, the capsule would detach from the rear rocket propeller and continue its course alone. Once the desired inclination was achieved, the front missile would transport it to the designated point on the western coast of Africa. At these coordinates, the astronaut would be ejected from the tower and the spacecraft would fall to the sea with the aid of a parachute.

If the GO sign on the monitor lit up, five minutes after takeoff, when the rocket would have used up the fuel and it was time to separate the spacecraft, the VELORT radar, capable of locating objects up to 680 miles away, would be activated in the Bermuda flight tracking station, over which the capsule would be flying at that moment, with a modern detector. The spacecraft had then a very small window to do the necessary 180 degree rotation needed to remain in orbit. Every six seconds, the processors estimated the coordinates of the point of land impact, where the spacecraft would fall in the case the mission had to be aborted If it managed to complete the three programmed orbits successfully, Goddard would calculate the precise moment to fire up the front propellers to take the capsule out of orbit and place it once again in the realm of gravity.

All the information processed in Maryland was sent to the Mercury Control Center in Florida in the form of binary messages at a speed of 1,000 bits per second. IBM had developed a security system to prevent reception errors. The messages were sent through four high-speed transmitters and were picked up by several other receivers in Cape Canaveral. There, three receivers were randomly selected and their messages were compared. They were only considered acceptable if at least two of them had identical messages.

Three years and two months had passed since the first meeting at the Langley Field headquarters. "Mr. Howe, President Eisenhower wants us to put an American in orbit." "Okay, Mr. Kraft, we'll do our best." Since that morning, Bud's team of 150 engineers, mathematicians and programmers had worked a total of 250 years to be able to develop the computers on time. They did amazing research which produced 159 inventions and 30 new patents in a very short period. They created science as they went along, working on concepts unknown at the time. Their first problem arose when they had to hire assistants. There was no one with that type of knowledge so they opted to call to Goddard the 25 most brilliant students of the five most prestigious universities in the country. The students attended aerospace engineering courses and were asked to note the theories emerging from what the scientists did in practice. They were privileged witnesses to a historical moment, which they themselves contributed to making a reality by helping the overwhelmed scientists of the Mercury Project.

February 20, 1962 arrived. That day, Bud Howe was more obsessed with the sky than ever. It couldn't have been otherwise. The whole Western World held its breath. His people had done an outstanding job. Throughout those months, he had to send dozens of telegrams that always ended with the same words of encouragement: "Congratulations on a job well done!" However, he couldn't permit excessive optimism. Less than a month before, Lieutenant Colonel John H. Glenn had entered the MA5 space capsule determined not to abandon it until he'd orbited the Earth three times at a speed of 17,500 miles per hour. He was in the capsule for an interminable five hours and three minutes and it never took off. Clouds hindered the cameras' visibility, which led officials to postpone the launch. A fiasco. A catastrophe. The American media reported on the public's disappointment the next day. The most optimistic forecasts for the American space race were a minimum delay of 17 months with respect to its competitors. The possibility of emulating the feat of Major Gherman Titov, who had managed to circle the globe 17 and a half times in August 1961, seemed increasingly far off. The Russians' supremacy triggered the paranoia of espionage syndrome. A classified report warned that: "Approximately 15 minutes after takeoff, our rescue efforts reported the presence of three Soviet ships (destroyers, I think) in the area slated for landing. I'm afraid they're not fishing. Signed: Al Layton."

But all that was in the past, and, as an air traffic controller had made clear that same morning, failure wasn't an option for America.

"Roger, the clock is ticking. We're underway." "Hear you loud and clear." "Little bumpy along about here." "Roger." Past the Max Q zone of maximum vibration, John Glenn was in space ready to go around the globe three times. He had a beautiful view, looking eastward across the Atlantic. He circled at an altitude of 124 miles and at an average of 90 minutes per orbit: Bermuda, Gran Canary, Kano, Zanzibar, the Indian Ocean, Muchea, Woomera, Canton, Hawaii, Guyana, California, Texas and Florida again. "*Gggggg*... Friendship 7, this is Canaveral Com Tech. How do you copy? Over." "*Gggggg*... Friendship 7 to Canaveral. Read you loud and clear." "*Gggggg*... Ah, do you have a retrofire time for 2 Bravo and 2 Charlie?" "This is Friendship 7. Ah, negative." "*Gggggg*... Okay, 2 Bravo, 01 50 00; 2 Charlie, 02 05 59. Over." "Roger, remaining fly-by-wire." "Seven, this is Cape. *Gggg*... The President will be talking to you and while he is speaking, I'll be sending Z and R cal. Roger."

Sixty million spectators had followed the television rebroadcast of the space launch. Four hours, 55 minutes and 23 seconds later, the capsule re-entered the atmosphere and fell into the Atlantic Ocean 800 miles southeast of Bermuda. John Glenn was rescued after 21 minutes' floating in the water. His physical signs were better than expected. Optimal. He had withstood anti-gravity without incident. Everything had gone according to plan. The only mystery that the astronaut brought back to Earth with him was the detailed description of the many fireflies that had appeared in space every time the sun rose on the horizon. This phenomenon remained a mystery for a long time until another astronaut, Scott Carpenter, accidently hit the wall of the spacecraft and disturbed a handful of those fluttering insects. They were actually tiny drops of dew that had accumulated in the reactors.

At Cape Canaveral, President Kennedy awarded the U.S. Marine Corps pilot the NASA Service Medal. In New York, 4 million people flooded the streets to watch the Lt. Col. Glenn's entourage pass by toward Rhinebeck Town Hall. There, Mayor Robert Wagner decorated Glenn with the Medal of Honor of the city. Glenn gave a speech at the

United Nations. *National Geographic* awarded him its top honor, reserved for a handful of legendary heroes, including Lindbergh and Amundsen. It was announced that the Friendship 7 would tour the world, with stops in 20 cities, so that it could be admired by people everywhere. In the winter of 1962, the sky incorporated a new star and no one wanted to miss the opportunity to celebrate him. The United States was throwing a party that had just started. J. J. Donegan, Mercury Program director general of operations, sent Bud a telegram: *Here at NASA, we are all aware of the vital contribution that your people provided to the success of the space mission. This could never have been done without the sweat, ulcers and sleepless nights of a group of hardworking people. Thanks for a job well done!*

At IBM, however, the party lasted just long enough. Just as soon as the high-sea rescue was completed and John Glenn climbed aboard the destroyer Noa, the director general of the IBM operations center in Maryland, Saul I. Gass, sent a clear message to everyone in Kingston to get back to work. "Now we have to put a man on the moon." The Gemini and Apollo projects immediately followed and IBM was responsible for creating the NASA Command Center in Houston, Texas. The story ended on July 20, 1969, the day Neil Armstrong stepped on the moon.

Bud couldn't help but think about his mother. He recalled her sitting in a swing on old Randolph's porch long before the dam was built. One summer evening, the whole family had gone outside to watch the shooting stars. The slight breeze coming off of Big Blue provided temporary relief from the sweltering summer heat of the Kansas plains. Mother Howe sighed, affectionately running her fingers through the hair of Nancy, her little girl. After looking warily at the sky, she said: "And to think that there are crazy people who believe a man will walk there someday…"

Today, as Bud helps me put duct tape around the suitcases, one, two, three times, he realizes those memories have been blurred by time. Of the 100 most solid U.S. companies in the 1950s, only 18 managed to survive to see the 21st century. During the golden years, big companies were accustomed to telling their clients what they needed and the clients would obediently buy it. At the Kingston plant, there were industrial yards measuring thousands of feet where 364 computers were personalized according to the specific needs of companies and organizations like Bank of America, the Department of the Treasury and the U.S. Bureau of Alcohol, Tobacco and Firearms. The engineers worked hard to program the thousands of grey computer boxes that were fed by long cables hanging from the ceiling. The scene changed dramatically in the 1980s. The economic giants collapsed. The adaptation of the market to PC clones caught IBM unprepared. The company suddenly saw the need to ask its regular clients to please buy something. This was when a very young Bill Gates appeared, offering IBM an operating system, Microsoft DOS. One of the members of the board, confusing him for a waiter, had asked him to bring him a cup of coffee and a donut.

After the Mercury Project, Bud's wife died following a long battle with cancer. Around the same time, Sarah's father, Harry Hill, died of a heart attack in Florida. My mother-in-law became a widow with five children. Bud had three. They met and decided to marry, like in the TV series *Eight Is Enough*. Sarah and Pam, Bud's young daughter, were inseparable friends, and couldn't believe their luck when they were told they would become sisters. Margaret Hill, who became Margaret Howe, although everyone calls her Peggy, remembers how Bud and his friend Scott Locken, then IBM vice president, used to tell her about projects that seemed like science fiction. "Very soon, Peggy, you'll go to the bank and a machine will serve you." "That's ridiculous," she said. But at the Kingston plant, the future was already on its way with the delivery of the first automatic teller machine in history under the number 3614. It was 1973 and a monumental revolution hit supermarkets with the installation of cash registers with glass prisms, optical lenses and lasers to read the prices. The world welcomed the bar code. When Bud began at IBM, the company's annual budget was $700 million. By the time he took early retirement in 1983—at his wife's suggestion because the heavy workload was taking its toll on his health—the budget had increased to $40 billion. No one suspected that just a decade later, the Kingston plant would close, leaving thousands of families without work and creating levels of unemployment never before known in the Hudson Valley. The business had changed and the top executives had been caught navel-gazing. It had to switch from manufacturing large machines to producing small components. There was too much space and the huge industrial yards were dismantled. "Since you left it hasn't been the same, Bud," complained the employees who ran into him on the streets of Rhinebeck. "Hi, Bud, it's not the same without you." Howe thanked them for their kindness but could not hide his disappointment and surprise. How was it possible for the giant company to which he had devoted the best years of his life, to suddenly teeter on the edge? Somebody should have taught those men who had obtained their PhDs from the country's most prestigious universities that you don't go through the storm stepping into every puddle along the way, since you don't know how deep they will be. "It's not the same without you, Bud." IBM would never be the same.

"It won't be the same without you guys. Nope," Bud tells me. Saying goodbye is always hard. Doing it twice, however, makes the goodbye ceremony somewhat easier. The effort on the first day is harder, trying to find the words that best describe your feelings, but now there's more time for hugs. On our second attempt to reach the airport, Raucci is at the wheel since Bruno couldn't make it. The kids wave goodbye through the windows. We go north on Route 9 toward the Kingston-Rhinecliff Bridge, past the hospital. I remember that our good friend David Hoffman just had a hip operation and I call him to ask how he's doing. "I'm okay. I'm home now. I was in the hospital for three days." Dr. Russell Tigges performed the operation. He is a respected surgeon who designed his own surgical instruments to reduce tissue damage. Russ performs an average of 400 knee and hip replacements a year. Perhaps for that reason, he tries to keep his own joints in good shape. Every morning, before going to the operating room of Northern Dutchess Hospital in

Rhinebeck, Russ rides 20 miles on his road bike, accompanied by his neighbor Steve Rosenberg, another nutcase willing to put a helmet on at 6:00 a.m. They cycle along Route 308 to the intersection with Rock City. Then they head north on Route 199 until the light at Red Hook. On the way back, they ride down Route 9G, which is lined with farms.

When he's not operating, Russ occasionally gives a talk at some U.S. hospital about the new method for doing joint replacements, which is currently practiced by some 100 surgeons around the country. The hip operation lasts an hour. Patients go straight to the operating room from their homes rather than spending the previous night at the hospital. Rehabilitation starts the next day in the same hospital. Recovery used to last between two and three months, but with the new procedure, David Hoffman says that he will be able to play tennis again in six weeks. "Did they also improve your serve?" I ask him. "No, I'm afraid not." Russ makes a 4-inch incision while most of his colleagues make 8-inch ones. If it were not for the prosthesis, Russ could work with his instrument in an even smaller space. He calculates that the operation affects between 30 percent and 50 percent less tissue than traditional procedures, since he takes advantage of the flexibility of the muscles to open a hole. And his patients do not need blood transfusions.

A computer called a CI helps Russ to position the implant at the ideal rotation angle. With a drill similar to the one in your garage, Russ makes a couple of one-and-a-half centimeter holes: one in the femur, the other in the tibia. He then screws two screws into the bone. The screws are attached to a tripod with infrared rays. With a pointer that has an antenna, he pricks the leg in 120 precise points so that the computer can identify the center of the tibia, the arc of the rotation of the bone and the exact position of the femur. With this information, the screen reproduces the patient's bones in 3D and indicates the exact location and inclination where the incision should be made. Russ then adjusts the antenna on his instrument and engages in a technique that looks like a video game. He observes the screen, which has a blue circle on the bone with a line marking the optimal spot. He places a plate with a slit in the middle on the patient's femur. The plate is reflected in the monitor as a yellow circle. When the circle is superimposed over the blue and both lines coincide, he screws it in. He applies the electric saw in the opening, cuts, lifts the plate and removes a piece of bone. Pure marksmanship. Now he just needs to insert the implant, which he does without taking his eyes from the monitor. A tiny error, which is easy to make if the surgeon relies solely on his vision, could slightly displace the natural angle of rotation and cause chaffing that would shorten the life of the prosthesis. David believes that his artificial hip will last at least 20 years. "So long?" "That's what the doctor said." "Okay, take care, David. I hope to be able to play a couple of sets before too long." "Okie-dokie." "You're so hip, man."

For such a small town, Rhinebeck is fortunate to have top-level professionals. The hospital is actually a nonprofit organization. If it depended on the economic contribution of insurance companies and the income from private consultations, it could not maintain its top-level medical staff and facilities. People know this, so they help out to guarantee their access to those services. One way they do this is through volunteer work, which totals 30,000 hours every year. Those who push wheelchairs down the halls, deliver food to the rooms, distribute instruments to nurses or drive emergency room staff to different facilities are students looking to enrich their CVs, explore the possibility of a career in medicine or simply want to get their required social work credit out of the way. The greeters at the hospital entrance and those who take notes on patients' ailments in the emergency room, show patients to doctors' offices, work in the gift shop, answer the phones or complete the payroll accounts in the administrative office are retired individuals who have opted to share with the community the knowledge acquired during professional careers or simply to help out to feel useful and maintain an active social life. The volunteer work means big savings for the hospital.

Private donations are always a source of joy, and the Northern Dutchess website proposes 21 different ideas for making a contribution.

For example: in lieu of flowers for a late patient's funeral, donations can be made to the hospital in the patient's memory. Or the hospital can be named as the beneficiary on a life insurance policy. The hospital's doctors, who are well aware of the direct benefits they will receive if the hospital operates smoothly, open their homes for benefit dinners and organize sports competitions to raise funds for the purchase of surgical equipment and supplies, dollar by dollar. The townspeople also make a huge effort to maintain Northern Dutchess's modern birth center, which features both midwives and conventional beds, and its emergency room, which offers top-ranked doctors.

Hiring stars like Russell Tigges is also part of the hospital's viability plan. He attracts powerful clientele from areas like Albany and New York City, who pay a fortune for private consultations. When Russ recently gave me the chance to witness hip and knee operations, I asked him whose fault it is that health care is so expensive in a country where doctors are expected to drive luxury cars and belong to exclusive clubs. He immediately launched into an explanation: "The pharmaceutical companies are to be partly blamed for having established a drug culture. Better living through chemistry, right? If I can eat 16 eggs a day and then have a pill to regulate my cholesterol, why should I eat only two eggs? The drug companies make a deal with the government. They make some medicines available to everybody, like inexpensive cholesterol-lowering drugs, but in exchange, they ask the government not to regulate the cost of medications for the 2,000 patient groups that have to pay exorbitant prices for their treatment. Insurance companies make a bundle of money, too. They use a lot of small print in their policies, for example, to inform you that a stem cell transplant won't be covered. But believe me, the drug companies are the most powerful."

Russ also mentioned the serious problem of patients' lack of health education. "Probably the biggest part of the blame," he says, "is that in the United States, everyone feels entitled to the best medical care. But people confuse the best with the most expensive. If a patient comes in with a cough, he or she will demand a chest scan to rule out lung cancer. Normally, a doctor would do an X-ray rather than a $1,000 MRI for symptoms that in 60 percent of the cases will disappear in a few weeks. But this is where the specter of malpractice comes in. If that patient does indeed develop lung cancer, he could sue either you or the hospital. If he goes for a second opinion to another doctor and that doctor orders an MRI, it is going to make you look like an idiot. It's a no-win situation. So you are pressured to order a scan, at a high cost to the system."

"For how much money can you sue a doctor for malpractice?" I asked Tigges. "Well, there is a protocol," he explained. "It is based on lost wages. Let's say the patient could not work for the past 10 years. In that case, we'd be talking about the money he or she would have made during those years. But there is another suit based on pain and suffering that is absolutely subjective. How do you measure that? Well, if you ask for less than $60,000, you would probably get it without litigation since legal costs are higher than that." That's something I know from personal experience. Recently, I had a very scary and unusual case of aspirated pneumonia that occurred during a routine procedure at Northern Dutchess Hospital, and which sent me back to its ER. I was surprised how many people encouraged me to sue the doctor and the hospital. I didn't. I wasn't raised to make money this way. It was an accident.

Russ says he once did a knee replacement on a man who unfortunately died the day afterward. "The hospital may have made some mistakes," he says, "but the guy weighed 350 pounds, was diabetic and had high blood pressure." The patient had requested the operation. The family already received $1 million from the hospital and is now suing Russ for another $1 million. Russ didn't do anything wrong. It's just a case of pain and suffering. That's why he has to pay $100,000 every year for an insurance policy that covers him up to $3 million. "A good hip replacement costs $8,000," he says. "If you had started exercising and improved your diet 10 years ago, resulting in a 75-pound weight loss, you could have avoided the cost of the replacement and the risks of the operation." The system needs more preventive medicine, Russ says, including vaccines and basic programs on healthy habits and the prevention of child obesity. There's even talk of a so-called "Fat Tax." Morbid obesity brings higher risks for infection, blood clots, heart attack … and diabetes! In the past 14 years, the number of diabetic children in the United States has skyrocketed.

After passing the hospital we drive by Williams Lumber, which is having a back-to-school sale including a huge selection of Boy Scout uniforms. I remember the ice. "Raucci, the ice." "What ice?" "The dry ice." Among the bags we are taking to Spain is an ice chest with some bison meat that Sunny gave me. "I don't know if they sell dry ice at Williams." "They told me in San Antonio that I could find it almost anywhere." "Why don't you go in and ask?" I do. They don't have any. They don't even know what I'm talking about. Dry ice? They explain that in the United States, ice is normally sold in gas stations and supermarkets. They've never heard of dry ice. "Thanks." "No problem, buddy." No place has it: not the Stop & Shop, Convenience Corner Gas nor any place else. "Shall we go to Kingston?" Raucci asks me. "There's no time, forget it. We'll take the cooler as is, filled with run-of-the-mill ice cubes."

We get on the highway. "Hey, John." "Yes?" "Wasn't there a third element?" "Another gas station?" "No, in your races. Besides running barefoot and breathing through the nose, didn't you mention a third principle that we never talked about?" "Oh, proper nutrition" he says. "You have to avoid preservatives, colorings and pre-cooked foods since their consumption produces toxins that overwhelm the natural filtering capacity of our liver and kidneys. When your mind treats the body well through natural foods, the body obeys the mind. You know what I mean?" "Not a clue, Losang Rampa."

"Just ask my son. He says that now, when another athlete is stronger than him, he asks his body to please give him a bit more speed. His fatigue suddenly disappears and he can run faster until he catches up and passes the other runner." "Is that so?" "Yep." "You must be kidding me…" "No. We are disconnected from the natural way of life and we are paying a big price for this. The Native Americans ate raw food without chemical products and just one type of food at a sitting. Thus, when they chewed meat, for example, the stomach detected its composition and activated the necessary enzymes to digest it. We usually mix several types of foods. Since the digestive organ doesn't have the capacity to send specific enzymes for each one, it digests the main food while the others become toxins. Disease and injury result." "Isn't that a gas station?" "Yes, do you want to stop?" "Just for a second, if you don't mind, to see if they have the damn dry ice." "I'll be right back." "*Papá*, get some potato chips!" "Okay."

"Hi, do you have any dry ice?" "No, we don't." "Thanks anyway." "Have a good one."

We're approaching the spot of yesterday's aquatic disaster. I recognize it because we just passed a fake tree that camouflages a cell phone tower. The trunk is metal, the branches plastic. It's just before a stone bridge in Mount Vernon. Half of the people here work in New York City and the other half in the splendid Connecticut mansions of bankers and stockbrokers. A friend who takes care of the dogs of one of those families, once brought us three garbage bags full of new clothes that the woman of the house had thrown out. Her husband runs a Wall Street firm. He leaves every day at 6:00 a.m. and returns at 10:00 p.m. He's very demanding and likes everything to be immaculate. If the children make a mark on the wall with a ball, his wife calls the painters in to touch it up before her husband gets home. The woman is a compulsive shopper and her husband periodically makes her throw out her many purchases. The trash bags our friend brought us contained name-brand European and American clothing—at least 15 dresses that have never been worn. Several boxes of wool socks with the sales receipt, a coat, a down jacket, stuffed animals, pants, shirts, 14 unopened CDs, a doll that cries (presumably because she hasn't left the box yet), an Easter bunny that sings and dances … everything went in the trash. We kept a couple of the things and distributed the rest among some needier people.

I wonder if Reverend Moon would be able to figure those tycoons out just by looking at them. Raucci tells me that he's decided to delve himself into the world of interpreting gestures. He's reading *Amazing Face Reading* by Mac Fulfer. Pinched lips signify greed. Bringing the palms together, as if praying, means lack of confidence. Grabbing one's own shoulders means you can't take anymore. Having four lines across the forehead, like Arnold Schwarzenegger's, means that the person is a perfectionist.

Fulfer's theory is that the face develops its physiology in keeping with the personality the individual develops. People whose ears stick out past the eyebrow line are capable of rapidly processing information. That's why they sometimes make decisions without thinking too much. On the contrary, when the ears fall below the mouth line, the individual processes information slowly. If you have thin eyebrows, it means that you can only do one thing at a time. But those who have bushy eyebrows are deep thinkers. "Fascinating," I say as I discreetly examine my eyebrows in the sun visor's mirror.

Moon used that knowledge to pair up his flock. He looked for a small variation in their facial features, a difference big enough to make things interesting, but not excessive. If he found a person with a sharp tongue, he wasn't going to match him with a very sensitive person. But sometimes he paired a Westerner with an Asian so that when the Westerner spoke brusquely, the Asian wouldn't view it as an insult, but instead would respond, "Thank you, thank you," and everyone would be happy. "The pairing didn't have anything to do with physical appearance," Raucci says. "The idea is to match ways of being, something that's hard for the American public to understand."

We arrive at the airport. "Kids, say goodbye to Raucci." "Byeee..." Raucci asks if we want him to wait for a minute in case there's a problem with the ice chest containing the bison meat. I tell him no, go ahead and leave. Max and Nico find some luggage carts. We're carrying quite a load. "What have you got there? Meat? Oh, I can't check that." "Why not?" "You can only take it on the plane if it's packed in dry ice."

"Could that be true?" "That's what I said." "Well, you've ruined my day. Do you know where I can buy dry ice?" "No. Not at the airport." "What can I do, then?" "Try to leave the cooler in storage and have a friend pick it up. That is if the airport storage center agrees to take it, which I doubt." "Could I speak with your supervisor?" "Whatever, good afternoon." "Afternoon, what seems to be the problem?" I give a summarized account of my current life: "I'm writing a book on America, I'm carrying meat from the bison of the legendary prairies so that Miguel Ansorena, the Navarran grill master, can prepare it, you know what I mean … " "No, I don't." I'm desperate. The bison has to reach Madrid somehow, if only so I can tell Sunny about the experience." "Sorry. So what's the problem with the ice cubes?" I keep trying. "The problem is a legal one: meat can thaw during the trip, then spoil and become a public health threat." I calculate the flying time. Eight hours. Hmmm. When I defrosted some of the bison meat in Rhinebeck so Charlie Rascoll could roast it, I had to leave it out overnight … in other words, it took eight hours! The worst that could happen is that it will be thawed when I arrive and we'll have to roast it the same day. I quickly turn around, take the package of vacuum-packed meat from the cooler and discreetly open a suitcase. I act like I'm looking for my phone charger and hide the meat among the clothes. All done. We check in. "These are your tickets." "Thanks." "You have to take the bags to the scanner." We drag them along with the cooler still packed with ice, which I don't know what to do with. "Luggage, please." I break out in a cold sweat. Is what I've just done illegal? They're going to ask me and I won't be able to lie. Lying is the worst of crimes in the United States. I hand over the bag with the bison meat. The handler asks me if it's locked. "No," I say. He takes all the bags. We walk away quickly before they ask us to open them. Now I need to get rid of the cooler—but where? There are no trashcans big enough. I consider leaving it in the bathroom. Forget it. The airport is on orange alert and a foreigner leaving a container in the bathroom can be given a life sentence. What should I do? We go outside. Police and military personnel are everywhere. Leaving it on the sidewalk would be like asking them to shoot me in the head. I take a deep breath. This time I breathe in through my mouth—sorry, Raucci. I finally decide to go up to a policeman and tell him my sob story. "Officer, they won't let me take this cooler on the plane and there's no trash can big enough to throw it out." He asks me to open it. I tell him it's empty. He tells me that it would be a shame to destroy it when someone else could use it. He looks at me kindly and tells me to leave it next to the wall, but with the top open so that everyone can see it's not dangerous. Someone will eventually pick it up. I do that and leave. Then I hear my name called over the loudspeaker. "There is an urgent message for passenger Guillermo..." how embarrassing. I deserve it for being such an idiot. "Passenger Guillermo ... Martinez Díaz, please go to the gate." Ufff! I breathe a sigh of relief. We board the plane and take our seats. The flight attendant approaches and asks me to accompany her. Oh, no. I wish the Earth would open up and swallow me whole. I look at the kids and say goodbye forever. I force a smile. I follow the flight attendant to the front of the plane. Another flight attendant informs me, with an enigmatic smile, that the Spanish pilot is a fan of *Gomaespuma*, and that he would like to upgrade me to first class. That's good. I go back to my family. "Good news," I tell Sarah. "I got you a seat in business class. Enjoy; I'll stay here with the kids." She smiles and throws me a kiss that floats like the astronauts in the Mercury capsule and stays by my side during the whole flight.

Epilogue

The Jewish community in Seville is not very big. Its active members number no more than 100, which seems especially small in light of the fact that Seville's extensive neighborhoods of Saint Cross and Saint Bartholomew were once combined and the area was home to the most extraordinary Jewish quarter of the medieval era. But those 100 Jewish Sevillanos could be considered an impressive number if we recall the difficulties this ethnic and religious group still faces in being acknowledged in Spanish daily life. Fortunately, the Jews of Seville have transformed the distinctive Andalusian sense of humor into an art. That's why the rabbi who guides them today, an Israeli of Italian origin and short physical stature, is affectionately known as "El Rabanito." This is how it works: In Spanish, rabbi is pronounced *rabino* and radish is pronounced *rabano*. Pretty close. To show affection, Andalucians add the suffix *ito* to the end of words. *Ito* is a diminutive meaning small, hence, *rabinito* means "little rabbi," and *rabanito* means "little radish."

The Cementerio de San Fernando, Seville's cemetery, is lined with cypress, palm, cedar and laurel trees. Tourists flock there in search of the tombs of illustrious bullfighters and flamenco singers and pay their respects before beautiful memorials such as the one that the great artist Mariano Benlliure created to honor the celebrated matador Joselito, "The Rooster." *Olé!*

Common mortals whose time on Earth came to end have also rested at the cemetery since 1852. By then, rapid population growth and several epidemics had collapsed the small graveyards of the numerous churches lining the streets of Seville. San Fernando was established under the blessing of the Catholic Church to be the only cemetery open to new customers. Nobody in Seville seems to know that San Fernando has a Jewish section, not even the local authorities. In fact, it took me three visits to the site to be able to find it in a secluded corner ... just outside the cemetery walls!

Prior to the establishment of the small Jewish subdivision in this graveyard, Jews had no choice but to bury their loved ones outside the borderlines of San Fernando Gardens— next to the wall, but in no man's land. Seville's City Hall took note and in the late 19th century, made the illegal burial ground kind of official, simply by enclosing the outside area and putting a lock on its gate, the key for which was given to the local Jewish community.

José Bendayan, a friendly man who has traveled widely around the globe in search of goods to be shipped in great cargo ships, has been the custodian of the Jewish funerary site for several years. In the right corner of this hidden cemetery, separated from the rest of the graves, he finds Rubin Decker's tomb for me. Oh, man. It doesn't have a tombstone. There is only a cement slab on the ground that time and weather has crumbled and practically turned to sand. "What is all that about, José?" I ask him. "Well," he says, "the gravedigger probably made a mistake because, at the time of the burial, the circumstances surrounding Decker's death were unknown. Marty's father died in August when most of us were on vacation. The gravedigger really didn't know who he was. He didn't even know if he was Jewish. Nobody told him. He thought he had committed suicide. The Sephardic rite dictates that those who have committed suicide must be placed apart from the rest. He decided to bury him out of compassion." Oh, man. I feel sick to my stomach. How am I going to deliver this news to Marty? He told me in Alaska that the American Consul agreed to cover the cost of his father's tombstone. José Bendayán shrugs his shoulders: "I imagine the Consul was probably expecting Marty or somebody else to be in charge and just send him an invoice afterwards. It's a misunderstanding which, through no one's fault, has left that promise unfulfilled." "It's okay, Guillermo," I tell myself. "Take a deep breath and everything is going to be back to normal." "José?" "Yes?" "Could Rubin's remains be exhumed and placed in a more dignified grave next to the others?" "No," he says. "The little radish won't like that idea. But don't worry, tell your friend that this space is very small and soon there will be other graves near his father's. Time will do him justice." "Really?" "Well…" "Could we at least put a tombstone there?" "Of course! Ask your friend what he wants on the inscription. The Jewish community will take care of that." Thank you, Mr Bendayán." I also mention Marty's concern that no religious ritual was performed during the burial. "Well, that's easy to solve," says José. "That part the little radish would like. I'll make sure there is a proper ceremony this time."

I write to Marty in Alaska inviting him and his family to spend a few days in Madrid with Sarah and me and travel together to Seville for the final *adios* to his father. I suggest that they come in late spring to be able to attend *Flamenco Pa Tos*, the Flamenco Festival that my radio partner and I put together every year to raise money for the Gomaespuma Foundation that we run. I suspect that for Marty to be part of that music celebration could be a good last tribute to his father;, the musician who traveled to Spain in search of flamenco melodies. I receive this response from him shortly afterward:

Hello G-Man, I am touched that my father's remains are still in Seville. Thanks for following up on that situation!! When he died, I was a penniless student and the best I could do was accept the government's offer to give him a plaque as a war veteran. Today I have a "big salary" as a schoolteacher and a fishing guide in Anchorage, but I think I could arrange something that would be more in keeping with his life as a musician and humanist. I'm relieved to think that, as his only son, I can still fulfill my responsibility to revive his memory. Twenty-seven years have passed, so there's no hurry. But if your offer is sincere, I will be happy to have the opportunity just to see you again, Conquistador! You are a true mensch. Thank you.

—Marty

It takes another six years for my friend Marty to make the move and the jump across the ocean to meet me in Spain, but during that time I stay in contact with José and continue encouraging him to convince *El Rabanito* to let us move Rubin closer to his people. But I always get "impossible" for an answer.

Then one late May morning, Marty, his wife, Karen, and his daughter, Emily, arrive in Madrid. I have informed José Bendayán of their arrival and asked him if he could make arrangements with El Rabanito. "I will," he promised. "Thanks so much." "No problem." "You know," I told José, "This would make a great story. Do you want me to call some press?" "Nope," he answered. "We don't want any publicity. We prefer to keep things intimate." I accepted his decision, impressed by his humility.

But wait a minute. Without inviting the press and their cameras to the cemetery in Seville, Spanish Jews are losing a great opportunity to normalize their life in my country. You see, I grew up in Madrid in the 1960s and was taught in school that in 1492 Spain expelled all the Jews and all the Muslims. Then everybody in Spain was a Christian. Period. But after I became a journalist and started to travel to other countries where Jews form part of the community, I had the opportunity to learn the meaning of the Jewish traditions that many people in Spain unknowingly keep without even realizing their origins. "Man," I once told a friend in Valencia, "That old doorbell that doesn't work in your parent's house is actually a mezuzah!" "A what?" "Unscrew it, dude. You'll see there is a different content inside than electrical wires." "Man," I told another guy in Santander, "Remember the barber that used to come every Saturday to your house?" "Yes, of course." "He was a rabbi, buddy." "A whaaat?!"

362

Then one day I had lunch with Enrique Múgica Herzog, a former Secretary of Justice and congressman, who by then was the Defender of the People—the Spanish Ombudsman that deals with complaints of bad administration and has the capacity to bring citizen's cases at the Constitutional Court. Múgica comes from the Basque countryside in the north of Spain where the people speak their own language: Euskera. Múgica, who was raised speaking Spanish, told me that he had grown up taking for granted that what his grandparents were speaking at home was Euskera. But it was not. One year, his brother Fernando came from Paris, where he was a student at the Sorbonne University, during Easter break, and broke the news: "Enrique, we're Jews! The language our grandparents speak is not Euskera, it's Yiddish. The family I'm staying with in Paris are Jewish and they say the same words." "Oh, man," Enrique Múgica recollected exclaiming in despair. "What are we going to do now?"

Spain is as Jewish as it gets. How could it not be? Of course a lot of Jews escaped the country in 1492. Hundreds of thousands of Sephardic Jews—from *Sefarad*, the Hebrew word for Spain—fled west to Portugal and subsequently to the Americas. Or went east to Italy and Turkey. Or north to the Netherlands, France and the Balkans. Or south to Morocco. But the majority pretended they had undergone a Christian conversion to avoid the Inquisition and stayed home where they belonged, with their friends and family. They've been hidden ever since then. And we are talking of merely 10 percent of the population of Spain in those years. Can you imagine?

The fact that Hitler helped Franco, the Spanish dictator that remained almost four decades in power (1939-1975), to win the Spanish Civil War didn't help us appreciate Spain's Jewish roots either. In 1984, after I reported on the air some news about the possibility of finding Auschwitz's notorious director of human experimentation, Dr. Josef Mengele's remains in Brazil, I got a phone call from Violeta Friedman, a Jewish Holocaust survivor. To make the story short, we became friends. I told her that my wife's father, Harry H. Hill, Jr., was a lawyer at the

Nuremberg Trials, and Violeta made me read so many books about Mengele's atrocities that I started having frequent nightmares about Nazis coming to get my family and we had to stop talking for several months.

Violeta Friedman, known to her friends and family as Ibi, was born in Marghita, Romania, in 1930. Before her 14th birthday, she and the rest of her family were deported by the Nazis to Auschwitz concentration camp, where her great-grandmothers, grandparents and parents were executed in gas chambers on the night of their arrival. She remained at Auschwitz-Birkenau until the camp was liberated by Russia in 1945. The high-heel shoes that her mother had given her on the train saved her life, making the Nazis think she was older and that she could therefore work. Upon arrival at the camp, anybody younger than 16 or older than 45 was immediately sent under Doctor Mengele's supervision to the gas chambers. The rest had the privilege of life ... working to death as slaves for the Third Reich. Violeta's feet were so swollen after standing so many hours on the train that brought the Hungarian and Romanian Jewish from Transylvania that her own shoes did not fit her anymore, so her mother took off hers and gave them to her daughter. It was night, and under the pale light of the train halt lamps, Violeta appeared much older to the eyes of Mengele who ordered the soldiers to push her to the left. Her mother, although she was only 40, looked exhausted and aged while standing near her own old mother, and both women were shoved to the right. Violeta would never see them again.

For almost 40 years, Violeta had remained silent about her traumatic experience. She didn't even discuss it with her own children. But she described everything thoroughly in a memoir that she had written secretly as part of her healing therapy. She let me read the manuscript and I convinced her of the importance of getting it published. "You have to give us your own testimony, Ibi," I told her one night at Barcelona Airport, where we were waiting for a plane to bring us back to Madrid after an emotional meeting with the Spanish survivors of Mauthausen concentration camp. "You have to speak up. Especially in a country like

Spain, where we don't have a clue about that period of history." So she let me publish an interview with her in *Epoca* magazine ... and then off she went on frequent visits to radio stations for interviews and to universities for public speeches, and eventually, in 1995, Violeta's memoir, *Mis Memorias* (*My Memories*), was published by a major Spanish publishing house. I always carry around with me these words from her book:

> My biggest wish is to prevent the seeds of hate from sprouting again, so the world will always be able to say: 'Never again.'

Violeta became so enthusiastic about upholding the truth that she even initiated a landmark legal fight against Holocaust denial. Her case was against León Degrelle, a Nazi who had sought asylum in Spain after the Belgian courts sentenced him to death. The infamous Butcher of Marseille released a statement in *Tiempo* magazine in which he denied the existence of the very gas chambers where Violeta's family had perished. In response to these statements, Violeta launched what would be a pivotal six-year judicial process against Degrelle. Since her daughter was very busy at the time and her son lived in Venezuela, sometimes she would ask me to accompany her to court. On the way out to the National Court, one of the most beautiful palaces in downtown Madrid, we were frequently confronted by neo-Nazi groups shouting anti-Semitic slogans. One day, after I put Violeta in a taxi, a group of shaved-headed neo-Nazis surrounded me. One guy looked at me right in the eye and whispered: "Dude, I love your radio show. You're amazing, but you should be ashamed of yourself for killing Jesus Christ!" Then he punched me in the eye and almost knocked me out. Me killing Jesus? Yes, that's how ignorant many of us Spaniards were at the time.

By the way, Violeta won her case after six years of legal fighting. In November 1991, the Constitutional Court of Spain found Degrelle guilty of Holocaust denial. According to the Spanish Constitution, "Freedom of expression may not legally be used to spread racist or xenophobic ideology." That crucial sentence became the precedent for Spain's recent reform of its penal code in relation to racism.

That's the end of the Violeta Friedman story; now back to San Fernando cemetery in Seville. Sorry about my parenthetical discussion of Holocaust denial, but now you may understand now how I felt when Jose Bendayán refused to allow the press to attend Rubin Decker's graveside ceremony. I understood and respected his decision, but I still think to this day that my country needs some good news about decent Jewish people to normalize their presence among us.

So the Decker family finally lands in Madrid. Since Sarah is in New York with the kids at the time, Marty, Karen, Emily and I go to Seville together. In the outskirts of San Fernando we meet with José. He greets Marty and his family, hands me a yarmulke and we all walk together to the cemetery. When he unlocks the gate my Alaskan friend's jaw drops to the ground. What a wonderful surprise! The Jewish community of Seville has had Rubin's remains moved to a new grave in the center of the enclosure. And they have installed a beautiful granite tombstone with the epitaph that Marty had emailed to José:

Rubin Decker
born in Cleveland, Ohio, August 12, 1915
Died in Seville, Spain, June 1, 1980
Musician, humanist and lover of life

Beneath the inscription, carved into the stone, is the image of a viola.

It's an intimate ceremony, simple and moving. Marty reads some poems from an English translation of "Stanzas to the Death of My Father" by Jorge Manrique:

Our lives are the rivers that run into the sea that is death. There go the great men, where their lives are finished and consumed. To this sea flow the mighty rivers, the mediocre rivers, and the streams. United in the sea of death, all rivers are made equal: those who lived by the labor of their hands and the rich ones.

It is a very appropriate elegy for the father of a fishing guide. Marty reads beautifully these great verses written by Manrique, a major Spanish poet and soldier in the 1400s whose book my cousin Valentina (who had taken her father to Alaska the previous summer on the same fishing trip I took) had given to Marty as a thank you gift. Wow! After the ceremony, Marty says he feels relieved. "My life is much richer now," he tells me. "Okay, *mi hermano*, let's go celebrate." The most magical restaurant in Seville, if you ever get there, is called Modesto. It's next to the Murillo Gardens. The taste of the grilled San Lucar shrimp there is to kill for. The white Barbadillo wine slides down your throat like water. Can anybody ask for a better treat? So you see, some stories do indeed end well. Batman doesn't always win. Or was Batman the good guy? I always get all those American superheroes confused.

Postscript

In August 2009, our family returned to Rhinebeck to embark on a second American adventure. Once again, I isolated myself from my world to write a film script (this time based on Sunny's amazing experience on his Texas bison ranch, and using the help of my talented screenwriter friend and neighbor Mark Burns) … and once again, I found myself distracted by other affairs. Like, for example, pairing up with Ricardo Gutierrez Zubiaurre, a wizard of camera work and editing, to produce TV news reports for Spain. *Vamonos, güey!*

On Saturday, May 29, 2010 at 4:00 in the afternoon, we had the good fortune to experience another unforgettable event in the Rhinebeck High School auditorium: a ceremony, led by the Spanish Consul General in New York, Fernando Villalonga. The proceedings were received with uproarious applause and tears and all 500 people in the audience stood and cheered when Íñigo Ramírez de Haro, the Spanish cultural attaché to New York, read aloud the following official document:

> *At the behest of the Secretary of State of Spain, Miguel Ángel Moratinos, and following deliberation of the ministerial cabinet, I hereby grant the Great Cross of Civil Merit to Mr. Anthony Joseph Orza, for his extraordinary services on behalf of the Spanish language and the good of our nation.*
>
> — King Juan Carlos I of Spain

Tony Orza, the Rhinebeck High School Spanish language teacher was retiring with honor. The Spanish government expressed its appreciation of Tony's teaching by awarding him the country's most prestigious medal given to a foreign citizen. The Spanish Secretary of Culture, Ángeles González Sinde, appeared on the giant screen to express her belief that "the most important thing people can do is to teach others" and that "to have a teacher like Mr. Orza can change lives and help people make decisions they would have never thought they would." Her appearance caused surprise, but even more surprises followed. Tony had touched so many lives that many former students were willing to return the favor during the ceremony. We enjoyed their many moving speeches along with a medley of contemporary Spanish music by two gifted high school students, Dylan Nowik and Finnegan Shanahan, who delighted the audience with their singing and violin and guitar-playing in the same way that the first concerts of Simon and Garfunkel must have amazed the attendees.

Two other people sent their greetings via the screen. First was Paloma San Basilio, a famous Spanish pop singer who had been the protagonist of many of Tony's lessons. She made the teacher from the Bronx blush when she blew him a kiss and promised to come to meet him in person one day. But the students stopped their complicit giggles when they realized that the next protagonist was Antonio Banderas—Zorro himself. Hollywood had also sent its blessings to Tony through one of its stars. The audience burst into laughter when Banderas confessed, "I'm increasingly forgetting my Spanish; when I forget it completely, I'll go to one of your classes in Rhinebeck, Tony, so you can remind me."

After the ceremony we moved to a tent on Sarah's mother's lawn. Some friends had contributed tables, others chairs, still others pitchers and serving dishes. Decorations included enormous fragrant white peonies from the garden of Jack and Carolyn Ackerman and many, many Spanish flags that Maxi and Joselu Igartua, our cousins from Connecticut, had ordered for us. Assisted by my garden partner, John Katomsky, Charlie Rascoll prepared some delicious rice paellas with ingredients donated by the Culinary Institute of America. Everyone went back for second helpings.

Several journalists also showed up, attracted by the miracle of a humble teacher from a small school in upstate New York who had received the highest honor from Spain. Debbie Rodriguez, a former student gave an excellent report that morning on CBS radio. Tony was also interviewed on WDST, the Woodstock radio station, and long articles about him appeared in both Kingston's *Daily Freeman* and the *Poughkeepsie Journal*. In Spain he made it to the national news. Correspondents from TVE and Antena 3 covered the ceremony. Mark Durand, the ESPN Films director who volunteers at Panda TV, the local television station based in Tivoli, lent us a camera and Daniel de La Calle, who by then had decided to forget about vegetarianism and keep to himself the Spanish chorizo that his mom was sending him from Spain, recorded every minute for a documentary ... which Ricardo and I still haven't edited yet. Oops.

When the party ended, a basket was filled with donations to establish a scholarship in the teacher's name. A lot of Tony's former students were very generous. The intention was to help low-income students who perform well academically to travel to Spain to improve their Spanish.

We slept well that night, with pleasant dreams, feeling like characters at the end of Frank Capra movies when the honorable man triumphs. To some people, Tony Orza may have sounded like an ogre. And maybe he was an ogre for some students. But if he was, then he was an ogre like Shrek, filled up with good intentions. All Tony wanted to be to his students was a modest man who demanded the daily application of common sense to the fullest extent possible, nothing more.

Tony Orza is one of those great teachers who increasingly go unnoticed. We people are sometimes too obsessed with sports heroes and forget to encourage the Mr. Smiths. But Americans need their Mr. Smiths to go to Washington to fight injustices and their Tony Orzas to inspire their children to accomplish things that would have seemed impossible otherwise. As for me, a Spaniard who came to America with the intention of writing a screenplay, I'd better stop talking and go back to work.

About the Author

Guillermo Fesser is a Spanish journalist mostly known in his country for his innovative morning radio talk show, *Gomaespuma*, which ran 25 years and had over 1 million listeners.

Fesser studied journalism at the Universidad Complutense of Madrid and filmmaking at the University of Southern California, Los Angeles via a Fulbright scholarship. He has written and directed films; edited and hosted television news programs; and published articles in the major Spanish newspapers *El Pais* and *El Mundo*.

Fesser lives with his family in Rhinebeck, New York, where he broadcasts weekly stories on life in small-town America to Onda Cero Radio in Spain and blogs for *The Huffington Post*.

CPSIA information can be obtained
at www.ICGtesting.com
Printed in the USA
LVHW110533191021
700831LV00001B/59